Corporate Trust
Administration and Management

Corporate Trust Administration and Management

FIFTH EDITION

*Robert I. Landau
and John E. Krueger*

COLUMBIA UNIVERSITY PRESS
NEW YORK

Columbia University Press
Publishers Since 1893
New York   Chichester, West Sussex

Copyright © 1961, 1974 New York University Press
Copyright © 1985, 1992, 1998 Columbia University Press
All rights reserved

∞

Casebound editions of Columbia University Press books are
printed on permanent and durable acid-free paper.

Printed in the United States of America

c 10 9 8 7 6 5 4 3 2 1

Contents

Part II: Management 289

Part III: Reference Material 335

Preface

Twenty-five years ago, I began the first revision to the then definitive work on corporate trust administration. Throughout each of the revisions, which appeared in 1974, 1985, and 1992, I have tried to maintain the original concept of a teaching vehicle. My objective was always to offer each new generation of account managers, administrators, and operations specialists a systematic approach to learning the fundamentals of indenture trustee administration.

In the third edition, I began to enlarge the scope of the book's coverage so that it would be useful also as an ongoing reference work for anyone who might be involved in or with the corporate trust industry. This modification, which was refined in the fourth edition and is continued in this edition, contains a separate part addressing the issues in managing the corporate trust business. This part also covers the training and development of both managers and the technical/professional staff, a compendium of sample forms and checklists, an extensive glossary of securities industry terms, and the complete text of the Trust Indenture Act of 1939, as amended.

My colleagues will note that John E. Krueger joins me as coauthor of the current edition. John and I have worked together on industry committees, conferences, and panels for more than twenty years. Most recently, we shared responsibility for managing the corporate trust business at NationsBank. John is an outstanding writer, teacher, and manager. He is, above all, a consummate professional with a wide breadth of securities industry knowledge and experience.

In the current edition, we have followed the same pattern used in earlier editions, but with extensive changes in content and emphasis. Many of the revisions reflect a much greater emphasis on municipal bond issues than on corporate debt issues. A new chapter on regulatory reporting, oversight, and risk management has been added, as well as a new chapter on acquisitions and divestitures. We have increased the coverage of collateral mortgage and asset-backed financings and have expanded the commentary on global finance issues, Rule 144A private placements, secondary market disclosure, and the securities depositories. Also included is a new section on project finance as an emerging opportunity for corporate trustees, a completely updated bankruptcy and reorganization chapter, and a new section dealing with litigation and discovery concerns for trustees. In addition, we have extensively revised and updated the exhibits and glossary.

The last six years have seen major shifts and realignments in the corporate trust business. The result is that a handful of formerly regional banks have become dominant participants in the industry, and many others now specialize in specific products or markets. We also have witnessed the emergence of the so-called middle office, which combines many of the functions and activities of relationship managers, administrators, and operations specialists. In addition, there is a growing trend to broaden the involvement of individual corporate trust departments in products and markets outside the traditional role of trust indenture administration.

It is evident that client service, both real and perceived, will continue to be a major factor in the decision to use a particular trustee. This—coupled with the increased use of computer applications, interfaces, and electronic movement of processed information by administrators—will be the significant differentiating factor among trustees competing for new business. On the management side, the increased sensitivity to risk exposure and potential liability has greatly increased the need for a professionally competent and thoroughly trained staff.

The changes during the past six years and the evolution of both the corporate trust business and the entire securities industry must be considered and understood by every participant in this business. The players are not limited to indenture account managers, administrators, and operations specialists but include all those persons drafting debt-financing instruments and documents and marketing bond issues, as well as those accountable for the enactment and implementation of statutes, rules, regulations, and other standards of performance applicable to the corporate trust industry.

As we enter the next century, the participants in the industry will have to function in an environment significantly and dramatically influenced by events, transactions, and general economic conditions in all the capital markets, both domestic and international. The future will demand not only attention to a changing and volatile financial environment but also the flexibility to meet the requirements of changing patterns of both debt financing and information processing. To become a successful corporate trust professional, however, still requires a sound understanding of the basic concepts and principles, together with a great deal of imagination, plain old savvy, and a deep commitment to acceptance of responsibility and initiative.

Both John and I wish to acknowledge, with our deep appreciation and thanks, the very important and meaningful contributions the following people made to this edition: Richard Bass, Ken Benton, Bill Berls, Peter Fowler, Sally Gleason, Tony Guthrie, John Hiott, Matt Holley, Bill Imhof, Pam Jones, Mike Klugman, Denis and Peggy McWhorter, Jane Pope, Jeff Powell, Linda Reavis, Mitch Sikora, Paul Williams, and especially David Retter. Any errors, minor or major, are ours alone.

As with the earlier editions, I owe a debt of gratitude to hundreds of people with whom I have worked, studied, and taught over the past thirty-seven years. This includes my former associates at Bankers Trust Company and NationsBank—many of whom have made me proud of their accomplishments and success in other organizations—individuals in other corporate trust organizations throughout the country, and scores of investment bankers, lawyers, members of federal regulatory agencies, and members of banking and securities industry associations—all of whom contributed to my education and understanding of this dynamic and constantly changing industry.

And on a personal note, for her constant and continuous professional assistance, my eternal thanks to my partner and wife, Valerie.

Robert I. Landau
March 1998

I

Administration

A trustee is held to something stricter than the morals of the marketplace. Not honesty alone, but the punctilio of an honor the most sensitive, is then the standard of behavior.   —Justice Benjamin N. Cardozo
Meinhard v. Salmon
249 N.Y. 458, 464 (1928)

An indenture trustee is not subject to the ordinary trustee's duty of undivided loyalty. Unlike the ordinary trustee, who has historic common-law duties imposed beyond those in the trust agreement, an indenture trustee is more like a stakeholder whose duties and obligations are exclusively defined by the terms of the indenture agreement.

—Judge Richard J. Cardamone
Meckel v. Continental Resources
758 F.2d 811 (2d Cir. 1985)

Introduction

The study of corporate trust and the administration of the provisions of indenture contracts, including the servicing of debt obligations issued under debentures, bond resolutions, and other agreements is difficult, time-consuming, and complex. It requires an understanding of the principles of corporate finance and fiduciary law and a knowledge of the federal legislation and regulations governing the rights, duties, and liabilities of the debt issuer, the corporate trustee, and the security holders.

The chapters in part I introduce to corporate trust administrators, account officers, operations supervisors, and managers such legislation and regulations, as well as relevant principles, policies, and procedures. Explanatory and supplementary footnotes provide additional clarity and references to appropriate books, articles, statutes, regulations, and judicial decisions.

Although the activities and responsibilities in administering the trust indenture contract and its related agency services have been evolving for the past one hundred years, it is the statutory and regulatory changes during the past fifteen years that perhaps stand out most prominently. Given the volatile nature of the securities market as it moves from a domestic to a global environment and the technological changes in processing information and delivering transactions, there is every reason to believe that this evolution will continue at an accelerated rate. Nevertheless, corporate trust professionals still must have the basic knowledge and skills to properly discharge their duties.

Some General Principles of Corporate and Municipal Finance

The corporate trust indenture is undoubtedly one of the most complicated financial documents ever devised. Even though the development of a simplified or plain-language form of indenture for issuing corporate securities has made the indenture provisions more widely and easily understood, administering an indenture still requires highly skilled and experienced personnel.[1]

Although a full discussion of the problems of corporate organization and finance is beyond the scope of this book, a basic knowledge and understanding of their main features are important even to the beginner in the field. As a preliminary, therefore, this chapter considers some of the essential concepts in the corporate form of business enterprise and its financing.

THE CORPORATE FORM OF BUSINESS ENTERPRISE

The most common form of business enterprise is the individual proprietorship, in which only the individual's own capital is invested. The owner operates the business alone or with one or more employees and is entitled to all the profits realized or, conversely, suffers all the losses. If the business should fail, not only the assets of the business but also all the personal assets of the proprietor are used to pay the business creditors.

[1] Model Simplified Indenture, 38 *Bus. Law.* 741 (Feb. 1983).

The partnership is similar and, in effect, is simply the association of two or more individual proprietors in a common business undertaking. The main features of both these forms are the direct participation of the owners in the operation of the business and their unlimited liability for the business's debts.[2]

The corporate form of business enterprise, however, is different. A creature of the Industrial Revolution, the corporation has been vital, from the time of the British mercantile companies organized for colonial development, to the growth and development of the industrialized economies with which we are familiar.

A corporation is a creature of the state and exists only by virtue of a charter granted by the state. In the early days of the United States, a corporation could be created only by special legislative enactment. This special charter was granted after careful consideration and usually was for a special and limited purpose. Some corporations still exist with charters so granted. Today, however, all states have general incorporation laws, and the creation of a corporation is relatively simple.

Because a corporation is a creature of the state, it can exercise only those powers specifically granted to it by the state. These powers are enumerated in the corporate charter that is a basic document of every corporation. Incorporators may include in a proposed charter any power not prohibited by law or contrary to public policy. It is therefore the general practice for every charter to include a broad grant of powers. From the viewpoint of corporate indenture financing, the essential powers are the right to borrow money and the right to mortgage and pledge the corporation's assets as security for this borrowed money. If a corporation performs or purports to perform an act for which its charter does not have authority, such an act is said to be *ultra vires* and, as such, may constitute a defense in a suit against the corporation arising from the act so performed.

A corporation is subject not only to the limitations contained in its charter but also to all the laws and regulations promulgated by the legislature or a regulatory authority of the state of incorporation, in addition to those of any federal agency having jurisdiction over the corporation or its business activities.

Another important corporate document is the corporate bylaws. Bylaws are the rules of procedure adopted by the stockholders, and they can be amended at any time by a vote of the stockholders. They spell out such

---

[2] Most states provide for the creation of limited partnerships, which limit the liability of the limited partners (as opposed to the general or managing partners) to the amount of money that each has invested in the business.

things as the form of the certificates of stock; the frequency, locations, and dates of stockholder meetings; the procedures for calling special meetings; the scope and functions of the board of directors and the various committees; the powers and duties of the principal officers; and other basic rules as necessary for or pertinent to the corporation's continued functioning.

The stockholders are the owners of the business and, as such, are entitled to a vote in the management of its affairs in proportion to their ownership of the outstanding stock. They are also entitled to share in the corporation's profits—but only through such dividends that may be declared from time to time by the corporate directors. These rights of ownership, however, differ markedly from those of other forms of business enterprises. For instance, the stockholders do not participate directly in managing the corporate business, and they are also protected by the limited liability in the corporate form of business. If a venture fails, the stockholders' investment in the business is likely to be lost, but their personal assets are not liable for the payment of the corporation's debts.

The purchase of stock in a particular corporation usually results from the desire to make a profitable investment of savings or excess funds rather than from the desire to participate in a particular type of business venture. Generally, such investments are for the purpose of receiving income from dividend payments or profits from the eventual sale of the stock at a higher price, or both. The concept of pooling the funds of many individuals to make possible the conduct of business on the vast scale we know today was the great contribution of the corporate form of business enterprise.

The management of a corporation is vested in a board of directors elected by the stockholders. In some cases, this board is made up entirely of people who are active officers of the corporation, but in publicly held corporations, it is more common for some of the directors to be drawn from prominent members of the community who are engaged primarily in other professions. The diversity of interests and viewpoints thus brought together is often helpful to the enterprise. Regardless of the composition of the board, the directors are primarily responsible for the affairs of the corporation and may become individually liable and accountable in other ways for unwarranted acts of the corporation.

The active management of corporate affairs is delegated to a corporate staff whose members work full time for the enterprise. These officers are appointed by the board, and their functions are described in the bylaws or are prescribed by resolutions of the board. An officer has only the authority specifically granted or necessarily implied, and anyone dealing with a corporation should be certain of the authority of the officials with whom he or she deals and of what constitutes proper authorization of any contract or undertaking.

CORPORATE FINANCIAL STATEMENTS

A corporation's activities are summarized in the records that the corporate officers are required to maintain. These records show the results of operations for designated periods and are forwarded periodically to stockholders, creditors, and others. It is customary to have these records audited at least annually by a firm of independent public accountants that furnishes a certificate of examination. Whenever a corporation issues securities publicly, it must file certified financial statements with the Securities and Exchange Commission (SEC) and with each corporate trustee of its public debt securities.

Regulated industries, such as railroads, public utilities, banks, and similar corporations, are required to maintain their records in a uniform manner as prescribed by the particular regulatory authority having jurisdiction over them. Other corporations are not so restricted, so there may be some differences in the details required from various types of companies. In general, however, the development of modern accounting techniques and procedures and the requirements of federal tax regulations ensure uniformity in the form and content of financial statements.

The corporate trust practitioner must be familiar with financial statements and the more commonly used financial ratios. Secured corporate financings typically require financial statement review and analysis skills. A discussion of the basic financial statements follows.

The Balance Sheet

The *balance sheet* presents a corporation's condition at a particular moment in its history. It also may be said to reflect the cumulative results of the company's operations from its inception to the date when the statement is rendered.

Assets are the things that the corporation owns or is owed, together with the investment or other use of funds that have come into its hands. Assets are customarily classified as either "current" or "fixed." *Current assets* include cash and such items that are converted into cash in the business's normal operations. Among such items are temporary investments, receivables (amounts owed by the company's customers), and inventories (either raw materials awaiting processing or finished goods available for sale). *Fixed assets* include whatever buildings and real property that the company owns and uses in the conduct of its business, permanent investments that the company may have in other companies, and other types of property that may be necessary or incidental to its operations but that are normally not held for resale. Such things as goodwill, patents, trademarks, and franchise rights are intangibles and may be classified as assets if they have a real value. Another term frequently employed is *tangible assets*, which include all assets other than goodwill, patents, and other intangibles that would have little, if any, value upon the liquidation of the business.

Assets are "balanced" against an equal amount of liabilities plus capital, which represent the source of funds with which the corporate assets were acquired. *Current liabilities* are the amounts due and payable within a specified period of time—usually a year—and incurred primarily in connection with normal business operations. The current asset and current liability accounts are considered the company's working capital accounts, and the excess of current assets over current liabilities is usually referred to as *working capital* or *net current assets*. Money borrowed for a period longer than one year is usually referred to as *funded debt* and is shown on the balance sheet as a *noncurrent liability*, although any portion of funded debt due within one year, because of either maturity or a sinking-fund obligation, is customarily included as a current liability.

Among the various forms of borrowing, the ordinary bank loan, generally used to provide additional working capital, matures in a relatively short time, although in recent years, such loans have been for terms longer than the traditional one to three years. Since many businesses operate on a cyclical basis during the year, there may be periods of heavy inventory accumulation, such as for the purchase of raw materials for fabrication or processing. These periods often require heavy bank borrowing to provide funds to purchase these raw materials. During the ensuing period of heavy sales, the finished goods are disposed of, inventory decreases, and the resulting surplus of cash is used to pay off the bank loans. It is much less expensive to meet temporary heavy cash requirements by means of bank credit than to provide enough permanent capital to meet the company's peak cash demands. All these transactions, as they occur, are reflected in the company's *working capital accounts*. Funds needed for capital or fixed property purposes are borrowed for longer periods of time, and it is this type of borrowing with which we will be concerned in our consideration of the trust indenture.

Another type of permanent capital is that supplied by the owners of the business, that is, the stockholders. The net amount invested by the owners—the amount paid in for the purchase of stock plus the undistributed earnings that have been reinvested in the business—accounts for the rest of the liability side of the balance sheet.

Income and Retained Earnings Statements

The principal source of a company's income is the sale of its products, and accordingly, the first item on the income statement is the amount of the net sales for the year, together with other earned income. This may include interest on temporary investments, income from investments in other companies, the excess of proceeds over book value realized from the sale of fixed assets no longer required in the business, and other similar items.

From this item is deducted the cost of the goods sold, including the cost of the raw materials and the costs directly chargeable to manufacturing operations. These costs tend to vary in almost direct proportion to the volume of goods produced. Costs that are more or less "fixed" without regard to fluctuations in the volume of business are the expenses of the sales force, advertising, general office, and other similar charges. These are usually shown separately on the income statement and in such detail as needed for proper presentation and understanding. To calculate the net income resulting from the year's operations, the manufacturing and general expenses from net sales are deducted.

The charge for *depreciation* is a noncash expense. Although certain assets represent permanent investments, they will in time become worn out as they are used in the manufacturing process and have to be replaced. It is therefore necessary to charge against each year's income an appropriate amount to represent the deterioration or decrease in the value of such fixed assets. This is the *depreciation charge*. There are a number of ways in which depreciation may be computed, but in general, the charge theoretically represents the portion of the total value of the fixed assets that were used up in the year's operations.

Other expense items that might be included in the depreciation charge are losses on sales of investments or fixed assets, amortization of discounts on funded debt obligations sold below par, and so on. The final deduction is the amount of income taxes incurred for the year, and the resulting balance is the corporation's net income from all activities during the period.

Retained earnings are the company's earnings that have been reinvested in the business rather than distributed to the stockholders.

Changes in the Financial Position Statement

The final example of a common type of financial statement is the Statement of Changes in Financial Position, also sometimes called a Sources and Uses of Funds statement.

This type of statement is helpful in considering a corporation's financial transactions. All corporate transactions are expressed in terms of dollars, even though many transactions take place each day without a concurrent transfer of dollars. For example, goods are bought to be paid for at a later date; wages, taxes, and other items of expense accrue that require cash outlays in the future; and similarly, sales are made on credit or services are performed to be paid for over a period of time.

Financial officers must plan to provide the cash, when required, to meet the payments called for by the corporate operations. Similarly, the primary concern of anyone extending credit to the company is that funds will be available to meet the service payments on the debt as they become due.

The Sources and Uses of Funds statement reflects the flow of cash through a company's operations for a stated period. This analysis can be extrapolated from the statements previously considered. More important to financial officers is the use of the statement's projections as a part of the budget preparation, to ensure that the company's financial obligations will be met promptly.

A single balance sheet provides little information other than the company's financial condition at a particular moment. It does not reflect the trend of the business. However, by comparing the balance sheets for the beginning and the end of a designated period, a great deal of information may be learned about the corporation's activities during that period. These records, combined with the income and retained earnings statements, offer enough information to construct a cash-flow statement for the period.

Assets represent the uses of funds; liabilities reflect the sources of funds. An increase in assets or a decrease in liabilities during a period thus shows the net use of corporate funds during that time. Similarly, the sum of the decrease in assets and the increase in liabilities reflects the net source of corporate funds for the period. Another type of Sources and

Uses of Funds statement can thus be constructed by rearranging the net increase and decrease in assets and liabilities reflected in the change in the balance sheet for the period in question. In fact, there are many thousands of sources and uses for any particular accounting period. For an adequate picture of the company's transactions, however, it is usually sufficient to summarize the net effect of all these transactions. Although an analysis of the balance sheets alone would provide such a picture, it would not be as complete as that obtained by considering also the income accounts for the period. In such an analysis, it is also common to regard the working capital accounts (current assets and current liabilities) as an entity. Thus, a net increase in working capital represents a use of funds, and a net decrease indicates a source.

FINANCING CAPITAL NEEDS

Corporate financial officers are continually faced with the problem of how to finance the business's money needs. Municipal or governmental officers have similar financing concerns. Although government entities are able to increase taxes to fund interest and principal for issued debt securities, additional monies to fund debt generally cannot be obtained without passing a referendum, by popular vote, to fund additional debt. Once a taxing referendum is passed, additional municipal debt is authorized by a governmental entity or a municipal resolution.

Municipal finance officers must also be concerned about the balance sheet, although such items as the inventory turnover are not applicable. Due to their ability to impose additional taxes to finance capital needs, municipalities were typically thought to be immune from financial difficulty. But in recent years, several cities and towns have declared bankruptcy owing to general economic conditions that made it difficult to collect needed taxes. Since that time, governmental entities have faced additional balance sheet scrutiny from public investors. Because concern about financing capital is normally not a problem that directly concerns the corporate trust administrator, we need not deal with it in detail here. An understanding of the basic principles is, however, helpful in understanding the reasons for some of the negotiations in drafting particular indenture provisions.

We noted that short-term working-capital needs are customarily financed by short-term bank loans. An additional and important source of short-term funds for companies with a strong credit standing is the sale of *commercial paper*. This refers to short-term promissory notes, usually unsecured, which are typically written in multiples of $5,000 with maturities of from three days to nine months.[3] These notes do not bear interest, as such. Instead, an effective interest rate is established by the sale of the notes at a discount from the face amount. Municipalities also use short-term note financing for their immediate needs or to manage debt issuance to take advantage of anticipated lower interest-rate markets, as discussed in chapter 4, "Municipal Trusts."

When the issuer needs additional security to obtain a top credit rating for its commercial paper, a bank issues an irrevocable letter of credit, on either a standby or a direct-draw basis.

Medium-term needs (e.g., the purchase of equipment that can be paid for in four to five years) might be financed through a bank term loan or an equipment lease transaction.[4] In recent years, corporations and municipalities have turned to using medium-term notes to address medium-term financing needs. Medium-term financing is described later in this chapter.

Corporate capital requirements are normally supplied from the capital markets or through the medium of retained earnings. Since this is the type of financing with which the corporate trustee is concerned, that it is what we will concentrate on here.

Capital requirements can be financed in one of four principal ways: (1) through some form of borrowing—the issuance of debt securities; (2) through the issuance of preferred stock (although this is a form of equity or ownership security, the holder is entitled to only a fixed return from the company's earnings—as opposed to a possibly larger return from common shares—but has a claim before that of common stockholders in the event of liquidation); (3) through the sale of additional common stock; or (4) through retained earnings. Even though conservative management normally retains a portion of earnings for use in the business (and this might be said not to be financing in the true sense), the retention of earnings is in effect a forced investment by the stockholders, and many of the considerations applicable to other types of capital financing are pertinent to the question of what portion of earnings should be retained, particularly if a change in the dividend policy is contemplated.[5]

---

[3] When the issuer needs additional security to obtain a top credit rating for its commercial paper, a bank will issue its irrevocable letter of credit, on either a standby or a direct-draw basis. In such instances, a bank is normally appointed as trustee and depository for the letter of credit.

[4] For a discussion of this type of financing and the role of the trustee bank, see chapter 15.

[5] Assuming that the company is viable, the decision is not whether to pay a dividend but when and how much to pay. Companies usually increase their dividend payments after an

Many factors affect the decision regarding the type of financing to be used for a particular project. Among the more important are (1) the nature of the project or expansion to be financed, how speculative it is, and its relationship in size, cost, and, profitability to the company's existing business; (2) the prospective earnings from the proposed investment and how precisely such earnings can be forecast; (3) the quality and durability of the company's existing earnings, the municipality's taxing ability for government entity borrowing, and the extent to which they are affected by cyclical changes in the general economy; (4) the company's existing capital structure, the government entity's financial condition, and the effect that alternative financing methods would have on this structure; and (5) the cost of alternative methods of raising the needed capital.

These factors can generally be reduced to a consideration of the risks in relation to the cost. It is assumed that the different types of capital are available at a price. If a particular method of financing is not available because of a prohibition in an existing contract, the quality of the borrower's credit, or for other reasons, the company's choices are either more limited or nonexistent.

It is axiomatic that—from the point of view of the borrower—the less expensive the method of financing is, the more risk it involves. Even though debt is usually the cheapest form of capital, there is some risk inherent in every type of debt financing, since debt financing entails fixed commitments that must be met regardless of the borrower's earnings or taxing power at that particular time. From the viewpoint of the common stockholder, issuing preferred stock is riskier than selling additional common stock, for it creates a class of holders with claims ranked higher than their own.

The cost of debt is the rate of interest that must be paid, but since interest paid by corporations is deductible under present tax laws in computing income tax, the actual cost of debt financing is less than half the nominal interest rate under present tax laws. The cost of using preferred stock is the *fixed dividend rate*. Because of its lower priority in case of insolvency, this rate is usually higher than the rate on debt for the same company. In addition, and possibly of greater significance, preferred dividends are not, with some exceptions, deductible for income tax purposes.

Another factor that is sometimes significant is the effect[6] on existing

---

improvement in their internal cash generation becomes apparent, and the payment is raised only to an amount that the management believes it can reasonably and safely maintain.

[6] A common assessment of an obligor's creditworthiness with respect to a debt issue is based on (1) the likelihood that the obligor will pay the interest and repay the principal, (2) the

capital structure that the proposed financing may have. Thus, maintaining a proper debt ratio is important not only because of the safety of having a sound equity base but also because of the adverse effect that excessive debt may have on the borrower's credit standing. There is no approved ratio, and anyway, each financial analyst uses a different measure for every class of borrower. Accordingly, a fairly high debt ratio might be acceptable for a particular industry, whereas the same ratio in another would be cause for serious concern. Historically, few companies have been able to justify a debt ratio over 50 percent, and for most, the maximum is 35 percent. When the ratio begins to exceed the theoretical ceiling, the company's security rating is affected, which makes additional debt financing more difficult and more expensive. Thus the proper proportion of equity to debt should be maintained at all times, and it is advisable to include a certain amount of equity financing while keeping a degree of flexibility, to take advantage of changing market conditions.

As stated earlier, security analysts consider the ability of governmental entities to impose additional taxation, as well as the short-, medium-, and long-term debt outstanding and the general economic condition of the governmental entity's geographical area. For example, some municipal debt is issued as revenue producing, such as tollways. In this case, the general need for a tollway and the projected traffic usage are taken into account when determining the issuer's ability to repay the borrowed funds.

Corporate and municipal finance is a volatile and constantly changing field, innovation and "creative financing" being the hallmarks of aggressive investment bankers. The expert of a decade ago emerging from a time capsule would find a strange world today. A number of factors introduced into the economy during the past ten years have contributed to these changes. One, of course, is the tremendous expansion that has taken place in the economy and that has created an unprecedented demand for investment funds, including the vast sums borrowed by states and municipalities. Another factor of equal or greater importance is the impact on corporations of the tax laws and regulations on their everyday activities. In addition, the global economy has changed the economic rules for borrowers. Big government and, especially, big taxes are always present, and it is no longer possible to make important decisions based on the economics of only the particular situation.

---

nature and provisions of the obligation, and (3) the protection afforded by the relative position of the obligation in the event of a bankruptcy or reorganization.

PRIVATE PLACEMENTS

One of the most important trends in the area of debt financing is the growth in the number and volume of *direct* or *private placement* contracts. Originally this was the direct result of concentrating funds in the hands of institutions that provided the bulk of available investment dollars—not only in savings bank and life insurance assets but also in both private and public pension funds, including the significant growth of individual retirement plans, such as IRAs and Keoghs.

Even though avoiding the uncertainties and expense of a public offering and complying with the registration requirements of the Securities Act of 1933 (33 Act) are frequently cited as the motivating factors, more important considerations are the ability to achieve greater flexibility—to tailor each financing to fit the particular circumstances—and the greater ease of securing amendments to the contract necessitated by changing conditions. Some institutional investors prefer this custom-made type of investment. They not only may be able to secure a somewhat better return but also can plan their investment operations more accurately by making commitments for fixed amounts at negotiated rates.

The private placement assumed major importance during the 1970s and 1980s when these placements accounted for approximately 50 percent of corporations' total capital debt financing. By 1991, private placements had shrunk to less than 3.0 percent of the total taxable market, but since 1994, this sector has hovered around 9.6 percent of the market. The adoption of certain initiatives by the SEC in April 1990 set the stage for another renaissance in the use of this financing sector. In 1990, the SEC adopted Rule 144A, which permits institutional investors with a minimum of $100 million invested in securities to trade in privately placed securities, eliminating the requirement that such securities be registered with the SEC as "public" securities under the 33 Act.[7] The effect of this new rule and the amendment to Rule 144, permitting the required holding period (usually two years) for private placements to begin the original issuance of the securities, in effect sets the stage for the creation of a secondary market in such securities.

These actions constituted the first step in liberalizing the private placement market, which has significantly increased its liquidity, making it more attractive to investors and reducing the cost to issuers of such financings. It has also increased the number of foreign issuers into this

[7] SEC Release 33–6862 and 34–27928 (Apr. 1990).

market—issuers that had been reluctant to subject themselves to the full registration requirements of the 33 Act.

Direct placement financing falls into three broad categories:

1. Issues that are secured by the traditional form of corporate indenture, either an existing mortgage or a new bond or debenture issue. Except for the number of holders and the likelihood of a home office payment agreement,[8] such an issue is almost the same as a publicly offered issue.

2. Special-purpose and third-party corporation financing. The variations are legion, and the security is more likely to involve leases, charter hires, throughput agreements, government-guaranteed home mortgages, or some form of contractual arrangement other than the traditional corporate mortgage. In this type of financing, the credit of the obligor issuer is seldom important, for in most cases it is a corporation specifically created for the purpose of issuing the debt obligation. The loan is made on the credit of the lessee or other contract party and its agreement to perform under its contract with the obligor issuer.

3. Note issues involving a direct unsecured loan without a trustee. Initially, these loans were similar to bank credit agreements, except they were for longer terms and normally for capital purposes. The borrowers were corporations with high credit ratings and usually little or no other funded debt. Frequently, only one institutional lender was involved, very seldom more than four or five. The loan agreements were uncomplicated, with few, if any, security covenants.

Inevitably, there was an increase in both the number of borrowers using this device and the variety and purpose of the loans. Credit agreements have become more complicated, with wider participation in individual loans. Eight to ten investors are fairly common, and many issues have had twenty-five to fifty participants. In private placement financing, these note agreements often replaced debenture financing, but without the flexibility, marketability, and uniformity of administration provided by the traditional debenture agreement with a competent and experienced corporate trustee.

We also note, though without extensive comment, several other significant trends in recent years:

1. The volatility and changing character of the domestic market. In an environment of economic uncertainties, wide swings in interest rates have prevailed, with innovative factors built into the particular financing

---

[8] This agreement provides that when payments of principal are mailed to the holder without requiring the obligation to be presented for notation of payment, the holder, before disposing of the note, will surrender it to the obligor (or its agent) for notation or issuance of a new note for the unpaid balance.

vehicle. These, together with the issuance of short- and mixed-term maturities, have ensured investors' continued interest in providing funds to both corporate and public-sector borrowers. Today's spectrum of financing structures includes floating-rate notes, deep discount and zero coupon issues, auction-rate securities, convertible securities (both mandatory and optional), variable-rate demand obligations, put/demand options, medium-term notes, and asset-backed securities. Asset-backed securities are collateralized by a wide and growing variety of asset classes, including mortgages, home equity loans, credit card receivables, auto and mobile home loans, student loans, and trade and medical receivables. The variations are almost endless, limited only by the imagination of investment bankers and the perceived appetite of the investing public.

2. Shelf registration under SEC Rule 415. This rule, permanently adopted as of December 31, 1983, permits top-tier corporations to register the offering or sale of their securities on a delayed or continuous basis in the future.[9] The effect of this rule is to allow such issuers almost instant access to the marketplace—whenever a "window" is available.

3. The increased popularity and rapid growth of medium-term notes (MTNs), an instrument modeled on the commercial paper issued by corporations to obtain short-term operating funds. The majority of MTNs are not sold through the traditional underwriting process but under a continuous offering procedure in which the issuer, acting through an investment bank(s) as sales agent(s), makes securities available to investors desiring specific maturities ranging from nine months to as long as fifteen years. The most important feature of an MTN program (i.e., issue) is the sales agent's ability to tailor the maturity date to satisfy the issuer's need for funds to the investor's need for a specific investment period. Most MTN programs provide for fixed, semiannual interest payments, although some issues have used a variable-rate feature, with the interest paid either monthly or quarterly.

4. The tremendous volume of public financing, including not only the continuous financing by the federal government in the management of the public debt but also the enormous amount of tax-exempt securities issued by states, state and local authorities, and municipalities. In addition to the increase in revenue bond financings, the broad-scale use of industrial development bonds (IDBs) had a major impact on the market during the early 1980s. The IDB activity was then curtailed during the late 1980s as the level of issuance was controlled by federal regulation to impose issuance caps at the state level, based on the state's population.

9 SEC Release 33–6499 (Nov. 1983).

Since municipal securities are typically exempt from federal taxation, the government became concerned about the number and amount of IDB securities issued annually. The primary purpose of IDBs was to make attractive the financing of new plants and/or the construction of pollution control facilities through use of the tax-exempt privilege.

5. Globalization of the securities markets is a new opportunity for corporate trustees. Although international project finance is by no means a new concept in funding the construction of infrastructure, there is an emerging trend requiring the services of a trustee. Previously, such financings were arranged and handled by a bank or syndicate of banks, with the operational needs filled by the lead bank. Increasingly, project finances are more complex in structure, more diverse in investor base, and more limited in recourse. Project sponsors and investors now are willing to risk capital in the international emerging markets in search of higher returns. There is also a strong need to diversify portfolios, forge alliances, and cultivate new relationships with international partners to compete effectively in the global marketplace. The flurry of activity is fueled by a fundamental disparity between the demands of the emerging markets and their ability to meet these demands. New projects are being developed in Latin America, eastern Europe, and the Pacific Rim. Although power projects lead the way for new project financings, there is a great need for other infrastructure development, such as toll roads, bridges, pollution control projects, airports, transportation, and industrial and manufacturing facilities.

As we move from one century to the next, fundamental changes are occurring in the international debt markets. Key among these are the following:

Changing population dynamics

Countries all over the world are facing the need to support aging populations, and this need will drive fundamental changes in the capital markets. As life expectancy increases at the same time that younger people are postponing marriage and having fewer children, the age profile in virtually all developed countries is changing drastically. In the United States, where ten people were working for every person retired in 1950, the ratio will be two working for every one retired in 2010.

Similar changes are taking place throughout Europe, Asia, and Latin America. They will put tremendous stress on state-sponsored retirement plans, especially in Europe and Asia, where the retirement systems are largely state financed and have necessarily been built on a "pay-as-you-go" basis. In addition, these demographic changes will force fundamental changes in current pension schemes, including their increasing privatization and a continuing search for higher-yielding investments with a greater emphasis on equities, as opposed to debt instruments.

National and local governments that have long been dependent on using state-run pension systems as a source of funding must now compete more aggressively for funding in the capital markets. This action will, in turn, force all issuers to broaden their search for debt capital, both geographically and by type of instrument.

More cross-border financings

Needs for investable funds, for both governmental and corporate projects, will grow across the globe, especially in the lesser-developed areas where funds are desperately needed for building basic infrastructure. The sources of capital, however, will remain concentrated in countries with large, stable economies and large pools of investable assets such as pension funds, mutual funds, and life insurance company assets. Financing will necessarily become more cross border as underwriters work to match needs with sources. Large, well-established borrowers, whether governmental or corporate, can be expected to increase their issuance of foreign currency issues as well as global issues with separate tranches of the same security issued in different markets and denominated in different currencies.

More complex financings

The increasing need for cross-border financings—with the greatest need for financing in some of the higher-risk locations—will generate a demand for more complex financings to attract limited investor capital. Underwriters can be expected to make greater use of more complex debt instruments such as securities with government guarantees or with "equity kickers," securitized instruments, instruments tied to specific revenue streams, instruments with obligations segmented into discrete portions for income versus principal and/or short versus long maturities, and multicurrency issues with debt service payable in different currencies.

Transition to a common currency

The planned conversion of several European currencies into the *EMU*, scheduled to commence in 1999, will lead to more complex instruments, at least during the transition period. We should expect to see multicurrency issues with income and principal payable in different currencies as well as "currency-optional" securities in which the holders choose the currency in which they wish to receive payment. Over the longer term, the emergence of a common currency in Europe will reduce the processing and accounting complexity as country-specific currencies are gradually eliminated.

Underwriting concentration

The more complex financing vehicles will include derivatives and migrate outward from the United States and the major centers in Europe and Asia. But the underwriting will remain localized in a few key centers because many, if not most, local markets will not have the internal capital and industry expertise to support these types of securities. Furthermore, the secondary markets for these securities, because they are dependent on liquidity and trading efficiency, will be concentrated in a few markets where the capital and the investment expertise can be brought together in one place.

TWO

The Trust Indenture

The *trust indenture* is a device by which a corporation or governmental entity borrows money from the general public or large institutional investors to issue securities. Securities issued by corporations are known in the industry as *corporates*, and securities issued by governmental entities are termed *munis*. The indenture provides the terms and conditions on which credit is extended; restricts the activities of the issuing corporation or governmental entity as long as the indenture securities are outstanding; sets forth remedies available to the security holders if there is a default in payment on the debt securities or in the terms of the indenture contract; and otherwise defines the rights, duties, and obligations of the obligor company or governmental entity, the security holders, and the trustee or trustees named in the instrument. If the indenture obligations are to be secured, the indenture creates or pledges the security and explains the terms and conditions for dealing with the security.

The use of a mortgage to secure the repayment of money is an ancient one. Likewise, the concept of a "use" or "trust" was developed at an early period in the common law, whereas the development of the *corporate mortgage*, or *trust indenture*, is fairly recent. It was first introduced around 1830, but until the latter part of the nineteenth century, the trust indenture was used infrequently. The reasons for this are many. First, early corporate financing was carried out primarily by means of *stock* rather than by the issuance of debt securities known as *bonds*. Also, the earlier corporations were generally created for special purposes and by special charter, and so their power to incur debt or mortgage their properties was strictly limited.

The growth and development of trust indentures closely parallel the growth of the corporate business enterprise. With the passage of general incorporation laws in most states, the organization of corporations became relatively simple, and as a result, the use of this form of business organization became common. The latter part of the nineteenth century was also a period of tremendous expansion and growth in the United States. Accordingly, there was a phenomenal increase in both the number and size of business corporations and the amount of capital required for their development.

The transaction of business by these vast enterprises came to involve both large stock financing and heavy borrowing. It became impractical to secure this financing through one bank, or even a group of banks, so a system of borrowing from the public at large was established through a multitude of small loans, each represented by the issuance of bonds of the corporation and all secured by the same mortgage to one individual or a small group of individuals. The corporate mortgage was at first used almost exclusively by railroad corporations, but with the growth of the corporate form of business enterprise and the development of large corporate systems, the practice was extended until now there are corporations and corporate and government bond issues that include terms and conditions for almost every type of business undertaking.

Although the indenture has become a necessary and important factor in the United States' economic life, it is still not well understood. Whereas many court decisions have been made regarding particular problems, the courts still have not agreed on the overall significance of the contract. Because the indenture device is little more than a century old and it developed mainly during the past fifty years, there has been no opportunity for a slow and gradual establishment of legal precedents. The courts have looked for guidance to cases with only a superficial similarity to the problems at hand, although the legal relationships appeared to be the same.

The trust indenture is an instrument sui generis, combining elements of several other legal relationships but without being identical with any of them. Although most courts now agree that the indenture does not create a trust relationship in the customary sense, some cases have indicated that the full extent of fiduciary responsibility may be imposed on the trustee. Indeed, it has been suggested that this responsibility be imposed by statute, even at the risk of seriously impairing its effective use.

Although every form of indenture has similar elements, the various types are designed for the different kinds of obligations to be issued, each with peculiarities of its own. The title of the indenture usually describes the type of obligations to be issued and the nature of the security, if any. For example, a mortgage indenture indicates that the principal security is a mortgage on the obligor's fixed property and that the obligations outstanding are mortgage bonds. A first mortgage indicates that the bonds are intended to be a first lien on such properties, a second mortgage a second lien, and so on. Normally, an indenture securing junior lien obligations contains provisions for refunding the prior lien bonds, and in that event, the indenture and the obligations issued are called, respectively, a *refunding mortgage* and *refunding mortgage bonds*, terms that sound more attractive than *second* or *third mortgage*. If the obligations have a first, or prior, lien on any property at all, the title *first and refunding mortgage* is frequently used. In some jurisdictions, the term *trust deed* is preferred to *mortgage*, although in most cases this is simply a variation in title. A *collateral trust agreement* usually denotes an indenture under which the obligations have a collateral rather than a direct lien. A *debenture agreement* usually, although not necessarily, indicates unsecured obligations. The many other variations, combinations, and different forms of designation depend on the type of obligation, the type of security, and other considerations. Although for most purposes, these distinctions do not affect the fundamental nature of the indenture or of the rights and obligations of the parties, they do involve different types of provisions and covenants and undoubtedly account to some extent for the confusion and contradictions in the relevant law.

The legal relationships of those features most common to the trust indenture are that of the mortgage, trust, and contract.

The Indenture as a Mortgage

Most secured indentures under which bonds are issued entail a mortgage of some kind. The nature and extent of the mortgage security depend on the particular circumstances of the issue, but the security usually involves a mortgage on the fixed property and equipment used by the issuer in its business. The property is usually described in detail by metes and bounds in the instrument, and the document is executed with great care to ensure that it conforms to the laws and customs of the jurisdictions where the property is located. The document is then properly filed and recorded at the relevant county and state offices. All efforts are made to ensure that the indenture creates the lien that it purports to do. The net effect of all this effort, however, is usually quite different from what the investors expect when told that they have a first mortgage security.

In the customary mortgage transaction, the borrower and lender are dealing with a security understood by both parties. In the absence of extraordinary developments, the property's intrinsic and realizable value usually is more than adequate to cover the amount of the loan, and if there is a default, the lender can foreclose and realize from the security the full amount of the loan.

A transaction like this differs from a mortgage on the property of a large business enterprise. The average investor who purchases bonds has no conception of the value of a large railroad system, for example, although a "mortgage" on the system may constitute the security. Even if the investors could examine each parcel, they would still be unable to ascertain its value, for in this case the value of the whole might be greater or less than the sum of the values of all its parts. As real estate, a railroad's right-of-way one mile long and thirty feet wide may have little value, although the railroad may have issued mortgage bonds to the extent of $300,000 or more per mile. Instead, the real value of a business enterprise's property is the enterprise's "going-concern." value. Considered separate and apart from its use for the business, the right-of-way's inadequacy as a security is readily apparent. In determining the value of securities, analysts thus are concerned with balance sheets, profit and loss statements, competitive conditions, economic trends, and other factors that may influence the business as a "going concern," and only infrequently do they consider the intrinsic value of the security, separate and apart, to be of substantial importance. A proper mortgage position is essential, not only for the value that may be realized on a possible future foreclosure and sale, but also for the prior claim on earnings or preferred position in the event of default, bankruptcy, or reorganization.

THE INDENTURE AS A TRUST

There is another important distinction between the trust indenture and the ordinary mortgage. In an ordinary mortgage, the mortgagee is usually the real party in interest, holding the mortgage as security for the credit it has extended. In the indenture, or corporate mortgage, immediately following the granting and habendum clauses, is a paragraph beginning with the words "In Trust, Nevertheless," which converts the mortgage into a trust deed and defines the terms and purposes for which the conveyance was made.

The trust so created, however, differs substantially from the usual *inter-vivos*, or *testamentary*, trust with which courts and practitioners are more familiar. The fundamental characteristic of the ordinary personal trust is possession by the trustee of a specific trust res that he or she holds and administers for the benefit of designated and usually well-known beneficiaries.

The trustee under an indenture, however, has no possession, or right to possession, of the mortgaged property until after a default has occurred, and even then, the trustee's rights are usually circumscribed and limited. It has no control of the obligor's business (and if it did, it would be disqualified from acting) or, except for infrequent and unusual circumstances, any voice in the management of its affairs. Efforts to subject it under these conditions to the same degree of care with respect to the security as is required of an ordinary trustee with respect to a specific trust res would make the position of the indenture trustee untenable and render financing of this type almost impossible. It would be unwise indeed, even if practicable, to try to substitute the judgment of the indenture trustee for that of the management of the issuing corporation.

In the case of the ordinary trust, usually a close and intimate relationship is formed between the trustee and the beneficiaries. The trustee is normally acquainted with their needs and can take the necessary actions. The trust instrument normally gives substantial discretionary powers to the trustee, with the resulting duties arising as much from the relationship with the beneficiaries as from the specific provisions of the trust document. In an extreme or doubtful case, the trustee can usually secure the direction of a court—or obtain the consent or waiver of all the interested parties—before taking action. It is also possible for accountings to be submitted periodically so that administration can be kept more or less up-to-date.

An indenture trustee is in the position of both a stakeholder and a trustee.[1] Its administration covers a long period of time, and it is frequently called on to make important and far-reaching decisions without being able to consult the security holders or seek the instructions of a court. In most cases, the beneficial owners of the indenture securities may be unknown to the trustee, and they change frequently so that an effort to secure their unanimous consent to a particular action is extremely difficult.[2] In addition, the indenture trustee normally has no predefault discretionary power and only limited authority. For instance, it has no authority

[1] See Sklar, "The Corporate Indenture Trustee: Genuine Fiduciary or Mere Stakeholder?" 106 *Banking L.J.* 1 (1989).

[2] Even with securities in fully registered form, registration may be in nominee or street name, especially when the securities are held in a depositary or by bank custodians, brokerage firms, and trust fund accounts.

to deal with or compromise the debt itself, no matter how desirable such a compromise might appear to be.

The trustee of a personal trust is responsible only to the beneficiaries, to administer the trust solely in their interests. Although the indenture trustee's primary fiduciary responsibility is to the indenture security holders, it also owes to the obligor important practical and fiduciary duties, and in the interest of all parties, it must be able to work cooperatively with the obligor.

A final and important distinction is the amount of compensation received by the two types of trustee. The fees of the trustee of an ordinary trust are measured by the amount of the trust res or the income from it. Although the trustee can be surcharged for a wrongful act or failure to exercise due care, the possible consequences of any particular course of action can normally be estimated with reasonable accuracy. The fees received by the indenture trustee are nominal in relation to the amount of indenture securities outstanding or the value of the trust estate. If it were to be held accountable for all the discretion and fiduciary responsibilities common to the ordinary trust, the amount for which it could be liable would be out of proportion to the compensation the obligor company or government entity could pay.

THE INDENTURE AS A CONTRACT

Even though it is similar to other legal relationships, the trust indenture is mainly a contract, and the courts have been in almost unanimous agreement in applying contractual principles to this relationship.

The parties to the contract, or the indenture, are the obligor company or government entity and the trustee, and only these parties execute the instrument. However, the participation of another party, or class of parties—the indenture security holders—is essential to make the contract operative. Three separate sets of contractual rights and obligations are created by each indenture: those between the obligor and the trustee, those between the obligor and the indenture security holders, and those between the trustee and the indenture security holders.

It is important to distinguish between the contractual rights, duties, and obligations relating primarily to the debt itself and those relating principally to the security for the debt. The indenture provisions that define the trustee's principal rights, duties, and obligations and its relationship with the obligor relate primarily to the security for the obligations issued or to be issued, whether it be the specific security conveyed or pledged by the indenture or the "negative" security determined and defined by the indenture covenants. These provisions contain the trustee's authority for dealing with this security and define the limitations and restrictions on the authority. They also restrict the issuing obligor in dealing with its property or in conducting its business. Since both the obligor and the trustee have an opportunity to read and examine the indenture before it becomes effective and both are signatory parties, some of the features of a true contract may be said to be present. Many are lacking, however, and it is important to remember that until the contract is executed, the trustee is acting not as a principal but only as a prospective fiduciary. The trustee does not negotiate the substantive terms of the contract, and so if it objects to particular provisions, it can only suggest, and not demand, that they be deleted or amended. The trustee's only recourse is to refuse to act, for it does not and cannot become an active participating party until the contract is actually signed and delivered.

The obligations issued under the indenture are directly those of the security holders and not of the trustee and are looked to primarily to define the relationship between the obligor and the security holders. It is therefore important that any provisions of the indenture that modify or affect this relationship, or limit the rights of the holders of these obligations, also be described in the bond or debenture that goes to the holder. Since the indenture describes in detail the rights, duties, and obligations of the parties (including the security holders) and the limitations on those rights, the security itself should embody those provisions by adequate reference. Obviously, the whole indenture cannot be fully defined in the bond, but it is usually sufficient to refer to the indenture in general terms. This is done by including in the bond (or other obligation) language substantially as follows:

> This bond is one of a duly authorized issue of bonds, issued and to be issued under, and all equally secured by a Mortgage and Deed of Trust dated as of _____, executed by _____ Company to the _____ Trust Company as Trustee, to which Indenture reference is hereby made for a description of the properties and franchises mortgaged, the nature and extent of the security, the rights of the holders of said bonds and of the trustee in respect of such security, and the terms and conditions under which the bonds are issued and secured.[3]

Although language like this is usually enough to put the security holder on notice about the existence of the indenture and to make its provisions

---

[3] For a plain language version, see para. 4, 38 *Bus. Law.*, *supra*, at 776.

binding on the holder, it is desirable to refer specifically to those provisions that directly affect the rights of the holder of the obligation itself. Such provisions include subordination and redemption provisions, sinking funds, transfers and exchanges of securities, any provisions permitting substantial modification of the indenture by fewer than all security holders, and waivers of default.

The substantive provisions of the indenture that must be referred to in the bond are printed on the reverse of the certificate, as a continuation of the bond form. An alternative procedure, made possible by the flexibility provided by article 8 of the Uniform Commercial Code (UCC) is to print a summary of the pertinent indenture provisions in less formal and more easily understood language.

Even though the holders of the indenture securities are parties to the indenture contract and are bound by its terms, it is more difficult, in their case, to find all the essential elements of a true contractual relationship. Because the holders cannot exist as such until after the contract has been executed and delivered, they cannot have a part in negotiating the indenture's terms, although the underwriting houses' counsel that is acting for the "purchasers" may do so on their behalf. In addition, the indenture is like a unilateral contract to which the security holders become parties by purchasing their security. But here, too, the analogy is somewhat strained, for the investor seldom reads the indenture before buying the securities. In fact, except for institutional or professional investors, the indenture is almost never read by the security holders, and if it were, many would not understand it. Nevertheless, for the proper functioning of these financing arrangements, it is essential that contractual principles be applied and that the indenture provisions be binding on the security holders as parties, even though in dealing with the obligor, the individual holder is at a disadvantage if there should be a default in payment of the principal or interest on the obligation held.

These considerations have led many courts not only to construe indenture provisions as being strictly against the obligor but also to try to find some other legal theory or precedent with which to protect the interests of the security holders. Such decisions have contributed to much of the confusion in the law, particularly as it relates to the third set of contractual relationships—those between the trustee and the security holders. The existence of a "trust" is necessary to create and define the trustee's interest in and relation to the security and the contract, but its relationship to the security and to the security holders is essentially contractual rather than fiduciary. The trust's principal function is to administer the contract in accordance with its terms. It has only the authority and powers granted by the indenture and is subject to all its restrictions and limitations. Except to the limited extent specified, the trustee has no right or authority to represent or act for the security holders or to substitute its judgment for theirs. The trustee should be held accountable for failing to carry out its duties properly, but there is no basis for holding, as some courts have tried to do, that the trustee owes to each holder duties or obligations not specifically spelled out in the contract[4] or required of it by statute or regulation.

When the trustee's obligation with respect to a particular subject matter is spelled out in the contract, there will be no difficulty if the obligation is carried out. There is a danger, however, that if the indenture is silent on a particular point, an implied obligation will be found in either the other indenture provisions or legal precedents evolved under different circumstances. It is therefore important to the trustee that the indenture clearly indicate its responsibilities in regard to all significant matters relating to the security or the obligations, even if it merely indicates that no responsibility exists. For example, in a mortgage indenture, the trustee's obligations, or lack thereof, with respect to maintenance, insurance, payment of taxes, and the like should be clearly spelled out to prevent the possibility of finding a substantial responsibility in the absence of any provision at all.[5]

TYPICAL PROVISIONS OF AN INDENTURE

Although the most important provisions of the indenture are discussed in later chapters in detail, we summarize them here. These examples were taken from a mortgage indenture of an industrial corporation; the general provisions for a municipal indenture are similar. Provisions of other indentures may differ in various respects, depending on the nature of the company or municipality, whether the obligations are secured or unsecured, the structure of the financing, and whether the indenture is qualified under the Trust Indenture Act of 1939 (TIA).[6] Municipal securities are not subject to the TIA.

---

[4] See *infra*, p. 60.

[5] For a discussion of the expanding scope of the trustee's potential liability, see chapter 3 and the discussion of secondary market disclosure in chapter 13.

[6] 15 U.S.C. secs. 77aaa *et seq.* (1990), as amended by the Trust Indenture Reform Act of 1990, P.L. 101–550 (TIRA). Subsequent references are to TIA section numbers, 301 through 328. For the complete text of the amended act, see the appendices.

Recitals

Each indenture begins by naming the parties and usually lists the reason for its creation. It declares the purpose of the issue and states that all legal requirements and authorizations have been fulfilled or obtained. It is important that such recitals be included because they may constitute an estoppel against a later assertion by the obligor that the mortgage or debt was not properly authorized.

The form of the bond, the interest coupon if it is a bearer bond,[7] and the trustee's (and authenticating agent's if any) certificate of authentication are also customarily set forth in full. As stated earlier, the form of bond should contain all the essential elements of the contract, either specifically or by appropriate reference to the indenture. Only those obligations conforming substantially to the form prescribed in the indenture should be authenticated by the trustee.

Granting Clauses

Following the recitals come the granting clauses that specify the security for the obligations to be issued. These clauses include a recital of the consideration, a specific grant to the trustee, and a description of the property to be mortgaged, in sufficient detail to enable the indenture to be properly recorded as a mortgage. If any securities or other properties are to be pledged, they are described. The specific property descriptions are usually followed by general descriptions of other properties intended to be included in the conveyance, such as appurtenances, franchises, and fixtures. The indenture should also explain the extent to which it is intended to become a lien on after-acquired property. It is also customary to enumerate the types or classes of property exempted from the conveyance and any other provisions that might help define the nature and scope of the security to be granted. The granting clauses conclude with the habendum and trust clauses, which create the trust relationship and specify the purposes and conditions on which the grant is made.

Definitions

All the important terms used in the indenture are usually defined, clearly and carefully, in a separate article. Not only is this a convenience for

[7] The Tax Equity and Fiscal Responsibility Act of 1982, Pub. L. 97–248, 96 Stat. 324, 576., effectively eliminated the issuance of corporate bearer bonds (as of January 1, 1983) and tax-

those who will later work with the indenture, but it also makes the job of drafting much easier. Throughout the indenture, defined terms that are in capital letters refer to the relevant definition article.

Amount, Form, Execution, Delivery, Registration, and Exchange of Bonds

Whether under this or a similar heading, these sections—amount, form, execution, delivery, registration, and exchange—contain important mechanical provisions for dealing with the obligations themselves and deserve careful attention at the time of drafting, particularly by those representatives of the trustee who will administer them. Included here are any limitations on the principal amount of bonds that may be issued or be outstanding at any one time under the indenture; the form of the bonds (if not included in the recitals), or the authority for the board of directors or municipal entity to determine the form, and other provisions with respect to any subsequent series; provisions regarding the manner in which the bonds are to be executed; a statement of who may sign; authorization of the use of facsimile seal or facsimile signatures if permitted by the law of the particular jurisdiction; authorization of temporary bonds in appropriate cases and provisions for their exchange for definitive bonds; appointment of a registrar and authorization of the issuance of bonds in registered form; provisions establishing the various denominations in which the bonds may be issued and prescribing the conditions on which bonds of one denomination may be exchanged for a bond or bonds of other denominations; provisions for issuing bonds to replace mutilated, destroyed, lost, or stolen bonds and the evidence and indemnity required; provisions with respect to treasury bonds or bonds reacquired by the obligor; language establishing and providing for the negotiability of the bonds; and similar provisions that may be deemed desirable to authorize and facilitate the efficient servicing of the obligations as long as they remain outstanding.[8]

Because most modern indentures, particularly open-end indentures, remain in existence for a long period of time, these provisions should be

---

exempt bearer bonds (as of July 1, 1983), by imposing adverse tax consequences on both issuer and investor.

[8] If the issue provides for book-entry-only certificates, the authorization should be included in this section. For specific sample provisions, see American Bar Association, Business Law Section, article 2, Sample Uncertificated Debt Indenture, draft dated January 28, 1991. See also Report of the Ad Hoc Committee on Uncertificated Debt Securities, *Bus. Law.* (May 1991).

made as broad and as flexible as possible so that both the obligor and the trustee can take advantage of changing and more efficient methods for processing and handling the indenture securities.

Issuance of Bonds

Included in the issuance of bonds section are the terms and conditions on which bonds may be issued under the indenture and the documents that must be furnished to the trustee on the basis of which it is authorized to authenticate and deliver the bonds.

Redemption of Bonds

If the obligor wants to reserve the right to retire the obligations, in whole or in part, before their stated maturity, this right must be reserved in the indenture. These provisions are included in a special article and specify the conditions under which bonds may be prepaid; the premium required, if any; the method of giving notice to the holders; and other pertinent requirements.

Sinking Fund

If the obligor is required to provide a sinking fund for retiring a portion of the outstanding bonds from time to time, this article will give the amount of the sinking fund, how it is to be paid, and the manner in which it must be applied by the trustee.

Particular Covenants

Covenants are an important part of each indenture contract and are normally discussed in a separate article. Most indentures, whether secured or unsecured, include covenants of some kind. They can be both affirmative—requiring the performance of certain things by the obligor, either continuously or at specified times—and negative—placing restrictions on particular activities of the obligor, such as incurring additional debt. These covenants provide additional security to the holders of the indenture securities, and the trustee has particular duties with respect to their enforcement.

Provisions in Regard to Pledged Collateral

If the indenture is in the form of a collateral trust, in which the security consists in whole or in part of securities or similar collateral pledged with the trustee, the indenture must explain in detail just how this collateral is to be administered. Matters such as the following should be covered: the form in which the collateral is to be held (whether bearer or registered and, if registered, in what name or names); collection and disposition of income; voting of stock; disposition of principal collected; enforcement of rights as a holder; action to be taken on default in payment or under the indenture securing the bonds or debentures held; release, substitution, replacement, and the like; and any other matters deemed to be pertinent to proper administration to achieve the purposes for which the pledge was made.[9]

Remedies of the Trustee and Bondholders

The article concerning remedies of the trustee and bondholders includes the default and remedial provisions. Events constituting a default under the indenture must be spelled out in detail, including grace periods, if any. Since the trustee has only the powers specifically granted by the contract, these powers must always include the alternative remedies available on default, with a grant of sufficient authority to pursue the remedies. The article must contain a statement of the rights of security holders under the indenture, individually or collectively, and, particularly, any limitation on the rights of security holders.

Immunity of the Incorporators, Stockholders, Officers, and Directors

Since the obligations are corporate and municipal obligations, a provision is almost always included that specifically grants immunity to the stockholders, directors, officers, elected officials, and so forth, with respect to the indenture or the securities to be issued. A similar provision is usually included in the form of the bond. Although this immunity is now fairly well established as a matter of general law, the provision is intended as protection against the possible application of some remote statutory or implied liability in a particular jurisdiction. It is doubtful that the protection would be applicable if fraudulent misrepresentations were involved. In fact, the 33 Act[10] has specific penalties for misrepresentations or misleading statements in a registration statement or prospectus.

---

[9]For a discussion of collateral represented by pools of assets, see chapter 15.
[10]15 U.S.C. sec. 77a (1976).

Consolidation, Merger, and Sale

The article regarding consolidation, merger, and sale lists the conditions under which corporate obligors may sell or lease all or substantially all its properties or may merge into or with another corporation. If the corporate obligor has subsidiary companies, they should also be specifically covered in these provisions, for the conditions affecting subsidiaries may be quite different from those applicable to the parent company. In many indentures, particularly debenture agreements, this article is an additional negative covenant. Typically, municipal or other governmental entities are not involved in merger provisions or subsidiary entities.

Releases

If the indenture is a secured indenture, and particularly if the security is a mortgage or collateral is held by the trustee, the obligor must be permitted to dispose of or substitute particular segments of the property as may be required or desirable from time to time. The indenture must describe the conditions under which this disposition or substitution may be made and the documents and consideration that must be furnished to the trustee.

Possession Until Default—Defeasance

Since the trustee's interest in the property is simply a security interest, the obligor is entitled to retain possession of it, at least until default, and this article—concerning retaining possession until default—confirms this right. It is also important to provide for a reconveyance to the obligor, and the terms and conditions on which it will be made, if the obligor performs all the terms and conditions of the indenture.

Concerning the Trustee

The article concerning the trustee is the most important and is explored in the next chapter. The trustee's specific duties, responsibilities, and liabilities are explained in detail, and the necessary and appropriate exculpatory and protective provisions are examined.

Requirements Regarding Evidence of Compliance with the Indenture's Provisions and Certificates

The TIA requires that certain statements or reports be furnished to the trustee as evidence of compliance with particular types of provisions, as well as the contents of certificates and opinions with respect to compliance with conditions and covenants.[11]

Supplemental Indentures, Bondholders' Meetings, Bondholders' Acts, Holdings, and Apparent Authority

The provisions for supplemental indentures, bondholders' meetings, bondholders' acts, holdings, and apparent authority explain the manner in which the indenture contract may be supplemented or amended. Some amendments may be made by the obligor and the trustee without reference to the security holders, and these are usually enumerated. In general, any provision that does not affect a substantive right of the security holders may be added without their consent. Other provisions may be changed with the consent of a specified percentage of the holders, whereas still others require 100 percent consent. If the holders' consent is required, the manner in which it is to be evidenced will be spelled out, as will the nature of the evidence on which the trustee may rely in establishing ownership of particular obligations.

Various miscellaneous provisions are embodied in a final article.

MODEL INDENTURES

Since the indenture was first used, approximately 165 years ago, it has developed into the largest and, in many respects, the most complex of legal documents. Language was added through the years in response to frequent court decisions interpreting particular provisions, but until 1962, little effort was made to reduce the excess verbiage or to standardize its provisions.

In 1962, the American Bar Foundation announced the adoption of the Corporate Debt Financing Project—A Project to Develop a Model Form of Corporate Debenture Indenture and Mortgage with Annotations and Comments.[12] The basic format, adopted in 1965 after extended discussions by the project committees, contains two documents. One document, called Model Provisions, consists solely of the traditional boilerplate provisions common to most corporate debt indentures. The second

---

[11] TIA secs. 314(c), (d), (e), and (f).

[12] For a detailed discussion of the background of the project, see Churchill Rodgers, "The Corporate Trust Indenture Project," 20 *Bus. Law.* 551 (1965).

document, sometimes called an Incorporating Indenture, incorporates by reference the Model Provisions, or as many of them as agreed to by the parties to the particular financing.

The incorporating indenture also contains the negotiated provisions, which usually include the principal amount, the interest rate, the stated maturity and the terms of redemption of the debenture issue, certain covenants, and other special provisions, all as negotiated by the parties. These documents were the result of many meetings and discussions by attorneys who had frequently represented the issuers or investors or investment bankers, a representative group of corporate trust officers, the SEC (with particular reference to conformity with the TIA), the New York Stock Exchange, and the Ad Hoc Consultative Committee of the American Institute of Certified Public Accountants. The final product inevitably contained many compromises. Nevertheless, it represented an important contribution by simplifying those provisions that were generally subject to negotiation in the drafting of indentures and providing standardized boilerplate for nonnegotiated provisions.[13]

The use of the 1965 Model Provisions (which provided for both bearer and fully registered debentures) was limited by the fact that by the time of its publication, many new issues were being offered in registered form only. In the latter part of 1964, while the 1965 Model Provisions were still in the drafting stage, the corporate trust group urged the project's directorate to prepare Model Debenture Indenture Provisions for "all-registered" issues. This corporate trust group secured general agreement on the basic procedures that should be incorporated in the model provisions, and early in 1966 the group published its recommendations.[14]

The result of this cooperative effort was the publication of a companion Sample Incorporating Indenture and a companion Model Provisions, which were tailored to all-registered issues of debentures but whose text was otherwise substantially the same as that of the two 1965 documents.[15]

The Model Provisions do not constitute an instrument but were intended as an exhibit to be attached to an indenture in the form recommended by the Sample Incorporating Indenture. It is, therefore, possible

[13] American Bar Foundation, Sample Incorporating Indenture—Model Debenture Indenture Provisions—1965.

[14] American Bankers Association, Corporate Trust Activities Committee, *Recommended Procedures for Registered Bond Issues* (1966). See also Joseph C. Kennedy and Robert I. Landau, "Recent Developments in Debt Financing and Corporate Trust Administration," 22 *Bus. Law.* 353 (1967).

[15] American Bar Foundation, Model Debenture Indenture Provisions—All Registered Issues—1967.

in the incorporating indenture to express specific deviations from the Model Provisions or to omit certain provisions by not incorporating them in the indenture.

The practice recommended by the project of incorporating the Model Provisions in the indenture by means of reference has rarely been used in practice because of its complexities, but the substantive provisions of the Sample Incorporating Indenture and the Model Provisions are often used as part of the modern indenture and are seldom modified or changed.

The publication of the Commentaries on Indentures[16] marked the third major step in achieving the project's objective. The Commentaries were intended to accomplish a number of things: to outline the Model Provisions and how they were to be used, to explain why the particular form used was adopted and why certain traditional but outmoded provisions could be safely eliminated, to deal with the theories underlying the negotiable positions of the indenture, and to offer sample alternative provisions that might be suitable for particular requirements.

With the publication in 1981 of the Model Mortgage Bond Indenture Form, the project completed its objectives, established nineteen years earlier.[17]

The Model Mortgage Form is structured as an integrated mortgage indenture, in place of the two-part technique used in the earlier models. It contains standardized model provisions and the negotiable provisions and includes many footnotes referring to the Debenture Commentaries, providing illustrations of alternative texts.

The next effort to streamline the trust indenture was the publication of a Model Simplified Indenture.[18] The model developed by the American Bar Association's Committee on Developments in Business Financing is relatively short—thirty-one pages—and is written in "plain English." The simplified model proceeds on the assumption

> that (except for provisions specifically required by the TIA) nearly all portions of an indenture are subject to negotiation in varying degrees, but seek to prescribe the language of frequently encountered provisions in such a way as to achieve a consensus generally acceptable to counsel accustomed to analyzing

[16] American Bar Foundation, Commentaries on Indentures, 1972.

[17] American Bar Foundation, Model Mortgage Bond Indenture, 1981. See also Brown, "Review of Mortgage Bond Indenture Forms," 36 *Bus. Law.* 1917 (1981).

[18] See chapter 1, note 1, *supra.*

[19] Id. at 742.

indenture terms from the points of view of debenture holders, corporate borrowers, lending institutions, investment bankers and indenture trustees.[19]

The extensive notes to the model are often explained with a comparison with the American Bar Foundation's model indentures and commentaries or with reference to stock exchange listing requirements or prevailing administrative practice.

The project's most recent endeavor is the Sample Uncertificated Debt Indenture, which provides for the issuance of corporate debt securities in either certificated or noncertificated form, at the holder's option.[20] Developed under the aegis of the Business Law Section of the American Bar Association by a group of distinguished securities lawyers, with advice from several corporate trust professionals, the proposed indenture attempts to provide for the issuance of corporate debt instruments in pure uncertificated (i.e., dematerialized) form, as contemplated by the 1977 UCC article 8 revisions, and the recommendations of the U.S. Working Committee of the Group of Thirty that "it is both desirable and achievable to eliminate use of the physical certificate by 1995 for the settlement of securities transactions."[21] In its report, the Ad Hoc Committee of the Business Law Section recognized that using this approach for municipal securities might be a problem, since

> many state laws require that municipal securities receive approval from local or state agencies other than the issuer thereof. Even when such statutes contemplate uncertificated securities, there may be a problem in the approving agency delegating its certification responsibility to the indenture trustee. Certain of such statutes could be construed to require approving agency signatures (albeit facsimiles) on each transaction statement

sent by the trustee to the seller and buyer involved.

The sum total of these efforts has produced valuable additions to the field of corporate finance, particularly the simplification and standardization of the corporate trust indenture.

[20] See note 8, *supra.*

[21] See U.S. Working Committee, Group of Thirty, Clearance and Settlement Project, *Status Report and Request for Comment* 8 (Aug. 1990).

THREE

The Corporate Trustee

DEVELOPMENT OF THE TRUSTEE CONCEPT

The development of a concept of the indenture trustee's duties and responsibilities has closely paralleled the growth and development of the
trust indenture itself. In the very early history of corporate mortgages, the
mortgage sometimes ran directly to the bondholders themselves, without
a trustee being named. The difficulties presented by such an arrangement
became apparent when the first default under such a mortgage occurred.
The court ruled that for the mortgage to be foreclosed, all bondholders
had to join in the petition. Consequently, the practice of using a trustee to
whom the mortgage would run for the benefit of all the bondholders was
adopted at an early date.

In the first years of this development, the trustee was usually one person, frequently an officer of the issuing corporation. Although this person's interests obviously opposed those of the bondholders, it made little
practical difference, for the trustee at that time was simply a convenience
for the mortgagor and had few, if any, actual duties to perform. The
trustee was, in almost every sense, a mere stakeholder.

With the growth in the number of indentures and the gradually increasing intricacies of corporate borrowing, criticism began to be directed at this officer–trustee device, and it soon became impractical. The
next step was designating an independent person as trustee. To give
added status to the issue, the persons selected were usually outstanding
citizens in the community.

The first instance of a bank being designated as an indenture trustee occurred in 1839, but the use of an institutional, as opposed to an individual, trustee did not become general practice until the latter part of the nineteenth century. The initial reason for the change was undoubtedly to avoid the problems presented by the death or incapacity of an individual trustee. After initial authentication of the bonds, there were few duties to be performed, and the responsibilities were not onerous.

As the use of the corporate indenture became more common and numerous problems were presented as a result of defaults, it was inevitable that greater power should be placed in the hands of the corporate trustee. As corporations grew and the size of their bond issues increased and became more complex, it became difficult for the bondholders themselves, either individually or collectively, to enforce their security in the event of default. Consequently, more and more restrictions were placed on lawsuits by individual holders, and most rights of action were concentrated in the trustee. It was much easier to create an appearance of protection, however, than it was to provide remedies adequate in fact. Several factors impeded the orderly growth and development of the trustee's duties and responsibilities.

Many banks viewed corporate trusteeships in the same way as they did escrows, and they accepted them, usually without compensation, as a service to their corporate banking customers. Laissez-faire was the guiding economic theory of the day, and it was not surprising that in this, as in other areas of corporate practice, a real sense of responsibility was slow in developing.

The growth in the trustee's duties was accompanied by an equivalent growth in the number and scope of exculpatory clauses. Early efforts to raise the fees for trustee services were resisted, and the trustee's resulting reluctance to undertake lengthy, expensive, and time-consuming legal proceedings was understandable.

As indicated earlier, there were no clear-cut legal precedents but, rather, considerable confusion in the minds of the courts about the exact nature of the indenture and the legal responsibility of the trustee for preserving and enforcing the security. The courts' reliance on different precedents and concepts led to many conflicting opinions and to the introduction of new and unusual provisions into each indenture. After each court decision, indenture drafters devised new language for the protection of the obligor and the trustee. As a result, the corporate indenture developed rapidly into one of the most complex of all legal documents, without offering a real solution to the problem of providing reasonable protection to security holders without exposing the trustee to undue and unwarranted liability.[1]

A start had been made, however. Many of the more responsible banks began to express concern over the losses suffered by bondholders and the apparent ineffectiveness of remedies after default. The volume of corporate trust business was now sufficient to warrant the establishment of separate corporate trust units in the larger institutions, and this led to a reexamination of policies and practices. The sense of responsibility grew, and more attention was paid to all phases of corporate trust activity. Even the older indentures, which contained little more than the basic mortgage provisions, took advantage of the "further assurance" clauses to update its information about the status of the security and the condition of the obligor's affairs. In newly drafted indentures, trustees began to insist on including additional protective provisions and covenants. A new pattern of responsibility rapidly emerged, and by the late 1920s, the corporate trustee had begun to be recognized as an important party to these financial transactions.

The pattern thus established by the more responsible institutions was not universal, however, and the practices still followed in a number of cases brought continued criticism by the courts and recognized authorities in the field. The financial collapse of 1929 and the ensuing Great Depression resulted in an increasing number of defaults and led to a critical examination of all phases of security practice. Although the broad generalities embodied in the conclusions and recommendations of the SEC report[2] were neither impartial nor fair, no serious student of the subject could question the desirability of establishing minimum standards to which the trust indentures and the conduct of corporate trustees should conform. The TIA, in effect, codified the more important practices that had been developed and were already being followed by the leading corporate trust departments. As indicated, the essential provisions of this act are now fairly standard for all corporate indentures, whether or not they are required to be qualified under the act, although private placement agreements usually do not impose the "prudent man" standard on the occurrence of a default.

Whereas by 1940, the practice of using an individual—as opposed to an institutional—trustee was nearly obsolete, the act required designating

[1] Not entirely whimsically, the corporate indenture has been defined as "the crystallized fears of five generations of lawyers."

[2] See SEC, *Report on the Study and Investigation of the Work, Activities, Personnel and Functions of Protective and Reorganization Committees*, part VI (1936).

an institutional corporate trustee meeting certain minimum standards of eligibility under all indentures to be qualified under the act.

ESSENTIAL FUNCTION OF THE CORPORATE TRUSTEE

In the following chapters, we will examine the duties of the trustee in regard to specific indenture provisions and the issuing and servicing of the indenture securities. First we consider briefly the principal areas of the trustee's responsibility.

As we pointed out in the preceding chapter, the trustee's main function is administering the security provisions of a contract between the issuing corporation and the holders of the indenture securities. There are three areas of responsibility.

First, if the issue is secured in any way, the trustee will hold and deal with the security. If the security consists in whole or in part of a mortgage on corporate real property, the trustee will be the mortgagee and must be concerned with problems related to maintenance, insurance, taxes, release, and replacement and, within the scope of the powers granted, must see that the security is maintained in the agreed manner. If the security for the bond issue is personal property, such as equipment, the trustee normally "perfects" its security interest in the property by filing a financing statement in accordance with the Uniform Commercial Code of the applicable state.

Second, as the administrator of the contract, the trustee is responsible for making sure that the covenants and other indenture provisions are performed in the agreed manner. This it does in large part by examining the reports and certificates it receives from the obligor or independent accountants, engineers, or other experts.

Finally, in the event of a default, the trustee is responsible for enforcing the contract's remedial provisions. As we will explain in greater detail in a later chapter, this responsibility has been greatly changed by the enactment of federal and state laws dealing with bankruptcy and creditors' rights. In addition to performing specifically enumerated duties, the modern corporate trustee contributes a great deal more to the relationship. Most larger institutions have a trained staff experienced in handling many types of indentures and the innumerable problems concerning them that have arisen over the years. Using this experience, corporate trust officers are able to contribute to the indenture-drafting process and frequently can suggest an appropriate course of action whenever difficulties arise. These professionals are also continually devising new and more efficient methods of handling the many administrative and operational details of processing and servicing securities through automation, as detailed in part II, "Management," thus achieving substantial savings for both issuers and security holders.

In many instances, an issuer sells long-term debt obligations to a limited number of institutional investors under a *direct placement* contract. This practice eliminates the necessity of registering such securities under the 33 Act or of qualifying an indenture. Occasionally, such securities are issued under purchase contracts with the separate investors, and no indenture or trustee is involved. This procedure can be quite proper in some cases. When security is involved, when more than a few investors purchase a single issue, when complicated sinking-fund or similar provisions are involved, or, again, when the terms of the contract are unusual and require frequent checking, the use of a trustee is recommended. From the investor's point of view, the trustee's activities supplement rather than supersede those of the investor institution. From the obligor's point of view, the convenience and service obtained usually outweigh the fairly nominal fees charged.

The terms of these issues are usually set in consultation with an investment banker and after discussion with one or more of the principal prospective purchasers. A special counsel appointed by the issuer to represent the purchaser traditionally drafts the financing documents. Although the flexibility available as a result of direct negotiations between the issuer and the purchaser is regarded as a major advantage of private placements, patterns of inflexibility developed when the major institutional investors established their own set of required covenants, sometimes without regard to the needs of a particular case. As a result, many of the existing note purchase agreements follow a more or less rigid pattern, which is not always in the best interests of either the issuer or the investor. For public and many private issues, an experienced corporate trustee, familiar with all types of financing arrangements, is an important addition to the team of experts who work out the operational details of the financing document. A similar contribution can be made in the case of privately placed note issues.

The use of a corporate trustee for such issues also helps solve problems encountered in the past and, on the positive side, provides numerous benefits, such as the following:

1. Uniform administration of the contract's security provisions.
2. Identification of the holders of notes entitled to the benefits of the

contract, provided by the trustee's authentication of the notes issued.

3. Improved marketability of the obligations. To qualify for exemption from the registration requirements of the 33 Act, the notes must be bought for investment and not for distribution. However, for an institutional investor, it is necessary that any obligation purchased be marketable: indeed, an increasing volume of obligations originally placed privately are being sold by the original investors. This trend can be expected to grow with the development of the secondary market for private placements, which SEC Rule 144A is intended to facilitate. Obvious problems are thus created, not only in carrying out these transactions, but also in determining the transferees' rights in the absence of an indenture and uniform provisions governing transfers or assignments.

4. Improved marketability to reduce the interest cost to obligors. Institutional investors usually insist, because of limited marketability, on a premium of ten to twenty basis points in the rate of interest paid on notes acquired in a private placement. Anything that improves marketability should reduce this spread.

5. Efficient servicing of the debt obligations, particularly in applying the amortization formula to ensure continuation of the investors' interests in the total debt. Many issuers now employ a bank as agent to render these services.

6. More efficient communication. Each investor usually receives a complete set of all documents at each note closing, although it is difficult to understand what real purpose they serve. If a complete set of documents were delivered to the trustee acting on behalf of all investors, all that any investor should require would be the note itself, a copy of the purchase agreement, and the opinion of its special counsel. This should represent a considerable saving to most institutional investors, as well as to the issuers.

ELIGIBILITY REQUIREMENTS

Section 310 of the TIA lists the requirements that an institution must meet to be eligible to serve as an indenture trustee. The act requires that there be at all times one or more trustees, at least one of which must be a corporation organized and doing business under the laws of the United States or of any state or territory or the District of Columbia. This trustee must be authorized under such laws to exercise corporate trust powers and be subject to supervision or examination by federal, state, territorial, or District of Columbia authority. It must have at all times a combined capital and surplus of not less than $150,000. Foreign institutions are now permitted to serve as corporate trustees under certain circumstances.[3] The act prohibits any obligor on the indenture securities—or any person directly or indirectly controlling, controlled by, or under the common control of this obligor—from acting as a trustee on the indenture securities.[4]

These requirements are minimal and enable almost any banking institution normally exercising trust powers to act. Many qualified indentures impose much more stringent requirements. For example, a customary minimum capital and surplus requirement is $5 million.[5] Often, the corporate trustee must have its principal office in one of the large financial centers, such as New York City. But this requirement is no longer as important, for many institutions throughout the country are now fully qualified and have the technology to act under most indentures. Instead, the experience and qualifications of the prospective trustee should be considered.

Inasmuch as the trustee will have been selected and will be acting at the time the indenture is executed and delivered, the purpose of the eligibility provision is to govern the selection of a successor trustee in the event the original trustee resigns or becomes incapable of acting. Because this is a substantive provision, a successor trustee that does not meet the specified standards cannot be named without the consent of all, or a specified percentage of, the security holders. In the unlikely event that no other trustee can be found that meets the requirements of the indenture and is willing to act, it has been held that a trustee not meeting such requirements can be appointed and can exercise all the rights and powers granted by the indenture. If such a situation should develop, however, it is recommended that judicial sanction for such an appointment first be obtained.

PROHIBITION OF CONFLICTING INTERESTS— QUALIFICATION OF THE TRUSTEE

The problem of conflicting interests is a troublesome one and one of which the trustee should always be conscious.[6] Issuing corporations often

---

[3] TIA sec. 310 (a)(1).

[4] TIA sec. 310 (a)(5).

[5] Many major corporate issuers insist on a potential trustee bank's having at least $25 million in combined capital and surplus.

[6] Even if the issue is exempt from the TIA, this does not necessarily mean that the trustee is exculpated from adhering to conduct that would be prohibited if the issue were qualified.

select one of their principal banks to act as indenture trustee. The familiarity of such an institution with the corporation's affairs and their close continuing relationship enable the institution to do a more thorough job for both the security holders and the issuing corporation. The administrative officers should thoroughly learn all relationships between their bank and the obligor corporation and ensure that the fairness and impartiality of the trustee's acts cannot be questioned. Although many corporations and municipalities do select their primary bank to serve as trustee, competitive pricing for trustee services has eroded some of the obligor's loyalties to these banks.

One of the innovations introduced by the TIA in 1939 was certain rules that would disqualify an institution from acting as a trustee for a qualified indenture. Recognizing that before default, the trustee's duties are essentially administrative and ministerial, the TIRA suspended the requirement of resigning because of a conflict of interest until a default occurs. These provisions are stated in section 310(b) and are now incorporated by force of law in all qualified indentures. This section does not, however, cover the whole field of conflicts or prohibit any interest that might be a conflict. The trustee is deemed to have a potential conflicting interest if it has one or more of ten different relationships. We next look at these relationships from the viewpoint of prohibited general interests or affiliations.

Trusteeship Under More Than One Indenture

Section 310(b)(1) identifies as a potential conflicting interest the same trustee acting under more than one indenture of the same obligor "or is trustee for more than one outstanding series of securities . . . under a single indenture of an obligor." The latter provision, which was unfortunately included in the TIRA, appears to mandate that there be separate trustees for each series of defaulted bonds issued under secured indentures, for example, utility and railroad mortgages. The SEC's broad exemptive powers, as well as the stay-of-resignation provisions absent a payment default, should, one hopes, resolve this problem, except in two situations. The first occurs when the qualified indenture is a collateral indenture, in which the only collateral consists of obligations issued under the other indenture. The second exception occurs when both issues are unsecured and confer on the holders substantially the same rights. It is required, however, that the qualified indenture specifically refer to the obligations under the other (prior) indenture. An exception is allowed when the second indenture is subsequently qualified under the act. On application, the SEC may permit trusteeship under more than one indenture after a default if it finds that the trusteeship is not likely to involve a material conflict of interest.

The significance of the same trustee acting under separate indentures is apparent. Although before default the trustee might act without difficulty under two indentures of the same obligor, in the event of default, this situation usually creates a conflict and prevents the trustee from adequately representing the holders under both indentures, for their interests are quite likely to be contradictory. Acting under separate indentures upon default becomes difficult when attempting to locate a successor trustee, and so large corporations often name a number of trustees for their debt security issues. The recent consolidation in the corporate trustee industry and the general banking industry, which is more fully discussed in part II, may make it difficult to locate a qualified trustee who is not already serving as a trustee for the obligor. The importance of having independent representation in the proceedings after a default was initially recognized in an 1895 decision of the federal court in New York, which permitted the intervention of individual bondholders in a foreclosure suit in which the trustee was acting under several indentures. Also, it was suggested that the trustee be subjected to a higher standard of care when it was acting under more than one indenture.

The term *obligor* is defined in the TIA as every person (including a guarantor) who is liable on the indenture securities.[7] Trusteeship under indentures of affiliated companies is permissible if the same company is not liable on the indenture securities issued under more than one of these indentures.

A difficult question arises when no guaranty in fact exists but the credit of one corporation is the primary security for the obligations issued by another. Such a situation would arise, for example, if corporation A issued securities for the construction of certain facilities to be leased to corporation B, the rental payments being sufficient to service the securities and the lease and the right to rents being pledged under the indenture. These facts alone are not sufficient to make corporation B an "obligor" on the securities, but greater care should be exercised in such a situation, and all the facts surrounding the proposed transaction should be considered to determine whether an actual, as distinguished from a technical, conflict is likely to arise.

---

[7] TIA sec. 303 (12).

Ownership of Securities

Subdivisions (5) to (9) of section 310(b) list the rules for disqualifying the trustee based on affiliations through security ownership. Disqualification under these subdivisions is not based on the actual control of, or any conflicting interest in fact, but the beneficial ownership of the specified percentage of securities is required to be made a conflicting interest as a part of the contract between the parties. A potential conflicting interest is deemed to exist, and upon default, the trustee will be disqualified from acting as such if any of the following situations exist:

1. Ten percent or more of the voting securities of the trustee is beneficially owned by an obligor or any director, partner, or executive officer of an obligor; 20 percent or more of such voting securities is collectively owned by any two or more of such persons; or 10 percent or more of such voting securities is beneficially owned by an underwriter for the obligor or any director, partner, or executive officer of it, or is beneficially and collectively owned by any two or more such persons.

2. Beneficial ownership by the trustee or the holding by the trustee as collateral security for an obligation that is in default as to principal for thirty days or more of (a) 5 percent or more of the voting securities of the obligor; (b) 10 percent or more of any other class of security of the obligor, excluding all securities issued under an indenture for which the trustee is acting as trustee; (c) 5 percent or more of the voting securities of a person who, to the knowledge of the trustee, owns 10 percent or more of the voting securities of, or controls directly or indirectly, or is under direct or indirect common control with, an obligor; (d) 10 percent or more of any class of security of a person who, to the knowledge of the trustee, owns 50 percent or more of the voting securities of an obligor; or (e) 10 percent or more of any class of security of an underwriter for an obligor.

Since a conflicting interest because of the trustee's ownership of the preceding percentage of securities is predicated on the existence of an adverse interest in the trustee, ownership of securities issued under the particular indenture in question, or under any other indenture for which the trustee also acts as trustee, is excluded.

3. Ownership by the trustee of securities in a fiduciary capacity. The trustee is required to check its holdings promptly after the date of a default on the indenture securities, and annually as long as the default continues, of the types of securities just enumerated in its capacity as executor, administrator, testamentary or *inter-vivos* trustee, guardian, committee, conservator, or any similar capacity. A potential conflicting

interest is deemed to exist if on such date, the trustee holds in such capacities an aggregate of 25 percent or more or any class of security, the beneficial ownership of a specified percentage of which would constitute a conflict. To eliminate the possibility of an inadvertent conflict arising through acquiring securities in new estates, the act provides that the conflict provisions will not apply, for a period not to exceed two years from the date of such acquisition, to the extent that such securities do not exceed 25 percent or more of the particular class outstanding.

If there is a default in the payment of principal or interest under an indenture that continues for thirty days, the trustee is required to promptly check its fiduciary holdings, and thereafter any ownership in this capacity of securities over which it has sole or joint control is to be deemed beneficial ownership for the purpose of determining whether a potential conflict exists.

Excluded from the operation of subdivisions (6) to (9) of section 310(b) is any security held by the trustee as collateral security for an obligation not in default; held as collateral security under the indenture, irrespective of any default; or held by it in the capacity of custodian, escrow agent, depositary, agent for collection, or any similar representative capacity.

Other Affiliations Between Trustee and Obligor or Underwriters

Four other situations are specified in section 310(b), the existence of any one of which constitute a potential conflict of interest.

In the first situation, the trustee or any of its directors or executive officers is an underwriter for an obligor. The TIRA defines an *underwriter* as any person who, within one year before the determination is made, was an underwriter of any security of an obligor.

In the second situation, the trustee or any of its directors or executive officers is a director, officer, partner, employee, appointee, or representative of an obligor or of any underwriter (other than the trustee itself) for an obligor. One person may be a director and/or executive officer of the trustee and a director and/or executive officer of an obligor if this person is not at the same time an executive officer of both. Also, if, and as long as, the number of directors of the trustee in office is more than nine, one additional person may be a director and/or executive officer of the trustee and a director of the obligor.[8]

---

[8] The SEC has indicated that "it is now our view that the term 'director' as defined in Sec-

In the third situation, the trustee directly or indirectly controls, is directly or indirectly controlled by, or is under direct or indirect common control with an underwriter for an obligor. The control referred to here is actual control, whether or not it involves ownership of a prohibited percentage of the securities referred to earlier. The question of whether or not actual control exists must be determined by the circumstances of each case.

Finally, a potential conflict of interest arises if the trustee is or becomes a creditor of the obligor. This new potential conflict codifies the existing practice of most major corporate trustees to resign a trusteeship for a financially troubled obligor when it is also a creditor. The credit policies for some banks prohibit acting as a corporate trustee if the bank is a lender. During the past few years, a number of banks have increased their credit policy focus on situations in which a dual trustee/creditor relationship may exist. Even though a bank is not prohibited from acting in a dual capacity, some bank credit officers have misinterpreted the TIA as prohibiting a dual role.

ADMINISTRATIVE RESPONSIBILITY UNDER CONFLICT PROVISIONS

Under a qualified indenture, if a conflict of interest as just outlined exists or develops, the trustee must either eliminate the conflict or resign within ninety days after default. The trustee should therefore establish procedures and checks that will reveal any conflict that may develop. No established routine is required, but the trustee should be able to show that it has exercised reasonable care, and it must report annually any change in its eligibility and qualifications to serve as trustee, and the creation of or any material change in any of the potential conflict of interest relationships set forth in TIA section 310(b)(1) through (10). A *material change* is any change that would cause the trustee to resign (if a default occurred) or would permit the bank to remain as trustee if there were a existing default under the indenture. It is recommended that an annual report be obtained from the obligor in regard to the latter's holding of trustee's securities, if

---

tion 303(5) of the [Trust Indenture] Act would not include emeritus, honorary or advisory directors who are appointed rather than elected and who serve merely as advisors without any other customary responsibilities or duties, including the right to vote, of directors." SEC letter, dated June 22, 1981, to James D. McLaughlin, Government Relations Counsel, American Bankers Association.

any; in regard to the outstanding securities of such obligor; and in regard to firms that have acted as underwriters for the obligor within the preceding year. Procedures in the trustee's office should be established to ensure the prompt reporting of such security holdings that might constitute a potential conflict. Although the obligor may report to the trustee only annually regarding potential conflicts, it is recommended that the trustee implement formal procedures to review potential conflicts quarterly. Larger trustees typically have implemented automated methods to review potential conflicts using standard industry codes, comparing the databases of the corporate trust department and the bank's credit department, and emphasizing general staff training.

Problems of Qualification in Foreign States

A corporation is a creature of the state in which it is incorporated, but it is a foreign entity insofar as other states are concerned. Although it is regarded as a "person" for many legal purposes, it is not entitled to the protection of the "privileges and immunities" clause of the U.S. Constitution. Accordingly, with certain exceptions relating to interstate or foreign commerce, a state may exclude a corporation of another state from doing business within its borders and from suing in its courts with respect to any prohibited transactions or otherwise engaging in activities over which the state has jurisdiction. It may also impose such terms and conditions as it deems proper for granting permission to do business within its borders. Most states have general statutes, whether on a basis of reciprocity or otherwise, relating to the conduct of business by foreign corporations.

In 1994, legislation was enacted that effectively paved the way for full interstate banking by mid-1997.[9] Banks are thus able to acquire other banks in any state or to establish branches in any state unless that state "opts out," as permitted by the 1994 legislation.

In addition, in late 1995 the Comptroller of the Currency ruled that

> a national bank that has been granted fiduciary powers may offer fiduciary services in, and have trust powers in, multiple states . . . . Such a national bank may exercise any of the fiduciary powers granted in section 92a (a) [of 12 U.S.C.] in any state unless that state both prohibits national banks and restricts its own state institutions from exercising that fiduciary power.[10]

[9]Riegle–Neal Interstate Banking and Branching Efficiency Act of 1994 (P.L. 103–328).
[10]Interpretative Letter No. 695, December 8, 1995, addressed to Banc One Corporation.

Note that this interpretation does not necessarily apply to state-chartered banks and trust companies.

Trustees may still have a problem with the "holding" of a mortgage on real property in a different state. Most larger corporations do business and own property in a number of states. When such a corporation wishes to execute a mortgage on its fixed properties to secure a bond issue, the question arises of whether the designated trustee may properly hold a security interest in property in all the states in which the property is located. It is impossible to establish a general rule for these situations because the law differs from state to state. Nonetheless, the following may be a basic guide: (1) When there is a specific statute prescribing conditions for the exercise of trust powers by foreign banking corporations, the trustee may need to qualify under this statute before accepting a mortgage or security interest in fixed property in that state; or (2) when there is no statutory provision, the trustee may normally hold such a security interest unless such act contravenes the general "doing of business" statutes. These are suggested as general guides only, however, because the statutes, and judicial interpretation of statutes, vary from state to state. Counsel should therefore be certain of the corporate trustee's proper authority in each situation.

If a corporate trustee acts without authority, it may not only subject itself to heavy penalties, but it may also, from the viewpoint of its fiduciary responsibility, be denied access to the state's courts to enforce the security if it becomes necessary.

The usual solution to this problem is to designate an individual to act as a cotrustee under the indenture. When only one state is in question, a banking corporation in that state may also be designated as a cotrustee. Under the U.S. Constitution, an individual citizen of a state is entitled to all the privileges and immunities of the citizens of other states and cannot be excluded from holding property or doing business, as can a foreign corporation. In any situation in which there is a question about the corporate trustee's authority, an individual cotrustee should be named.

Care must be exercised in drafting the appropriate indenture provisions. The usual provision, and a requirement of the TIA for qualified indentures, is that all rights, powers, duties, and obligations conferred or imposed on the trustees be conferred or imposed on and exercised by the institutional corporate trustee, or the institutional trustee and the cotrustee jointly, except to the extent that under any law of any jurisdiction in which any act or acts are to be performed, the institutional trustee is incompetent or unqualified to perform this act or acts, in which event the cotrustee must exercise and perform these rights, powers, duties, and obligations.

Since all rights, powers, and duties are to be performed by the corporate trustee, except for those functions it is incapable of performing, the corporate trustee is usually given the right, either alone or jointly with the obligor, to remove the designated individual trustee at any time and to appoint another individual to act. It is also a common practice to reserve for the corporate trustee and obligor the right to designate a cotrustee or an additional cotrustee at any time if such a designation is necessary or desirable for carrying out a specific duty. This is done even though in the first instance a cotrustee may not be required, for it avoids the possibility that the corporate trustee cannot act and no mechanism is available for resolving the difficulty.

Although any individual citizen may be designated as a cotrustee, the usual practice is for an officer of the corporate trustee to be designated as the individual cotrustee. This facilitates the exercise of powers or the performance of duties, such as executing releases of supplemental indentures, that the trustees are required to perform jointly.

Two states (Florida and Missouri) prohibit the exercise of trust powers by other than a corporation or individual citizen of that state. Although such statutes probably do not exclude an individual citizen of another state from holding or enforcing a security interest in property, it is advisable to comply with the letter of the law and to designate an individual or a bank in that state as the cotrustee. When administering indentures with an individual cotrustee, it is important to obtain from the cotrustee a signed, undated notice of resignation and keep it on file. Because indentures typically involve issuing debt securities with maturities as long as thirty years, individual trustees can be difficult to locate after many years. The signed resignation on file can thus facilitate the appointment of a replacement individual cotrustee.

These problems do not arise in the case of an unsecured debenture or note agreement, or in other indentures in which no property is mortgaged or pledged, for the trustee normally performs no acts outside its principal office.

SPECIAL PROVISIONS RELATING TO THE TRUSTEE

In addition to the matters just discussed, certain general provisions relating to the trustee should be incorporated in all indentures. These are usually found in the separate "Trustee" article.

First is the acceptance by the trustee of the trusts and obligations imposed on it by the indenture. Although the act of execution undoubtedly constitutes a sufficient acceptance, it is customary to include in the indenture an affirmative statement to this effect.

Second is a provision relating to the trustee's compensation and expenses. Rather than setting specific rates of compensation, the common practice is to entitle the trustee to reasonable compensation not limited by any statutory provision governing the compensation of trustees. This practice avoids the possibility of statutes, which exist in many states, that fix the maximum compensation for executors and trustees of testamentary or inter-vivos trusts that would be held applicable to these agreements. It is also desirable for the trustee to include a provision in which the obligor agrees to indemnify it with respect to any liability incurred or damage suffered by it resulting from other than its own negligence. The trustee should also be permitted, but not required, to make advances to preserve the mortgaged property to pay taxes or for other purposes. All these items, including all expenses and disbursements made by the trustee, should be payable by the obligor on demand (with interest in the case of any funds advanced by the trustee). If the indenture is a secured indenture, the trustee is usually given a lien on the security (before that of the indenture securities) to ensure payment of its compensation, expenses, advances, and liabilities. This is desirable, although one would be hard pressed to find a case in which the full implications of such priority of lien have been upheld.

Third, the trustee should be given authority to act through agents or attorneys in carrying out its duties, and it is customarily provided that the trustee will not be liable for the acts of these agents or attorneys if reasonable care is exercised in their selection.

Finally, the indenture should contain appropriate provisions regarding the resignation or removal of the trustee. As we indicated, a conflict of interest may require the trustee's resignation. The trustee should also be permitted to submit its resignation at any time for any reason it deems sufficient, or for no reason if it no longer wishes to serve. The indenture should provide appropriate procedures for resigning and for appointing a successor, which must be eligible and qualified to act. A majority in principal amount of the indenture security holders are usually given the absolute right to designate the successor trustee, but until they exercise this right, any successor appointed by the obligor has the full authority and power to act. As a practical matter, a successor trustee is usually appointed by the obligor and seldom by the bondholders. If the trustee is involved in a merger or consolidation with another institution, the surviving corporation, if it is eligible and qualified, usually succeeds to the trusteeship without further action.

A majority in principal amount of the indenture security holders are customarily given the absolute right, at any time and with or without cause, to remove the trustee. Because the trustee is supposed to serve their interests, it is appropriate that the security holders have the power, by majority action, to remove the trustee and substitute another if for any reason they believe their interests are not being served properly. The obligor, however, should never be given the right by unilateral action to remove the trustee. During the past decade, municipal obligors have increasingly requested the right to remove the trustee if there is no potential or actual default. The trustee should resist this request, as it appears to conflict with the general principles of appointing a corporate trustee for the benefit of the investors.

If the trustee submits its resignation and no successor is appointed within a reasonable time, the trustee or any security holder may petition a court to appoint a successor, and an institution so appointed is qualified to act.

EXCULPATORY PROVISIONS

Among the provisions that were the subject of much comment, criticism, and controversy in pre-TIA days were the "exculpatory clauses," which had come to be more or less standard in all indentures. The general legal effect of these provisions was to exempt the trustee from liability for any act or failure to act, short of willful misconduct or gross negligence. Much could be written for and against on this matter, for these clauses were enlarged and expanded over a lengthy period. This was due in no small part to the misunderstandings by security holders and courts concerning the trustee's function and their attempt to hold the trustee accountable in some way for every unfortunate and unwise investment. Under these conditions, even conscientious trustees and their counsel had to protect themselves. Notwithstanding the validity of arguments that could be, and were, made in favor of these provisions, they had two unfortunate results. First, they protected even those trustees indifferent to their fiduciary responsibility, and second, they subjected all trustees to criticism, even those who were diligent and conscientious in performing their duties, the latter comprising the great majority of trustees.

One result of the TIA's enactment was the prohibition of such broad immunity provisions.[11] A qualified indenture may not contain provisions relieving the trustee of liability for its own negligent action, its own negligent failure to act, or its own willful misconduct, although the trustee must be protected from liability for any error of judgment made in good faith by a responsible officer when the trustee was not negligent in ascertaining the pertinent facts. This has become the accepted practice for almost all modern indentures, whether qualified or not.

Certain exculpatory provisions are still proper and permissible if they do not contravene the foregoing prohibition. Trustees should try to have them included to prevent a court's reading into an indenture an implied covenant or duty on the part of the trustee when none was intended. Several cases have made it apparent, however, that trustees can no longer be absolutely assured that such exculpatory provisions do provide the protection intended. These cases seem to fall into two categories: those holding that only a trial can determine whether the trustee's duties extended beyond the indenture's provisions[12] and those that question the trustee's protection in relying on information and advice given it by the obligor, bond counsel, and even its own legal counsel.[13]

Despite these cases, the trustee's counsel should ensure that in the absence of any express duty in the indenture, or only to the extent of any duty specifically imposed, the following provisions are included:

1. The trustee has no obligation or duty to record the indenture.
2. The trustee has no responsibility for the truth or accuracy of the recitals in the indenture.
3. The trustee has no responsibility in regard to the application of the proceeds of any bonds or with respect to the use or application of any property or monies released or paid out in accordance with the indenture's provisions. An exception may be municipal indentures that direct the trustee to accept bond proceeds and invest and distribute them on the written direction of the obligor.
4. The trustee may consult with counsel and be held harmless for anything done, in good faith, in accordance with the opinion of this counsel.

[11] TIA sec. 315(d).

[12] Cronin v. Midwestern Oklahoma Development Authority, 619 F.2d 856 (10th Cir. 1980); Nelson v. Quimby Island Reclamation District Facilities Corporation, 491 F. Supp. 1364 (N.D. Cal. 1980).

[13] Matthew's v. Fischer, 1979–80 Fed. Sec. L. Rptr. para. 97,336 (S.D. Ohio 1978); Woods v. Holmes & Structures of Pittsburgh, Kansas, 489 F. Supp. 1270 (Kan. 1980).

5. The trustee is not responsible for the validity of the indenture or of any securities issued thereunder or for the obligor's title to, or the value of, the security held.

6. In the absence of bad faith, the trustee may rely on any certificates, opinions, documents, or other papers furnished to it and believed by it to be genuine and to be signed by the proper party or parties. The trustee is obligated, however, to examine any instruments furnished to it in accordance with an indenture provision to make sure that they comply with this provision.

7. The trustee is not liable for any action taken at the request or direction of the holders of a majority in principal amount of the indenture securities.

PRESCRIBED STANDARDS OF CONDUCT

What should be the prescribed standard of conduct for an indenture trustee?[14] A clear distinction should be made between the duties before a default and those after a default when the security holder's investment is in jeopardy. Normally, the obligor performs its obligations and covenants, and the investor's principal concern is in receiving interest and principal when due. Under these circumstances, the trustee's duties are largely administrative. It is important, however, that the security holders' interests be protected at all times, no matter how solvent or secure the obligor may appear. The trustee's active and vigilant administration is necessary at all times to ensure, if possible, that there is no default or, if there is a default, that the security holders will have the security for which they bargained from which to recover. If the trustee is concerned about a potential default or is uncertain about an appropriate course of action, it should consult with competent counsel or other experts. The overriding standard of conduct, in accordance with custom and practice in the industry, is that the trustee must act reasonably under the particular circumstances.

By offering its services to the public, the trustee undertakes an inherent obligation to perform these services in good faith, in a professional and competent manner, and, when appropriate, in accordance with the custom and practice of other professional corporate trustees.

---

[14] It is the board of directors that is ultimately responsible for the proper exercise of fiduciary powers by every national bank. All pertinent matters—including the determination of policies, the investment and disposition of property held in a fiduciary capacity, and the direction and review of all officers, employees, and committees used by the bank in the exercise of its fiduciary powers—are the responsibility of the board. See 12 CFR sec. 9.7(a)(1) (1989).

In this connection, corporate trust administrative officers should refer to exhibit 1, a Fiduciary Obligations Review, which outlines the recommended policies and procedures governing the conduct and performance of the bank acting as a corporate trustee.

The nature and extent of the trustee's duties vary with each indenture, depending on its terms. Because the indenture is a contract between the obligor and the trustee, it not only prescribes the rules of conduct for the former but also defines the limits of the trustee's authority, and the trustee may do only what the indenture either in express terms or by necessary implication authorizes it to do.

As authorized by the TIA before default, (1) the trustee shall be liable only for the performance of such duties as specifically set forth in the indenture; (2) the extent of such duties shall be determined solely by the express provisions of the indenture; and (3) no implied duties or covenants on the part of the trustee shall be read into the indenture.[15]

Most early court decisions dealing with the issue of fiduciary responsibilities pertained to indentures that did not contain this language, and many courts found duties implied but not expressed, frequently basing their decisions on the nature of the agreement itself. The majority of indentures still contain language that imply, but do not specify, certain duties. For example, usually a trustee may, on its own initiative, make independent investigations or require further evidence of the obligor's performance of its covenants. Such a provision is highly desirable, but it is recommended that an express qualification be inserted to the effect that the trustee is under no duty to undertake these measures. Some courts have indicated that the trustee is under an implied duty to do whatever may be necessary to preserve the trust estate and that to this extent, this duty cannot be abridged even by agreement.[16]

A real problem exists whenever the trustee deems it necessary to act beyond the scope of its express duties and powers. It is possible that an even higher standard of care may be imposed with respect to any such action, and the trustee may lose the benefit of the exculpatory clauses. If it is imperative that action be taken, the trustee should consult with counsel, and every effort should be made to find an indenture provision on which to base this action.

The TIA requires that on the occurrence of an event of default, the trustee shall exercise such of the rights and powers vested in it by the

---

[15] TIA sec. 315(a).

[16] See generally, Schreiber and Wood, "Caveat Indenture Trustees: Avoiding the Expanding Scope of Sutton's Law," 121/1 *Trusts and Estate* 48 (Jan. 1982).

indenture and shall use the same degree of care and skill in their exercise as a prudent man would exercise or use under the circumstances in the conduct of his own affairs.[17]

Despite some earlier court cases that held that trustees may have pre-default obligations beyond those set forth in the indenture,[18] it is generally accepted now that prior to a default, under an indenture the trustee's responsibilities are defined and determined solely by the terms of the indenture.[19] In *Meckel v. Continental Resources Co.*, the court concluded that "unlike the ordinary trustee, who has historic common-law duties imposed beyond those in the trust agreement, an indenture trustee is more like a stakeholder whose duties and obligations are exclusively defined by the terms of the indenture agreement."[20] Further reinforcing this doctrine, the court in *Elliott Associates v. J. Henry Schroder Bank & Trust Co.* stated that "we therefore conclude that, so long as the trustee fulfills its obligations under the express terms of the indenture, it owes the debenture holders no additional, implicit pre-default duties or obligations except to avoid conflicts of interest."[21]

It does not appear however, that this is a settled issue in all jurisdictions, since the TIA recognizes,[22] and courts have held, that states may regulate trust indentures as long as the regulation does not conflict with the TIA.[23]

[17] When the TIA was initially introduced in the Senate, it required the inclusion of a provision in every qualified indenture that the trustee had to discharge its predefault duties and obligations in a manner consistent with what a "prudent man" would assume and perform [S.2065, 76th Cong., 1st sess., sec. 315(a) (1939)]. The version of the act introduced in the House of Representatives excluded the imposition of a predefault "prudent man" duty on the trustee [H.R. 5220, 76th Cong., 1st sess., sec. 315 (1939)], which was ultimately the version enacted as section 315(c).

[18] Dabney v. Chase National Bank, 196 F.2d 668 (2d Cir. 1952), *appeal dismissed*, 346 U.S. 863 (1953); Van Gemert v. Boeing Co., 520 F.2d 1373 (2d Cir. 1975), *cert. denied*, 423 U.S. 947 (1975).

[19] Meckel v. Continental Resources Co., 758 F.2d 811 (2d Cir. 1985); Elliott Associates v. J. Henry Schroder Bank & Trust Co., 838 F.2d 66 (2d Cir. 1988). In Lorenz v. CSX, 736 F. Supp. 650 (W.D.Pa 1990), involving a non-TIA indenture, the court reached the same conclusion.

[20] 758 F.2d at 816.

[21] 838 F.2d at 71.

[22] TIA sec. 326.

[23] See, for example, United States Trust Company v. First Nat'l City Bank, 410 N.Y.S.2d 580(1980) (holding that the TIA does not abrogate an indenture trustee's common law, predefault, fiduciary duty of loyalty). For an excellent discussion of the complexity and confusion that courts have demonstrated in this area, see *In re* E.F. Hutton Southwest Properties II, Ltd., 953 F2d 963 (5th Cir. 1992).

OTHER RELATIONS BETWEEN TRUSTEE AND OBLIGOR

A trustee is generally selected from among the banks with which the obligor has a banking relationship. However, as discussed earlier, competitive fee pricing for trustee services has made this loyalty less common. Competitive fee pricing is perfectly proper, and the indenture usually contains provisions permitting all other normal and customary relationships. The trustee, in its individual capacity, may own indenture securities and, as a holder, has the same rights and privileges as do other holders. It may act as a depositary, custodian, transfer agent, registrar, paying agent, fiscal agent, or escrow agent or in any similar capacity.[24] Subject to the qualification provisions of the indenture, the trustee may also act as the trustee for the obligor, whether under an indenture or otherwise.

Although a creditor relationship between the obligor and the trustee did not create a conflict of interest under the TIA as originally enacted, the TIRA added such a relationship as a potential conflict of interest. This was a logical step in view of the suspension of the conflict-of-interest provisions until default, since the bank as the obligor's creditor may be in a position adverse to that of the bank as the trustee for the obligor's security holders whenever the obligor is in a difficult financial position or faces insolvency.

Section 311 of the TIA as originally enacted was an effort to address the creditor relationship in a different way, and in view of the TIRA, it remains something of an anachronism, although presumably it will govern the contractual rights of a trustee that has received payment on debt of the obligor within three months of an indenture default, or those of a former trustee/creditor that has resigned upon an indenture default. This section provides that if the trustee is, or will become, a creditor, directly or indirectly, of an obligor on the indenture securities within three months before a default in the payment of principal or interest on the indenture securities, it may not enforce any preferential collection of its claim against the obligor except under the conditions specified. Under these circumstances, the trustee bank must set aside, in a special account for the benefit of itself and the indenture security holders, (1) an amount equal to any and all reductions in the amount due and owing on any claim as a creditor on the principal and interest effected after the beginning of the three-month period and (2) all property received for any claim as a creditor, either as

[24] TIA sec. 310(b)(4)(C).

security therefor or in satisfaction or composition thereof, after the beginning of the three-month period, or an amount equal to the proceeds of such property, if it has been disposed of.

The trustee bank is entitled (1) to exercise any right of setoff it could have exercised if a petition in bankruptcy had been filed by or against the obligor on the date of the default; (2) to retain for its own account payments made on account of its claim by a third person, and/or distributions made in cash, securities, or other property in regard to claims filed against the obligor in bankruptcy or receivership or in proceedings for reorganization pursuant to a bankruptcy act or applicable state laws; (3) to realize for its own account on any property held as collateral security for such claim before the beginning of the three-month period; (4) to realize for its own account on any property received as security simultaneously with the creation of such claim if the trustee bank became a creditor after the beginning of the three-month period and had no reasonable cause to believe that a default would occur; and (5) to receive payment on any claim against the release of any property held as security to the extent of its fair value. Property substituted after the beginning of the three-month period has the same status as property released to the extent of the fair value of the latter, and any renewal after the beginning of this period has the same status as the preexisting claim.

The language in Section 311 regarding the disposition of any funds or property segregated in a special account is somewhat laborious. It appears that the property in the account cannot be apportioned until the obligor has gone through bankruptcy, receivership, or reorganization proceedings. The court with jurisdiction over these proceedings is given the right to apportion the property in accordance with TIA Section 311(a) or, in lieu of this apportionment, to give due consideration to these provisions in determining the fairness of the distributions to be made to the security holders and the trustee bank in the proceedings.

The formula according to which the property in the account is to be distributed is quite simple. Secured portions of the claims of both the security holders and the trustee bank are to be disregarded, and the respective claims are to be reduced to the extent of the distribution of these portions. The funds in the special account are then to be allocated so that the security holders and the trustee bank receive the same proportion of the unsecured portions of their claims from this account and from dividends paid from the obligor's estate in regard to the unsecured portions. The problem is applying the formula. Anyone familiar with reorganization proceedings can appreciate the difficulty of even approximating the value of a lien position or of the securities and interests distributed in reorganization. Calculating these values so as to allocate a fund according to an exact mathematical formula is all but impossible.

If the trustee resigns or is removed after the beginning of the three-month period, it still is subject to these provisions. If the resignation or removal came before this period, the trustee bank is subject to these provisions only if the property was received or the claim occurred after the beginning of the three-month period and within three months after the resignation or removal.

Certain creditor relationships may be excluded from the provisions of this section. These are the creditor relationships arising from (1) the ownership or acquisition of securities issued under an indenture, or any security with a maturity of one year or more at the time of its acquisition by the trustee; (2) advances for the purpose of preserving the trust estate or discharging taxes, prior liens, and the like authorized by the indenture, or by a bankruptcy or receivership court, if notice of the advance is given as provided in the indenture; (3) disbursements made in the ordinary course of business as the trustee under an indenture, transfer agent, registrar, custodian, paying agent, fiscal agent, depositary, or similar capacity; (4) indebtedness created as a result of services rendered or premises rented or as a result of goods or securities sold in a cash transaction; (5) the ownership of stock or of other securities of a corporation organized under the provisions of Section 25(a) of the Federal Reserve Act, as amended, that is directly or indirectly a creditor of the obligor; or (6) the acquisition, ownership, acceptance, or negotiation of any drafts, bills of exchange, acceptances, or obligations that can be classified as self-liquidating paper.

The increased use of the subordinated debenture issue raises special problems for a bank that is also a creditor of the issuer. In addition to prior funded indebtedness, these issues are usually made subordinate to all existing bank indebtedness and all future bank indebtedness, up to specified amounts.

What is the status of a trustee bank that is or becomes the holder of preferred indebtedness to which the debentures issued under the indenture are specifically subordinated? The intent is clear, but an ambiguity is created by the provisions of TIA Section 311, unless the preferred indebtedness to which the debentures are subordinate is specifically excepted. Indebtedness to the bank with a maturity of more than one year at the time of its creation is undoubtedly exempt from this section, for a note is a "security" within the meaning of the TIA, and securities with a maturity of more than one year are exempt from the provisions of Section 311. In regard to shorter-term indebtedness, a court might well consider the expressed intent of the parties in making an allocation in a bankruptcy or reorganization proceeding, although there is no assurance that it would do this.

Although the SEC has not conceded that the section is not operative, historically it has permitted the inclusion of a provision qualifying the preferential collection of claims provisions to the extent that the trustee is entitled to all the rights (in the indenture) with respect to any senior indebtedness at any time held by it to the same extent as is any other holder of senior indebtedness and that no other section of the indenture should be construed to deprive the trustee of any of its rights as a holder. Now that the TIA provisions are deemed incorporated into every qualified indenture and no longer are specified, trustees should include such a qualifying provision in the subordination provisions.

Despite the possibly inequitable treatment on a basis different from that accorded to other holders of the same indebtedness, until this question has been clarified by statutory amendment or judicial decision, trustees should assume that they will be required to operate in accordance with Section 311, even though they hold an obligation that by its terms is superior to the indenture securities. If they are unwilling to continue on the basis of such an assumption, the alternative is to refuse an appointment as trustee under a subordinated indenture.

THE TRUSTEE'S ROLE IN RULE 144A PRIVATE PLACEMENT TRANSACTIONS

As noted in chapter 1, the growth of Rule 144A issues since 1992 has been steady and, in the current economic environment, has assumed a useful and established part of the securities markets. For corporate trustees, this growth has presented an opportunity to provide services, even though the TIA does not apply to such issues. In particular, these services would include record keeping, collateral custody and investments, interest and principal payments, covenant monitoring, and postdefault administration.

The technical features of Rule 144A issues as they affect corporate trustees are as follows:

1. Purchasers of Rule 144A securities must be eligible as qualified institutional buyers (QIBs). These include banks, brokers, and private institutions meeting certain capital requirements.

2. The trustee should monitor transfers of Rule 144A securities to ensure that the transferee is a QIB. Many trustees require that a purchaser that may not be a well-known institution provide a simple certification that it meets the rule requirements as a QIB. It is recommended that the trustees for Rule 144A issues have operational procedures in place to monitor the QIB requirements to avoid any potential liability issues.

3. Rule 144A securities can be traded at any time and are exempt from the two-year trading restriction applied to other, nonqualified private placements.

4. A trustee does not have any unusual duties simply because the private placement issue has qualified under Rule 144A. It is, however, incumbent on the trustee to be mindful of any monitoring responsibilities imposed on it by the institutional holders in the financing documents.

LITIGATION AND DISCOVERY

Although it is not within the scope of this book to cover litigation in any detail, it is important for corporate trust professionals to appreciate that they work in an environment fraught with litigation risk. This risk is due, in large measure, to the fact that when an obligor is unable to redeem its debt obligations, security holders will seek to recover their loan from as many participants in the financing as possible. The list of potential defendants includes the obligor's underwriter, financial adviser, law firm, and accounting firm, as well as bond counsel and the corporate trustee and its counsel and agents.

The bank acting as the corporate trustee for a defaulted bond issue is an attractive target for lawsuits because of the nature of the trustee's duties and responsibilities in a postdefault situation. The trustee's performance (i.e., both its actions and its nonactions) is measured, in hindsight, against three "standards": (1) the provisions of the indenture covering the trustee's postdefault duties and responsibilities; (2) the custom and practice in the corporate trust industry in similar defaults; and (3) when applicable—the "prudent-man" rule, which may result in very different opinions by attorneys, experts, and, ultimately, judges and juries. In addition, the trustee's predefault performance and even its activities leading up to the date it legally became the trustee may be subject to examination and review by plaintiffs against both the trustee's policies and procedures and the custom and practice in the corporate trust industry.

From the trustee's perspective, it is unfortunate that the better its records are, the more thorough and complete its written policies and procedures are, and the more requirements for which it must create paper trails and document audit concerns, the easier it will be for plaintiffs to measure the trustee's actual performance against a standard of care that may not have been adhered to completely. Much of this information is obtained through both a litigation process known as *discovery* and the deposition testimony of the trustee's employees and managers. The discovery process often elicits information that gives plaintiffs new allegations of negligence or breach of fiduciary duty or supports allegations made in the original complaint.

Although we cannot address all the concerns of which trustees should be aware, the following are among the most important:

1. Account acceptance. Make sure that the bank's policies specifically authorize designated "positions" to accept a new trusteeship and that no departmental document indicates any exception to this policy. Under the Comptroller of the Currency's Regulation 9, all fiduciary accounts must be accepted by the bank's board of directors[25] It is therefore essential that the corporate trust department have a process by which the minutes of the corporate trust committee (or similar committee) are reviewed and approved, in writing, by a committee of the board or other entity specifically authorized by the board to accept fiduciary business. See exhibit 2 as an example of an acceptance worksheet documenting the review of new business before it is presented to the corporate trust committee or other designated entity.

2. Document review. In connection with a new appointment, the trustee should read only those documents relating to its duties and responsibilities. Trustee's counsel, however, should read every document related to the financing and advise the trustee about the impact or implication of any relevant statute or regulation. The trustee's duties and obligations should be limited to those contained in either the indenture or another specifically identified document. The trustee must completely understand all words, phrases, and terms of the proposed indenture or associated document. He or she should not accept a term or phrase on the basis of "don't worry, it doesn't apply," or "it will never happen," or "it's required by some law or regulation."

3. Preclosing activities. Ensure that care is exercised in the level of involvement in the financing transaction before the closing. An overly active role creates the risk that the trustee will be treated as a substantial

[25] 12 CFR 9.4(a) (*revised* Jan. 29, 1997).

participant in the offer and sale of the securities.[26] Chapter 4 has more to say about the trustee's reliance on information in the preliminary and final offering statements.

4. Conclusive reliance. Conclusive reliance is one of the most important trustee protection provisions in the indenture, with the language of the TIA version being the preferred one to use. Remember that the negligence standard requires the trustee to examine each certificate or written opinion to ensure that (a) it is responsive to the requirements of the specific indenture provision or other document, (b) it is understandable and unqualified in any way, and (c) that it is signed by an authorized person. Note that the attendant good-faith requirement means that the trustee does not have actual knowledge that contradicts the information in the particular certificate or opinion.

5. File documents. Keep only those documents and papers that are essential to the acceptance and administration of the account. Internal memoranda that support any significant decisions or discretionary actions by the trustee should also be retained. All the trustee's files are subject to discovery in litigation, even handwritten notes that may be in the document files. This includes the minutes of trust committee meetings, which should be drafted accordingly, as well as the reports of any internal audits and responses.

6. Counsel fees. Subject to the bank's own requirements, the trustee should agree on the parameters of any engagement with counsel, including the basis for its billing (e.g., fee per hour). It is important to get periodic bills that include the backup data to support all billed hours. This is essential if the bank expects to recover its ongoing legal expenses in a bankruptcy proceeding or other litigation. If additional counsel is required, particularly from another jurisdiction, the trustee should ensure that it has written justification for such retention in its files, with the same fee-monitoring process in place.

7. Fees. Ensure that your fee letter (or fee schedule) is explicit as to the fees for each service or activity. All contemplated services or operational activities, as well as provisions for reimbursement of out-of-pocket expenses, should be covered. If the bank is to receive the value of any float on balances, this should be so noted in your letter or schedule. Also make sure that you retain sufficient data to support your bills and reimbursable expenses.

[26] See generally, Robert P. Varian, "The Demise of the Aider-and-Abettor Liability Under Rule 10b-5: The Implications for Banks and Trust Companies," 112 *Banking L.J.* 246 (Mar. 1995).

FOUR

Municipal Trusts

During the past decade, a large portion of tax-exempt financing has been in the form of revenue bond issues. In such instances, it has become customary to appoint a bank as the trustee pursuant to a bond resolution of a municipal authority. Often, trustees in close geographical proximity to the financed project are given an opportunity to bid for the appointment. The growth in local trustee-bidding opportunities, competitively priced operating software, a lifestyle change as corporate trust professionals searched for non-money center cities to make their living, and the continuing search by banks for additional fee income all offered opportunities for local and regional banks to expand their corporate trust businesses. In part II we will see that the expansion of the business during the past decade has increased the number of corporate trust acquisitions and divestitures, especially since 1994. These changes have, in turn, sharpened the focus on tax-exempt financing appointments by larger corporate trustees.

Three of the most common types of tax-exempt financing have been for the construction of hospitals, educational facilities (including dormitories), and single and multifamily housing units. In addition, issues of industrial revenue bonds have been used for multiple purposes under legislation permitting the use of the tax-exempt bonds to build or modernize the plant facilities of private corporations.

As with any document related to the particular financing, the trustee should carefully examine, in conjunction with its counsel, the relevant bond resolution, the opinion of bond counsel, and the bond purchase agreement. Even though it is not a document that the trustee needs to read, the preliminary official statement can be useful to understanding the business intent of the financing and the general cash flow of the financing. The governing indenture or resolution must always serve as the source document for administering the trust. The trustee or agent is not a party to, and should not rely on, the preliminary or official statement in administering the trustee's duties. From time to time, there will be areas of conflict between the official statements and the governing indenture or resolution.

In addition to being appointed as the trustee, the trustee is generally appointed as the paying agent. And as the result of the Tax Equity and Fiscal Responsibility Act (TEFRA) of 1982,[1] the trustee may also be appointed as the registrar. This last appointment entails the traditional registration of transfer services and the accounting for and, where physical certificates have been issued, the destruction of canceled certificates.

The traditional long-term, fixed-rate, semiannual interest payment transaction consisting of serial maturities and term bonds, once referred to as a *plain vanilla deal*, gradually changed shape during the 1980s, soon after trustees and paying agents managed to enhance system capabilities to service the addition of capital accumulation, or zero coupon bonds. Fixed-rate transactions rapidly became a vehicle of the past as variable-rate securities, with demand features, grew in popularity. With the enactment of the Tax Reform Act of 1986 (86 Act),[2] restrictions were placed on municipal debt issuers, including (among other things) restrictions on the amount of tax-exempt debt that any tax-exempt organization[3] could have outstanding at one time, the introduction of state volume caps for "private activity bonds," requirements for issuers to perform complex arbitrage rebate calculations, and restrictions on the percentage of gross proceeds that can be applied to the costs of issuing securities.

During the 1990s, municipal revenue bonds began to closely resemble securities generally associated with the corporate sector. Multimodal, variable-rate, variable-term, variable-interest, and principal payment instruments (similar to commercial paper); medium-term notes (MTNs); and even taxable municipals emerged. The proliferation of changes placed extraordinary demands on software providers while also increasing the use of the personal computer at the corporate trust administrative officer's desk.

[1] See chapter 2, note 7, *supra*.
[2] Pub. Law 99–514 (1986).
[3] See Internal Revenue Code, sec. 501(c)(3), for specific types of organizations.

MUNICIPAL POOL FINANCING

The basic objective of any borrowing entity is to raise funds at the lowest possible cost. For issuers of tax-exempt or taxable debt securities, three factors in achieving this objective are (1) to obtain the most favorable interest rate possible, (2) to structure the financing to appeal to a wide market, and (3) to limit the costs of actually issuing the securities. One way of lowering the cost of borrowing is for entities to apply for a loan from a state, county, or city authority that issues tax-exempt bonds, such as a state bond bank. The proceeds from the sale of bonds by the issuing authority are lent to the entity at a more favorable tax-exempt rate than if it had borrowed the money under its own name. As provided for in the loan agreement between the issuer and the borrowing entity, the loan repayments are deposited in a bond fund established in accordance with the trust indenture and used to pay the debt service on the bonds.

Smaller entities applying to the issuing authority could be at a disadvantage, however, as the interest rate it obtained might not be as favorable as what a larger issuing entity could get. In fact, the cost of issuance could be prohibitive for a smaller issuer. In addition, the market interest in purchasing the securities could be relatively limited, if for no other reason than little may be known about the issuer.

A financial structure designed to address the needs of both smaller and larger borrowing entities is the *loan pool vehicle*, in which the proceeds from the same pool of bonds are lent to several similar entities with comparable financing needs. A group of hospitals or school districts are examples. Each issuer obtains approval from the issuing authority for a loan and then draws (borrows) against the pool of funds. Because the costs of issuance are distributed pro rata among the borrowing entities, a more favorable rate is generally obtained.

The 1986 Act eliminated "blind pools." In many cases, a large percentage of the proceeds from the bond pool issuance was not lent, resulting in early calls for redemption of the bonds and arbitrage on the bond proceeds. Now, under the 1986 regulations, the issuing authority must have a reasonable expectation that a major percentage of the proceeds will be expended (lent) within a specific time. Consequently, the issuing authority must obtain firm commitments from the issuers wishing to borrow funds from a specific pool before the bonds may be issued.

Pool-financing transactions place additional accounting and record-keeping responsibilities on the trustee. Many trustees created computerized subaccounting and management-reporting vehicles to meet the demands of the bond pool financing. In addition to the routine accounting for the custody of collateral and the maintenance of funds established in accordance with the indenture, the trustee is also responsible for administering and accounting for the loan. Each borrowing entity's loan must be administered and accounted for separately. The loan repayments are collected from each entity, and the aggregate funds are then transferred to the appropriate debt service accounts. Currently, twenty-two states have legislation authorizing bond banks. Some of the more active ones are Maine, New Hampshire, Vermont, and Indiana.

ANTICIPATION NOTES

In chapter 1, we examined the problems that corporations encounter in financing their short-term working-capital needs. Municipalities face similar cash-flow challenges. Although operating expenses must be paid throughout the year, major income items such as property taxes are often collected at stated intervals during the year. By issuing tax anticipation notes (TANs) and other types of revenue anticipation notes, a municipality can finance its working capital during periods of cash-flow shortfall. Generally, if the anticipation note is not outstanding for more than thirteen months and the principal amount of obligations issued is less than the anticipated maximum cumulative cash-flow deficit,[4] the issuer is permitted to invest all the proceeds of the TAN sale at an unrestricted yield.

Anticipation notes are issued in accordance with a resolution generally requiring the services of a paying agent, since a trustee is not typically appointed. As we show later, the benefits of pool financing combined with the unrestricted yield from the investment of the anticipation notes' proceeds, among other things, have resulted in programs that may require the services of an indenture trustee.

MASTER TRUSTEE

Another way of pooling like entities to borrow to meet capital needs is by forming an obligated group. The members of this group need not be

---

[4] *Maximum cumulative cash-flow deficit* is defined as the sum of (1) the amount the issuer will expend from the beginning of the period to the computation date that would ordinarily be paid out of or financed by anticipated tax or other revenues, plus (2) the amount of the anticipated expenditures for a period of one month after the computation date, minus (3) the sum of

affiliated entities, but for practical reasons, they usually are. Health institutions, with multiple facilities, are the predominant users of this type of structure. Individual entities become members of the group (i.e., obligated issuers) by executing a note issued in accordance with a master trust indenture. By executing the note, each obligated issuer agrees that it will duly and punctually pay the principal, interest, and any applicable premium in accordance with its terms. In addition, each obligated issuer jointly and severally guarantees and promises to pay any and all amounts payable under any note issued in accordance with the master trust indenture.

The master trustee is responsible for registering the note, enforcing the covenants of the master indenture, and, in some instances, collecting the principal and interest payments on the notes. Master notes are frequently issued along with one or more revenue bond transactions. The master notes are then registered to the issuer of the revenue bonds in the same aggregate principal amount as the bonds issued under the indenture. The issuer then assigns all its right, title, and interest in the master notes to the bond trustee. If there is more than one related revenue bond financing, the same procedure applies to each of the issuers and bond trustees. The payments by the obligated issuers in accordance with the provisions of the master note are then made directly to the bond trustee or trustees to provide for debt service. Because the master trustee must take prompt action in the event of a default, the master trustee and the related trustees must establish procedures to ensure that they are promptly notified of a default on any note payment. Because there is a potential for conflict between the role of the bond trustee and that of the master indenture trustee, the same entity should generally not act in both capacities.

ADVANCE-FUNDING PROGRAM NOTES

Tax-exempt issuing authorities also pool similar borrowing entities by issuing advance-funding program notes. The proceeds from the sale of the program notes are advanced to the participating entities to resolve cash-flow deficiencies in the current fiscal year. The program participants issue TANs that are purchased by the issuer. Each participating entity pledges to the issuing authority a security interest in all revenues derived by it from taxes and other revenues, by executing an advance-refunding

the amounts (other than the proceeds of the issue in question) that will be available for the payment of such expenditures during this period.

agreement. The program notes issued through the authority must comply with the anticipation note regulations (referred to earlier) in order for the proceeds to be treated as invested during a temporary period in accordance with the Internal Revenue Code.[5] The repayments by the participating entities of the tax and revenue anticipation notes plus the interest earnings on any funds held in accordance with the trust indenture are transferred to the debt service fund to pay the principal and interest on the program notes as they become due.

As with other types of pooled arrangements, the trustee may be responsible for administering and accounting for the loan in addition to its duties as indenture trustee, registrar, and paying agent.

VARIABLE-RATE SECURITIES

Since the early 1980s, different forms of variable-rate securities have been popular investment vehicles in the tax-exempt market. They are designed to approximate interest-rate changes to keep the value of the security at or as close to par as possible. The earliest issues paid an interest rate based on a percentage of an established index, often tied to a particular bank's prime lending rate. These issues were typically private placements.

The next development involved bonds allowing bondholders to tender their bonds back to the issuer at par through a "put" or "demand" feature. The benefit to the issuer is that it pays a short-term interest rate (largely based on the time between tenders) instead of the usual long-term rate based on the maturity of the bonds. The spread between the short-term variable rate and the long-term fixed rate results in savings to the issuer, which can be offset by the fees of the various agents required to run the program. Clearly, the greater the spread between short-term and long-term rates in the credit markets, the more likely that variable-rate securities will be issued.

Securities with a "put" or "demand" feature typically involve a remarketing agent, a liquidity facility provider, and a tender agent. The *remarketing agent*, usually an investment bank, is responsible for setting new interest rates, for remarketing or reselling any securities that are tendered, and for providing the new registration information and remarketing proceeds to the tender agent. Except in unusual circumstances,

[5] Sec. 1.103–14(c).

the remarketing agent is usually successful in selling the tendered securities to new investors.

The *liquidity facility* can be provided in various forms, including letters of credit (L/Cs), insurance, or standby purchase agreements. Letters of credit are the most popular liquidity vehicles. Letter of credit banks in effect guarantee that in the event of the remarketing agent's failure to remarket the securities, the L/C bank will step in and purchase the securities. This "guarantee" of liquidity on a tendered security helps keep the interest rate low. Note that the rating of the securities is usually the same as the rating of the liquidity facility provider. The "guarantee" is only as strong as the ability of the liquidity facility provider to make payments if called on to do so.

The *tender agent* receives notices of tender from security holders; notifies the remarketing agent, liquidity facility provider, issuer, and trustee of receipt of the notice and the securities being tendered; pays the tendering holders with the appropriate funds; and, in a coregistrar capacity, reissues new securities to the new purchaser. These tasks may also be performed by the trustee.

Tender bonds come in two types. The first is a *put bond*, which the bondholder can tender only during certain preset times, usually between fifteen to thirty days before the payment date. Semiannual and annual tender bonds are the most common examples. In some security issues, the "put" option is permitted to operate only in designated years.

The other type of tender bond is the *demand bond*, for which the bondholder can demand payment at any time after giving the appropriate notice. These are often called *variable-rate demand bonds* (VRDBs), of which weekly demand bonds are the most popular. Other kinds are daily and monthly demand bonds. The interest rate of a weekly VRDB is reset each week by the remarketing agent at a rate that allows the bonds to be remarketed at par. This ability to reset the rate helps the remarketing agent resell bonds that are tendered.

Commercial paper mode bonds are a hybrid of the two types of tender bonds. During their existence in a commercial paper mode, bonds can be issued with maturities ranging anywhere from one to 270 days, as in typical commercial paper programs. The benefit to the issuer of commercial paper mode securities is the flexibility to use shorter or longer mandatory "tender" dates. These dates are determined during remarketings based on buyer demand and current or anticipated changes in the interest rate. An interesting feature of most variable-rate securities is the ability to convert from one rate mode to another. For example, a weekly mode security can be converted to a fixed-rate mode or a daily-rate mode. Some issues allow for only a single conversion, to a fixed rate, but most can be changed into any one of several different modes, by means of a mandatory tender. When a security issue is offered, some portions of the issue may be in different modes at the same time, and so the issue is designated a *multimodal structure instrument*.

A typical tender by a holder takes place as follows: Those security holders who want to tender their bonds give the tender agent or trustee a notice or demand. This notice, which is usually available from the trustee, states the holder's irrevocable intention to tender a specific principal amount of bonds for settlement on a specific date. This notice includes the numbers of the securities being tendered. The tender agent or the trustee then notifies the remarketing agent, the liquidity facility provider, and the issuer of the receipt of the notice. At this point, the remarketing agent looks for a new buyer for the securities. If successful in selling the securities, the proceeds are forwarded to the tender agent or trustee to pay the tendering holder upon presentation of the securities. In the case of an unsuccessful remarketing, the tender agent or trustee draws on (borrows from) the liquidity facility provider to pay for the tendered securities. The new securities are then registered in the new buyer's or the liquidity facility provider's name, whichever is appropriate. Variable-rate security tenders must be carefully planned and orchestrated by all parties to the transaction. Failing to process a tender in a timely fashion can result in operating losses for the trustee and/or agent. Preparing the notices, remarketing the securities, and arranging for the liquidity draw are usually timed to occur within short periods of time. To ensure that the transaction is processed accurately and promptly, the trustee and its counsel should review the timing, administrative, and operational requirements during the initial governing document preparation and review.

Preparing, Executing, and Recording Indentures

SELECTING THE METHOD OF FINANCING

It is the responsibility of corporate and municipal financial officers to secure the necessary funds to expand and operate the corporate enterprise and governmental entity, in the amounts and at the times they are required. If these funds are not generated from the business's operations or, in the case of a municipality, through its general taxing powers, they must be obtained in the highly competitive and often volatile financial markets. The officers must try to secure the most favorable terms with the fewest possible restrictions placed on the obligor's freedom of action.

Of the many reasons for capital financing, the most common is providing new facilities in the form of plant and equipment for the business's expanded needs, such as a new office building to house the executive and administrative staffs. If additional working capital is required or funds are needed for a maturity, existing indebtedness may be refunded on more favorable terms. During the late 1980s, much of the corporate debt financing was fueled by the rapid growth and widespread use of leveraged buyouts and mergers. Because capital financing is expensive even for large municipalities and major corporations with a high credit rating, it needs to be carefully planned to minimize visits to the capital markets. Many companies resort to their commercial banks for interim financing, with the understanding that at periodic intervals or within an agreed period, funded debt will be issued and the bank loans paid off.

The factors considered when determining the form and method of financing include the purpose of the loan, the credit standing of the issuer, the existing capital structure, the availability of investment funds, and market conditions. Although the exact terms are determined by negotiation, the obligor's officials, usually with the assistance of qualified financial advisers, make a preliminary determination of the amount of the issue, whether it will be secured or unsecured, the approximate amount that can be repaid annually through a sinking fund, the restrictive provisions that will be permitted, and the final maturity date. They then decide how the issue will be marketed or distributed. Despite the many investment bankers with innovative and creative financing ideas, there are essentially three methods by which financing needs are met: negotiated transactions, public bids, and direct placements.

In a *negotiated transaction*, an investment-banking firm is selected to underwrite the issue, and the substantive terms of the issue are negotiated with this firm. When this method of marketing is used, the investment bankers usually, although not necessarily, act for all issues of the particular obligor and are thoroughly familiar with the obligor's financial affairs and programs. In addition to underwriting the company's public offerings, the firm may be retained as a general financial consultant and is able to offer valuable collateral services to the corporate officials. The investment bankers usually participate in discussions from the beginning; their familiarity with security markets and the obligor's affairs enable them to tailor the issue to meet the obligor's requirements and current market conditions. The underwriters' compensation is provided by the "spread" between the wholesale price they pay for the entire issue and the retail price at which the securities are sold to the investors (often referred to as the *underwriters' discount*). Usually the principal or lead underwriter brings together a number of other firms (called a *syndicate*) to market the issue, with each firm being responsible for, and assuming the risk of, a percentage of the total issue. The amount of the underwriter's "spread" varies, but it is calculated to provide a reasonable profit based on the work involved and the risk assumed in the particular financing.

Another method for marketing debt securities issues is through a *public invitation for bids*. All companies subject to the jurisdiction of the SEC under the Public Utility Holding Company Act are required to sell their securities in this manner unless specifically exempted. Other public bodies having jurisdiction over regulated industries may or may not prescribe or influence the manner in which securities are offered, but they must approve the method selected and the terms of the sale. Under the method of public bidding, the issuing corporation engages experienced, independent attorneys to represent the prospective purchasers of the securities, and the terms and details of the offering are negotiated between the company and the attorneys, except for the price, which is determined by the public bids. Occasionally the company retains investment bankers as advisers who work for a fee and do not participate in the bidding. Usually the company and counsel know the investment houses that head the various syndicates likely to participate in the bidding, and these firms may be consulted in advance about some of the proposed terms of the issue. Since market conditions determine the price at which securities can be offered successfully, most bids are very close to one another, and the competition revolves around the amount of the underwriter's commission. The use of public bids, as opposed to the negotiated method, has certain advantages and disadvantages. Some regulatory bodies feel that the obligor obtains a better price through public bids, although experts differ on this matter. This advantage can be weighed against the value of a continuing relationship with, and the advice received from, investment bankers in a negotiated transaction.

A third method of marketing that is frequently used by more mature companies with a high credit rating is *direct placement* (i.e., private placement). Under this method, the issue is not underwritten at all, but negotiations are conducted with a group of institutional investors who are the actual purchasers of the securities. The corporation usually retains an investment house or the corporate finance department of a major bank as an agent to find interested purchasers and negotiate the terms, although the corporation may elect to do this itself. Such an issue does not have to be registered under the securities acts, and the indenture is not qualified. In some instances when the issue is unsecured, only a few purchasers are involved, the terms are not complicated, and an indenture and trustee are not used. The company executes separate but identical agreements with each purchaser, embodying all the terms of the contract.

These three methods are the principal ones used in distributing debt securities, but others are sometimes used, such as offering convertible debentures, which may or may not be underwritten, to existing stockholders. Mergers, acquisitions, recapitalizations, reorganizations, and similar transactions usually entail offering securities to existing security holders of either the issuing or a different corporation. The corporation itself may elect to market its securities publicly without the assistance of an underwriting firm, although this practice is rare. Moreover, with the adoption of SEC rule 415 permitting shelf registrations to be filed, a corporation gains both tremendous flexibility by issuing debt securities and almost instant access to the capital markets.

PREPARING THE INDENTURE

Because the indenture, when executed, becomes a contract binding on the security holders, the obligor, and the trustee, establishing the obligations and rights of the parties and setting limitations on the rights of all, it follows that preparing the indenture is one of the most important steps in the whole process. It is here that the security holders stand in the greatest need of protection, and it is here that they frequently lack adequate representation. The substantive terms are established by agreement between the issuer and the underwriter, or counsel appointed to represent the underwriter. Although this process offers some protection—for the leading investment houses feel some moral responsibility for issues they sponsor—the underwriter's primary concern is securing terms that will make the issue readily marketable and not necessarily terms that a security holder, in retrospect, might have considered desirable.

Over the years, a number of developments have substantially resolved this problem, with the result that the typical indenture is a fairly sound financial document with reasonably adequate safeguards designed to protect the investor. Among such developments are the following:

1. The increasing influence of the institutional investor. Whereas the direct placement contract is the only situation in which the investors actually negotiate the terms of an issue, the institutional purchaser is also important to publicly distributed issues, and both issuers and underwriters try to make the issue and the terms of the contract attractive to professional investors.
2. The minimum standards set forth in the TIA. They now are applicable, as a matter of law, to every qualified indenture and should not be written into the indenture itself. It may be helpful, however, to include a TIA section reference page at the beginning of each qualified indenture. An example is shown in exhibit 3.
3. The disclosure provisions of the 33 Act. Most public corporate issues of securities are required to be registered under this act, which requires full disclosure of both the history and current financial condition of the issuer and all important terms and provisions of the indenture and the securities to be issued. This information, or a summary of it, is required to be included in a prospectus, preliminary offering statement, or offering memorandum that must be given to all prospective investors. Thus, the investor has available all information necessary to make an

informed investment decision. If the investor fails to use or comprehend this information (assuming it is accurate), he or she has no one else to blame.

4. The regulatory powers of the SEC and other regulatory agencies. These agencies have set certain minimum standards required in cases when they have the authority to approve or prescribe the terms and conditions of the proposed financing.

5. The patterns for typical indentures that have become established among investment houses, institutional investors, and bond counsel.

6. The influence of the more experienced corporate trustees and their counsel.

Once the essential terms of the indenture have been agreed upon, drafting it is relatively simple. An earlier indenture, frequently of the same obligor, is selected as a model. Many of the provisions remain exactly the same. Clauses not appropriate to the current transaction or that experience has shown to be troublesome are eliminated; new provisions that embody the terms of the contract are added, as are any new clauses that the evolutionary process has revealed as beneficial or desirable. Once an initial draft of the new indenture is ready, copies are distributed to all interested parties, and the document is modified until all parties are reasonably satisfied.

THE TRUSTEE'S FUNCTION

At some point, the corporate trustee must be selected, usually by the issuer itself but, in many instances, on the advice and recommendation of its investment banker, underwriter, or attorneys. The trustee should be chosen at the earliest possible moment, for the trustee can make important contributions to the process of finalizing the terms of the indenture. Although it has no responsibility for the substantive provisions of the contract and, under normal circumstances, should never undertake to alter the terms of the basic contract, it is the trustee that will have to administer the agreement and so should be allowed to participate fully in all discussions relative to translating the contract into indenture language.

Given the importance of all phases of the indenture preparation process, the trustee should always be represented by experienced legal counsel and should work closely with counsel until the indenture has been executed and the initial bonds delivered. Although some corporate trustees follow the practice of relinquishing to counsel the conduct of all matters during this preliminary process, this is not advisable. A number of business and operational, as well as legal, considerations are involved, and the trustee cannot delegate, nor should it permit counsel to usurp, the trustee's responsibility for making decisions. But the corporate trustee should consult with counsel on all legal questions.

It would be difficult to describe the exact procedure the trustee should follow in its examination and review of the terms of the proposed indenture, but the following are some of the general principles:[1]

1. Since the recitals are not part of the substantive contract and the trustee has no responsibility for them, there is a tendency to skip over these clauses. It is important, however, that the obligor's authorization of all acts relating to creating the indenture, issuing the securities, and mortgaging or pledging the property be stated. Whereas appropriate evidence of this authorization should be obtained and examined, the recitals may constitute an estoppel against the obligor if it should subsequently claim a lack of proper authorization.

2. The form of bond as set forth in the indenture should be examined closely. Since the bonds, when executed, become separate instruments and constitute separate contracts and obligations running directly to their holders, the bond form should contain specific reference to the indenture and should also explain in detail any provision of the indenture that modifies or affects the obligation contained in the bond or that imposes any limitations on the rights of the holder. In any lawsuit by a bondholder, if the provisions of the indenture are in direct conflict with the provisions of the bond itself, the latter are controlling.

3. The adequacy of the granting clauses to convey the property and create the lien (or "perfect" the security interest) intended is a legal matter and should be a concern primarily for counsel. The trustee should secure appropriate legal opinions covering these points. A detailed examination of the property descriptions would serve no purpose, for the trustee usually has nothing against which to check or compare such descriptions and must rely on the obligor and its counsel, although the use of a title company can be helpful. The trustee should make sure, however, that it is qualified to hold property as mortgagee in the various jurisdictions in which the property is located. If there is any question, a qualified cotrustee might be appointed. When the ownership of franchises, rights, or permits is essential to the obligor's business, the trustee should make certain that these are included with the mortgaged property. The same care should be taken with regard to any important leases,

---

[1] To facilitate this effort, it is useful to prepare checklists as a guide. Exhibit 4 is a comprehensive guide for reviewing new and additional securities issues under indentures.

easements, contracts, rights of way, and so forth, the purpose being to ensure that the lien covers the obligor's property as a "going concern." If any important franchises, leases, contracts, and so forth should expire before the maturity date of the securities to be issued, any renewal privileges or the securing of alternative rights should be investigated to avoid a substantial diminution of security or a default. If an after-acquired property clause is included, the trustee should ensure that it clearly indicates what subsequently acquired property is to be covered. If any property is to be assigned or pledged, a proper record should be made so that an executed assignment or physical delivery of the property is obtained at the closing. If any part of the property is in the possession of another trustee, proper notification should be given to the other trustee and a tickler record prepared to obtain possession of the property on satisfaction of the other lien. If a leasehold estate is mortgaged, the last day of the term of each lease should be specifically excluded. This avoids creating for the trustee an estate identical with that of the obligor-lessee, as well as the possibility of a claim that the trustee is liable for performing the lessee's obligations under the lease. Finally, special laws or regulations may be applicable in those jurisdictions where the property is located, the mortgage contract is executed and delivered, or a financing statement is to be filed.

4. Although the trustee is not responsible for the substantive provisions of the contract or for the covenants that may be included, it should review these provisions carefully to make certain that they are clear and unambiguous and adequately express the intent of the parties.

5. The trustee should examine carefully the evidence it is to receive of compliance by the obligor with the various indenture covenants to ensure its adequacy. Note that section 314 (a) (4) of the TIA requires the obligor to give the trustee annually a certificate "from the principal executive officer, principal financial officer or principal accounting officer as to his or her knowledge of such obligor's compliance with all conditions and covenants under the indenture" (i.e., a "no-default" certificate). This should be in addition to specific evidence for the more important covenants. Although municipal indentures are not qualified under the TIA, it is wise to request a similar annual certificate from a principal municipal official.

6. It is the obligor's, and not the trustee's, responsibility to see that an indenture to be qualified does not contain provisions contrary to the TIA. A diligent trustee carefully reviews the indenture language and advises the obligor (or its counsel) of any inconsistent language.

7. The trustee has a particular responsibility for the operational provisions relating to the servicing of the indenture securities. It should verify

that they are workable and do not conflict with its established practices and procedures or applicable state law (e.g., escheatment). The greatest amount of flexibility consistent with clarity should be retained. Whenever possible, the manner in which a particular operation is to be conducted should be left to the discretion of the trustee rather than set forth in detail. This permits a change in procedure to conform with evolving and more efficient methods and system developments and is not only proper but also desirable as long as substantive rights are not affected.

8. Particular attention should be paid to the remedial provisions and to the trustee article. The rights, powers, duties, and responsibilities of the trustee and any limitation on its rights and powers are governed by the general provisions of these articles. The trustee should ascertain that it has all requisite power and authority to carry out its duties. It should also make sure that the appropriate exculpatory and protective provisions are included, for the potential liability is substantial.

9. Finally, after each section has been carefully read, the contract should be considered as an entity. It is important that the various provisions and covenants be consistent, for the indenture must be considered and construed as a single document. The trustee should have a clear understanding of the essential purpose and intent of the transaction, and the provisions of the indenture, considered together, should clearly express and carry out this purpose and intent.

THE REGISTRATION STATEMENT AND QUALIFICATION OF THE INDENTURE

Issuing securities is not only a delicate marketing operation but also a matter of careful planning and timing. The many different transactions that together constitute a unified operation must be initiated at the appropriate time so that everything will be completed on the date set for delivering the securities. Time is usually of the essence, and the customary procedure is to select a date for selling the securities and to tie all other activities to this date.

When the securities are to be distributed publicly, they must be registered under the 33 Act. Unless the issuer has filed an SEC Rule 415 shelf registration,[2] it can take several weeks for a registration to be cleared and to become effective. A copy of the indenture must be filed as an exhibit to the registration statement, and the indenture should be in as complete and

2 See chapter 1, note 9, *supra*.

final a form as possible to minimize the number of amendments that have to be filed.

The contents of the registration statement and the prospectus are the responsibility of the obligor and not the trustee. It is advisable for the latter to review copies of these documents to ensure that they disclose no information that might affect its rights or obligations or that might be contrary to its understanding of the transaction. In particular, the sections summarizing the indenture provisions should be carefully reviewed. The trustee must exercise caution during the review of these documents to make sure that it is not deemed to be participating in the offering of the securities.

The TIA requires any information and documents that the Commission may prescribe to be filed with each registration statement, to enable it to determine whether any person designated to act as trustee is eligible and qualified. The SEC has prescribed the form in which this information is to be furnished. Form T-1 is required for domestic institutional trustees, T-2 for individual trustees, and T-6 for foreign trustees. Form T-1 requires filing, among other documents, the trustee's most recent report of condition, a copy of its articles of association or incorporation, a certificate of authority to commence business, a copy of its bylaws, and the consent of the trustee that copies of reports of examination by federal, state, territorial, or district authorities may be furnished to the Commission. Forms T-1, T-2, and T-6 require information sufficient to enable the Commission to determine whether the proposed trustee is qualified to act under Section 310 (a) of the TIA.[3] Electronically filing the documents associated with the registration of a new corporate security issue has cut the amount of time required to receive approval from the SEC. The trustee is expected to conform with electronic filing requirements. Bond counsel often assumes the responsibility for collecting the electronic media information from all parties to the financing.

EXECUTING, DELIVERING, AND RECORDING THE INDENTURE

As soon as the registration statement has become effective and all other authorizations and approvals have been obtained, the indenture may be

[3] The text and instructions for Forms T-1, T-2, and T-6 are given in 17 CFR 269.1, 269.2, and 269.9, respectively. See also "Rules and Forms to Implement the Trust Indenture Reform Act of 1990," SEC Release Nos. 33–6892 and 39–2263 (May 8, 1991).

executed and the securities delivered (often referred to as the *bond closing*). The trustee should make certain that the officers or officials of the obligor who execute the indenture have been authorized to do so. The trustee is also usually requested to furnish an appropriate certificate of the authority of its officers who join in executing the indenture (i.e., the trustee's certificate of incumbency).

The indenture customarily contains an express statement that the laws of a particular state apply with respect to all questions that may arise in its interpretation. This is important, for the laws of different states may vary substantially in important respects. It is desirable, although not essential, that the state specified be that in which the office of the trustee is located, for its laws are the ones with which it is presumably most familiar. In the absence of an express provision, the law applied is that of the state in which the contract is executed and delivered. If delivery takes place at the office of the trustee, there is no problem. If the laws that are to govern are those of another state, there may be a problem, since the trustee may not be qualified to do business in that state. More important, the trustee may be barred in that state from bringing an action against the obligor if this should be necessary. If it is impossible to negotiate a change in the language of the "governing law" provision, the trustee should make every effort to have additional language inserted stating that the trustee's rights, duties, liabilities, and obligations be governed by and construed in accordance with the laws of its state of incorporation or principal place of business. The parties to the indenture also must agree that any action by the obligor against the trustee be brought in the district or state courts in the state where the trustee is located and that the parties consent to this forum.

When the indenture is delivered, the trustee should receive documents establishing the authorization of all proceedings in connection with the indenture and the securities. Counsel should be consulted about the documents required and their form and content.

If the indenture grants a mortgage or lien on any property, one of the first steps to be taken after it has been executed is having it recorded in all jurisdictions in which the property is located. Sometimes this is done before or simultaneously with delivery of the securities, but it is usually sufficient if done promptly thereafter. Whereas the contract is binding on the obligor when delivered, the importance of recording it is to give public notice of the lien and to prevent a third party from obtaining a lien prior to that of the trustee. Recording is the responsibility of the counsel to the issuing corporation. If a number of jurisdictions are involved, local counsel familiar with the laws of each jurisdiction are used to ensure strict adherence to recording requirements.

If the indenture creates a security interest in real estate, including a lease or rents *and* in any personal property or fixtures, the filing provisions of article 9 of the UCC are applicable to "perfect" the security interest in the personal property. The appropriate filing must be done, even though the mortgage or supplemental mortgage creating the lien on real and personal property is properly recorded as a real estate mortgage. (If, however, the mortgage or supplement creating the lien was properly recorded as a mortgage of real property before the effective date of the UCC, no filing is necessary.)

If all the collateral under an indenture is in the trustee's possession, that alone will "perfect" the security interest, and no filing is necessary. In the usual collateral trust indenture, this consists of negotiable instruments or securities such as stock and bonds.

When filing is necessary, the UCC prescribes the formal requisites for the financing statement. Most states have adopted a standard form for this purpose. Completion is merely a matter of filling in the blank spaces and having the form signed by the obligor (the debtor) and the trustee (the secured party). Although the indenture itself may be filed if it meets the particular state's requirements, as a practical matter it is simpler to use the prescribed form for this purpose.

The trustee should obtain appropriate evidence of this recording and/or filing. The recorded counterparts of the indenture and/or a filing counterpart of each financing statement showing the recording or filing data are usually returned to and retained by the trustee.

In addition, the obligor must furnish the trustee with a legal opinion or opinions on the sufficiency of the recording and/or filing. This requirement provides that the obligor will give the trustee (1) promptly after the execution and delivery of the indenture and of each supplemental indenture, an opinion of counsel either stating that in the opinion of the counsel that the indenture has been properly recorded and/or filed so as to make effective the lien or security interest intended to be created and reciting the details of the action or stating that in the opinion of the counsel, no action is necessary to make the lien or security interest effective; and (2) at least annually thereafter an opinion of counsel either stating that in its opinion, this action has been taken with respect to the recording, filing, rerecording, and refiling of the indenture and of each supplement as is necessary to maintain the lien or security interest of the indenture and reciting the details of this action or stating that in the opinion of the counsel, no action is necessary to maintain the lien or security interest.[4]

Although a mortgage of real property usually need not be recorded to maintain the lien, a financing statement perfecting a security interest in personal property will lapse five years after the filing date unless a continuation statement is filed within six months before the expiration of the five-year period. Some governing jurisdictions have varying lengths of time before the financing statement or continuation statement expires. After the timely filing of the continuation statements, the original statement will continue to be effective for successive five-year periods or other periods as prescribed by governing jurisdictions.

One of the first actions that the trustee should take after the indenture is executed and delivered is to review all the indenture's provisions and establish an appropriate tickler record in regard to all actions that the obligor or trustee must take in connection with administering the indenture. These include such things as the dates on which the sinking fund is to operate and the date when certificates and opinions must be filed. No particular form of record is required, provided the form used is adequate to ensure that appropriate timely reminders will be brought to the attention of the administrative officers and that the monitoring of uncompleted items can be followed up. Some trustees use technology to maintain automated ticklers and follow-up. Details of this automation are more fully described in part II.

SUPPLEMENTAL INDENTURES

In addition to the original indenture, supplemental indentures for various purposes may be executed from time to time. They may provide the terms of additional series of securities to be issued under the indenture; they may convey additional property or pledge additional security; they may modify or amend provisions of the original contract; they may impose additional restrictions on the obligor; or they may be executed for other reasons that require that the original contract be supplemented or amended.

The same care should be used as for the original indenture in regard to the proper authorization, execution, delivery, recording, and filing of these instruments. The trustee should also ensure that each supplement is consistent with and is authorized, either explicitly or by necessary implication, by the original indenture.

[4]TIA secs. 314(b)(1) and (2).

Once the supplement has been executed and delivered, it becomes part of the contract and the original indenture, and all supplemental indentures must be read together to determine the rights, duties, and obligations of the parties.

Since the effect of many provisions in the TIRA is to relax restrictions previously imposed on the trustee and since the act does not preclude the trustee from "agreeing" to more rigorous contractual provisions, it is wise to include in any supplemental indenture to a pre–November 15, 1990, qualified indenture, language substantially as follows: "Except to the extent specifically provided therein, no provision of this supplemental indenture or any future supplemental indenture is intended to modify, and the parties do hereby adopt and confirm, the provisions of section 318 (c) of the Trust Indenture Act that amend and supersede the provisions of the [indenture] in effect before November 15, 1990."

Issuing Indenture Securities

THE TRUSTEE'S RESPONSIBILITIES

Since the purpose of the indenture is to provide security for the outstanding securities and to spell out the terms and conditions on which they can be issued, the proceedings surrounding the authentication and delivery of the indenture securities are among the trustee's most important responsibilities. The issuance of securities in uncertificated form (more commonly known as *book-entry securities*) and, as is less likely in the future, in certificated form is governed by the indenture's provisions. The trustee is responsible for seeing that the necessary conditions have been fulfilled.[1] When the trustee receives the documents called for by the indenture, it is entitled to rely on them and does not need to examine independently the facts certified. If the trustee acts in good faith, it will be protected even if it turns out that the certificates were false. When the requisite conditions do not exist and the trustee fails to receive the requisite documents, when the documents are not in the required form, or when they disclose facts that put the trustee on notice that the requisite

[1] Note the distinction between a pure "book-entry" system, in which no physical securities certificates are issued and all transfers of ownership are made through entries on the issuer's books of record, and an "immobilized clearance" system. In the latter case, a large portion of an outstanding issue is held in a depository facility represented by one or more jumbo certificates with changes in record ownership entered in the depository's books. The balance of the issue is held in certificate form by the investors, with certificates flowing in and out of the depository as the public's need for securities certificates fluctuates.

conditions do not exist, the trustee may be held liable by the security holders. The amount of liability has been held to be the same as would be required to put the security holders in the same position as they would be if the requisite conditions existed

All securities physically issued under the indenture must be authenticated by the trustee with original signatures. This is done by applying the trustee's signature to a certificate imprinted on each bond or debenture. The form of this certificate seldom varies from the standard phraseology: "This bond is one of the bonds, of the series designated therein, described in the within mentioned indenture." The bond should provide that it will not become valid for any purpose until this certificate has been executed by the trustee.

The purpose of the authentication certification is to enable the trustee to control the amount of the issue outstanding and to prevent an overissuance. It ensures that the obligor cannot sell bonds in excess of the amount authorized. The authentication certificate is not a guaranty, nor is it an implied warranty of the sufficiency of the security or the regularity of the obligor's conduct in issuing bonds. The trustee should be careful that the certificate contains no representation, lest it be held responsible for ascertaining the accuracy of the facts represented. For example, a certificate stating that this is a "convertible subordinated sinking-fund debenture" may be held to be a representation by the trustee. Although a diligent trustee will, to the best of its ability, ascertain that all representations made by the obligor are accurate, it is seldom in a position to check all the facts, and a representation that it has done so is neither required nor advisable.[2]

THE FORM AND CONTENT OF SECURITIES

Because the trustee is authorized to authenticate only the securities provided for in the indenture, it must see that the securities do conform with the indenture's provisions. The indenture provides the form and text of the securities authorized, and the trustee should compare the text of the security itself with the text given in the indenture. Minor variations in detail are permissible, but each variation should be noted and reviewed. To avoid possible embarrassment, the trustee should arrange to examine

[2]For potential liability regarding additional representations, see Nelson v. Quimby Island Reclamation District Facilities Corporation, 491 F. Supp. 1371 (N.D. Cal. 1980).

proofs of all securities before they are prepared in final form. As a practical matter, the bank note companies that prepare these securities generally require approval by the trustee before they prepare the final securities. Despite this preliminary check, a final examination should be made of one bond of each denomination before the securities are released, although as uncertificated bonds have increased in popularity, bonds are printed in "blank" unlimited form to accommodate all requested denominations permitted by the indenture and to facilitate the operational issuance of bonds.

Not only should the text be compared, but the securities also must be in the form required by the indenture. The various requirements for form are explained in detail and are designed to comply with stock exchange regulations for corporate securities or with general usage. The New York Stock Exchange probably has the most detailed regulations of any national exchange for the form of securities, whose purpose is to guard against duplication, alteration, or forgery. These regulations require that the border, vignette, denomination or "money" boxes, promise-to-pay clause, and certain other standard provisions of the bond be engraved. Variable parts of the text, including those that appear on the reverse side, may be lithographed or printed.

Municipal securities are not subject to the same strict bond form regulations, since they are not listed on national exchanges. Accordingly, it is not uncommon for small municipal bond issues to be printed by local printers on preprinted stock border paper. With the advent of the personal computer, It has also become increasingly popular to prepare some smaller municipal bond issue bond forms on safety paper. Whether the bond forms are printed by local printers on blank border stock or on safety paper, they still must be authenticated by the trustee with the trustee's original signature. Bond forms that are not printed by nationally recognized bond printers can be difficult to print by automation.

Before 1964, most corporate debt securities were issued in bearer form, for bearer bonds were the only security form that constituted a good delivery when sold. Municipal debt issues, on the other hand, were issued primarily in bearer form until July 1, 1983.[3] The indenture usually provided that the holder could have the bond registered as principal, in which case it could be transferred only by assignment of the registered holder. It also customarily enabled the bonds to be issued in fully registered form, without coupons, in which both principal and interest were payable only to a

---

[3] See chapter 2, note 7, *supra.*

registered holder. As the institutional investors became more important, a number of corporate trustees urged issuers to liberalize the exchange provisions to encourage increased holding of large registered pieces by these investors. As the result of such efforts and the cooperation of the underwriters and dealers, as well as increased awareness by the investing public of the advantages, the number of corporate issues sold only in fully registered form grew steadily each year until by the end of 1982, 99 percent of new corporate issues marketed were in such form. The major exception to this change was the sale of debt securities by domestic corporations to nonresident alien investors, the so-called Eurobond issues. Because of investors' reluctance to hold these debt obligations in registered form, almost all these issues have been sold in bearer form with coupons.[4]

The indenture states the denominations in which the securities may be issued, with no other denominations authorized or to be authenticated by the trustee. The customary and recommended practice for corporate issues is to authorize them in $1,000 denominations and in any denomination that is a multiple of $1,000. Municipal issues, however, are customarily issued in minimum denominations of $5,000 and multiples of $5,000.

The huge volume of all registered issues, the greater use of automated equipment to process the certificates, and the continuing storage problem have dictated the need for using the uniform "stock certificate size" approved by the American National Standards Institute (ANSI). As explained earlier, the substantive provisions of the indenture or summaries of the pertinent provisions are printed on the reverse of the certificates as a continuation of the bond form. The use of certificates with preprinted denominations is also desirable, as well as "blank" or unspecified denomination certificates. In addition to the standard $1,000 denomination certificate, both $5,000 and $10,000 certificates probably should be prepared for corporate issues in excess of $100 million. It is more common to use preprinted certificates when trustees do not have the sophisticated technology to use blank certificates. The inability to employ sophisticated technology often places trustees at a disadvantage, however, owing to the added cost incurred by the obligor in printing additional denominations. However, for those bond registrars using computer-generated certificates, the use of only "blank" denominated certificates may be especially attractive.

---

[4] The sale of bearer bonds of issues sold after July 18, 1984, to offshore investors has been affected by the repeal of the 30 percent withholding tax on interest paid. See sec. 127, Tax Reform Act of 1984, P.O. 98–369, 98 Stat. 552. To qualify for the exemption, certain procedures are prescribed by the Internal Revenue Service. See IRC sec. 163 (f)(2)(B) and IRS Regulations, sec. 1.163–65(c)T.

For a "good delivery" of certificates of issues listed on the New York Stock Exchange, the denomination amount should be engraved in both upper corners of the face of the certificate, with the bond number printed directly below. "Blank" denomination certificates up to $100,000 are also acceptable, provided the numeric amount is macerated or "matrixed" on the certificate. Such blank certificates need have only the numeric dollar amount recorded in the upper right corner, with the upper left corner used for the bond number. For unlisted corporate issues and municipal issues, the same requirements are recommended.[5] As more and more trustees use computers to register bonds, they are finding it easier to use the matrix format for all bonds to simplify the certificate formatting and issuance process.

The indenture also specifies the manner in which the bonds are to be executed by the obligor, and the trustee should see that this provision is followed strictly. All signatures should appear on the face of the certificate, and whenever possible, those of the obligor should be facsimile. A limited number of municipal issues require manual obligor signatures. This usually delays the processing, as it can be difficult to locate appropriate municipal officials who understand the bond issue. The trustee's authentication should, however, never be other than a manual signature. The corporate seal on the bond is usually a facsimile, but this also should be specifically authorized by the indenture.

Not only should the trustee compare the text of the bonds of each denomination with that of the indenture, but the trustee also should examine each bond to see that it is properly signed and sealed; that the text on both face and reverse is complete (to guard against a mechanical printing failure); that the bonds are numbered consecutively; and that the aggregate amount of bonds so executed is the amount authorized to be authenticated. Computer-generated certificates usually reprint the bond's certificate number on the certificate to verify the accuracy of data entry on the bond registration software.

The trustee is responsible for controlling the total principal amount of bonds authenticated and delivered. The records established to maintain this control should note each bond received, authenticated, delivered, canceled, replaced for lost or stolen securities, or otherwise dealt with by the trustee so that at any time it can certify the bonds outstanding.

---

[5] For specific recommendations on certificate format and paper quality standards, see American Bankers Association, *Recommended Certificate Standards for Registered Bond Issues, Corporate Trust Activities Committee* (1974); American National Standards Institute, *Specifications for Fully Registered Municipal Securities*, X9.12–1983.

UNCERTIFICATED SECURITIES

As the result of the back-office paper crisis that occurred on Wall Street in the late 1960s, several far-reaching innovations were instituted, the goal being to make the transfer of securities more efficient. Among the most significant innovations was eliminating the use of the physical certificate as evidence of ownership in a corporation and as evidence of indebtedness of both public and private corporations.

The U.S. Treasury was the first to eliminate paper certificates, and in 1967 it began eliminating physical Treasury Bill securities. By 1986 all marketable U.S. Treasury obligations were in book-entry form, as are currently all securities issued by the Federal National Mortgage Association, the Student Loan Marketing Association, and the Federal Home Loan Mortgage Association.

By 1977 comprehensive revisions of article 8 of the UCC were completed and promulgated, including provisions that permit the issuance of pure uncertificated securities and govern the legal relationships and liabilities of the parties dealing with them.

Despite these efforts over the past thirty years, the most visible progress toward eliminating the security certificate has been the development of the "immobilized clearance" system by the Depository Trust Company (DTC), which by 1997 accounted for more than 75 percent of the outstanding shares and 90 percent of public debt securities of companies listed on the New York Stock Exchange, as well as more than 95 percent of outstanding municipal securities. In most cases, DTC holds the physical certificates that are registered by the issuer's transfer agent/bond registrar in the name of Cede & Co., their nominee. However, for a significant percentage of municipal issues and a growing number of corporate issues, the so-called book-entry-only process for debt securities has been implemented—the difference between it and a pure book-entry system is that in this case one jumbo certificate is prepared and registered by the bond registrar in the name of Cede & Co. To avoid having to issue a new jumbo certificate each time securities move in or out of DTC's position, many bond registrars indicate on the certificate itself that the face amount of the certificate is "such amount as shall be shown on the securities registrar from time to time as the amount payable to Cede & Co."

The trend of the future is clearly toward eliminating the paper certificate, and significant progress has been made. The movement has been reinforced by the recommendations of the U.S. Working Committee of the Group of Thirty (an independent, nonpartisan, nonprofit organization established in 1978 to address public policy issues around the world). In its August 1990 interim report, the U.S. Working Committee reached the preliminary conclusion/recommendation that "it is both desirable and achievable to eliminate the use of the physical certificate by 1995 for the settlement of securities transactions and transfers." Substantial progress was made in the 1994 Same Day Funds Task Force Recommendations to the Group of Thirty, in which the following guidelines were recommended: "Effective January 1, 1995, all new issues must be made depository-eligible by meeting depository eligibility requirements and must be structured so that all payments to depositories of principal and income must be made in same day funds on payment date. Such issues can be in certificated or book-entry-only (BEO) form."[6]

Despite the slow progress over the past twenty-five years, it is evident that within the next five years, paper certificates may very well be found only in attics and antique shops!

DISPOSING OF BOND PROCEEDS

Without express provisions in the indenture, the trustee is under no duty to direct the application of the bonds' proceeds, and the indenture will usually so provide. In a few cases, the courts have found an implied duty even in the face of an express provision to the contrary, but in all these cases, a specific use was spelled out, and the facts indicated that the trustee had actual knowledge of misapplication.

Generally, when the indenture provides for the bonds' proceeds to be used for a specific purpose, it should require that the appropriate evidence be furnished to the trustee of the application. In such cases, the trustee should be authorized to retain possession of the bonds' proceeds and disburse them as required upon receipt of the proper certificates. A typical example is a bond issue authorized for the construction of a specific project. For a newly formed corporation that has no substantial property or when the proposed expenditure is substantial in relation to a company's net worth, protective provisions are essential, and a trustee should not accept an appointment unless they are included. Normally, however, when all conditions for the authentication and delivery of bonds have been fulfilled, the trustee should not be concerned about the actual use of the proceeds.

[6]"Implementing the G30 Recommendations," *Securities Processing Digest*, no. 25, Winter 1994.

TYPICAL PROVISIONS GOVERNING THE ISSUANCE OF BONDS

The indenture must specify the terms and conditions by which the indenture securities may be issued. The usual debenture or note agreement provides for the initial issuance of all authorized securities, so that each issue of such obligations is covered by a separate agreement or indenture. But this is not always the case, and it is proper for such an indenture to permit the creation and issuance of additional series of obligations, provided that such obligations are of the same class. The condition for issuing additional obligations under such an agreement usually is the existence of no default, and if the indenture requires maintenance of specified financial ratios, these ratios must exist after the additional obligations have been issued.

As distinguished from the usual debenture or note agreement, a typical mortgage bond indenture is open ended and is designed to provide not only for the current financing but also for all future bond financing of the corporation. The reasons for this are obvious. Not only would the creation of a separate indenture for each financing be expensive, but also the use of a single mortgage indenture is the only way in which secured obligations, ranking *pari passu*, can be issued from time to time over a period of years. Because a first-mortgage obligation normally commands a better price and is more readily marketable than one with a junior lien position, it is desirable to provide a vehicle under which senior securities can continue to be issued.

Such an indenture describes the provisions of the first series of bonds to be issued and stipulates the manner in which the terms and provisions of later series are to be established. This is done by either a resolution of the corporation's board of directors or a supplemental indenture, or usually both, for such a supplement must be approved by the board. It is recommended that a supplemental indenture always be used. Recording the original indenture gives public notice of only the initial series of bonds. Although the lien created will probably be effective until specifically discharged, it is desirable that public notice be given of additional debt secured, particularly if the maturity date of the later series extends beyond that of the initial series. This notice is given by the proper execution and recording of the supplemental indenture.

The indenture authorizes the initial authentication and delivery of a specified principal amount of bonds. These bonds are usually authorized to be authenticated and delivered on the request of specified officers of the corporation, without compliance by the corporation with any conditions other than the execution and delivery of the indenture and the furnishing of the requisite documents and authorities to support the execution and delivery.

Additional issuance can be secured only after specified conditions have been met. Bondholders contract for specific security coverage for their obligations as a condition for extending credit. Each additional creation of debt, ranking equally with that outstanding, automatically depletes the security interest of each bondholder in the property existing at that time. The purpose of the detailed provisions governing the creation of additional indebtedness is to ensure that the security interest is not reduced proportionately (in regard to the aggregate value of the property) below the minimum contracted for in the indenture. This is the basic concept that the trustee should have in mind when reviewing these sections of every proposed secured indenture.

We cannot describe every purpose for which additional bonds might be authorized, but we will summarize the most common purposes.

1. To provide funds for the construction of property additions or to reimburse the company for expenditures made in such construction. Property additions should always be specifically defined, but they normally are any type of property included in the company's fixed property accounts, in accordance with accepted accounting practices. All property owned by the corporation at the date of the indenture (or, frequently, as of the end of the fiscal period immediately before or after this date) is regarded as "funded" and is not available for use as a basis for issuing additional bonds or for any other purpose under the indenture. Property acquired after this date can be so used. Under an after-acquired property clause, such property becomes subject to the lien of the indenture as acquired but remains "unfunded" until it has been used for the specific purpose under the indenture, at which time its character changes to that of being funded.

An active corporation is almost continuously adding property and retiring property that has become worn out or obsolete. For the proper security to be maintained, only "net property additions" should be taken into account when considering the amount of property that can be "bonded" (i.e., used to support the issuance of additional bonds). Sometimes the computations to determine this become quite complicated, for frequently other indenture provisions and their use of property have to be taken into account. The general process, however, is to deduct from the gross amount of all unfunded property additions those additions from the book value of all property retired to determine the net property additions. The value at which the gross property additions may be taken into account is the lesser of the cost to the company or the fair market value as of the date of the certification.

When the net value of property additions has been determined, it is then necessary to compute the amount of bonds that can be issued on that basis. Rarely are companies permitted to issue bonds to the full value of such property. We have mentioned the importance of the debt ratio, and bondholders should always insist on a reasonable margin of security. A percentage often found in utility mortgages, for example, is 60 percent, which means that for each $1,000 of net value added to the fixed property account, a maximum of $600 of additional secured indebtedness is permitted.

2. To retire prior lien obligations. When prior liens exist on all or any part of the property mortgaged, provisions should always be made for their retirement. Even if no such liens exist when the indenture is created, this problem should be considered, for often additional property is acquired that is subject to a lien at the time of acquisition. If such additional property is used as a basis for issuing bonds, the amount of the prior lien should first be deducted from the bondable value of the property. It is then appropriate to permit refunding of the prior lien by issuing additional bonds under the indenture.

This is one of the situations in which the trustee is responsible for properly applying the bond proceeds. A common requirement is surrendering the prior lien obligations to the trustee as a condition for issuing the bonds. This is usually the case when the prior lien is only partially retired, and quite often the prior lien obligations are required to be held alive by the trustee. The desirability of such a provision is questionable, for it is unlikely that the trustee could claim a position *pari passu* with the remaining holders of prior lien obligations to the extent of the obligations that the trustee holds. A certificate of the prior lien trustee with respect to the cancellation of a specified amount of prior lien obligations seems to afford the same protection as their delivery to the trustee, and an indenture provision to this effect should be acceptable.

When the prior lien is to be retired in whole, the trustee should be protected in paying the proceeds to the prior lien trustee or to the company if it receives a duly executed and recorded counterpart of the satisfaction of the prior lien obligation.

3. Refunding of outstanding indenture securities. This is obviously a proper purpose, for it results merely in the substitution of one indenture obligation for another. When bonds are acquired by the obligor company

by purchase or otherwise, their surrender to the trustee for cancellation is sufficient for the authentication and delivery of an equivalent amount of bonds of another series. When a preceding series is to be redeemed in whole or in part, it is sufficient if the trustee holds, in trust, funds sufficient to effect such a redemption and is authorized to take the necessary steps required. Any premium or interest payable on the redemption must be supplied separately by the obligor.

Previously issued bonds often are retired or redeemed without the concurrent issuance of additional bonds, but the obligor may wish to reserve the right to issue bonds on the basis of their retirement. This is perfectly proper, and it is unnecessary to require that previously issued bonds be held alive in the company's treasury to preserve this right.

Bonds retired through a sinking fund or similar provisions should normally not be permitted as the basis for issuing additional bonds under the indenture. This would result in an indirect depletion of the bondholders' security.

4. Issuing bonds against a deposit of cash. A common indenture provision permits the issuance of bonds against the deposit with the trustee of an equivalent amount of cash. The cash so deposited is subject to withdrawal upon the company's establishing its right to the authentication and delivery of an equivalent amount of bonds under other provisions of the indenture. Each bond financing is expensive. When a company contemplates a substantial expansion program or when such a program and a refunding are being considered, it may take down its estimated total requirements through one issue against the deposit of cash with the trustee. As property additions are completed, it makes the necessary certifications to the trustee and withdraws cash in an amount equal to the principal amount of bonds that it can issue on the basis of this property. The net result is the same. This was once a frequently used provision, although it is more common now for corporations to resort to interim bank financing to fund construction programs, deferring permanent bond financing until the program is nearly completed. This practice tends to reduce interest costs. But bond financing rather than interim bank credit might be more advantageous when the bond market is favorable, with low interest rates.

One final point should be noted. If a default should occur after bonds have been issued under such a provision and before the cash is withdrawn, this cash becomes part of the general trust estate securing all bonds outstanding and cannot be set aside for the benefit of the holders of the specific series issued against its deposit. Without express and specific provisions to the contrary, all indenture securities are equal in regard to their claims against the trust estate and the obligor.

Evidence Required by the Trustee of Compliance with Conditions

The indenture specifies the particular documents to be delivered to the trustee to establish the company's right to the authentication and delivery of the bonds requested. The trustee must examine all such documents to see that they comply with all the conditions, and it must also make sure that the documents are in the form required by the indenture. Because of the importance of these transactions, the trustee should always have counsel review the documents.

The documents received are determined by the particular purpose for which the bonds are to be issued. Three documents should be received in all cases, however, including a resolution by the company's board of directors (or in the case of tax-exempt bonds, of the directors or governing body of the tax-exempt entity) authorizing the issuance of the bonds, describing the purpose for which they are to be issued, directing the execution of the bonds by specified officers, providing for the execution and delivery of necessary documents to the trustee, and requesting the authentication and delivery of the bonds by the trustee. The trustee should also receive a certificate executed by authorized officers of the company to the effect that there is no default under the indenture and that all conditions for the authentication and delivery of the bonds requested have been satisfied. This should be accompanied by an opinion of counsel that all these conditions have been fulfilled.

When the authentication and delivery of bonds is on the basis of property additions, these property additions should be certified to the trustee by authorized officers in sufficient detail to permit their identification. The certification should also include an appropriate computation of the net bondable value of the property to establish the company's right to issue the bonds requested. This certificate should be accompanied by a separate certificate from an engineer, appraiser, or other expert giving the value of the property additions. Under certain circumstances, the engineer's certificate must be executed by an independent engineer or appraiser not under the obligor's control.

Frequently, an earnings requirement is included as a condition. The customary form of this condition is that for a specified period, the company's net earnings available for interest (or the average earnings if the period is more than a year) must be so many times the interest charges on all indebtedness, including the bonds to be issued. Compliance with this condition should be established by an accountant's certificate, which under certain conditions must be a certificate of an independent public accountant.

When property additions are made the basis for issuing bonds, the trustee should receive the opinion of counsel on the instruments of conveyance required to subject the property to the lien of the indenture or the assurance that no instruments are necessary. As we indicated earlier, if the bonds to be issued are a new series, a supplemental indenture is desirable. A specific conveyance of the property is customarily included in the same supplement.

If the authorization of any regulatory agency or public body is required, evidence of the authorization should be secured.[7] If the bonds are to be issued publicly, registration requirements under the 33 Act must be completed, including the filing of a new Form T-1.

For the administrator's convenience, it is helpful to use a guide sheet for each new issue of securities, as outlined in exhibit 4 (for trustee appointment) or exhibit 5 (for agency appointments). These guide sheets call attention to the various matters that should be considered, or the actions to be taken, and, when completed, can be added to the bond issue

---

[7] For a discussion of problems relating to the public utilities bonding of nuclear-generating facilities, see American Bankers Association, Corporate Trust Activities Committee, *The Bondability of Nuclear Facilities* (1977).

SEVEN

Sinking-Fund and Maintenance Provisions

A common type of covenant found in indentures is the *sinking-fund provision*. This is a device for amortizing the debt, or a part of it, over the life of a security issue. It is an important provision of the security issue and is almost always found in an unsecured debenture or note agreement. This provision is also common to bond indentures. If a security issue is created for the construction or purchase of certain fixed property or facilities, the holders' security will be depleted unless the amount of the debt is reduced proportionately by the depreciation or loss in value of the property as it is used in the business. A common use for cash generated by the depreciation charge is the reduction of the debt incurred to purchase the property. Even though it is not related to specific property or security, a sinking fund is a convenient device for reducing corporate and municipal funded debt.

In mortgage indentures, particularly those of utility and railroad corporations and hospital- and housing-related securities, a maintenance covenant is often included in lieu of, and sometimes in addition to, a sinking-fund provision. This type of covenant is not the simple maintenance covenant undertaken by the obligor to keep the mortgaged property in good working order and condition. A simple maintenance covenant should be part of all mortgage indentures. Rather, a *maintenance covenant* is the expenditure of a stated amount of money to renew and replace the property. The theory of this covenant is that in lieu of retiring debt as the value of the property depreciates, the company will maintain the value of the security by expending an equivalent amount to construct or acquire additional property.

The operation and purpose of this covenant can be illustrated by a simple example. Let us suppose that a corporation acquires a new plant for $100 million with an estimated productive economic life of twenty-five years. For convenience, we assume that the value depreciates on a level basis, or at the rate of $4 million per year. The plant is financed with $40 million of equity money and $60 million of bonds, secured by a mortgage on the property. Clearly, for the bondholders to maintain their margin of security, $2.4 million in bonds would have to be retired each year. This would be done through a sinking fund. An alternative method would be for the company to maintain the security at $100 million, by mortgaging entirely new facilities, by adding to the existing plant, or by replacing portions of the plant as they become old or worn out. This alternative undertaking is described in a maintenance or a renewal and replacement covenant. The common term for the retirement and replacement of mortgaged property is *property deletions and additions*. Schedules to denote the appropriate changes are typically maintained by the trustee and obligor to substantiate the current value of the collateral underlying the outstanding securities.

SINKING-FUND COVENANTS

A *sinking-fund covenant* may take any of a different number of forms, and the exact terms result from the negotiations leading up to the issue. Some indentures do not contain a sinking fund, although investors usually insist on including an orderly procedure to retire debt. This is particularly true in the case of an unsecured debenture or note issue. It is uncommon for an agreement of this kind not to include a sinking fund. An alternative method for retiring debt is to have the securities mature in series. Usually, serial maturities are scheduled as annual maturities, rather than all maturing at the same time. Serial issues are very common in state and municipal bonds. Purchasers of corporate bonds, however, prefer term bonds with a sinking fund rather than serial maturities. Consequently, serial maturities are not often found in industrial companies' issues.

The trustee has substantial duties and responsibilities for the proper operation of the sinking fund. The indenture provisions should receive attention during the drafting of the indenture and in connection with each sinking-fund operation, since if the trustee misapplies the funds, it may incur substantial liability. The trustee should review its role as the paying agent to verify that the sinking-fund provisions can be managed efficiently within the capabilities of the operating system and with sufficient notice to the bondholders.

Method of Computation

A sinking fund may operate annually, semiannually, or even at more frequent intervals. Because each operation may be quite expensive, it is not advisable for the sinking fund to operate more often than needed to carry out the basic purpose of the contract. Each sinking-fund payment may be computed in different ways, with no particular preference or advantage for one method over another. Rather, the method of computation should be the one best suited to obtain the desired result.

The most common used methods are (1) payment of a fixed dollar amount, (2) payment of an amount calculated as a percentage of the maximum amount of securities that have been at any time authenticated and outstanding, or (3) payment of an amount sufficient to retire a fixed percentage of the bonds. The last might be the preferred method when a redemption premium on a declining scale is involved in a sinking-fund operation, for it ensures the retirement of a level rather than a variable amount of bonds.

Although most sinking funds are fixed in some definite amount or according to a specified formula, a variable sinking fund is often used. Such a sinking fund might be measured by a percentage of net earnings, either of the company's total net earnings or from a specified source. It also might be a combination of several factors; for example, a minimum fixed sinking fund might be provided, to which is added a percentage of net earnings over a specified amount. This type might be desirable for a company whose earnings tend to fluctuate greatly with cyclical changes in the economy, ensuring greater retirement of the debt during financially successful years and providing some measure of protection in less successful years.

It is also common for the amount of the fixed sinking-fund payment to vary from year to year, for instance, retiring a smaller percentage of bonds during the earlier years and an increasing percentage during the later years. This method is almost always used when the principal security is a lease or contract obligation. Level amortization payments are provided to cover both the interest and the sinking fund. The amount required for interest decreases with each payment, leaving a greater amount available to retire the principal.

When several series of bonds are outstanding under the same indenture, different procedures may be followed. A separate sinking fund may be created for each series, and a number of separate payments are made, at either the same or different times. Each requires an entirely separate operation related to the securities of the particular series involved. Or a single sinking fund may be established that can be applied to the bonds of any or all series. The only change that takes place when a new series is created is that the amount of each sinking fund is usually increased.

When a single sinking-fund payment is made for bonds of different series with different interest rates and maturity dates, the trustee should apply the monies carefully and should always see that the indenture spells out the exact procedure to be followed. The usual provision requires the retirement of bonds that, computed on the basis of the price to be paid, provide the highest yield to maturity. This application is the most advantageous to the obligor company, results in the greatest reduction in annual fixed charges, and thus might be said to be the most beneficial to the trust estate. Whereas the usual effect is to eliminate certain series of bonds from participating in the sinking fund and thus might be said to be unfair in this respect, it should be kept in mind that it is part of their contract, and theoretically at least, the holders of the series could have bargained for a separate sinking fund allocable to their series of bonds if they had so desired.

To avoid conflicts with securities to be issued, the trustee should review the provisions of those sinking funds of securities for which it currently serves as trustee. The trustee should make certain that the indenture specifies how the interest and premium (if any) required to be paid in connection with any sinking-fund retirement are to be provided. It may be evident from the manner in which the sinking fund is computed, but if not, the indenture should specify whether the company is to provide these amounts separately or whether they are chargeable against the sinking fund.

Inasmuch as bonds can usually be retired through a sinking fund without a premium, or at a lower premium than for the optional redemption, the obligor company has no right to increase the amount of a sinking fund or to anticipate sinking-fund payments unless it has this right. If the indenture includes this reservation, there should also be no doubt about whether the obligor is entitled to a credit against subsequent sinking-fund payments for any amounts anticipated or paid beyond normal requirements.

Method of Applying Sinking-Fund Monies

The trustee should ensure that the method of applying sinking-fund monies is clearly stated in the indenture and, if alternative methods are provided, that the indenture specifies the order in which such methods are to be used or the conditions used to select the particular method.

Once specific bonds have been selected for purchase or redemption by the sinking fund and all steps necessary to effect the purchase or redemption have been taken except the actual surrender of the bonds, the funds in the hands of the trustee cease to be general trust estate funds and become specifically allocated to the particular bond or bonds selected. In the event of a subsequent default, the holder is entitled to payment upon surrender of his or her bond, regardless of what the other indenture security holders may realize.

A more difficult problem is presented, however, when a default occurs before the monies have been applied or before all steps necessary to retire specific bonds have been taken. The problem is complicated if the sinking-fund payment was made for a particular series of bonds or if the trustee has selected specific bonds for retirement but has not mailed the notice of redemption.

The law applicable to such a situation is not clear, so the trustee's action should be guided by counsel. As a general rule, all further action should be suspended, any preliminary steps that may have been taken should be revoked, and the funds should be retained by the trustee without application until the default has been cured or waived or until the trustee receives judicial direction on disposing of the funds. Even when only one series of bonds is involved, applying the funds to retire specific bonds with knowledge of a default might entangle the trustee in an unlawful preference for which it might be held liable. Aside from the question of the trustee's liability, this application would be unfair if as a result of the default, the remaining security holders received less than their full claim.

The obligor company is frequently given the right to receive credit against its sinking-fund obligation for any bonds it surrenders to the trustee for cancellation. (This right may, in the case of a convertible debenture issue, also include the principal amount of debentures already converted.) This enables the obligor company to acquire bonds throughout the year in the open market, taking advantage of favorable market conditions, and some companies continuously satisfy their entire sinking-fund obligations in this manner. The amount of the credit the company receives for bonds surrendered may be the par value of the bonds, the actual cost of the bonds to the company not above the par value, or the current sinking-fund redemption price if more than par.

If the obligor does not have a specific right to surrender bonds against credit or in lieu of a sinking-fund payment, a question arises about the trustee's right, in applying sinking-fund monies, to acquire or purchase bonds held by the obligor company in its treasury. It is preferable that this right be specified, although such actions are a more or less accepted practice and, without an express prohibition, would seem to be in order. But such an acquisition should at or below the price at which equivalent bonds could be purchased from other holders.

The trustee may be directed to use sinking-fund monies to buy bonds in the open market at a price not higher than the current redemption price. If the bonds are noncallable, the indenture will set a more or less arbitrary price. The interest and commission paid on such purchases are usually, although not necessarily, separately reimbursed by the obligor. If not, then these amounts should be added when computing the maximum price that can be offered. A time limit is customarily set for this method of operation, and if the funds cannot be exhausted within this time, a different method must be followed for the remaining funds.

Another method of operation is for the trustee to invite tenders of bonds. This is regarded by some as a fairer method of operation, although it usually results in paying a higher average price than would be the case in an open-market operation. When the current market price is higher than the maximum price at which tenders can be accepted (usually the sinking-fund redemption price), an invitation for tenders is essentially an idle gesture, and when the trustee can decide on the method to be followed, this fact should be considered.

The procedure to be followed when tenders are invited is relatively simple, but it still requires care. A date is selected for the submission of tenders, with both the hour and the day specified. The invitation is then mailed in accordance with the indenture's provisions to all registered holders of securities. (If bearer bonds are outstanding, the notice must be published, and copies mailed to all holders who may have filed their names with the trustee for the purpose of receiving reports and notices.) It is desirable to request the submission of sealed tenders, and all other conditions should be clearly stated in the notice. The right to reject tenders in whole or in part should always be specifically reserved. To avoid error, some form of dual control should be established for all tenders received. A record of their receipt should be kept and the tenders deposited in a locked container. If any tenders are received unsealed, they should be examined to see that all necessary information is included and then immediately sealed and deposited. No record of prices should be kept, and until the tenders have been opened and examined at the appointed time, no information should be disclosed to anyone, including the obligor company.

When the appointed hour has arrived, the tenders should be opened, examined, and listed, and the prices at which the bonds are offered should be reviewed. In the case of different issues with different interest rates and maturity dates, the price should be computed on the basis of yield to maturity, with the higher the yield, the lower the price. Enough bonds should then be accepted at the lowest prices offered to exhaust the monies available. When the notice of acceptance is mailed, the contract is completed.

A final method of operation is selecting bonds for redemption through the indenture's redemption provisions. Bonds are usually redeemable at par for the purpose of the sinking fund, or at prices lower than would be required for an optional redemption. The particular bonds to be redeemed are selected according to the indenture. It is customary for the trustee to select them. When drafting these provisions, it is desirable for the trustee to retain flexibility, and so it is better to have a provision allowing for the selection to be made in a manner that the trustee deems equitable, rather than to have the mechanics spelled out in detail. Once the particular bonds to be redeemed have been selected, the trustee arranges to mail an appropriate notice in the manner prescribed by the indenture.[1] Once the notice has been mailed, the designated bonds become due and payable on the date specified, and the necessary funds should be segregated by the trustee and held in an account specifically for their payment.

In the case of direct placements, in which all securities are held by institutional investors, it is customary to provide that in lieu of application by lot, sinking-fund monies proportionate to their holdings are allocated among the owners. The provision should be carefully drafted and administered, the objective being for each holder to retain, as nearly as possible, its proportional percentage of the debt obligations. Normally, bonds must be retired in even multiples of $1,000 for corporate securities and in multiples of $5,000 for municipal securities. There is no problem when the sinking-fund percentage is applied to each holding result in an uneven multiple of the permitted denomination of $1,000 or $5,000. This seldom happens, however, and so it is necessary for the trustee to devise an appropriate formula for each operation. No particular formula is required so long as the same one is used consistently year after year and produces the desired allocation. Although the operating systems used by most trustees and agents perform pro-rata redemptions, it is helpful to understand how they complete the redemption process. Exhibit 6 describes a typical formula and illustrates its application.

---

[1] If bonds are outstanding in bearer form, an appropriate notice must also be published.

Bonds retired through a sinking fund are usually canceled by the trustee and cannot be reissued or used by the obligor as a credit under any other indenture provision.

Maintenance and Replacement Covenants

As we said earlier, a maintenance and replacement covenant is sometimes used instead of, or in addition to, a sinking fund. This is more common in the case of a regulated company, such as an electric utility, which requires a more or less continuous supply of funds for capital purposes and for which a somewhat higher debt ratio is permissible. The fund established by such a covenant is more properly a renewal and replacement fund than a maintenance fund. Every corporation is expected to provide funds for the normal maintenance of its properties, which constitute expenses chargeable to its income account. The fund we are considering here is a capital fund, and its expenditures are normally chargeable to fixed property accounts.

There is no fixed formula by which the amount of such fund is to be computed, and it varies with the type of company, its properties, and other considerations. In the case of regulated companies, the regulatory authority may require a particular formula, or it may otherwise be determined as part of the negotiations for drafting the indenture. Ordinarily, the formula depends on the amount of the obligor's annual depreciation charges and, in any event, should be designed to provide the amount that will enable the company to preserve the value of the property securing its outstanding bonds.

As an illustration, a more or less arbitrary rule was at one time applied to electric utilities. As a general average, the investment of $4 in fixed plant was required to produce $1 of gross annual revenue. Also, as a general average, using those amounts for the entire property account resulting from applying the required depreciation percentages to specified classes of property indicated an annual average depreciation charge of 3¾ percent. Using these figures, a covenant to expend 15 percent of annual gross revenues from operations for maintenance and replacement was frequently used in these obligors' indentures. This percentage might vary when the character of a obligor's property differed substantially from the norm. More recent indentures have tailored the covenant to the circumstances of the particular obligor rather than follow a preestablished percentage.

The indenture requires annually filing with the trustee a certificate detailed enough to show compliance with the covenant. All computations should be shown, and the trustee should check them against the governing indenture covenants and also check the data included against the financial statements and other information it may receive from the obligor.

All property acquired by the obligor and certified to the trustee in compliance with this covenant becomes funded property and cannot be used as a basis for issuing bonds or other purposes. Accordingly, the trustee should receive all the supplemental documents relevant to the property as it would receive if the property were being used as a basis for issuing bonds. These documents include an engineer's certificate of value, an opinion of counsel, and an officer's certificate regarding the company's title to the property and the lien of the indenture, and any required instruments of specific conveyance.

As distinguished from issuing bonds, property additions can be taken under this covenant at 100 percent rather than at the bondable percentage of their value. If any such property is subject to a prior lien, it is necessary to deduct an amount equivalent to the bondable property value of the lien. For example, if the bondable percentage of property additions under the indenture is 60 percent, $166\frac{2}{3}$ percent of any prior lien bonds is deducted in such a computation.

Usually the maintenance covenant is combined with a renewal and replacement covenant, to allow the obligor to take the expenditures for normal repairs and maintenance as a credit. It is also necessary, as it is when issuing bonds, to deduct the book value of the property retirements from the gross property expenditures to determine the net credit to be allowed.

One of the difficult administrative problems is dealing with property certificates under a number of different indenture provisions.[2] Although the value of a particular addition can be used only once, the value of the addition may be above the amount certified for a particular purpose, and the excess can be used for another purpose. Similarly, the property retirements or prior liens can be deducted only once. The certificates should be drawn so as to enable the trustee to check these facts.

During any year, if the obligor expends more than the required percentage for maintenance and replacement, it is normally allowed a credit for the excess against the requirement of subsequent years. This credit may be unlimited in that it can be taken at any time, or it may have to be used within a specified time. If the latter is the case, we offer a word of caution.

[2] See chapter 6, note 7, *supra*.

For example, if the use of the credit is limited to the three succeeding years and the company has excess expenditures for four successive years, the amount of the credit for the first of the four years will no longer be available. This may seem obvious, except that the certificates may be drawn to indicate that in each year, the company first uses the credit for the preceding year and the resulting larger credit for the current year is allocable to that year and not to both years. The result may be to carry forward indefinitely a substantial credit that would otherwise have lapsed.

If the computation indicates that the company has not expended the required percentage during the year, a deficit for the year results. This deficit may be offset by the amount of any credit the company was entitled to carry forward from previous years. To the extent it is not offset, the obligor must deposit cash or bonds with the trustee, which may be subsequently withdrawn against certification of property additions or on the basis of a credit shown in a subsequent maintenance certificate. If the company desires, any bonds so deposited may be canceled as a credit against the maintenance requirements. The canceled bonds have the same status as sinking-fund bonds and cannot be reissued or used as a basis for any other action under the indenture.

EIGHT

Release and Substitution of Property

Another major segment of the indenture contract dealing with the maintenance and preservation of the bondholders' security is the section dealing with the release and substitution of property. These provisions are not, of course, pertinent to the unsecured debenture or note agreement, but in almost every case in which specific property is mortgaged to or pledged with the trustee, the indenture contains detailed provisions for how the obligor should deal with its properties and prescribes conditions for the release and substitution of specific properties on which the indenture is a lien. During the early history of the corporate trust business, most provisions for the release and substitution of property were contained in utility companies' indentures. Most of the utility indentures were served by financial center trustees. In recent years, municipal securities for hospitals and single and multifamily housing have required that more and more trustees located outside financial centers become familiar with related property clauses in governing indentures.

The necessity for and importance of such provisions become clear when one considers that in the usual case, the real security is the business of the obligor as a going concern and not the aggregate of the individual parcels of property. It is customary for mortgage indentures to continue for an indefinite period, and the needs of the mortgagor obligor are likely to change considerably while the indenture is in operation. Also, many parts of the original property wear out and become unfit for use in the obligor's business. The primary purpose of the release provisions is to enable the obligor to dispose of obsolete and unproductive properties, free from the lien of the indenture, and to use the proceeds to acquire additional properties or improvements necessary or useful in its business operations. Because it is desirable to provide for almost every contingency, the release provisions cannot be limited to the mere disposition of worn-out or obsolete properties but usually cover any property that the obligor may sell or otherwise dispose of.

Inasmuch as the trustee's primary responsibilities revolve around the preservation of the bondholders' security, the duties discussed in this and the two preceding chapters might be regarded as the tripartite base on which most of the predefault administrative provisions of a secured indenture are founded. The sections dealing with the issuance of bonds limit the creation of additional debt to a prescribed percentage of the additional value added to the security and are designed to ensure that the requisite equity is maintained. The sinking-fund and maintenance provisions have as their purpose the continuation of the predetermined minimum ratio of security value to debt. The minimum ratio is ensured through the retirement of debt in proportion to the effect of depreciation and obsolescence factors on the obligor's properties. Finally, the release provisions enable the obligor to deal with its properties efficiently and expeditiously, provided that equivalent value is substituted for any properties sold or otherwise disposed of. Once this basic concept is understood, the proper foundation can be laid for the intelligent consideration of applications or certificates filed under any of the various sections. Although the entire indenture constitutes, and must be considered as, a single contract, it is important that these three segments be complementary. In reviewing the terms of a proposed new mortgage indenture, the trustee should make sure that the various provisions are consistent and designed to carry out the purposes just outlined.

From the viewpoint of both the obligor and the trustee, the release provisions are of the greatest importance, and some of the most intricate problems in indenture administration have to do with the release of property. It is simple enough to state the basic proposition that the trustee's duty is discharged if equivalent value is received for value surrendered, but how is "value" in such an instance to be determined? If a piece of property is sold as a result of arm's length bargaining, isn't the sale price fairly conclusive in relation to the "value" involved? But this means that we are dealing solely with intrinsic values. What happens to the concept that the important consideration is maintaining the value of the business as a going concern and not the intrinsic value of the individual pieces of property? Given the "going concern" theory, is it ever proper for the trustee to accept less than the intrinsic value of the specific property being disposed of? In some situations, should it insist on receiving a great deal more?

The problem is complicated by the trustee's dual fiduciary responsibilities. Preserving the security is the trustee's fundamental responsibility, and to this end, its fiduciary duty to the bondholders is absolute. Conversely, before default, the obligor has the right within the terms of its contract to deal with its property in a manner that seems to be in the best interest of all parties, and the obligor is in a much better position than the trustee to make this determination. The release provisions are a part of the contract between the obligor and the trustee, and if the necessary conditions are fulfilled, the trustee must assent to a requested release and may be liable if it refuses to do so.

This essential problem is as follows: Assume that two extensive railway systems—railroad A and railroad B—serve exactly the same territory between two points on their lines approximately two hundred miles apart and that for this distance, their lines roughly parallel each other. The property of each is heavily mortgaged. As a result of detailed studies and with approval of the Interstate Commerce Commission (ICC), the companies agree that railroad A will grant to railroad B the right in perpetuity to use A's tracks between the points in question and that B will abandon its trackage and right-of-way. The remaining single line is capable of handling all traffic and will lose no revenue. In fact, several million dollars will be saved annually from reductions in property taxes, maintenance, and terminal expenses. Railroad B applies to its mortgage trustee for the release of its entire two-hundred-mile line, the consideration being the mortgaging of the trackage right from railroad A and the deposit of all proceeds of the salvage, with the proceeds to be used to enlarge and improve certain facilities on the new joint line to facilitate the handling of the increased traffic. What should the mortgage trustee's attitude be? Despite the economic desirability of effectuating the agreement, isn't the value of the trust estate being diminished? Does the trust estate benefit at all from the savings realized, unless they are set aside and used to reduce outstanding indebtedness? It is doubtful that the trustee could successfully impose this as a condition for the release if it receives an engineer's certification that the value of the trackage rights is at least equal to the value of the right-of-way to be abandoned.

Railroad A's trustee also has a problem, although possibly not so great as that of railroad B's trustee. The latter would have to insist that the rights granted be superior to all mortgages on railroad A's property, although this would result in a substantial encumbrance ranking ahead of the lien of railroad A's mortgage, requiring a consent or release by its trustee. Again, the consideration could only be the savings in expense, which might or might not directly benefit the trust estate.

In administering the release provisions, the trustee must always insist on receiving the certificates and other documents required and must examine them to see that the proper statements and certifications have been made. The question is the extent, if any, to which the trustee should examine the practical aspects and possible consequences of the proposed transaction and interpose its independent judgment. The matter is complicated when the action requested is unusual and there is uncertainty about whether it is specifically authorized by the indenture's provisions. The trustee has a difficult decision to make in these cases, even though the contemplated action appears to be clearly in the interest of the bondholders. If the trustee assents to the proposed release without the requisite authority and suffers a loss, it may be liable for acting beyond the scope of its powers. Conversely, if it refuses to execute a release and suffers a loss, it may be liable to both the security holders and the obligor if in fact the transaction was within the scope of the indenture. All too frequently, time is of the essence, and it is impossible in these situations to obtain a judicial construction of the trustee's language.

The problem of releases has been the subject of considerable comment over the years, both in judicial decisions and by writers on the subject. Unfortunately, no consistent pattern has been established that might serve as a guide to the trustee. The cases considered have, for the most part, involved situations in which substantial losses have resulted and the trustees were subjected to severe criticism, even though the facts indicated that the terms of the indenture had been strictly followed.

In other cases in which trustees departed from the indenture's restrictions and logically might be subject to criticism, their actions were upheld. A striking example of the latter situation is presented by the numerous cases involving the substitution of buses for municipal railway systems. Few of the railway system indentures provided for the release of lines of railway, and in fact, many contained an express prohibition against it. Most companies, however, would have faced serious financial trouble and a possible loss of franchises if a way had not been found to change the method of transportation. Almost without exception, the courts were able to find enough implied authority in the indenture to permit the transactions. One court held that bondholders acquired their obligations with implied knowledge of a possible change in methods of conducting business and that this was implicit in the agreement.[1] Another found the requisite authority in the provisions reserving to the company, before default, the right to possess, manage, and operate the mortgaged properties.[2]

The extent to which a trustee may go in refusing to execute a release when it appears that the bondholders' security will be impaired, even though the necessary conditions exist, is problematic. Two cases on this point, both decided by New York courts, demonstrate the problem.

The first case entailed a collateral trust indenture in which the collateral consisted largely of bonds secured by real estate mortgages. The indenture provided that the bonds could be accepted as collateral only when accompanied by appraisals showing that the unpaid balance was not more than 75 percent of the value of the real estate. The indenture further provided that whenever the principal amount of bonds outstanding under the indenture was less than 83 ⅓ percent of the par value of collateral pledged, the excess collateral could be withdrawn until the percentage was reached. The case was the application to withdraw $8 million of the excess collateral computed on this basis. The trustee refused to comply, arguing that even though the collateral bonds were adequately secured at the time of deposit, depreciation in real estate values had wiped out the 25 percent margin and that in many cases, the value of the underlying real estate was less than the face amount of the bonds. The trustee's position was upheld by the court, which ruled that the release provisions were qualified by an implied intent that a 25 percent margin in security for all collateral be maintained.[3]

The second case was of a mortgage indenture that contained a rather unusual provision permitting, upon deposit with the trustee, the release of a stated proportion of the consideration for which the property was sold, the percentage varying with the property's gross sales price. On December 18, the obligor notified the trustee that it would default on the interest installment due on the next January 1. On December 30, it applied for the release of certain property, tendering 20 percent of the sales price, which was the required percentage under the applicable indenture clause. The trustee refused to release the property, but the courts upheld

[1] Mayor et al. of City of Baltimore v. United Railways and Electric Company of Baltimore City, 108 Md. 64, 69 Atl. 436 (1908).

[2] New York State Railways v. Security Trust Company of Rochester, 135 Misc. 456, 238 N.Y.S. 354 (1929).

[3] Prudence Company Inc. v. Central Hanover Bank and Trust Company, 261 N.Y. 420, 184 N.E. 687 (1933).

the company's suit for specific performance, holding that since a default did not exist on the date of application, the trustee had no right to refuse.[4]

Under the TIA, the trustee is protected if it relies in good faith on certificates furnished to it by to the indenture provisions, but it must examine the certificates to ensure that they do conform to the provisions.[5] In most situations, if the trustee follows this rule, there will be no problem. No hard-and-fast rule can be established, however, to guide the trustee in unusual or special situations. The requirement of good faith means that it cannot free itself from considering the practical aspects and potential consequences of the proposed transaction.

In regard to the indenture's customary provision relating to these matters, we will deal separately with the mortgage indenture and the collateral indenture. Although both kinds of indentures have the same purpose, they have different problems.

DEALING WITH PROPERTY UNDER MORTGAGE INDENTURES

Before default, the mortgagor obligor has the absolute right to possess, manage, and operate its properties free from restriction or interference, provided only that it complies with the covenants and provisions of the indenture. It is customary for this right to be specifically affirmed in general terms by the indenture. The first sections of the release article then enumerate specific rights retained by the mortgagor in furtherance of this general affirmation.

The first provision deals with the company's right to remove and dispose of property and equipment that has become obsolete or unserviceable or is no longer useful to the company's business. This can be done without the necessity of release or other action by the trustee. The only condition is that the property disposed of be replaced by other property of at least equal value or that, to the extent of any deficiency, cash be deposited with the trustee. Mechanically, the most feasible method of ensuring compliance is to require filing with the trustee an annual certificate of the aggregate value of property retired, the value of property substituted, and the amount of the cash deficiency, if any.

---

[4] Indian River Islands Corporation v. Manufacturers Trust Company et al., 253 App. Div. 549, 2 N.Y.S. 2d 860 (1938).

[5] TIA sec. 315(a)(2).

A second section gives the obligor the right to relocate machinery or equipment; to move any of the property from one location to another; to alter, remodel, or change the location of any building or structure; or to make any similar change or alteration as long as the aggregate value of the mortgaged property is not diminished. Because these rights do not affect the lien of the indenture, no accounting to the trustee is necessary.

Finally, the mortgagor is given the right to alter or amend any lease, contract, easement, license, franchise, or similar right or to enter into any such agreements. This right is usually conditioned on a finding by the obligor's board of directors that the alteration or amendment will not prejudice the obligor's activities or the trust estate or that it will be in the best interests of the obligor and its bondholders. Other conditions may be imposed as appropriate to the obligor's circumstances. For example, if the obligor is given the right to grant leases or other interests in its property, these usually must be made subject to the prior rights of the trustee as the mortgagee.

This reservation of rights in the obligor is a necessary and integral part of its right to possession and use of the property and is to be exercised without reference to or action by the trustee. Normally, however, on the obligor's request, the trustee executes the release or other documents that may be necessary or desirable to confirm the company's action in any particular situation.

Because the trustee has no control over dealing with its security, it should carefully examine these sections to ensure that the security will not be prejudiced by any such action. Likewise, the restrictions on and qualifications for the obligor's unilateral action under these sections should not be so broad as to prejudice the action the obligor can take with the concurrence of the trustee, under the general release provisions. In one situation, a provision prohibiting the granting of leases, except subject to the indenture's prior lien, raised a serious question. A trustee was presented with an application for the release of a leasehold estate to enable the separate financing of substantial improvements to a particular property, without a clear right to execute such a release. It would have been simple to make the restriction applicable only to unilateral action by the obligor, carrying out the obvious intent of the parties.

Whereas the sections permitting unilateral action by an obligor should be fairly restrictive, a great deal of flexibility is desirable with respect to the action that may be taken with the consent and concurrence of the trustee. As long as the security's essential character is preserved, the obligor should be given the right to obtain the release of any property it wishes to dispose of, upon the substitution of property of equivalent value or an appropriate reduction in the amount of the secured indebtedness.

The conditions for the obligor's right to secure a release of property and the documents required to substantiate compliance with such conditions are given in section 314(d) of the TIA.

Many indentures provide that property cannot be released unless the obligor has sold or contracted to sell the specific property in question. Although this appears not to present a problem, sometimes it has proved to be too restrictive. Occasionally it may be desirable to change the terms of a lease, contract, easement, or other property right in which no actual sale is involved and under circumstances requiring the consent or participation of the trustee. Any general limitation or restriction should be questioned.

One of the basic documents required is a resolution of the obligor's board of directors reciting the essential facts surrounding the transaction, containing an adequate description of the property and requesting the execution of a release by the trustee. Though seldom required, it is desirable also to have the resolution specify that the obligor is not in default and that the requested release will not impair the security of the indenture in contravention of the provisions. These are required conditions and must be covered in other certificates. The purpose of requiring a resolution, in addition to seeing that the requisite authority is given to the obligor officers, is to make certain that the transaction has been referred to and authorized by the senior responsible body of the obligor, and it is desirable to require affirmation of all aspects of the transaction.

The value of the property to be released is determined by the certificate of an engineer, appraiser, or other expert. This certification must also state that the proposed release will not impair the security of the indenture. Under certain circumstances, when the value of the property to be released is above a specified amount, this certification must be made by an independent engineer, appraiser, or expert having no affiliation with the obligor. The certificate must describe in detail the scope of the examination and investigation that formed the basis of the opinion certified. Normally, the obligor is given the right to select the engineer or appraiser, but the selection should be approved by the trustee. In view of the importance of this certificate, the trustee should insist on receiving an adequate statement of the expert's qualifications and then should evaluate them.

Two additional documents are always required—a certificate from designated officers of the company and an opinion of counsel—each of which must state that all conditions for the requested release exist or have been satisfied and recount in detail the examination and investigation made by the signers to ascertain these facts. In addition to this general statement, it is customary for the officers to certify affirmatively all pertinent facts—that there is no default, that the property has been sold or a release is necessary for the reasons given, that the release is desirable in the conduct of the company's business and will not impair the security of the indenture, and other facts appropriate to the situation.

Finally, a consideration for the release must be furnished. This should equal the greater of the fair value of the property released or the consideration received by the company on its sale. This consideration is normally in the form of cash or other real or personal property, but occasionally it may be purchase-money obligations secured by the property released. If the last, it should be limited to a fixed percentage (usually 66$\frac{2}{3}$ percent) of the property's value. It is also desirable to limit the aggregate amount of the obligations that may be held. Even though they may be perfectly good security, they may diminish the working capital of any corporation that is not in the business of investing in mortgages.

Any cash received is deposited with the trustee and may be withdrawn by the company to reimburse itself for any additional property acquired and subjected to the lien of the indenture, in an amount equal to the lesser of the cost or the fair value of the property to the company. The indenture should be reviewed before any investment of cash is considered. Municipal mortgage indentures are likely to provide for the investment of proceeds from the sale of the mortgaged property. Corporate indentures are often silent, and any proceeds from the sale of property should be invested only on the written approval and appropriate indemnification of the obligor. When investing these proceeds, the obligor should be consulted about the length of time the funds will be on deposit. The obligor should provide written direction even if the investment is specifically allowed by the governing indenture. Whenever any property is subjected to the lien of the indenture, either as the basis for the release of other property or for the withdrawal of cash, substantially the same documents must be filed as in the case of the issuance of bonds on the basis of property additions. These must include an engineer's or appraiser's certificate of the fair value of the property to the company; an opinion of counsel that all conditions for the withdrawal have been complied with and that the property is subject to the lien of the indenture; and an officers' certificate that the property is useful and desirable to the conduct of the company's business and that all conditions for the transaction have been met. If counsel indicates that instruments of conveyance are necessary or desirable to perfect the lien of the indenture on the property, these instruments must be executed and recorded and become supplements to the indenture.

An inexperienced administrator is often confused by complex provisions that may be included in open-ended mortgages, which try to classify properties used as a basis for releases and to permit their reuse at a later date under other provisions of the indenture. The reason for this will become clear if the distinction between funded and unfunded property is borne in mind. *Funded* property has been bonded or used as a basis for credit under a sinking fund, maintenance, or similar provision. *Unfunded* property, though subject to the lien of the indenture, is excess property available for use by the company in certifying compliance with the pertinent indenture sections. Property substituted for other property released should retain the latter status, and when this is unfunded, the new property still remains available to be used for other purposes, even though it is certified to the trustee as a basis for releasing other unfunded property.

It is desirable also to include a provision that, although used infrequently, permits the trustee to apply any cash deposited to the purchase or redemption of bonds. Normally, the application should be at the option of the obligor.

Miscellaneous Provisions

For the general purposes of the release clauses and for special situations or contingencies, it is customary to include a number of general sections in the release article, most of which become operative only for particular events.

When frequent sales of property are likely, it is desirable to include a provision permitting the obligor, without application to or release by the trustee, to sell up to a specified aggregate amount each year. Preparing individual release applications is time-consuming and expensive, and so this provision saves much time and expense. The obligor must provide a single annual accounting to the trustee. Although it is seldom required, it is desirable to have a single release covering all such properties executed annually. The conveyance of property without the specific release of a mortgage lien creates a possible cloud on the title that may be expensive to remove at a later date. Sometimes it is difficult to identify a particular parcel as one that was properly sold under such a general section, and the trustee is placed in an embarrassing position when it is requested, years later, to join in a confirmatory release.

A statement should always be included to the effect that the purchaser of any property released by the trustee is protected and under no duty to inquire into the particular circumstances or the propriety of any such release. When the trustee executes a release improperly or without the requisite authority, it is not clear what the effect on the title of the purchaser may be. Some cases have held that a release so executed is invalid and that the purchaser does not acquire good title. Other courts have held, however, that when the indenture contains a provision protecting the purchaser, the provision is controlling and the purchaser is protected, even though the trustee's action was *ultra vires*. No one should question the desirability or equity of this rule.

Provisions should always be included that deal with the disposition of property taken through the power of eminent domain or by the right of any government, bureau, or agency, or any public or quasi-public body to condemn or take possession of or title to any property or interest in it. The award granted for any property taken is paid to the trustee. As discussed earlier, the governing indenture provisions should be reviewed if the proceeds are to be invested, and appropriate authority and indemnification should be obtained from the obligor. It is desirable to include a greater degree of flexibility, however, and the procedure will be simplified if the obligor is given the right to compromise or settle its claim in such a situation. The practice usually followed is to proceed under the general release section, but sometimes the conditions are not completely satisfied, and because it is a special situation—not subject to the company's control—it is better to deal with it as such. An appropriate certificate of the fairness of the proposed settlement can serve as a basis for releasing the property. This enables the obligor to use the proceeds promptly to acquire substitute property and to avoid the delay and expense of pursuing the condemnation route.

The normal release provisions are operative only if no default exists under the indenture. There may be a problem if there is a default. Ordinarily, the rights of the obligor under the release article are exercised by a trustee appointed in bankruptcy or reorganization proceedings. As a practical matter, this official operates under the orders of the court having jurisdiction, which may direct the sale of particular property, whether or not there is indenture authorization, but it is desirable, nevertheless, to provide for this contingency.

It is more complicated when no formal proceedings have been instituted. Here the trustee is required to use more discretion and judgment, and the release sections are usually made permissive. If in the judgment of the trustee, the proposed transaction seems desirable, it is granted authority to execute a release but is permitted to refuse to do so. The trustee should receive the same certifications and documents as in the case of a predefault release and may require additional evidence to enable it to reach an appropriate conclusion.

Finally, provisions are needed to deal with any special situation or special properties of the obligor. These provisions depend on the special circumstances. Certain property or classes of property may be important enough to the financing arrangement to warrant a prohibition against their disposal or a provision that the proceeds can be applied only to retiring the debt. Acquiring particular classes of property with trust monies may be forbidden or may be limited to a fixed aggregate amount or a percentage of the indenture securities outstanding. The trustee should ensure that it understands the purpose intended and that the provisions inserted are designed properly for the purpose.

PROVISIONS FOR PLEDGED COLLATERAL

The traditional collateral trust indenture is not now as important to corporate financing as it was in the 1920s and 1930s.[6] This was the era of the growth and influence of the large holding company systems, particularly in the public utilities. The parent companies in these systems, and often the companies on the second and even third tiers of the intracorporate structure, owned no physical operating properties at all but merely held securities of the system's subsidiary and affiliated companies. Capital debt financing by these corporations was arranged through a collateral trust device, under which the affiliated companies' securities were the sole security for the outstanding obligations. The rapid expansion of these systems and the numerous recapitalizations led to a pyramided debt and frequent withdrawals and substitutions of collateral under the various indentures.

A number of events greatly lessened the relative significance of these arrangements. Most important was the enactment of the Public Utility Holding Company Act, under which the giant systems either disappeared or were greatly curtailed. During the reorganization, the old indentures were satisfied through the exchange of securities. The companies' capital structures were simplified, and their valuation became more realistic. A

[6]For a discussion of various types of collateral used in asset-backed transactions, see chapter 15.

system's debt securities are not usually issued by the subsidiary operating companies when operating properties rather than collateral constitute the security. Public financing by the parent holding company is normally through sales of equities. When debt securities are issued, it is on an unsecured basis.

When securities are held as part of the trust estate, the requirements governing their release are now substantially the same as those relating to real property. Important is the requirement of certificates of value for the collateral being released as well as that being substituted for other property. These certificates must be made by experts who must cite the criteria for their appraisal, which can be subjected to objective scrutiny. In particular situations, these certificates must be furnished by independent appraisers.

Despite the decline in importance of the traditional collateral trust indenture, the handling of collateral security is a significant factor in many mortgage indentures and asset-backed financing vehicles. Numerous companies still conduct a portion of their business through subsidiary or affiliated companies. To provide security on the complete business operation, it is necessary to create a combined mortgage and collateral trust indenture. The significance of the pledge of securities, however, lies not in their current market value but in the granting of a collateral lien on the parent company's allied or subsidiary operations conducted through the companies whose securities are pledged. The pertinent indenture provisions should therefore be designed for this purpose.

All the securities of the affiliates or subsidiaries owned by the obligor must be included in the pledge. This need not necessarily cover open-book advances, although these, too, are frequently included through a requirement for the execution and pledge of an unsecured note. In the case of a real property mortgage, the creation of a prior lien is effectively prevented by recording requirements. A collateral lien can, however, be impaired by issuing senior securities ranking ahead of those pledged. Without a specific requirement for the pledge of any such securities, protection should be obtained in the form of negative covenants controlling the amount of securities that can be issued.

Before default, no particular action is required of the trustee other than the custody of the securities pledged. The obligor is entitled to all income from them and should be permitted to exercise all voting rights except on matters that might affect the value of the collateral lien. Enforcing the principal of any debt obligations pledged is not important, and the trustee may properly be freed from any duty in this connection. Despite the lien nature of the pledge, however, any payments made on account of principal or received on retirement of equity securities should be sent to the trustee. This requirement is roughly equivalent to the maintenance requirement for mortgaged property.

Adequate provisions should be included to facilitate any exchange, recapitalization, merger, or other type of intracompany transactions that may occur from time to time. These should authorize the trustee—upon receipt of the appropriate resolutions and certificates establishing the desirability of the proposed arrangement—to execute the documents or give any consent that may be required.

Because of the special purpose of this collateral pledge, normally no part of the securities of any particular company held (except on payment, exchange, or for a similar reason) should be released unless all the company's securities are disposed of simultaneously.

As in the case of real property, special situations should be dealt with separately, and appropriate authority should be included in the indenture for the trustee's guidance.

After default, the trustee should have all rights of ownership with respect to pledged securities, including the right to receive and return income, the right of sale or other disposition, and the right to exercise full voting control.

NINE

Indenture Covenants

In addition to provisions relating specifically to the trust estate or to the debt and the rights of the relevant parties, most indentures contain a number of covenants designed to restrict the obligor's activities. The number and nature of the covenants included result from negotiations between the obligor and the person or persons representing the prospective purchasers of the securities (in a public issue, normally the counsel to the underwriters). The type of covenants included depends to a large extent on the obligor's business, the term of the loan, the purpose for which it is being made, whether it is secured or unsecured, the extent and nature of other outstanding obligations, and other, similar considerations.[1] Corporate indentures typically contain more financial covenants than do municipal indentures.

The trustee is not, of course, responsible for what covenants are or are not included in a particular indenture, for this is part of the contract between the borrower and the lender. Even though the trustee does not draft the covenants, it should review all of them and insist on language that gives it the options to exercise its duties and responsibilities in a timely and flexible manner to protect the bondholders' interests. Once the contract is executed, however, the trustee has the primary duty of enforcing it and therefore must be concerned with all its provisions. The trustee is more effective if it understands not only the language but also the purpose it is intended to accomplish and why the provision was included in that particular indenture. Unfortunately, some drafters have special provisions

[1] See TIA sec. 314. The TIRA converted several frequently used covenants, designed to supply information to the trustee about the obligor's affairs, into legislatively mandated obligations.

they like and sometimes insert them without regard to their relevance to the contract. An astute trustee examines these provisions closely and makes sure their relevance and purpose are understood by the parties to the contract. Once the indenture is executed and delivered, it is difficult and expensive—and sometimes even impossible—to have it modified. It is unfortunate when a particular covenant, designed to enhance the credit and protect the investor, actually threatens the primary security and places the obligor in a difficult situation. When faced with such a development, the trustee is put in an unenviable position that might have been avoided if greater care had been taken when the contract was still in draft form.

Of paramount importance, of course, is the cardinal rule applicable to all indenture language—that its meaning be clear and unambiguous. One of the trustee's most difficult tasks is interpreting and applying a particular provision to a situation not contemplated at the time the provision was drafted and that the covenant was not designed to address. No matter how sincere and honest corporate financial officers may be, they tend to interpret provisions in light of the particular problem with which they may be faced from time to time, with the language taking on different shades of meaning as the obligor's circumstances change. Since many covenants require only unilateral action by the obligor, a default may occur unintentionally because of an incorrect or slightly distorted interpretation by the obligor officials.

Of equal importance is that the covenant be drafted so that any violation can be easily detected. If only the obligor knows particular facts or prohibited acts or situations, and they are not likely to be readily disclosed by the financial statements or other information furnished to the trustee, every effort should be made to obtain periodic certification of compliance with the covenant. Compliance should be stated either as part of a general certification or with adequate detail about the facts indicating compliance or noncompliance with the specific provision.

In general, covenants should be related to and designed to facilitate the implementation of each loan contract. It is impossible to detail or recite all covenants that might be desirable, and so the following enumeration is intended to present only those covenants most commonly used. Many of those listed would not be applicable to particular indentures, but an understanding of their uses and purposes should be useful to indenture administrators in most situations.

Covenants may be classified in a number of ways, but probably the simplest is to distinguish between *affirmative* covenants, which require specific action by the obligor, either continuously or at specified periods, and *negative* covenants, which are prohibitive or restrictive and require refraining from taking certain actions.

Affirmative Covenants

As the name implies, an affirmative covenant requires some positive or definite action by the obligor. It requires taking specific action continuously, from time to time, or at specified times. A sinking-fund covenant is, of course, of this type, although it is almost always covered in a separate section of the indenture and is not included in the enumeration. Many affirmative covenants are pertinent only to mortgage indentures and relate to the mortgage security, whereas others are equally applicable whether the issue is secured or unsecured.

Some provisions are frequently included in the covenant section, although they are more like warranties. Typical of such provisions are the following:

1. A covenant that the obligor has complied with all legal requirements and is duly authorized to execute and deliver the indenture and to issue the indenture securities and that the indenture securities in the hands of the holders are valid and enforceable obligations.
2. A covenant that the obligor legally possesses the mortgaged and pledged property and has good right and lawful authority to mortgage and pledge it.
3. A covenant that the obligor will warrant and defend the title to the property and the trustee's security interest in it against all claims and demands.

These provisions may be included as recitals in the indenture instead of, or in addition to, being included as specific covenants. It probably makes little difference where they appear, for the conditions obviously mean that a violation would provide a basis for immediately prematuring the debt and bringing the remedial provisions into play. Their inclusion as specific covenants creates a direct relationship with the default and remedial section and is preferred for that reason. Whether included as covenants or recitals, or both, the provisions serve as an estoppel against the corporation and prevent its questioning the validity of its acts, even though there may have been a technical failure to secure due and proper authorization of the indenture, the indenture securities, or the mortgage. An estoppel would not be effective against third parties who obtained rights for value and in good faith. Its inclusion in the indenture, therefore, does not mean that the trustee and its counsel should be less diligent in assuring themselves about the due and proper authorization of the indenture and the obligations issued.

Other types of affirmative covenants are applicable only to secured indentures and are usually found—in one form or another—in most mortgage indentures. Some of these may be included as parts of other covenants or undertakings but are listed separately for clarity.

4. A covenant to maintain and preserve the lien of the indenture.
5. A covenant to give further assurances.
6. A covenant to subject to the lien of the indenture, by supplement if necessary, all property acquired after the date of the indenture and intended to be covered by it.

All these covenants are meant to give further assurances and provide a basis for a trustee's demand that additional documents be executed or things be done that will ensure the maintenance of the security for which the indenture was created, and to extend the lien on it to additionally acquired property should there be any questions about the effectiveness of an after-acquired property clause in any jurisdiction. For example, the further assurances covenant has been used as a basis for a request, in a nonqualified indenture, for an annual certificate of after-acquired property and an annual opinion on the timely recording and filing of the indenture and the necessity for any periodic rerecording or refiling.

7. A covenant to record the indenture and all supplements and to furnish opinions of counsel, after each recording and annually, about the recording and the necessity for any rerecording or refiling to preserve the lien.

Section 314(b)(1) of the TIA imposes such a requirement for all indentures thus qualified that include a mortgage or pledge of property. The matter of recording is so obviously important that this is more or less a standard provision in all mortgage indentures even if not qualified under the act. Because of the many jurisdictions frequently involved and the diversity of recording statutes, counsel who are familiar with the laws of the various states where the property is located should be relied on.

8. Covenants with respect to prior lien bonds.

When prior lien bonds are outstanding, it is customary to include provisions regarding prior liens. These provisions are designed to prevent a default under the prior lien and its extension or refunding afterward with other prior lien obligations. The indenture therefore usually contains covenants to the effect that the obligor will comply with all provisions of prior lien indentures; that it will pay the obligations when due and will not consent to the extension of the maturity (the indenture usually contains provisions for refunding prior lien obligations); and that upon satisfaction of any prior lien indenture, it will cause the trustee to surrender to the trustee all specific property pledged with the prior lien trustee. When prior lien obligations are retired in part or are acquired by the obligor, the indenture often provides that they will be held alive and pledged with the trustee. The theory of such a provision is that to the extent of the obligations held, the trustee will acquire rights *pari passu* with the other holders of prior lien obligations. The validity of this theory is doubtful, however, except to the extent of the value actually paid by the trustee for the obligations.

Many other affirmative covenants are equally applicable to secured or unsecured indentures, although their context or purpose may differ depending on the obligor and the indenture. Some of the more common covenants of this type are listed next.

> 9. A covenant that the obligor will duly and punctually pay the principal of and interest and premium, if any, on all the indenture securities outstanding according to the terms.

Inasmuch as the obligations themselves contain an absolute promise to pay, including this provision in the indenture might seem unnecessary and redundant. The obligation in the securities, however, runs directly to the holders and not to the trustee. The indenture covenant runs to the trustee and enables it to enforce the obligation for the benefit of the security holders if there should be a default in the payment of any installment of principal or interest.

> 10. A covenant to maintain an office or agency where the bonds may be presented for payment and where notices and demands may be served on the obligor.

It is customary to provide that an office or agency be maintained in one or more specified cities and that if the obligor fails to keep or provide such an office, presentation may be made, and notices and demands served, at the principal office of the trustee. As a practical matter, the trustee's office is almost always designated as the office or agency, and in any event, any demands and inquiries by security holders are directed to the trustee.

> 11. A covenant to pay all taxes, assessments, and other changes or claims imposed on the obligor's property, on the income or profits from it, or on the lien on or the trustee's interest in the property or income.

It is usually also provided that the obligor may delay payment of any such claim as long as it is, in good faith, contesting its validity by means of appropriate legal proceedings. The purpose of this covenant is to prevent the creation of a lien or claim that might be given preference by law to the indenture securities.

12. A covenant to maintain its corporate existence and to maintain, preserve, and renew all rights, powers, privileges, and franchises owned by it.

The purpose of this undertaking is obvious. Because the loan is based on the corporation's credit as a "going concern," all rights essential to its continuing as such must be preserved. This covenant is usually made subject to the merger clause and occasionally to the release and other provisions of the indenture.

13. A covenant to maintain, preserve, and keep its properties in good repair, working order, and condition.
14. A covenant to set aside from earnings each year enough reserves for renewals and replacements, obsolescence, depletion, exhaustion, and depreciation.

These are customary covenants in most indentures, whether secured or unsecured, which emphasize further the importance of the "going concern" concept of the business and to maintain the security for the debt. In some types of mortgage indentures—particularly those of regulated companies such as public utilities and railroads—the covenants are combined and enlarged into an elaborate maintenance covenant, as outlined and discussed in chapter 7.

15. Covenant to maintain insurance.

Some indentures require maintaining specific types of insurance; for example, in some businesses, public liability insurance may be important, and failing to provide it in the correct amounts might result in a severe loss for the obligor and prejudice to the security holders' claims. Needs and requirements tend to change over the years, however, and as a general rule, it is unwise to be too specific. A more desirable form is to provide that insurance of such kinds and amounts will be maintained as is customary in the industry or as is customarily maintained by other companies operating similar businesses. As long as the covenant requires adequate insurance, it is desirable to permit as much flexibility as possible. The obligor should be permitted to select the insurance companies, to participate in an insurance pool, or, if desired, to provide its own system of self-insurance. When the properties are widely scattered, with no great percentage of the total value concentrated in one place, this last may be the most desirable arrangement. Other innovations may also be suitable in particular cases, such as including a deductible clause of a substantial amount to avoid a multiplicity of small claims and correspondingly heavier premium charges. In any system of self-insurance, the trustee should insist that the indenture contain requirements for appropriate certification to it of the adequacy of such a system and the reserves maintained.

In many of the old type of indentures, the insurance policies were required to be deposited with the trustee. The modern practice is to provide instead for a periodic certificate to be furnished, usually annually. This certificate should spell out the kinds and amounts of insurance and the names of the companies and contain a statement of the adequacy of the insurance coverage. Although such a detailed statement is not as essential in an unsecured indenture, it is often inserted, or the trustee is given the right to request it. If the certificate indicates that the policies will expire before the next certificate is to be furnished, an appropriate tickler should be established and followed up to see that the insurance is renewed. It is common for municipal indentures to specify the amount and type of insurance coverage to be carried by the obligor. The insurance certificate should be reviewed regarding the indenture's requirement, to verify compliance with the indenture's covenants.

When the indenture constitutes a lien on the obligor's properties, the trustee should be named in the policies as a named payee, so that it will receive any proceeds of the insurance. Usually these proceeds, up to a specified amount, are turned over immediately to the obligor, but the trustee should keep amounts above this until receiving evidence that the property has been restored or replaced.

16. A covenant to honor obligations as the lessee.

If an important part of the obligor's property consists of leaseholds or ground rent estates, it is advisable to include a covenant that the obligor will perform all covenants and obligations as the lessee, will see that the lessor observes all its covenants and obligations in the leases, and will renew the terms of any leases that expire before the maturity date of the indenture obligations.

17. A covenant to continue to engage in a particular business or in the business in which the obligor is presently engaged.

This is an example of the type of covenant that should be examined carefully and used only if particular circumstances make it appropriate. If the indenture is to run for a long period of time, there is a danger in such an undertaking, as any harness maker could verify. In a majority of indentures, it is obviously unnecessary. It might be necessary when the loan is of relatively short duration and the principal security is a special inventory or special-purpose machinery and equipment suitable only for a particular business.

18. A covenant to keep true books of record and account.
19. A covenant to file with the trustee all balance sheets, income and surplus statements, and other pertinent financial statements.
20. A covenant to furnish copies of all reports forwarded to stock-holders or filed with the SEC and any other information that may be prescribed from time to time by regulations of the SEC.[2]
21. A covenant to permit a representative of the trustee at all reasonable times, upon request, to inspect the obligor's books and properties.
22. A covenant to furnish such other data and information pertaining to the obligor's affairs as the trustee may reasonably request.

All these covenants relate to keeping proper financial and accounting records and filing with the trustee periodic reports of the obligor's financial affairs. Section 314(a)(1) of the TIA requires that the obligor file with the trustee copies of the reports required to be filed with the SEC according to sections 13 or 15(d) of the 34 Act. These sections require filing periodic financial reports and supplementary reports to keep current various data filed with the original registration statement. In addition, copies of the annual audited statements certified by independent public accountants must be filed within a specified period after the close of the obligor's fiscal year.[3] Interim statements may also be required in some cases, and it is usually sufficient to have these certified by one of the obligor's financial officers. If the condition of the business is subject to rapid change and the maintenance of certain ratios or a minimum amount of working capital is important, a more frequent check on the obligor's condition than is provided by the annual audited statements may be desirable.

How detailed an examination and analysis of the financial statements the trustee should make is not prescribed. Some corporate trust departments follow the practice of having all such statements reviewed by out-

[2] See TIA sec. 314(a)(2). The obligor's annual report should be accompanied by a certificate or opinion of independent public accountants regarding the obligor's compliance with those conditions or covenants in the indenture that are subject to verification by accountants.

[3] TIA sec. 314(a)(2).

side accountants. But this seems extreme and, except in a most unusual situation, should not be necessary. Finance is a bank's business, and a trust company that purports to act as a corporate trustee should have personnel qualified to make whatever analysis is indicated. The trustee should know any facts that would be revealed by a reasonable examination, and the minimum requirement seems to be to check to see that there has been no violation of any indenture provision. An experienced administrator or account officer also should review the pertinent footnotes and commentary, the latter often called Management's Discussion and Analysis or something similar. Any unfavorable trend or situation that might warrant a more careful follow-up should be noted. The nature of the business, the financial standing of the obligor, the purpose of the loan, the specific responsibilities of the trustee, and other similar considerations should serve as a guide to the degree of care and attention that should be devoted to the examination beyond the limits indicated.

23. A covenant to furnish to the trustee annually a certificate signed by "the principal executive officer, principal financial officer or principal accounting officer as to his or her knowledge of such obligor's compliance with all conditions and covenants under the indenture."[4]

For pre-TIRA indentures requiring a different certification or signatures by different officers, both the requirements of the indenture and the section must be complied with. In most cases, these can be satisfied by a certification reciting what the TIA requires and any other indenture requirement, signed by two "officers" (as defined in the indenture), one of whom is the principal executive, financial, or accounting officer.

Recognizing the importance of this certification, the TIRA converted what was a commonly used affirmative undertaking into a new, legislatively mandated covenant. Not only does it give the trustee appropriate evidence on which it is entitled to rely, but more important, by making this certification a federal law requirement for all qualified indentures, criminal sanctions and civil suits are possible in the event of late, missed, or untrue certificates.

NEGATIVE COVENANTS

The difference between negative and affirmative covenants is not so much in the phraseology used, for almost any covenant can be expressed

---

[4] See TIA sec. 314(a)(4). This certification need not include the four compliance statements stated in sec. 314(e).

in either positive or negative terms. Instead, the distinction is that the so-called negative covenants generally restrict the activities of the obligor in order to protect the interests of the investor or lender. Although some of these covenants are common to both bond and debenture agreements, the negative covenant is most commonly associated with the debenture indenture, or unsecured financing. Their main purpose is to ensure, to the extent possible, that the investor for whose benefit they are made will remain in essentially the same relative position (in regard to that of other creditors) as at the time the credit is extended.

The use of negative covenants has been severely criticized from time to time, particularly in an early report by the SEC.[5] The SEC's argument was that these covenants tended to lead the investor into a sense of false security and were of limited value because of the ease with which they could be violated and the lack of any effective legal remedy to prevent such violations.

The statement that no effective remedy exists to prevent the violation of these clauses is also doubtful. Theoretically, an action for specific performance or for injunctive relief should be possible, although it is likely that these remedies will offer little protection because the trustee will probably not know about the violation until the assets have been transferred or pledged or a prohibited loan or advance has been obtained. To have such a transaction set aside would require proof not only of the violation but also of knowledge on the part of the pledger or transferee. There is one remedy, however, that can be effective: the right to declare a default under the indenture and premature the indenture obligations. Although this may not place the security holders in as good a position as they were before and so cannot be said to constitute full protection, it is a potent weapon that should deter all but the most callous. Faced with such a threat, the obligor is more likely to try to resolve a difficult situation through frank disclosure and negotiation rather than through intentional violation of a restrictive covenant.

In many cases, an unsecured obligation under a carefully drawn indenture provides as much protection and security to the investor as a mortgage bond does. The principal considerations in either case are the credit of the obligor as a going concern and the caliber of its management. In some cases, the borrower's unsecured credit is so good that few restrictions or covenants are necessary. When the investors are obtaining a senior creditor position, all that is reasonably required are provisions in the agreement that under normal conditions will ensure the retention of such a position. It is impossible to protect against every possible contingency,

[5] See chapter 3, note 2, *supra*.

and an effort to do so by placing overly restrictive conditions on the business's continued operation is as likely to prejudice as to improve the security holders' position.

It is possible, however, that the lack of strong restrictive covenants can imperil the value of bondholders' investments. This became evident during the 1980s when the growth of complex and diverse financial instruments, coupled with the explosion of novel and debt-laden corporate capital structures, had a major impact on the holders of bonds issued during the preceding twenty years. In the mid-1980s to mid-1990s, there was a widespread trend by major corporate issuers to reduce the number of restrictive covenants applicable to their new issues, particularly those restricting the payment of dividends or incurring additional debt.[6]

The losses incurred by bondholders who had purchased high-grade debt instruments and ended up with so-called junk bonds reinforced a reversal of that trend. Institutional investors, in particular, demanded much greater protection against recapitalization transactions, commonly called *event risk*, which can have a devastating impact on the value of their investments. It is evident that

> the tension between restrictive financial covenants and business flexibility for the issuer has led the marketplace away from covenants which measure the "symptoms" of a worsening financial condition to covenants designed to identify the events which cause the condition and provide an immediate bailout opportunity for the holder upon the occurrence of those events.[7]

Public corporate issues offer the opportunity for monitoring the obligor's financial conditions through filings with the Securities and Exchange Commission, but municipal issues do not offer the same access to financial information and covenant satisfaction. The efforts to improve this information availability for municipal issues are discussed in chapter 13, "Secondary Market Disclosure."

The original "poison put" provision was designed to ward off unfriendly takeovers and did not normally operate in the event of a friendly takeover (e.g., a management buyout). But the latter event can be just as disastrous to the bondholders as any hostile acquisition, with the result that institutional investors have increased their insistence on including "super poison put" covenants, which eliminate the distinction between

[6]Morey W. McDaniel, "Bondholders and Corporate Governance," 41 *Bus. Law.* 413, 425–27 (1986).

[7]Patricia A. Vlahakis, "Old Indentures—New Transactions," 929 *Law J.* (Seminars Press) 19 (1989).

friendly and hostile transactions. These covenants can include change-of-control tests and others directed at the obligor's creditworthiness, such as

1. Net worth call. This provides for the acceleration of a sinking fund in the event that the obligor's net worth falls below a specified level.
2. Poison puts. An immediate tender can be made back to the obligor if the debt-to-equity ratio increases above a specified amount or if the obligor's credit rating falls.
3. Interest-rate reset. This provides for a set increase in the interest rate if certain specified ratios are not maintained.
4. Automatic redemption. This covenant mandates an automatic redemption with a premium, either fixed or based on a spread over long-term U.S. Treasury bonds.[8]

Because it is impossible to foresee every contingency, it is desirable to provide for some degree of flexibility, but this is difficult. When the notes or debentures are purchased directly by informed institutional investors, this situation can be resolved by the holders agreeing to amend the indenture or to modify or waive a particular provision either permanently or temporarily during a period of stress. A different problem is presented when an issue is sold publicly. The first principle to be observed is to include only those restrictive covenants that under reasonably foreseeable conditions are not likely to cause undue hardship or seriously impede the normal conduct of the obligor's business. If the credit is not good enough under those conditions, it is best avoided.

It is also desirable to include a provision permitting modification of the indenture by the holders of a specified percentage of the indenture securities. The customary percentage used is 66⅔ percent. Although it may be almost impossible to contact all holders of a publicly held issue, the consent of a reasonable percentage can normally be obtained, with foresight and preparation, if the modification proposed is reasonable and desirable.[9]

The trustee is frequently asked to consent to a temporary waiver or modification of a particular provision, or at least to consent to take no action for some period of time after a breach. Under the circumstances in which it is presented, the obligor's proposed action usually appears reasonable and often highly desirable from the security holders' viewpoint.

---

[8] See also Patricia A. Vlahakis, "Deleveraging: A Search for Rules in a Financial Free-for-All," 2 *M & A and Corporate Governance Law Reptr.*, 290 (Oct. 1990); Clemens, "Poison Debt: The New Takeover Defense," 42 *Bus. Law.* 747 (May 1987).

[9] See TIA secs. 316(a)(1)(B) and 316(c).

Whereas a good argument can be made for granting such discretionary powers to a trustee, under the usual indenture it has no such power and no authority or right to give a consent or waiver.

Once a breach has occurred and matured into a default under the indenture, the trustee's conduct is subject to the prudent man standard of judgment. It is unfortunate that relatively few judicial precedents exist for the trustee's guidance in such situations, since in their absence, the trustee may logically be inclined to take immediate action under the remedial provisions to avoid being subjected to substantial potential liability.

In many cases, though, patience and a reasonable degree of judgment and discretion enable the situation to be worked out without subjecting the obligor and the security holders to the substantial expense and virtually inevitable losses incurred in a reorganization proceeding. To avoid this, some indentures provide that a default will not occur for breach of an indenture covenant of this type unless and until the trustee has received notice from a specified percentage of the security holders. But this type of provision is generally undesirable because it tends to restrict too greatly the trustee's right to take action. A more desirable provision, and one that is common in most indentures, permits a majority in principal amount of the security holders to waive a default or to direct the trustee's course of conduct in the event of a default.[10]

As in the case of affirmative covenants, the types of negative clauses are many and varied. It is desirable, therefore, to include restrictive provisions to fit the circumstances of each case rather than to try to apply a set pattern or formula to each situation. The following provisions are some of the more common covenants used. Remember that because the obligor conducts part of its operations through subsidiaries, or may subsequently do so, the covenants should be phrased so as to apply to subsidiaries as well as to the obligor itself.

1. Covenants relating to the maintenance of working capital.

Covenants of this type relate to the maintenance of working capital (sometimes called *net current assets* and representing an excess of current assets over current liabilities) at a certain minimum level. The covenant takes different forms. Sometimes the obligor is required to maintain a specified amount of working capital. Sometimes the current ratio (current assets divided by current liabilities) cannot fall below a prescribed minimum. Frequently, the covenant requires the maintenance of working capital as a stated percentage of funded debt. Occasionally, there

[10] Id.

is a combination of several requirements of this type. It is a common practice to combine this requirement with other negative covenants. For example, the obligor may be permitted to borrow additional funds as long as the net working capital is maintained at the required percentage of total funded debt.

This type of covenant is important and is almost always included when the principal purpose of the credit being arranged is for working capital, for such purposes as expanding inventory. Regardless of the proposed use of funds, if the business requires a large amount of working capital, this is one indicator that should be monitored closely when examining the obligor's financial statements. It is desirable to provide some basis for action if there are signs that the obligor's position may be deteriorating.

2. A covenant against the creation of additional debt.

This is a covenant commonly found in most debenture agreements. Because the obligations to be issued are unsecured, it is obvious that continued unrestricted borrowing might seriously prejudice the security holders' position or impair the equity on whose basis they extended credit.

The basic prohibition is against creating additional funded debt (usually defined as that having a maturity of more than one year at the time incurred), but it is sometimes extended to include current debt or current borrowings above a stated amount.

There are normally a number of permitted exceptions to this restriction that can be expressed in several ways. Always exempt from its operation are liabilities (other than for borrowed money) incurred in the ordinary course of business, accrual of taxes, claims for labor, and other similar accruals essential to the business's orderly operation.

As indicated, the restriction is frequently made inoperative as long as certain ratios are maintained. The ratios most often used are working capital to total debt and net tangible assets to debt. The latter restriction can be expressed in another way: aggregate debt is limited to a certain percentage of the obligor's total capitalization. These requirements are usually combined with an earnings requirement. An example of this is the provision that the average profit before interest and taxes during the past five years—and for each of the two preceding years—that is available to pay interest must have been at least nine times the total interest requirements on all debt, including that proposed to be issued.

Finally, the limitation of debt may be merely a total dollar limitation, expressed either with or without the exclusion of liabilities incurred in the ordinary course of business.

3. A covenant against sale and leaseback.

Under this type of financing, a obligor that owns substantial real estate, such as office buildings, warehouses, or retail stores, arranges for the sale of this property to one or more investors and takes back a noncancelable lease for a specified term at a rental aggregating the purchase price plus an amount equivalent to the going rate of interest on the unamortized purchase price. This not only provides a convenient method of raising funds but also enables the obligor to keep its capital invested in its primary business rather than in the ownership and operation of real estate.

The covenant is designed to prohibit or limit such arrangements during the terms of the loan. The limitation may be expressed in many ways, such as a dollar limitation on the gross value of property transferred, a limitation on the aggregate annual rentals equal to a percentage of the net earnings for a prescribed period, or, as in the case of the preceding covenant, a limitation in terms of maintaining certain ratios of working capital or net tangible assets to debt, in which the aggregate of all leaseback sales is added to the debt.

The purpose of the covenant is twofold. The first consideration is substantially the same as the restriction against debt. Rentals under the leases become fixed obligations, and a limitation on incurring such obligations is usually important. A second consideration is related to the "negative pledge" clause and is a prohibition against selling productive facilities to which recourse might be made in the event of a default. Thus in some cases, the sale of an office building or similar holding may be permitted, but the sale of factories, warehouses, or other essential productive property is restricted.

4. A covenant against the execution or lease of real property or equipment.
5. A covenant against the rental or lease of personal property sold by the obligor or acquired by an investor for rental or lease to the obligor.

These covenants are similar and serve the same purpose as the restriction on sale and leaseback arrangements. Here again, the prohibition may be absolute or expressed in terms of certain limitations or exceptions. These limitations may be expressed in terms of a maximum dollar amount of annual rentals or aggregate rentals as a percentage of net earnings, or such leases may be permitted if their terms (including renewals) do not exceed a stated period, usually not more than five years.

6. A covenant against the creation of prior liens (negative pledge clause).

This restriction is designed to prohibit the creation of claims or obligations paramount to those of the indenture securities, so as to ensure the maintenance of the holders' same priority position as existing at the time the credit is extended. This may be accomplished in either of two ways; the covenant is frequently expressed as either absolutely restricting the creation of liens on the obligor's property or permitting their creation only on condition that the indenture's obligations are equally secured at the same time.[11]

To permit the orderly conduct of the obligor's business, certain logical exceptions to the restriction are usually permitted. These include (1) liens for taxes not yet due; (2) liens existing on the property at the time of its acquisition by the obligor or purchase-money mortgages created in connection with the acquisition of additional property (these liens may be limited to a certain percentage of the property's value, and it is usually expressly provided that they cannot be extended to any other property of the obligor. It is customary to include a maximum dollar limitation on the aggregate of all such liens); (3) renewals or extension of liens referred to in (2), provided they have not been increased and do not extend to other property; (4) liens incurred in the ordinary course of business not involving the borrowing of money; and (5) deposits of money or property to secure performance of a contract or obligation, such as deposits required by worker's compensation laws, under government contracts, and in connection with self-insurance arrangements.

This covenant is frequently referred to as a "negative pledge" clause, which is actually a misnomer. The clause does not create a pledge of any assets, nor does it give an equitable lien on any property that may be pledged or transferred in violation of the covenant.

7. A covenant against loans, advances, and guarantees.
8. A covenant against a pledge or discount of receivables or their sale at less than par.
9. A covenant against the mortgage of patents, copyrights, or similar property.
10. A covenant against the ownership of securities, except stock or indebtedness of subsidiaries or obligations of the United States.

These covenants fall into the same general category as the preceding

---

[11] For an excellent review of this topic, see Morey W. McDaniel, "Are Negative Pledge Clauses in Public Debt Issues Obsolete?" 38 *Bus. Law.* 867 (May 1983).

one and are intended to prevent the encumbrance, dissipation, or use of the obligor's assets except in the orderly conduct of its business. The covenant against loans, advances, and guarantees usually includes an exemption for intrasystem transactions if a portion of the obligor's business is conducted through subsidiaries, and the restrictive covenants in the indenture apply to both the obligor and its subsidiaries. Transactions in the ordinary course of business may also be exempted if guarantees are normally granted as a part of the business's conduct.

11. A covenant restricting the payment of dividends or the purchase or retirement of stock.

Equity capital, or the stockholders' investment in a business, is made up of not only the stated capital and surplus, which the stockholders have paid into the business as consideration for the issuance of their shares, but also the amount of the earned surplus, which represents the aggregate of the earnings that the obligor has retained for use in the business. Generally speaking, earned surplus is not subject to any restrictions and can be paid out or distributed as dividends to stockholders at any time. This distribution can be in cash or property.

One of the principal concerns of an investor when extending credit is the amount of the stockholders' equity, particularly in relation to the amount of the debt that will be outstanding. Because debt represents a priority claim against the obligor's assets, any excessive distribution to stockholders may be regarded as a preferential distribution to a subordinate claimant.

It is therefore quite common for all indentures, whether secured or unsecured, to include a provision that will prevent any unwarranted distribution. This is usually done by placing a substantial portion of the unrestricted earned surplus in a restricted category for the duration of the loan. A portion of the surplus is usually left in an unrestricted category available for dividends, the amount being a matter for negotiation, but often it represents a sum approximately equal to one year's dividends on the stock. In working out the other terms of the credit, the amount unrestricted is usually disregarded by the investor, and the amount retained provides an additional cushion to bolster the credit extended.

The covenant usually provides that no dividends will be distributed to stockholders or that any funds of the corporation will be applied to the purchase, redemption, or other retirement of shares of stock in excess of the sum of (1) the amount of the earned surplus left in an unrestricted category, (2) the obligor's net earnings after a stated date (usually the end of the next fiscal year), and (3) the amount received by the obligor as proceeds of the sale of additional shares of stock.

The payment of dividends or other distributions to stockholders is always made contingent on there being no default under the arrangement and, often, on the existence of certain minimum ratios at the time of declaration.

12. Covenants relating to subsidiaries, the most common being (a) against the sale of stock or debt of a subsidiary, (b) against the issue of stock of a subsidiary except to the parent obligor or to another subsidiary, and (c) against permitting a subsidiary to issue preferred stock except to the obligor or another subsidiary.

As indicated, when subsidiary companies are important to a system's operation, all general restrictive covenants, such as those against additional debt or against the creation of liens, are made applicable alike to the parent company and its subsidiaries. Because the companies are viewed as an entity for the purpose of the credit, intrasystem transactions are customarily excluded from these restrictions. It is therefore necessary to add other restrictions to prevent weakening the entity by reducing the system percentage ownership of any subsidiary obligor.

The first of the covenants prohibits the disposal of the investment in a subsidiary. To permit flexibility, the restrictive provision usually states that no stock or indebtedness of a subsidiary may be sold except as an entirety and then only if (1) the operations conducted by such subsidiary do not represent a significant part of the system's operations; (2) in the judgment of the obligor's board of directors, retention of the investment in it is no longer necessary for the system's operations; (3) the sale is for a cash consideration representing the full value of the system's investment in the subsidiary; and (4) the subsidiary owns no stock in or indebtedness of another subsidiary.

For subsidiary companies that are less than 100 percent owned by the system, covenant (b) above, is usually qualified to prohibit any issuance of stock that would decrease the system's pro-rata interest.

The reason for prohibiting a public issue of preferred stock of a subsidiary follows the same theory as the prohibition against prior liens. As far as the obligor itself is concerned, the indenture securities have priority over any preferred stock issue. The stock of a subsidiary company is, however, an asset of the obligor, and permitting the issuance of another class of stock having priority would be equivalent to subjecting the property represented by this asset to a prior claim.

13. A covenant against a merger of the obligor or the sale or lease of all or substantially all of its assets.

The indenture usually contains a separate section dealing with mergers, consolidations, and so on. It is included here because it is, in effect, a restrictive covenant. There is usually no absolute prohibition against mergers or consolidations or the sale of the obligor's assets, but these activities are permitted only under certain conditions, which should be explicitly stated. The following conditions are usually included:

a. Either the obligor must be the surviving corporation, or the obligations under the indenture must be expressly assumed in writing (usually by supplemental indenture) by the survivor.
b. There must be no default under the indenture, and no default can exist after the merger is completed.
c. If any other debt will become a lien on any properties of the obligor when the merger is completed, the indenture securities must be secured by a mortgage or other lien on the obligor's properties before the merger.
d. If the surviving corporation will have secured debt outstanding above a given amount (whether or not the obligor's property will become subject to this lien), the indenture securities must be first secured by a lien on the obligor's properties.
e. If the indenture requires the maintenance of certain specified ratios (such as minimum working capital, working capital to debt, or net tangible assets to debt), these ratios usually must exist in the prescribed minimum amount immediately following the merger.

In reviewing a draft of a proposed indenture contract, all the provisions should be read together as in the aggregate constituting a single entity. This is particularly true of all the indenture's covenants. In addition, the administrator should ensure that none of them is inconsistent with any of the obligations/covenants mandated by the TIA. To administer a contract properly, the trustee must understand it. This means not only making sense out of the language of each provision considered separately but also understanding the meaning and purpose of the whole indenture as a single contract. The investor is willing to extend credit on certain terms and conditions that the borrower is willing to meet. The indenture contract should spell out those terms and conditions completely and unambiguously. All the provisions should fit together like a puzzle. Once the concept of the entire contract is understood, each covenant will assume its proper meaning, and the job of administration will be made much easier.

Payment and Redemption of Bonds

Although the "perpetual debenture" without a fixed maturity has been used with success in the United Kingdom and some of the Commonwealth countries, this practice never became popular in the United States. Such obligations are frequently regarded more as stock than debt, and certainly they have many of the aspects of permanent equity capital. Almost without exception, corporate debt obligations issued in this country under indentures have a fixed maturity. This is, of course, an essential condition for the negotiability of the securities.

The fixed obligation in the securities and the corresponding indenture covenants to pay the principal and interest as they become due are the obligor's most important undertakings. On or before the debt's fixed maturity, funds must be provided to make payment, although this is not always easy. As we noted earlier, one device is the use of the sinking fund, in which a portion of the debt is retired each year over its life, thereby eliminating, or substantially reducing, the problem presented at the final maturity. Another common device used in states' and municipalities' issues is to provide for serial maturities, in which a portion of the debt falls due each year. This practice has seldom been used in business corporations' issues, as market acceptance can make it more difficult to sell the securities.

It is unusual, and sometimes not prudent from a cash management perspective, for an obligor to pay a large fixed principal maturity out of available cash. Even when a sinking-fund covenant is included, often a substantial portion of the obligations must be paid at final maturity. The obligor's financial officer must therefore plan the cash flow in advance of the maturity date to ensure that funds will be available to pay the obligations at maturity. Some form of refunding that involves the issuance of other securities to provide the cash to pay the maturing issue is usually necessary. As we pointed out in chapter 5, among the purposes for which additional securities are customarily authorized to be issued under open-end indentures is refunding prior lien securities or other series of securities outstanding under the indenture.

When the obligor has a good credit rating and the contracts for the obligor's financial undertaking were thoughtfully drafted, the approaching debt maturity date does not present any difficulty. An important question may be, however, timing and cost. If an obligor is faced with having to meet a maturity during a period of higher interest rates, its annual fixed charges may be greatly increased. From the obligor's point of view, therefore, a considerable degree of flexibility should be reserved in the indenture to facilitate its dealing with its debt obligations.

To provide this flexibility, the indenture's redemption provisions are important. These usually appear in a separate article of the indenture. The redemption provisions constitute the reservation by the obligor of the privilege of prepaying its securities, or designated portions, at its option, before their stated maturity. To exercise this privilege, the obligor may be required to pay a price, in the form of a redemption premium, in addition to the principal and accrued interest to the date of the prepayment. The right of redemption before maturity is a significant right. The terms on which it may be exercised, including the amount of premium that must be paid, are important elements in the original negotiations. It is common, however, to set the initial redemption premium at an amount equivalent to one year's interest on the securities. This premium is then scaled down, in roughly equal amounts throughout the life of the issue. Generally, no premium is paid during the last year.

Because this provision affects the rights of the securities' holders, the redemption privilege must be spelled out in the text of the securities, as well as in the indenture. The language should be understandable to the holder regarding the terms and conditions on which the obligation may be called for prepayment.

During periods of high interest rates, investors prefer to protect themselves against the possibility that the obligations they purchase will be refunded as soon as a change in market conditions makes it advantageous for the issuer to do so. When there is a rapid change in market conditions and a substantial decline in interest rates, obligors may call their securities, even if they have been outstanding for less than a year. As a result, investors may suffer substantial losses because they sold other securities (or passed up other investment opportunities) to purchase these obligations whose subsequent redemption necessitated reinvestment at much lower yields.

The protection against such a possibility takes the form of a noncallable or nonrefundable provision in the security and indenture. A *noncallable provision* means merely that the obligor may not redeem its securities (except for sinking-fund purposes) for a stated period of time. A *nonrefundable provision* permits redemption but specifies that this cannot be done with other funds borrowed at a rate of interest less than that borne by the indenture securities. These restrictions are usually limited to a specified period of time following the date of a security issue—commonly five or ten years.

A noncallable provision is easily administered, whereas a nonrefundable provision may present difficulties. The trustee should insist that the indenture include a provision for receiving a certificate from appropriate officials of the obligor. This certificate should state that a proposed redemption does not violate the restriction, and the trustee should be authorized to rely conclusively on the certificate.

Some indentures provide that the obligor, at its discretion, may purchase securities on the open market and submit them to the trustee in satisfaction of a mandatory sinking-fund redemption and in lieu of redeeming securities. Corporate obligors are particularly likely to do this during periods when the current market prices for the securities are lower than the call price. Indentures permitting this alternative should state that the obligor must provide a certificate to the trustee well in advance of the date specified for the trustee to select securities to be called, describing exactly how a particular sinking fund will be satisfied. Typically, the obligor's certificate is provided at least sixty days before the redemption date, to allow the trustee sufficient time to process the redemption and provide notice in accordance with the indenture's governing provisions.

Whether or not an indenture provides for a sinking fund, it may permit the obligor to purchase securities on the open market and submit them to the trustee for cancellation. Many corporate obligors take advantage of this in periods of favorable market conditions, to reduce the outstanding debt and related carrying costs. In this situation, the trustee should receive an appropriate certification well in advance when it would normally begin to select securities for redemption. It is important for the trustee to maintain accurate records of credits applied to future sinking-fund obligations.

It is common for obligors to satisfy sinking-fund requirements several years in advance if market prices permit the purchase of securities below the redemption price.

Another alternative to a sinking-fund call in some indentures, particularly municipal revenue issues, is the obligor's right to instruct the trustee to use accumulated cash deposits in the sinking fund to conduct a tender offer for securities. The trustee selects enough securities from among all those tendered to satisfy the sinking-fund requirement. The indenture should spell out the mechanics of such a procedure, including the timing of and criteria for notifying holders and selecting security certificates.

A different form of redemption giving the security holder the right to sell the security back to the issuer, at par, is also used. In issues with this provision, the holder receives a "put" or "demand" option, the difference being that in the *put option*, the security may be sold back *only* on a fixed date or specific dates. In the *demand option*, the right may be exercised at any time, usually on one to seven days' notice. In either situation, the underlying agreement must spell out the holder's option rights.

Put and demand options evolved during the late 1970s and 1980s in response to investors' desire for greater liquidity in periods of economic uncertainty and interest-rate volatility. Obligors have used one-to-seven-day put security issues as alternatives to issuing commercial paper. Although initially, puts were associated primarily with municipal securities, they have been used in many forms by corporate issuers. One variety, developed as part of the corporate antitakeover strategy is the *poison put*, in which holders may put their securities back to the issuer, as, for example, in event of a significant change in the obligor's ownership (i.e., a hostile takeover).

Although some securities are issued without put or demand features, they have put options attached to them by investment bankers to improve their marketability in times of sharply rising interest rates. Certificates representing these *added on* options are separate from the security itself, and the terms are specified in a separate option agreement. Usually the security holder pays a price—either deducted from interest payments or otherwise paid—for the right to the put option in these situations.

Issues that give the holder a put or demand option also may entitle the obligor to the right to redeem the issue on the put date or upon notice to the holders in the case of a demand option. Generally, the right to redemption by the obligor can be exercised at its option.

It is common for a tender agent to be appointed independent of the trustee. Managing a put feature requires extraordinary coordination among the tender agent, trustee, the paying agent, and the applicable operations department, requiring each party to the transaction to understand the rules and the timing in which the put will operate. Puts require cautious interpretation, as they often contain restrictions that may not be fully understood by the security holder.

Risk and Liability Concerns

Because of the great surge in number and amount of security redemptions in the late 1980s and 1990s, trustees and paying agents have been subjected to increasing pressure from the investment community and the public to compensate holders for losses resulting from their failure to present and redeem called securities in a timely manner. In seeking such compensation, holders frequently claim that the trustee/paying agent was "unjustly enriched" as a result of the holder's failing to submit a called security until sometime after the redemption date. In such situations, the holder may allege that he or she did not receive proper notification of the security call. To establish industry guidance for paying such claims, the American Bankers Association (ABA), through its Fiduciary and Securities Operations Division, developed its Compensation Guidelines for time frames and conditions for paying called debt securities. The guidelines establish parameters for paying compensation in the event of error or noncompliance by the trustees and paying agents.[1]

These guidelines, which were approved and disseminated to trustees and paying agents, apply to all corporate and municipal debt securities and to the presentation of called securities through either physical or book-entry delivery.

Uniform standards for redemption notices and compensation claims are important to limiting risk to trustees/paying agents in processing calls of zero coupon securities. Because these obligations do not pay interest periodically, a holder who misses a security call may not be aware that his or her security was called until presenting it years later for payment on final maturity. At that time, when finding that the security can be redeemed for only the accreted value as of the call date many years earlier, a holder may lodge a claim or file a lawsuit against the trustee/paying agent. The redemption standards approved by the American National Standards

---

[1] For recommended redemption notification guidelines, see this chapter, note 2, *infra*.

Institute (and discussed later) contain special provisions for zero coupon securities that require one additional notice of an early redemption to be sent within a year after the redemption date, via secure means. But the ability to maintain current addresses of security holders for zero coupon corporate securities is hampered because fewer notices need to be mailed, under the reformation of the Trust Indenture Act. As an added service, trustees and agents may ask obligors to consider periodically mailing a special notice to zero coupon security holders to verify their current addresses.

Of related concern to the trustee/paying agent is the liability that may result from the method of giving notice to security holders. Although an indenture for a fully or partly registered issue may require that notice be given by publication only, it is wise for the trustee also to mail notices to the registered holders to avoid claims and possible litigation. The redemption standards mentioned later in this chapter contain a provision for marking the outside of envelopes containing redemption notices with a notice reading "IMPORTANT NOTICE OF REDEMPTION ENCLOSED."

For both partial and full redemptions, an appropriate affidavit of mailing should be prepared by the trustee and filed as part of its records. This affidavit should include, as attachments, the redemption notice and a listing of all registered holders with called securities. In the case of bearer security issues, the list of the serial numbers arranged numerically by maturity should be included as part of the redemption notice to be published and mailed. The trustee should also obtain affidavits of both the publication and the mailing.

Another area of concern in risk management is redeeming structured financing transactions. The trustee/paying agent must be careful to execute redemptions in accordance with the operative documents, because failing to do so may adversely affect the cash-flow coverage of future debt service and could destroy the integrity of nonrecourse financing. In financings requiring a "strip call" or involving zero coupon securities, failing to call the correct securities on just one occasion may have an escalating negative effect over future years. Credit enhancement providers and rating agencies monitor the trustee's/paying agent's performance in these areas, and the trustee/paying agent may be held liable for damage to cash flows from errors in redemption processing. Examples of structured financings to which these concerns are critical are those involving multifamily housing, single family housing, and collateralized mortgage obligations.

MECHANICAL PROVISIONS

Terms and Conditions

The terms and conditions on which the securities may be called for pre-payment should be spelled out in the indenture. Although it is the obligor that theoretically exercises this right, as a practical matter the trustee is usually asked to see to all the details. (See exhibit 7 for a Full Redemption Procedure Guide and exhibit 8 for a Partial Redemption Procedure Guide.) Therefore, these provisions should receive careful attention by the trustee as it reviews the prospective contract. Under an open-end indenture providing for different series of securities, the redemption terms (other than the amount of premium payable) are usually given in the original indenture and apply to all series of securities, including those to be issued in the future. As an alternative, the terms of the original indenture may be made applicable only to the initial series of securities, with the terms and conditions for subsequent series inserted in the supplemental indenture or board resolution creating each series. Although not frequently used, the latter practice is recommended, as it offers more flexibility.

The first condition to which attention should be directed is the nature and extent of the right. Subject to any provisions for nonrefundability, this right should be as broadly based as possible. The right should be reserved to redeem all, or any part, of the indenture securities at any time or from time to time. Occasionally, redemption is restricted to a minimum principal amount, and this restriction is proper from the point of view of both the obligor and the investor. Some indentures restrict the redemption to an interest payment date, and other indentures may not allow redemption at any time.

The redemption premiums should be explicit. They are customarily expressed as a percentage of the principal amount. If a formula for a declining percentage is to be used, it should be worked out before the indenture is executed and the actual prices (by dates) are stated in the indenture and in the securities. This formula avoids any possibility of error or misunderstanding at a later date. For a sinking fund, the securities normally are callable at par, without a premium.

For the practical handling of redemptions, two provisions are desirable for the trustee: for registered securities, no endorsement or assignment should be required if payment is to be made to the registered holder. The securities must be presented to obtain payment unless a home office payment agreement is allowed by the governing indenture. Home office payment agreements typically apply to private placement securities owned by institutional investors. When redemption is on an interest payment date, the interest check should be mailed in the normal manner to the registered holders as of the record date. In the case of bearer securities, the holders should be instructed to detach and present separately the interest coupon maturing on that date; otherwise, subsequent accountings may create confusion.

Notices

Notice of redemption must be given to the holders of the securities. The indenture must specify not only the method of giving notice but also the period of time before the redemption date when such notice must be given. A minimum of thirty days' notice is ordinarily required, and it is also common for a maximum period to be specified. The usual provision is to require the first notice to be given not less than thirty, or more than sixty, days before the date designated for the redemption.

The indenture should specify the information to be included in the notice, such as a full description of the issue as printed on the security certificate: name, date of issue, maturity dates, interest rates, date of redemption, redemption price payable, CUSIP number, certificate numbers and called amounts for each certificate (for partial calls), place or places of payment to which the called securities should be presented, total principal amount called if less than the entire issue is called and if a new security will be issued for any unredeemed portion, and any other information that may be pertinent to the particular situation or required by law or regulation.

The notice should state that on the designated redemption date, the called securities (or portions of them) will become due and payable and that on and after this date, all interest will cease to accrue and the holders will cease to be entitled to the benefits of the indenture, as their rights are limited to receiving the redemption price in the hands of the trustee, or paying agent, upon presentation of their securities for cancellation. As we stated earlier, it is common for security holders to allege that they did not receive a notice of redemption and to claim additional interest. An additional way of avoiding future interest claims from security holders is to cite the redemption or the final maturity on the interest check of each applicable security holder. The endorsement block on the check can state that the holder's endorsement includes acknowledgment of notice of the redemption or final maturity. This notice typically is programmed into the operating system.

To overcome problems in the redemption notification of securities, the SEC and the American Bankers Association (ABA) established standards and guidelines based on a consensus of opinions expressed by major securities industry associations, self-regulatory organizations, and federal regulatory agencies.[2] The standards were that

1. Notices of security redemptions should contain the preceding information.
2. All notices should be sent in a secure fashion (e.g., by certified mail or overnight express) to all registered securities depositories and to the national information services that disseminate such information.
3. Notices allow a thirty-day period between the notice date and the redemption date.
4. Notices be sent to the registered depositories before the publication date (a guideline generally not acceptable to corporate trustees).
5. Second notices of advance refundings be given thirty days before the redemption date.
6. The CUSIP number be indicated on all redemption payments (checks and wires).[3]

These guidelines were disseminated as Recommended Guidelines for Processing Bond Calls by the ABA's corporate trust committee in the summer of 1989. To encourage industrywide acceptance of these guidelines (with even greater specificity), the American National Standards Institute, working through its X9D Committee, drew up a revised set of standards, which were approved and published on December 11, 1992, as the *Called Securities Processing—Securities Subject to Early Redemption*. These standards include notice of redemption, publication of notice of redemption, follow-up notices, and suggested trust indenture language.

It has become standard practice for all parties to a new financing to abide by these standards. During the indenture review period, trustees should monitor the redemption provisions to verify that the standards are being followed. For older municipal indentures, it may be difficult to provide a thirty-day advance notice of the redemption, as the standards require. Accordingly, some older indentures require a shorter advance notice period.

[2] SEC Release 34–23856 (Dec. 3, 1986), 51 Fed. Reg. 235 at 44398 (Dec. 9, 1986).

[3] See Van Gemert v. Boeing Co. 520 F. 2d 1373 (2d. Cir.), *cert. denied*, 423 U.S. 947 (1975).

The redemption notice standards have also been incorporated in securities depositories' required procedures and operating arrangements. Trustees and agents should be familiar with the procedures and should maintain current copies of them provided by the securities depositories.

For a partial call of a fully registered security issue, the traditional notice listing all the security numbers and applicable principal amounts being called for redemption can be avoided by using a letter form of notice incorporating the required details of redemption. This notice should be accompanied by a special form addressed to each holder affected by the call, specifying the principal amount of holdings selected for redemption and the security number(s) against which the selection was allocated, to be presented for payment. Copies of this form can also be used for follow-up and posting operations. This notice should be sent by mail to the registered holders at their addresses as indicated in the security register. The notice needs to be sent only to the registered holders of securities selected for redemption. Notice by registered or certified mail should never be required. A certificate of mailing should be prepared, indicating that the notice was mailed on a specified date, that a count of notices mailed was reconciled with the number of registered holders whose securities were called, and that the notices were properly addressed and deposited in a postal facility.

The indenture should not contain any requirements for the publication of the notice, for this is expensive and unnecessary when all securities are registered. However, when an issue is actively traded, it is desirable to make available the information services specified in the preceding guidelines and also a list of the numbers of the called securities to any securities exchange on which the securities are listed, in addition to the securities depositories, which often require that these data be provided by the trustee.

When securities are outstanding in bearer form, notice is given by publication in an authorized newspaper. What constitutes an "authorized newspaper" should be defined in the indenture. Published notices should comply with the standards specified in the SEC and ABA guidelines. For corporate issues, copies should also be sent to any securities exchanges on which the securities are listed.

In addition to publishing the required notice, which should also indicate the serial numbers of the bearer securities to be redeemed and the coupons that must be attached to them, a copy should be sent to each registered holder of the called securities. The trustee should make sure that these are mailed and at the same time as the initial publication.

Bearer security holders often have asked trustees and agents to keep their names and addresses on file for future notices. Since the few outstanding bearer security issues typically allow for the issuance of registered securities, trustees should consider abandoning the practice of agreeing to maintain bearer holder addresses for future notice, so as to limit potential compensation claims from holders.

If the redemption is for the sinking fund or uses special funds that are part of the trust estate, the notice should be mailed (or published) under the name of trustee (or sinking-fund agent, if other than the trustee) unless the indenture specifies otherwise. If redemption is for an option right reserved for the obligor, it should be mailed (or published) under the name of the obligor, even though it was actually prepared and disseminated by the trustee.

Payment Provisions

Provision should be made for depositing with the trustee those funds required for the redemption. It is not necessary that this be done before the selection and mailing (or publication) of notice, although the funds should be deposited on or before the date of payment and in the full amount. The deposit should be made in trust, and the funds held in a special account for payment of the securities to be redeemed.

The same-day funds payment rules recommended by the Group of Thirty became effective on February 22, 1996. The rules are a requirement for all dividend, interest, and principal payments on securities and requires funds to be received at the offices of depositories early in the afternoon on the payable date. Meeting this deadline allows the depositories to pay their participants on the payable date. Municipal and corporate obligors must be instructed to deposit federal funds early on the payable date so as to comply with the same-day funds requirements. Because many municipal issuers prefer to make their debt service payments by check, special provisions must be made with the depositing obligor to allow sufficient time for the check to clear. Trustees and paying agents must control the receipt of funds to determine whether the funds have been collected at the time they are paid to the depository. Monitoring the receipt and disbursement of debt service funds avoids the risk of incurring daylight overdrafts. Trustees should consult each depository's operating procedures to understand the rules, in case a payment is made to the depository in error and it is necessary to retrieve the funds from the depository. On heavy redemption dates, the amounts being wired to the depositories may exceed their bank's daylight overdraft cap. Thus each trustee must be aware of the daylight overdraft rules established by the Federal Reserve System.

Managing the timely receipt and immediate disbursement of funds is one of the many operating challenges of the trustee and or agent. If the deposit is made with a paying agent other than the trustee, it should be placed in a special trust account in the name of the trustee and should be under its control rather than the obligor's. An appropriate letter to this effect should also be obtained from the paying agent unless such an undertaking is included in a general letter at the time the indenture is executed. If not deposited, or if the obligor acts as its own paying agent and retains the redemption funds under its control, the called securities should not be discharged from the trustee's records until the trustee actually receives and cancels the securities.

If because of a refunding or for other reasons, the funds necessary for the redemption are deposited before the date of the mailing (or first publication) of notice, an early payment is sometimes offered. This is an offer to pay the full redemption price upon presentation of the securities at any time after the notice is mailed (or published), even if the presentation is before the redemption date. Such an offer is acceptable, although seldom used, but it should be made at the discretion of the obligor and must be made if the indenture so requires. The trustee should not, by agreement with anyone other than the obligor, offer to make an early payment, even though it may possess the funds.

When payment is made for redeemed securities, the trustee/paying agent must ensure that proper procedures have been established in the operational area so that IRS Form 1099B is issued for each payment made. These forms should be issued on the redemption date and for the year in which the redemption date occurs, regardless of when the redeemed securities are actually presented for payment. The issuance of Form 1099B also serves as an additional notice to security holders if they have failed to present their security on time. This, of course, applies to all securities redeemed, whether the interest on such securities is taxable or tax exempt. Since most municipal securities are tax exempt, it is common for municipal security holders to argue that no notice to the IRS is required. Notice to the IRS on Form 1099B can serve as notice of a potential capital gain or loss on a municipal security. If the trustee/paying agent has not previously received a certified taxpayer identification number for a payee on IRS Form W-8 or W-9, it must obtain certification before disbursing the redemption proceeds. As stated in the Interest and

Dividend Tax Compliance Act of 1983, as amended, the trustee may be required to withhold 31 percent of the total redemption proceeds for a payment in the event the payee fails to provide certain certifications or if the trustee/paying agent is ordered by the IRS to withhold it. Most operating systems are able to maintain accurate filing information. Any required interest is generally withheld by the trustee/agent's operating system.

PARTIAL REDEMPTIONS

When fewer than all the securities of an issue are to be redeemed, particular securities should be selected by the trustee, following the same method as when selecting securities for redemption by a sinking fund. As noted in chapter 7, the indenture should give the trustee flexibility in the selection process. Rather than detail the particular procedures to be employed, indenture drafters should leave this to the trustee's discretion. The only requirement should be that the method adopted be fair and equitable to all holders. In this way, the trustee can keep up with current practices rather than be bound by possibly antiquated procedures.

The traditional method of selection has been by security number, with a basic unit of $1,000 for corporate issues and $5,000 for municipal securities. Securities of larger denominations are assigned as many unit numbers as there are multiples of $1,000 or $5,000. Other methods of selection may be equally fair, depending on the particular case. For an all-registered issue, the indenture may require the trustee to make the selection pro rata by holder and then allocate the portions selected from a particular security or securities. The significance of this method is that each holder receives a portion of the redemption proceeds.

Some structured financings with serial securities require a partial call so that the aggregate annual debt service requirement is reduced proportionately for each serial maturity. For this type of call, known as a *strip call*, securities must be selected across all maturities, including maturities composed of zero coupon securities, for a proportionate reduction. The proper execution of these calls in accordance with indenture provisions can be critical to future cash flows.

The necessity of closing the security register during the selection period is obvious, and there is no way in which changes in the holders or numbers of outstanding registered securities can be permitted. The indenture should provide that the privilege of transfer or exchange of securities may be suspended for a period of fifteen days preceding the mailing or publication. It is incumbent on the trustee, however, to use its best efforts to minimize the suspension time, especially for an active security issue, so that the registration of transfers as a result of trading is not unduly disrupted. If the parties desire, an interim receipt can be issued for a security presented for registration of transfer or in exchange during the time the security register is closed. In such an event, however, the registrar should place a legend on the receipt to the effect that the security register is closed for the purpose of selecting securities for redemption at a designated price on a designated date; that the security presented for registration of transfer or exchange is subject to selection for redemption in whole or in part; and that in the event of their selection, any new security(s) registered, as indicated on the receipt, for the uncalled portion will be delivered in exchange for the receipt, together with a redemption ticket redeemable on the redemption date, for the called portion of such security.

Once the selection has been made and the notice mailed (or first published), the securities selected become due and payable on the date designated. On this date, they cease to be outstanding for any purpose of the indenture except to receive payment and should be removed from the classification of outstanding securities by an entry in the trustee's records. It is desirable to control them in a subsidiary redemption ledger, with the entry being made as the securities are actually surrendered and paid.

Because some of the securities will not be presented promptly, care should be taken on the next record date for payment of interest that appropriate stop payments are noted on the registrar's records. For bearer securities, the stop payment should be noted against the coupons appurtenant to all such securities that remain outstanding. This will prevent an unauthorized payment and also facilitate notifying those holders who have not surrendered their called securities.

After the selection has been completed and the security register reopened, any security not affected by the call may be transferred, exchanged, or otherwise dealt with. When a portion of a security has been selected for redemption and the security has been presented for transfer or exchange before the redemption date, it is proper to make the requested transaction with respect to the uncalled portion of the security. The original security, now representing only the called portion, should be retained by the trustee (or forwarded by the registrar to the trustee or paying agent) for payment on the redemption date. It has been suggested that provision be made for registering the transfer of called securities between the selection date and the redemption date. It is difficult to understand why this should be desired, for the status of the obligation has now been changed. It represents only the right to receive payment of the redemption price on the redemption date and can no longer be used to settle a contract to deliver a "security" of the issue.

If the entire issue has been called for redemption, it may be desirable to continue the registering the transfers and to permit the trading of "called" securities. In this situation, any securities delivered should be overstamped with an appropriate legend of the redemption.

The process of selecting securities for redemption and special precautions to avoid future payments on called securities is delegated, in most trustee and agent offices today, to the operating systems. The redemption standards and increasing numbers of redemptions can best be managed by sophisticated operating systems.

CONVERTIBLE SECURITIES

Debt securities that can be converted, at the option of the holder, into other types of securities of the issuer require the trustee to protect this privilege. The common practice when any securities are called for redemption is to continue the conversion privilege up to and including the redemption date. The trustee should request that such a provision be included in the indenture. Some issues provide that a conversion privilege will terminate several days before the redemption date. No matter how carefully it is spelled out in the notice, however, many holders invariably miss the cutoff date and consequently suffer a loss.

In preparing the redemption notice, it is recommended that the conversion privilege, if of value, be stated separately so that the holder's attention is drawn to it. It is inevitable that some holders will lose their privilege through misunderstanding or carelessness, but every effort should be made to keep such losses at a minimum.[4]

For convertible issues, the trustee should insist that the indenture provisions contain specific time frames before a redemption date in which the obligor may notify the trustee of its election to redeem securities. Discretion for the trustee to determine that a shorter notice period is satisfactory may lead to claims or litigation by holders if the economic return to the holders resulting from the conversion and redemption timing is unsatisfactory.

[4] See TIA sec. 314(a)(4). This certification need not include the four compliance statements stated in sec. 314(e).

Funds held in the redemption account for payment of converted securities are usually returned to the obligor. This is proper, for in effect, the payment for the securities has been made by issuing other securities (e.g., stock). The trustee should make certain that this is explicitly covered in the indenture.

Satisfaction and Defeasance

An important part of every indenture is the section pertaining to satisfaction and discharge, or defeasance. *Defeasance* refers to the "undoing" or release from the lien of the indenture or the mortgage of property originally pledged or mortgaged to secure the payment of principal and interest and to ensure that the obligor carries out its covenants. For any type of secured issue, including a mortgage bond indenture, defeasance entitles the obligor or mortgagor to receive its pledged or mortgaged property free and clear from the lien of the indenture.

This defeasance should not be confused with *in-substance defeasance* (also referred to as *taxable defeasance*, *de facto defeasance*, and *effective defeasance*), which are transactions intended to satisfy debt obligations in substance, although there is no legal discharge of the obligation. In effect, an issuer purchases U.S. government obligations at a discount and places them in a trust, pledging the government's future income and principal to pay the interest and principal on its own outstanding security issue. This transaction may be advantageous to the issuer in that it can (1) enhance its financial statements, (2) upgrade its debt rating, and (3) result in effectively retiring an outstanding security issue without having to repurchase the securities.[1] Next we examine special concerns with these transactions.

In most cases, the indenture covenants are included as additional

---

[1] See Financial Accounting Standards Board, *Statement of Financial Accounting Standards No. 76, Extinguishment of Debt* (Nov. 1983); and SEC Interpretive Release Nos. 33–6501, 34–20509, 35–23176, FR-15 (Dec. 22, 1983).

security provisions to guarantee performance of the basic covenant, namely, to pay the indenture obligations as they become due. Accordingly, if all obligations have been paid, or satisfactory provision has been made for them, the obligor is entitled to a satisfaction, even though a default may have occurred or may at the time exist under a particular security covenant.

The obligor must, however, have discharged, or provided for the discharge of, all its obligations to the security holders. For example, if the securities contain a convertible provision, an option to purchase stock, or any other condition or provision that constitutes an additional consideration for purchasing the securities by the holders, it is not sufficient merely to pay the principal and interest on the indenture securities. All other conditions must be performed or their performance provided for before the obligor is entitled to a formal satisfaction and discharge of the indenture.

The obligor must also have discharged all obligations owed to the trustee and other agents. These include payment of all disbursements, repayment of all advances (with interest if properly chargeable), and payment of all fees and other compensation due, including reasonable fees for executing a satisfaction and any other duties required to be performed subsequently.

If the trustee executes and delivers a satisfaction improperly, it will be liable for legal damages to anyone injured by its action. Conversely, if it improperly withholds a satisfaction, it may be liable to the obligor. The trustee must therefore exercise due care in all matters relating to the satisfaction and discharge of the indenture.

It would be impractical and unfair to require actual payment of all the outstanding securities before the obligor could obtain a satisfaction. Over a long time, some securities become misplaced or lost, or holders are slow in presenting them for payment. Occasionally, a small percentage of the obligations are never presented, and in many instances, several years may elapse before all the obligations are actually retired. Nevertheless, the security holders are entitled to their security until they receive payment for their securities, and it is important that payment be secured for them before the indenture is satisfied.

The usual provision is to require depositing with the trustee, in trust, enough funds to pay all principal and interest on the securities to the maturity date or the redemption date if the securities have been called and for the indenture to provide that upon this deposit, the obligor becomes entitled to a satisfaction of the indenture. If any facts must be established or any conditions satisfied, the indenture should provide that the trustee will be protected if it accepts and relies in good faith on an officers' certificate and opinion of counsel as to the existence of these facts or the satisfaction of these conditions.

It is not essential that all steps be taken to make the redemption before the conditions are satisfied. This fact may be important if the redemption funds are being provided by refunding under another indenture. In order that the obligor give a proper lien under the new indenture—which is essential to enable it to secure the necessary funds—it must at the same time be able to secure a legal discharge of the former lien. It is sufficient if the requisite funds are deposited with the trustee, together with irrevocable instructions to perform all acts necessary to make the redemption.

ACCOUNTING ANALYSIS

For the trustee to determine what funds are required, an appropriate accounting may have to be prepared. This may take any form as long as it is reasonably detailed and accurate and includes all obligations that have become due under the indenture and the provision made for their discharge. If the appropriate records have been accurately maintained throughout the life of the issue (especially if bearer obligations are involved), the analysis for a final maturity (or a full redemption) should not present a problem. But if this is not done or if the records are out of proof, then the task may be enormous.

Analyzing principal means accounting for the total principal amount authenticated by the trustee at any time under any provision of the indenture. Because securities will have been issued because of registration of transfer, exchange, or replacement or for other purposes, the total obligations to be accounted for usually exceeds the amount outstanding at any time under the indenture.[2] Offsetting principal obligations so authenticated is the aggregate of all such obligations that have been canceled by the trustee. Ordinarily, the evidence of a cancellation is the executed destruction certificate in the trustee's possession. If the trustee does not have destruction certificates or canceled securities for all the securities, the trustee should satisfy itself that the canceled obligations have been properly disposed of. If the trustee's records do not show the cancellation of these obligations, it should insist on their surrender to ensure their

---

[2] If a database system contains certificate cancellation data and can produce a report covering specified time periods, it should not be necessary to detail the reason for the certificate cancellation in the final accounting. See also chapter 16, *supra*.

proper disposition. Subtracting the principal amount of obligations canceled from the aggregate amount authenticated gives the remaining principal to be accounted for. This may be offset by funds on deposit with the trustee, by monies to be deposited, or by satisfactory indemnity bonds on file.

In preparing any interest accounting, the principal amount of obligations outstanding on each interest payment date should be ascertained and the interest calculated for each date. The amount of registered interest paid, the aggregate amount of coupons canceled, and the coupons paid against the bonds of indemnity for each period should be shown separately. The sum of these subtracted from the interest due leaves the balance due for each interest date represented by outstanding unpresented coupons. The total of these amounts should represent the funds on deposit with the trustee or paying agent.

If the trustee is not the agent to pay the registered interest, it should receive an appropriate certificate of a responsible disbursing agent. This should be examined and compared with the total amount of the registered interest due, and a record should be kept for later accounting. When the trustee is not the paying agent, the trustee must remember to reduce the principal outstanding on its operating system at the time the agent certifies the payment.

After being paid, coupons are customarily destroyed by the trustee, and the destruction certificates provide the evidence necessary to support this phase of the accounting. When the paying agents are other than the trustee, they should arrange to have all interest obligations periodically surrendered to them for verification and destruction. In lieu of surrender, the trustee may accept a destruction certificate from a reliable agent, although good practice should prohibit its accepting a certificate of the obligor without independent verification.

Most indentures permit the replacement of lost, stolen, or destroyed obligations, or their payment, in lieu of replacement, upon documentation of loss, theft, or destruction and the provision of satisfactory indemnity. These replacement securities, however, constitute additional contractual obligations entitled to the security of the indenture. In connection with a final accounting, it is customary to give credit for all obligations covered by a satisfactory bond of indemnity if an original counterpart is on file with the trustee and if the latter is named as an obligee. This is a matter for the trustee's discretion, however. If the security afforded by such bonds of indemnity is not in all respects satisfactory, the trustee is entitled to insist on adequate security or the deposit of funds to cover such obligations.

DEPOSIT OF FUNDS

The trustee is entitled to, and should insist on, receiving the deposit of all funds due for all outstanding obligations before it executes a satisfaction. If funds to meet matured and unpresented obligations are on deposit with other agents, arrangements should be made for their transfer to the trustee, even if the deposit with the other agent is in trust. The fact that a statute of limitations may have run against particular interest obligations is immaterial unless the indenture contains a specific provision that no further claim may be asserted.

In the exceptional cases when the deposit with the trustee is not feasible, because the latter is not an authorized depositary or for other reasons, the depositary should be satisfactory to and approved by the trustee, and the deposit should be under the trustee's exclusive control. In this case, the trustee is not liable if reasonable care was used in selecting the depositary, even if the funds are subsequently lost through the failure of the depositary.

The issuer's obligation contained in its securities runs directly to the holders. When the requisite funds for their payment are deposited with the trustee, however, it has been held that this is equivalent to paying the holders, and the issuer is not liable if the trustee misapplies the funds or becomes bankrupt. This is true, however, only from and after the date on which funds in the hands of the trustee become available to the security holders upon surrender of their securities.

DOCUMENTATION

When all requisite accountings have been prepared and checked and the trustee has satisfied itself that it has funds in its possession to pay all obligations shown to be still outstanding; when it has received an officers' certificate and an opinion of counsel on compliance by the obligor with all conditions; and when it has received from the obligor irrevocable instructions to complete all conditions requisite to redeeming those securities not previously completed, it is then in a position to execute and deliver a satisfaction and discharge of the indenture.

The instruments of satisfaction are usually prepared by counsel for the obligor, but the trustee should check them carefully.

In the case of a debenture agreement or unsecured indenture, execution of a formal instrument of satisfaction is not absolutely necessary, for no property has to be reconveyed. It is good practice, however, to acknowledge formally the obligor's compliance with its obligations, and this is almost always observed. Complete and final accountings should be prepared in any event, as in the case of a mortgage indenture.

Under a mortgage indenture, the instrument of satisfaction constitutes a reconveyance of all the trustee's interest in the mortgaged property.[3] It must, therefore, be in a form that can be recorded in the necessary jurisdictions to discharge the lien of the indenture of record. The instrument must be in the form of a release or quitclaim deed and contain no warranties. It is good practice for the instrument to contain a statement that the instrument has been executed without covenant or warranty, express or implied, and without recourse against the trustee in any event. The instrument should always run to the obligor and never to a third party. As the securities are paid in full, corporations typically incorporate a release of the lien of the indenture into their payment procedures. Municipalities often fail to request the release on such entities as hospitals and housing projects when the security issues are paid in full. Several years can pass until the municipal entity realizes that it did not receive the appropriate satisfaction document, and it can become difficult to secure the satisfaction several years later. In general, the consolidation of the corporate trust industry and banks can make retrieving records more difficult.

Typically when the need for satisfaction documents is realized, it is an urgent need.

"In Substance" Defeasance

For various economic and financial reasons, and particularly during periods when short-term interest rates are lower than those born by an obligor's securities, an obligor may elect to defease an indenture, with the securities to be redeemed at a future date or dates. Indentures for tax-exempt issues frequently permit this type of defeasance, and tax-exempt obligors often use refunding securities to finance such transactions. One reason for this type of defeasance is that the securities are "call protected," that is, not subject to an optional redemption until a future date, if at all. Indentures may permit such a transaction, stating that cash or government securities be deposited with the trustee, provided that such securities and

---

[3] In the case of a collateral trust indenture, in which the trustee perfected its security interest by filing a financing statement under the UCC, its security interest is released by filing a termination statement.

cash, together with the interest to be earned on them, are sufficient to pay all the principal, premiums, if any, and interest on the outstanding securities as they become due by their term or through redemption. Some indentures, however, require that enough cash to pay all future debt service be deposited for the defeasance. The trustee should be careful to distinguish this type of defeasance (sometimes termed *gross defeasance*) from the first type, which allows future investment earnings to be factored into the equation (*net defeasance*). For either type of "in substance" defeasance, the trustee should request that the obligor obtain and provide an accounting from a recognized accounting firm clearly showing that the cash, securities, and investment income, if any, will cover all debt service in future years, up to and including final maturity or redemption.

In most instances, for tax-exempt financings, the trustee and obligor enter into a separate escrow deposit agreement, stating the obligations and duties of both parties until all the securities are redeemed or mature by their terms. The escrow deposit agreement should include all the provisions from the defeased indenture with regard to the registration of transfer and the payment of the securities, as well as exculpation, indemnification, and protection for the trustee in its new capacity as escrow agent. Although structured as an escrow agreement, the funds are nevertheless held in trust by the escrow agent for the benefit of the security holders. The agreement also should spell out the agent's responsibility for the future investment and reinvestment of cash, securities, and investment income and the disposition of any excess funds not required to pay principal and interest as they become due.

When an "in substance" defeasance is for a tax-exempt issue, the trustee would be wise also to ask a nationally recognized municipal bond counsel whether the defeasance will adversely affect the securities' tax-exempt status, in addition to any other opinions required by the indenture as a condition for the defeasance.

DISPOSING OF COLLATERAL, FUNDS, AND RECORDS

For all defeasances, arrangements should be made to return to the obligor the pledged collateral, unclaimed debt service funds, or other items of property that are physically in the possession of the trustee but are not required to be held as part of an escrow or otherwise for future payments to security holders. In this connection, the trustee should make sure that no junior lienor is entitled to possess the property. If such a lien does exist, arrangements should be made to surrender the property to the trustee of the junior lien, with the proper receipt. This may include the right to the proceeds of any released property, insurance proceeds, or similar funds in the hands of the trustee.

It is desirable for every indenture to provide for the return to the obligor of all unclaimed funds deposited to pay the indenture obligations after a specified number of years have elapsed following the satisfaction of the indenture. The most common period used is six years, but the length is not material as long as some period is specified. Without such a provision, the trustee may be required to retain permanently a small balance on its books, for it is unlikely that each obligation will be presented to it.[4]

Without the appropriate indenture authority, the trustee runs a risk in returning any unclaimed funds to the obligor, no matter how many years may have elapsed, for the obligor has no legal right to this return. Similarly, the obligor is not entitled to have such funds invested for its benefit, and if they are, the trustee may be liable for any loss.

Most states have complicated the problems of corporate financial officers, municipalities, corporate trustees, and paying agents by enacting sundry escheat or abandoned-property laws. The general purport of these statutes is to require the transfer to the state of all funds and, in some states, securities held unclaimed for a stated period of time. In 1981, the Commissioners on Uniform State Laws promulgated the Uniform Unclaimed Property Act, which has been adopted by a majority of the states. The 1981 act incorporated a 1965 U.S. Supreme Court decision that the right and power to escheat belongs to the state of the creditor's last known address, as shown on the debtor's books and records.

Since theoretically a state can seize only that property belonging to its residents, a difficult problem was encountered when funds were held for the payment of bearer securities. In a 1993 decision, the U.S. Supreme Court held that an intermediary holding property in its own name generally is deemed to be the "debtor."[5] And if the "debtor's" records do not reflect a last known address, then the unclaimed property should be escheated to the "debtor's" state of domicile. This decision was incorporated into the Uniform Unclaimed Property Act of 1995, which is under consideration by the individual state legislatures.

In addition to establishing that the state where the financial intermediary

---

[4] An informal survey of twenty-eight major banks in early 1997 by the authors indicated that of the original principal amount of an issue, approximately 3 percent of bearer bonds and 1 percent of registered bonds remain outstanding a year after their redemption or maturity.

[5] Delaware v. New York, 113 S.Ct. 1550 (1993).

(e.g., trustee/paying agent) is located is entitled to the escheatment of un-claimed bearer funds and securities, the act also provides that both the principal amount of a registered bond and its interest become excheatable five years after the first interest payment is returned as undeliverable. In the case of bearer bonds and original discount bonds, the five-year dormancy period begins after their date of maturity.

The indenture provisions relating to the disposition of unclaimed moneys should therefore be drafted in accordance with any applicable escheat or abandoned property law. When an appropriate indenture provision is lacking, the trustee must make a difficult decision when asked to execute a satisfaction. For example, let us assume that during the life of a particular issue, the obligor has paid several thousand dollars according to an escheat law requiring the transfer of all interest monies held unclaimed for six years. The issue matures, and the obligor tenders, to the trustee, funds to pay the principal and all unclaimed interest due during the preceding six years and demands the execution of an instrument of satisfaction. Should the trustee comply or should it insist on the deposit of an amount equivalent to the funds previously escheated? This is not an easy decision, but unless the escheat law was sufficient to discharge the trustee's obligation with respect to such unclaimed interest, the trustee may act at its peril if it executes a satisfaction without adequately securing the unpaid interest, whose coupons may be subsequently presented to the trustee. Under such circumstances, the trustee would be well advised to secure at least an appropriate indemnity from the obligor.

One final problem remains. Now that the indenture has been satisfied and appropriate provision has been made to pay all outstanding obligations, what should be the disposition of the mountain of documents and papers that the trustee has accumulated during the life of the indenture? Obviously the answer depends to some extent on any laws or regulations in the jurisdiction of the trustee relating to the disposition of fiduciary records. Most corporate trustees tend to be very conservative and to hold on to papers and documents for many years beyond the time when they can serve any conceivable purpose. This is an expensive folly, and it is urged that each trustee consider establishing a reasonable schedule for the systematic disposition of obsolete records.

Some records accumulated by a corporate trustee should, however, be retained permanently, including one original executed counterpart of the indenture and of the instrument of satisfaction; a copy of its final accounting with respect to all indenture securities; copies of all destruction certificates; originals of all bonds of indemnity or assumptions of liability of others with respect to any indenture securities or other obligations; and any document relating to an obligation or undertaking beyond the maturity of the indenture securities or essential to establishing the basic historical continuity of the trusteeship, such as an assumption agreement by a successor obligor.

Most other documents can be disposed of within a reasonable time after termination of the appointment or after applicable statutes of limitation. More and more trustees are imaging documentation to avoid storage costs in future years.

Once the indenture has been satisfied, the recorded counterparts of the indenture and all supplements are no longer of any value to the trustee. They may be returned to the obligor corporation if it desires them. Otherwise they should be destroyed.

The original counterparts of indentures executed before 1966 bear canceled federal documentary stamps evidencing payment of the original issue tax and should be dealt with carefully. Because they document the payment of an obligation by the obligor, they may be returned to the obligor if the latter wishes. A receipt should be obtained that lists the principal amount of canceled tax obligations. If the obligor does not wish to have this document returned, which is usually the case, the trustee may destroy it. The destruction certificates should include a statement of the face amount of those tax stamps destroyed.

Default and Remedial Provisions

The administration of indentures after default is the greatest test of the corporate trust officer's skill and expertise. In addition to the requirements of the TIA, most indentures provide that before default the trustee be charged with performing only those duties specified in the indenture. The instrument itself serves as the guide for the action to be taken for each problem that arises. However, there are often no applicable precedents to follow, and the trustee may find itself navigating in uncharted waters. The consolidation of the corporate trust industry has prompted many of the remaining trustees to create special default units with the purpose of navigating these waters. (See exhibit 9, Default Report Form, which may be used to report the status of defaulted accounts to the corporate trust committee or senior management.)

It is impossible to prescribe the exact conduct to be followed in the event of a default. The indenture is essentially a security instrument and should reflect the premise that the trustee's primary objective, both before and after default, is to protect the security position of the indenture security holders. If liquidation or reorganization becomes necessary, the trustee should see that the security holders realize their claims in full or to the greatest extent possible.

Except for the duties imposed by the TIA,[1] the trustee's rights and powers after default are derived from the authority granted by the indenture, or those that may be properly inferred from the authority expressly

---

[1] Secs. 315(a) and (c) and 317(a).

granted. Before discussing the general principles of default indenture administration, we should consider the default and remedial provisions customarily included in trust indentures.

EVENTS OF DEFAULT

The events that constitute a default and give rise to the remedial provisions must be stated clearly in the indenture.[2] Although there is occasional variance because of particular circumstances, the general provisions are fairly uniform:

1. Default in the payment of the principal of any of the indenture securities when they become due, whether at maturity, by call, by declaration, or otherwise. Because of the serious nature of this type of default, no grace period is provided, for it is unlikely to happen by inadvertence. Also, prompt action by the trustee may be indicated, and it should not be hampered by having to wait through a grace period.
2. Default in the payment of any installment of interest on any of the indenture securities when it becomes due. Most indentures provide a grace period, usually thirty to sixty days, within which time the obligor may cure such a default. The remedies provided in the indenture are stayed until this grace period has expired.
3. If the indenture provides for a sinking fund or a purchase fund or similar payments to be made to the trustee, failing to make these payments will constitute an *Event of Default*. It is desirable to allow a grace period to cure the default, and such a provision is customarily, although not always, included.
4. If there are prior lien securities outstanding, or other obligations that constitute a lien before the lien of the indenture securities on the trust estate or some part of it, a covenant to pay the prior liens and comply with all provisions of the indenture securing it should be included in the indenture. Failing to discharge these prior lien obligations when due should be made a default under the indenture after a grace period. There is a sound reason for this. Although failing to discharge the prior lien normally constitutes a default under the prior lien obligation, its holder may

[2]Note that a so-called lower-case default will ripen into an Event of Default when there is no grace period, the appropriate grace period in the indenture has expired, or the trustee gives notice, as prescribed in the indenture. The indenture's remedial provisions become operative only upon an Event of Default.

take no action to enforce the obligation. Unless this also constituted an Event of Default under the indenture securing the junior obligations, the holders of the latter may be unable to take steps to protect their equity in the property until it has been substantially dissipated.

5. It is an *Event of Default* if the obligor, according to or within the meaning of any federal or state bankruptcy law, commences a voluntary case, consents to the entry of an order for relief against it in an involuntary case, consents to the appointment of a custodian of it or for all or substantially all its property, or makes a general assignment for the benefit of its creditors; or a court of competent jurisdiction enters an order or decree under any bankruptcy law that is for relief against the obligor in an involuntary case, appoints a custodian of the obligor or for all or substantially all its property, or orders the liquidation of the obligor and the order or decree remains unstayed and in effect for sixty days.[3]

6. Finally, the breach of any covenant or the failure of the obligor to meet any condition provided for in the indenture in turn leads to a default. It is customarily provided that an Event of Default will not occur for this reason until a stated period of time has expired after the trustee or a specified percentage of the indenture security holders have notified the obligor in writing of the breach of the covenant or condition.

Whereas both a notice and a grace period should be provided in the event of a breach of most indenture covenants, either or both may be unwise. For example, in the case of certain negative covenants, such as those against incurring indebtedness, creating prior liens, transferring properties, or declaring dividends, time may be of the essence, and the trustee should have the right to move promptly if such action seems warranted. This should include obtaining injunctive relief from an appropriate court. Although the trustee does not draft these provisions, it should insist on flexibility during the indenture review and negotiation sessions with the issuer (or its counsel).

The trustee and the obligor may disagree about whether a default has in fact occurred under the terms of the indenture. This may result from

---

[3] Derived from the Federal Bankruptcy Code, 11 U.S.C.A., secs. 301 and 303 (h) (2), Pub. L. No. 95–598, 92 Stat. 2549 (1978); and the Model Simplified Indenture, at 756. See also Committee on Developments in Business Financing, "Structuring and Documenting Business Financing Transactions Under the Federal Bankruptcy Code of 1978," 35 *Bus. Law.* 1645 (1980).

differing opinions of counsel (to the obligor and to the trustee) on the proper interpretation or application of a particular indenture covenant. In this case, the trustee should consider instituting a declaratory judgment action against the obligor in federal court, seeking a judicial determination of whether a default has in fact occurred.[4] Thus, the trustee may be able to avoid future litigation, by either the obligor or the security holders, for it will have received judicial approval of its action or nonaction.

REMEDIAL PROVISIONS

The indenture contains various remedial provisions that, theoretically, may become operational once an Event of Default has occurred. To the average security holder, the powers of enforcement granted to the trustee seem adequate, and an investor may therefore not understand why in many situations the repayment of securities is less than bargained for. Unfortunately, remedial action normally requires judicial proceedings of some kind, and the courts and lawyers are familiar with the usual remedies. When the intrinsic value of the security is sufficient, these remedies might be adequate. In the case of the usual corporate obligor, however, they are often inadequate, unenforceable, or impractical.

The remedies found most frequently in secured indentures are the following:

1. The right to accelerate the maturity of the indenture securities and to declare all principal due.
2. The right of the trustee to recover judgment in its own name and as the trustee of an express trust.
3. The right to sue in equity or at law for the specific performance of any covenant or agreement, for the enforcement of any rights of the trustee and security holders, or for the enforcement of any appropriate equitable or legal remedy.
4. The right of entry to and possession of the mortgaged property by a custodian, agents or, otherwise, this possession to continue until all defaults are cured.
5. The right to sell the trust estate at public auction, with or without entry.
6. In the case of a collateral indenture, the exercise of full rights of ownership with respect to any collateral held.
7. The right to the appointment of a custodian or receiver of the

[4] This action may be possible under the Declaratory Judgment Act, 28 U.S.C.A., sec. 2201.

mortgaged property and to foreclosure on it by appropriate judicial action.

8. The right to file proofs of claim on behalf of all the security holders in any judicial proceedings.

In the case of an unsecured indenture, the same remedies usually are included, except for items 4, 5, 6, and 7, which relate to specific action for realizing on the indenture security. The unsecured indenture customarily contains a general provision permitting the trustee to have appointed a custodian or receiver of the obligor's property and to bring suit to foreclose on the property to satisfy its judgment for the amounts owed on the indenture securities. The advantage of the mortgage indenture is that the lien on the properties is already established.

To aid in the trustee's powers of enforcement, the remedial sections usually contain three covenants by the obligor:

1. In the event of a default in payment of the principal or interest (whether at maturity, on redemption, or by declaration), to pay to the trustee promptly all amounts then due and owing. Because it is obvious that if the obligor could do this, no default would have occurred, the provision may appear meaningless. But it is intended to aid the trustee's obtaining a prompt judgment to enable it to enforce other remedies.

2. Upon the commencement of any action, suit, or proceeding by the trustee to waive the issuance and service of process and to enter its voluntary appearance in such an action, suit, or proceeding and to consent to the entry of judgment in favor of the trustee for all amounts owing under the indenture.

3. As far as it lawfully and effectively may, to waive and relinquish the benefit and advantage of any and all valuation, stay, appraisement, extension, or redemption laws then existing or afterward enacted.

THE TRUSTEE'S RIGHTS AND DUTIES UPON DEFAULT

The Trustee's Responsibilities

Before the TIA was enacted, most indentures provided that the trustee was under no duty to take action to enforce the indenture's remedial provisions until it had received an official demand by a specified percentage of the indenture's security holders, together with whatever indemnity might be required to protect it against expense and liability. This provision was accompanied by broad exculpatory clauses that relieved the trustee of liability except for acts amounting to willful misconduct or gross negligence.

Despite the great criticism of these provisions, there was a sound and logical basis for their existence. Initially, as has been noted, the trustee was a mere stakeholder, and its function was limited to holding the specific security for the benefit of the bondholders. Despite the grant of broad rights and powers to the trustee, this concept did not disappear entirely. Even though the trustee was given the right to proceed on its own to enforce the remedial provisions, in practice it continued to be regarded primarily as the instrument of the security holders in exercising this right. Accordingly, the customary procedure whenever a default occurred or seemed imminent was for the trustee (1) to confer with the obligor to ascertain the facts and, if possible, to work out a tentative program or course of action; (2) to take those actions, with the cooperation of the obligor if possible, necessary to preserve the status quo insofar as possible; (3) to communicate the essential facts to the indenture's security holders and, if indicated, to assist in organizing a committee to represent the security holders; and (4) to work with the security holders and their committee and to take action to enforce the indenture remedial provisions decided on by the trustee and the committee. Whenever possible, an effort was made to work out a compromise solution without resorting to the drastic indenture remedies.

This process was, of course, time-consuming. These indenture provisions were included to protect the trustee to enable it to delay pursuing the indenture remedies until it could consult with the security holders on its action.

Whereas this procedure was the one most frequently followed, sometimes the trustee initiated action without awaiting the direction of the security holders. It is possible, though by no means certain, that if this had been done more often, some of the consequences might have been less serious. In any event, the security holders were regarded as having an inherent right to decide for themselves whether their interests would be served best by compromise or by strict enforcement of the indenture remedies.

The trustee's position was made more difficult by the incorporation in all qualified indentures, and in most other indentures since 1940, of certain provisions required by the TIA. Although no specific course of action was prescribed, the act established a new standard for trustees after default. Section 315(c) required the inclusion in each qualified indenture executed before November 15, 1990, of a provision that the indenture trustee should exercise, *in case of default*, those rights and powers vested in it by the indenture and should use the same degree of care and skill in their exercise as a prudent man would exercise or use under similar circumstances in the conduct of his own affairs. The TIRA made this duty a legislatively mandated standard of care.

The "prudent man" standard was not a novel concept, as it existed in the law of numerous states as the fiduciary standard for executors, administrators, or inter-vivos trustees and under early judicial decisions.[5] Precedent is a significant factor in determining compliance in a particular case, and in relation to the various types of "personal" trusts, precedent is not too difficult to establish. Because of the generally high level of economic activity from 1950 to 1987, there were relatively few defaults under qualified indentures. As a result, the indenture act provisions were not fully tested and adjudicated. Even with the significant increase in the number of defaults during the past decade, there has not been a major acceleration in the development of legal principles related to the trustee's role in this area. Many of the "precedents" that still exist for the conduct of indenture trustees are those of pre-TIA days. These should not be relied on in the future, for it must be assumed that the primary reason for changing the rules was dissatisfaction with these precedents.

More important is the fact that the trustee still has only limited powers. It is axiomatic that the imposition of responsibility should be accompanied by the grant of sufficient power and authority to discharge it properly. Yet what occurred was the establishment of a new standard of conduct for the indenture trustees without any change in its limited authority. The prudent man in managing his own affairs can take *any* action that seems to be indicated by the circumstances, and the same is generally true for the classes of fiduciaries to which the rule has been applied in the past. As applied to indenture trustees, the trustee is limited to exercising the rights and powers vested in it by the indenture. The review of the customary remedial provisions earlier in this chapter shows that they contemplate action to be taken only for the most serious type of default. What course of action should the trustee follow when prudence dictates remedies or procedures not included in the rights and powers vested in it by the indenture?

This question will arise many times, and so for illustration, let us consider two possible "defaults." The first is the default in a covenant to maintain working capital in a specified amount. The obligor's financial condition remains basically sound, but because of circumstances beyond its control, its working capital falls below the minimum required. No judicial action can remedy the situation. What should the trustee do?

---

5 See Sturges v. Knapp, 31 Vt 1 (1858); Harvard College v. Amory, Pick. 446, 461 (Mass. 1931).

The second situation involves a sinking-fund default. Owing to depressed business conditions, the obligor is unable to meet its large principal payments. It appears, however, that rearranging the maturity schedule by deferring a portion of the current installments will resolve the difficulty. Can the trustee properly cooperate in securing the necessary adjustment, especially when it may require a substantial period of time to secure the requisite consents?

The answer to these and other questions must await future court decisions. In the meantime, indenture trustees should consider the following possibilities:

1. Because the limitation of liability to the performance of duties specified in the indenture is, by the terms of the indenture, related to predefault activities, the courts may very well find implied discretionary powers to perform acts or take action not specifically embraced in the indenture language.
2. Despite this possibility, the trustee should take great care in any action taken for which express authority is not given in the indenture, as the trustee may be subject to a stricter level of liability.
3. The trustee's right to rely conclusively on certificates or opinions conforming to indenture requirements is limited to certificates with respect to predefault activities.[6] After a default occurs, these certificates and opinions may not constitute adequate protection if an independent investigation would have disclosed a different facts or resulted in a different conclusion.
4. In appropriate situations, full advantage should be taken of the indenture provisions permitting amendment of the indenture with the consent of a requisite percentage of security holders. The two hypothetical cases cited earlier would be suitable situations for resorting to this provision. Because this would seem to be the prudent course, the trustee should be fully protected in cooperating with the obligor in presenting a proposal to the security holders and requesting their consent. Care must be taken to see that there is no material adverse change in the situation during the interim.
5. When the default is merely technical, seemingly temporary, or, in the trustee's judgment, is capable of being cured or resolved through negotiation or adjustment with the obligor, the trustee undoubtedly has sufficient authority to take the necessary action

[6]TIA sec. 315 (a) (2).

without consulting with the security holders or without resorting to the remedial sections. This authority is necessarily implicit in other provisions of the indenture.

6. When a serious default occurs, the trustee is obligated to take appropriate action. It is doubtful that the changes imposed by the TIA were intended to alter the basic concept of the trustee's responsibility. Accordingly, if the trustee acts reasonably and in a manner calculated to preserve the status quo until it has an opportunity to consult with the indenture security holders, this should normally be sufficient. The circumstances of each case, however, determine the degree of care and course of action that should be followed. Although the trustee is responsible for taking prompt and decisive action, no specific action can be prescribed for every situation, but each must be carefully considered at the time. It is unfortunate, but the trustee's action or lack of action is almost always judged in hindsight.

Notice of Default

One of the first problems with which the trustee is confronted is whether or not to notify the indenture security holders of the occurrence of a default. In qualified indentures, the trustee must promptly give security holders notice of all defaults known to it. This notice must be given within ninety days after the default occurs. Giving notice is mandatory with respect to any default in the payment of the principal of, or interest on, any security or in the payment of any sinking-fund or purchase-fund installment.[7] The trustee is protected in withholding notice of other defaults as long as its board of directors, executive committee, or trust committee determines in good faith that withholding notice is in the interest of the indenture security holders.

Before the TIA, under most indentures, the trustee had no express duty to notify the security holders of a default. Although a general notice was sometimes given, it was the exception rather than the rule. When action by security holders seemed indicated, the trustee frequently contacted institutional and other holders of substantial amounts of securities known to it and also consulted with any security holders who made inquiries. But a general notification of security holders was usually deferred until it was determined that organizing a committee was desirable,

---

[7] TIA sec. 315 (b). In practice, most trustees give holders notice of default within ten days of its occurrence or after the expiration of any applicable grace period.

and then notice was given by committee representatives rather than by the trustee. In other situations when some arrangement or adjustment appeared feasible, the trustee would work out an appropriate proposal with the obligor, which the obligor would then submit to the security holders.

The absence of a specific indenture requirement did not, however, always fully protect the trustee in withholding notice. In one case, an indenture contained a covenant that the obligor would not consolidate or merge with another corporation. With the knowledge of the trustee, the obligor merged into another corporation, and the trustee continued to pay interest. Subsequently, bankruptcy ensued. The court held that the trustee was guilty of gross negligence and bad faith in failing to give notice of the default, even though the indenture provided that the trustee need take no notice of a default unless notified by a specified percentage of the bondholders.[8]

Another court held that in a suit brought against it by bondholders, the trustee was responsible for explaining why it had permitted a default for several years without notifying the bondholders or protecting their interests.[9]

When the trustee uses its own funds to meet interest payments and thus prevents the bondholders from learning about the obligor's default, it may be liable for any resulting reduction in the security's value. It has also been held in such a situation that the trustee is not entitled to claim reimbursement for or to share pro rata with the bondholders a subsequent sale of the property. Similarly, it has been held that when engaged in marketing its securities, the controlling stockholder of the obligor uses its own money to pay coupons to prevent notice of default, these coupons are paid and not purchased and are not entitled to either priority to or equality against the obligor's assets.

As we noted, when the paying agent for the obligor's securities is other than the trustee, the paying agent must notify the trustee in case the obligor defaults on any installment of principal or interest when it falls due.

Most indentures provide that the trustee may, at its sole discretion, advance monies to pay taxes, insurance, rentals under leases, or other items for preserving the trust estate. It is also provided that to secure such advances, the trustee is entitled to a lien on the trust estate before the lien of any securities issued under the indenture. This type of advance is, however, exclusively for preserving the trust estate or to prevent the creation of a prior lien on it. It should be distinguished from the type of advance

[8] Seelig et al. v. First National Bank of Chicago, 20 F. Supp. 61 (D.C.N.D. Ill. 1936).
[9] Boylston v. Senate Apartment Building Corporation, 11 N.E. 2d 636 (1937).

referred to earlier, which prevents security holders from learning of a serious default.

In the case of advances by the trustee to preserve the trust estate, the trustee is required under the TIA to give notice within ninety days of making an advance if the amount of advances remaining unpaid totals more than 10 percent of the principal amount of indenture securities outstanding.[10] The trustee must also include in an annual report to security holders a report of any advances made by it that remain unpaid on the date of the report if the unpaid advances total more than one-half of 1 percent of the principal amount of the indenture securities outstanding on that date.[11]

There is still some inconsistency in the TIA provisions in this regard. As noted, the report sections require notice of advances only when they aggregate certain specified minimum amounts. Section 311 appears, however, to protect the trustee's lien and right to prior repayment only with respect to advances that have been reported to the security holders, regardless of the amount. Except under special circumstances, it is unlikely that the trustee would make advances unless the obligor had defaulted. Notice of such s default would have to be reported unless it were withheld for the reasons permitted by the indenture. If these reasons are sufficient for withholding notice, the trustee should not be penalized by losing its lien or right to prior repayment. It is likely that the omission in section 311 is unintentional and that the trustee would be protected if it complied with the requirements for reporting outlined in other sections of the act. If such a situation arises, however, these provisions should receive the attention of the trustee and its counsel.

It is important that the trustee be given broad discretion in the matter of withholding notice of default and that it be protected in the exercise of this discretion. The security holders are entitled to prompt notice if their security or their investment is prejudiced, and the trustee should be prompt in notifying them of any serious default. As indicated, such notice is mandatory in the case of a default on the payment of principal or interest. The primary objective of all parties should, however, be to prevent a default or to remedy the situation. If this is possible, then too hasty action in publicizing the default can cause irreparable damage. The trustee should always have sufficient time to explore the possibility of curing a default or of working out some arrangement to prevent a serious loss to security holders.

[10] TIA sec. 313 (b) (2).
[11] TIA sec. 313 (a) (3).

The duty to act with care includes the responsibility for withholding, as well as giving, notice in appropriate situations. The trustee should consider that withholding notice of technical default may result in preventing the holders from exercising their rights (e.g., declaring an Event of Default), and therefore it may be held accountable for any resultant loss. In a doubtful or borderline case, notice should be given. All facts should be investigated promptly and weighed carefully. Whatever the conclusion of the administrative officer, it is recommended that the final decision in each case be made, with the advice of counsel, by the trust committee or, if there is none, by the executive committee or board of directors of the trustee.

The Trustee and the Indenture's Remedial Provisions

Even though under modern practice, with certain special exceptions, recourse is seldom made to the remedial provisions specified in the indenture, we will describe briefly the general principles applicable to their use.

1. Trustee's discretion regarding remedy. Subject to the right of a majority in principal amount of the indenture security holders to direct the time, method, and place of conducting any proceeding for any remedy available to the trustee—which exists under most indentures—the trustee has broad discretion with respect to the particular remedy to be pursued. As long as it acts in good faith and not in a wholly unreasonable and arbitrary manner, a court should not interfere with the trustee's exercise of discretion. This is true even though the trustee may have a conflicting interest. Likewise, the trustee will not be held liable for any error of judgment made in good faith by a responsible officer unless it can be shown that the trustee was negligent in ascertaining the pertinent facts.[12]

Although the trustee's powers are strictly limited by the indenture, a court may find implied powers or responsibilities or, in a particular situation, may authorize the trustee to perform acts it would otherwise have no power to perform. Thus, in a case in which depressed economic conditions made it impossible for the obligor to perform a covenant in an indenture secured by real estate securities relating to the maintenance of certain value ratios, and in which the only alternative was foreclosure,

---

[12]TIA sec. 315 (d) (2). The act does not define "responsible officer." However, the Model Provisions (see chapter 2, note 13, *supra*) define the term to include senior officers and designated junior officers of the trustee and any other officer of the trustee customarily performing functions similar to those performed by the two designated officers, and with respect to any particular corporate trust matter, any other officer to whom such matter is referred because of his or her knowledge or any familiarity with the particular subject.

the trustee was permitted to enter into a working agreement with the obligor, allowing the latter to retain possession.[13] In another case in which the security consisted of various collateral, the court held that it had the power to authorize the trustee to secure a loan on the collateral and make a distribution to the security holders rather than dispose of it at a forced sale.[14]

In pursuing a course of action not specifically authorized or permitted by the indenture, however, the trustee should obtain an outside legal opinion or expert opinion and, in appropriate cases, the authority of a court or the permission of a majority in principal amount of the security holders. If the trustee tries to act on its own without authority, even though in good faith and in an honest effort to preserve the security for the bondholders, it may be liable for any loss resulting from its action.

2. Rights incident to other remedies. The first two remedies enumerated are included primarily to enable the more adequate enforcement of other remedies.

The first of these is the right to accelerate the maturity of the indenture securities. This right is given to the trustee alone and, frequently, to a specified percentage of the indenture security holders acting without the trustee's concurrence. The purpose of the provision is to enable conversion of the obligor's obligation into a matured debt so that foreclosure or other proceedings may be undertaken to the same extent as if there had been a principal default. If the indenture does not contain such a provision, the trustee may not be able to foreclose in the event of a default in interest, except to the extent of past due interest. This would necessitate successive actions until the principal debt matures. It is therefore important that every indenture contain an acceleration clause.

Another provision in all qualified indentures is giving the trustee the right to recover judgment in its own name in the event of a default in the payment of principal or interest. Inasmuch as the trustee's duties relate primarily to enforcing the security, and the security holders themselves own the debt, a serious question arose about the extent of the trustee's rights in the absence of this power. Some courts have held that on foreclosure, the trustee could not recover a deficiency judgment in the absence of such a provision.

3. Rights of entry, sale, and foreclosure. Some of the powers given to the trustee in the case of default are seldom exercised. One of these is

---

[13] N.J. National Bank & Trust Co. v. Lincoln Mortgage & Title Guaranty Company et al., 105 N.J. Eq. 557, 148 Atl. 713 (1930).

[14] Seigle et al. v. First National Company et al., 338 Mo. 417, 90 S.W. 2d 776 (1936).

the right of entry and possession until the default is cured. The theory underlying the right is preventing mismanagement of the property and diverting the rents and profits from it to purposes other than paying interest and principal on the indenture securities. The theory is that the trustee should be able to take possession, receive the rents and profits until all defaults are cured, and then return the property in good condition to the mortgagor. Although such a procedure might be feasible in the case of a real estate mortgage, it is not practicable in the case of the usual industrial or utility mortgage whose management is highly specialized. When a trustee is in possession according to such a provision, however, it has all the rights of a mortgagee-in-possession and is accountable to the mortgagor only after all payments required by the indenture have been made to the bondholders.

Another remedy seldom pursued any longer is that of sale without judicial proceedings. It is usually impossible for an outright sale of property to an independent purchaser, and the sale of the properties is therefore only incidental to some form of reorganization proceedings and actually is unnecessary under existing provisions of the bankruptcy statutes. This power has been used in particular situations, such as under a railroad equipment trust agreement. It may also be of value when the trustee holds marketable collateral securities. Except for such situations, however, the power of sale is not an effective usable remedy.

One of the important rights on default, which is incidental to the concept of the indenture as a mortgage, is the right of foreclosure. Before enactment of sections 77 and 77B of the old Bankruptcy Act, this was the most important remedy available and was used frequently for an effective reorganization. For this reason, the courts customarily found sufficient power invested in the trustee to initiate foreclosure proceedings, even when the indenture provisions were not clear or seemed to qualify the right. For example, when the only provision was an authorization for the trustee to foreclose on the request of a specified percentage in principal amount of bondholders, it was held to have the right to do so on its own initiative.

Incidental to foreclosure proceedings or other remedies, an application should be made to appoint a custodian for the benefit of the indenture trustee and the security holders. This is important to those provisions relating to the assignment of rents and profits. The usual indenture is so drafted that the indenture trustee has no right to rents or profits until it takes possession. It has been held that a provision stating that an Event of Default would act as an automatic assignment of rents and profits is valid and enforceable. In any case, however, it is desirable to apply for the appointment of a custodian and for the segregation of rents and profits for the benefit of the trustee and bondholders.

One of the problems that arose in connection with foreclosure proceedings was the trustee's right to bid on the property. When this power was not granted, the trustee's rights have been held to be limited to taking steps that would lead to a cash distribution to the bondholders and, therefore, not a right to purchase the property. Other courts have held that this power could be implied or, if not expressly given, could be authorized by the court. Unless expressly required by the indenture, the trustee cannot be compelled to bid on the property. But when the trustee does bid on the property, it has an implied power to resell it for the best price obtainable.

ENVIRONMENTAL LIABILITY

During the past several years, concerns have been raised over an indenture trustee's potential liability in dealing with possibly contaminated property. The basis of these concerns was the possible applicability of the Comprehensive Environmental Response, Compensation, and Liability Act of 1980 (CERCLA) to security issues that are secured by property on which there may be hazardous waste.[15] The law provided that a current owner or operator could be held liable whether or not it had caused the contamination.[16]

The courts have occasionally extended the liability to those who lent money on the property where it was found that the lender could control the operation that caused the contamination[17] or when the lender foreclosed, thus becoming the "owner."[18] Although the U.S. Environmental Protection Agency (EPA) sought to limit this liability, inconsistent federal policy, state policy, and court decisions caused uncertainty by making it difficult for secured real estate lenders (and therefore the trustees of secured bond issues) to evaluate potential liabilities.

[15] 42 U.S.C. secs. 9601 et seq. (1980).

[16] See, for example, Resource Conservation and Recovery Act (RCRA), 42 U.S.C. secs. 6990 et seq.

[17] United States v. Fleet Factors Corp., 901 F. 2d 1550 (11th Cir. 1990), cert. denied, 498 U.S. 1046 (1991) (suggesting that a lender's mere power to affect or influence a borrower's operation might be sufficient to subject the lender to liability).

[18] See, for example, United States v. Maryland Bank & Trust Co., 732 F. Supp. 556 (W.D. PA. 1989).

This uncertainty for lenders and trustees was resolved by the enactment in September 1996 of the Lender and Fiduciary Liability Limitations Amendments.[19] These amendments, which expressly adopted the EPA's policy, protect real estate lenders and indenture trustees that act only to protect their security interest in the property.[20] This exculpation from liability applies as long as the ownership is held primarily to protect the security interest and the trustee does not participate in managing the facility.

In addition, the act provides that a trustee's liability for any environmental contamination is limited to the assets of the trust for which it is a fiduciary. No longer can a trustee be held personally liable for environmental contamination for simply serving in a such capacity. If however, the contamination is caused by or contributed to through the negligence of the trustee, its liability will not be limited to the trust's assets.

CERCLA still holds owners/operators who "participate in management" of the facility strictly liable for environmental contamination. However, the new act narrowly defines this participation as actual and active participation, not simply having the "capacity to influence." Simply holding an ownership/security interest, without "exercising decision making control over environmental compliance for the facility" or "exercising control at a level comparable to that of a manager of the facility," does not create personal liability.

Thus, trustees will not be liable if they (1) monitor or undertake one or more inspections of the property or (2) administer the provisions of an indenture/agreement covering a facility that was contaminated before the trustee relationship began, provided that they do not participate in managing the facility.

INHERENT DIFFICULTIES OF DEFAULT ADMINISTRATION

Having considered the various indenture provisions relating to default, we will now summarize the problems facing the trustee on default and the difficulty in dealing with them effectively.

Although it is essential to include indentures' broad remedial provisions, one of the unfortunate consequences is the false sense of security created in the minds of individual security holders. As we emphasized,

[19] Part of the Asset Conservation, Lender Liability and Deposit Insurance Protection Act of 1996 (42 U.S.C. 9607).

[20] The liability amendments apply to both RCRA and CERCLA.

the real security for security holders is the "going concern" value of the obligor and the income and profits realized from the operation of its business. The indenture covenants constitute a strong deterrent, and if the business is profitable, the obligor is mainly concerned with seeing that no default occurs, so that it may remain in the undisturbed possession and enjoyment of its properties. If the business becomes unprofitable, this "going concern" value, and hence the bondholders' real security, will be depleted. The obligor will be unable to meet its obligations, and the realizable value of the property—as distinguished from its value to the operation of the business for which it was intended—is usually insufficient to discharge these obligations. This is particularly true when the default occurs during a period of general economic recession or when the industry of which the obligor is a part is undergoing strain or depressed conditions. These are economic facts. They are the risks that each investor must personally evaluate, and no contract provisions can give the investor complete protection against them. This scenario is especially true for unsecured issues, whereas in a collateralized bond issue, the real security depends almost entirely on the value of the collateral itself, independent of the obligor as a "going concern."

A serious indenture default usually is accompanied by the obligor's general inability to meet its obligations or by insolvency. In such a situation, the obligor can protect itself against the strict enforcement of the indenture's remedial provisions by seeking protection under the Federal Bankruptcy Code.[21] This in fact is what usually occurs. The trustee is than enjoined by the court from instituting or continuing any proceedings to enforce the indenture provisions.

Of even greater significance than the rights, powers, and remedies available to the trustee are those it does not have, by either express limitation or the absence of a grant. The provisions customarily included that have become more or less standard are derived from traditional common law remedies developed for small, readily identifiable properties with inherent intrinsic values. They were not designed for large industrial properties devoted to corporate rather than individual use. They contemplate some form of liquidation and sale, which in most cases is undesirable and impractical.

Even if it were possible to enforce the remedial provisions according to the letter of the contract, this is seldom desirable, at least during the initial phases of most defaults. What is called for is some form of cooperative working arrangement to enable the obligor alone, or in conjunction with

[21] See note 3, *supra*.

its major creditors, to try to resolve its financial problems outside the bankruptcy laws. It is in this area that the trustee can act only in a conciliatory mode, since it is almost without power or authority to act independently. It is true that action can be taken with the support and consent of certain percentages in principal amount of the indenture security holders, but the delay necessarily involved, as well as the occasional harassment by individual or minority groups of holders, is unfortunate. As a result, the trustee must frequently walk a rather precarious path. As suggested earlier, further obstacles may have been created by the imposition of a stricter standard without a concurrent grant of broader authority.

Whether an indenture trustee should be given additional or broader powers is debatable. It has been argued that the default section should allow the trustee to take legal action even when no monetary or other default has occurred but when the very security of the bond issue may be impaired (e.g., when there is an effort to transfer assets to another entity before a principal payment or redemption). In such situations, the trustee should have the right to obtain judicial determination to prevent any such impairment of the rights or interests of the bondholders or the trustee under the indenture.[22] It is certain that the trustees themselves would resist this grant unless it included adequate provisions to protect them when exercising discretion, as well as assurance that their expenses and appropriate compensation would be paid. Most corporate trust organizations are not staffed to make the necessary studies and investigations and so in most cases must hire experts.

This grant of power would also mean delegating authority that traditionally has been reserved for the security holders themselves. Some authority for dealing with the situation during an interim period until the security holders can be organized would be desirable if accompanied by appropriate immunity, protective provisions, and compensation.

In general, the powers granted to the trustee relate solely to strictly enforcing the contractual rights under the indenture. To the extent that the obligor can be compelled, through judicial proceedings or otherwise, to perform its covenants and obligations under the indenture, or to the extent that a sale or foreclosure under the indenture is indicated and can be effected, the trustee has requisite authority.

Because the usual corporate indenture involves important and necessary operating properties, liquidation such as is contemplated by sale or

[22] See James Spiotto, *The Problems of Indenture Trustees and Bondholders*, Course Handbook Series No. 343 (1990) at 671.

foreclosure is seldom feasible. Security holders usually realize more through a reorganization or readjustment of the obligor's capital structure than through liquidation, even if the latter is permitted. Accordingly, when a major default occurs, the object of most proceedings is the reorganization of the obligor's financial structure.

Although the trustee's authority in these proceedings is usually sufficient to enable it to take all preliminary steps, there are strict limitations on its rights to represent the security holders. A reorganization generally is possible only if the security holders are willing to accept the reorganized obligor's other securities in satisfaction of their claims. This normally involves some compromise of claims.

The trustee has no power or authority to make such a compromise on behalf of the indenture security holders or to accept anything but cash in satisfaction of their claim. The trustee has no title to, or interest in, the debt secured, except to the extent that it may recover judgment against the obligor incidental to the enforcement of the security. The debt secured cannot be compromised or discharged except by judicial decree or, if specifically provided for in the indenture, with the consent of the security holders themselves.

Unusual circumstances may justify an exception to this general rule, however. In *United States v. Freeman*,[23] the court held that indenture trustees had the power and authority to consent to a compromise settlement binding on bondholders. The case involved a liquidation proceeding following a terminated unsuccessful effort to reorganize a railroad. One of the trustees' powers was the right to take possession, operate the properties, and pay taxes and other proper charges superior to the lien of the mortgage. Although the trustees were not in possession and had been specifically enjoined from enforcing indenture remedies, the court found that since the amount realized from the liquidation was less than the claims alleged to be prior to the indenture lien, the trustees had a right to enter into an agreement compromising all claims and that "this right of the trustees to assent on behalf of the bondholders was unquestioned."

In view of the limitations on the trustee's rights and powers, it is important to consider the rights and powers of the indenture security holders, both individually and collectively, which we will do in the next chapter before discussing the problems in bankruptcy and reorganization proceedings.

[23] D.C., S.D.N.Y. (1/25/60).

Rights of Security Holders

The main purpose of an indenture is to protect the holders of the securities issued under it. The covenants and remedial provisions are of no avail unless ample power of enforcing them is given. In the previous chapter, we considered the trustee's rights and duties to protect the security holders' interests. We noted, however, that these rights are not all-inclusive but are limited to those expressly granted in the indenture. Therefore, it is important to consider the rights that the security holders have under the indenture, the enforcement of these provisions, and the claims represented by the securities they hold.

These considerations present a difficult question, and one that still remains to be resolved fully and satisfactorily. It is important to remember a distinction already made. The obligation of the issuer or obligor to pay principal and interest on the individual securities runs directly to the security holders themselves and therefore is an obligation that may be enforced by the holders themselves. Indentures typically recognize that the ownership of the debt represented by the securities rests in each individual. As a result, no one should be permitted to amend, modify, prejudice, or deal with the debt without the express consent of its owner.

The difficulty arises when it is necessary to distinguish between the claim of an individual holder, which may be represented by only one of many thousands of obligations identical in terms, and claims under the indenture, which secures the entire debt represented by all obligations outstanding. From the viewpoint of the issuer, the obligor, and the trustee, the debt secured by the indenture is a single obligation and is dealt with as such.

The trustee's rights, duties, and responsibilities all relate to enforcing the security provisions of the indenture that secures this entire debt. Its rights to sue and recover judgment for the debt are part of this enforcement. Although the trustee has a duty to each individual holder, its primary responsibility is to the security holders as a class, and it cannot permit the claim of an individual holder to prejudice the rights of the holders as a group. In addition, even though the law is not settled in this regard, the trustee may have a duty to protect the interests of the minority holders if their rights are being prejudiced by the actions of the majority. For example, if the obligor enters into a side agreement with several large holders to "take out" their securities in exchange for their consent to make changes in certain covenants, the trustee must still ensure that these actions do not result in the unfair impairment of the minority holders' interests.

This discussion assumes that the duties and covenants that may be enforced only by the trustee are limited to indentures under which the securities issued are collateralized, but not to unsecured debt. In reality, all covenants under all indentures, secured and unsecured, are enforceable only by the trustee, except for (1) payment covenants or (2) when the holders have made a demand on the trustee and given it sixty days' notice and indemnity and the trustee has refused to enforce a remedial provision, also known as the *no-action clause*.

Also, during the life of a security issue, the obligor answers to the trustee with respect to its duties and obligations under the indenture. One of the advantages to an obligor of the indenture–trustee device is that it has only one entity to deal with for most problems that arise. Whereas most obligors try to provide any reasonable information requested by an individual holder, they cannot, for practical reasons, deal with many thousands of such holders individually.

A distinction should be made between the holders of obligations issued publicly and the holders who acquire obligations through a "private placement." In the latter case, besides executing an indenture with the trustee, the obligor often enters into a separate "purchase agreement" with each purchaser of a part of the debt. In these agreements, the purchasers usually require filing periodic financial and other information directly with them. These rights are, however, acquired under separate agreements with the obligor and not under the indenture. In such cases, these rights may also be "personal" in that they may not be transferred on sale of the obligations to a subsequent purchaser. These rights depend on the transfer/assignment provisions in the purchase agreement. Rule 144A securities are not easily transferred because of securities laws, so in such transactions, it's not the "rights" but, rather, the "securities" that cannot be easily transferred.[1]

Whereas in relation to enforcement, many of the rules that would apply to holders of a publicly sold issue would also apply to holders under private placement contracts, we will be concerned only with the former.

RIGHTS BEFORE DEFAULT

Information and Disclosure Provisions

Adequate protection of the investor's interest entails factors over and above enforcement and the indenture's remedial provisions. Under the securities laws, the investor generally is entitled to have complete information about the obligations offered for purchase. The investor is entitled to be kept reasonably informed of developments that may affect the investment so long as it is held. The investor is also entitled to have knowledge of his or her rights in the event that action is required to enforce the claim represented by the investment.

One purpose of the 33 Act was to require full disclosure of information about new securities being issued publicly. The act's provisions were expanded by the TIA, which requires "qualification of an indenture in connection with registrations of new securities." Summaries of the indenture's important provisions must be included in the registration statement. Pertinent financial and other information contained in this statement, including summaries of the indenture provisions, must be incorporated in the prospectus prepared in connection with the sale of the securities. Each purchaser must receive a copy of the prospectus so that the investor has available all information pertinent to making an intelligent decision.

The security itself refers to important sections of the indenture, particularly any that impose limitations on the rights of the holder. If further information is desired, the trustee will always make a copy of the indenture available for the holder's inspection or advise the holder about the contents of particular sections that are of concern.

Although not directly related to the individual security holder, the SEC's activities under the 34 Act, the 33 Act, and the 40 Act (which applies to special situations, not bonds generally) are designed to protect

---

[1] See the discussion of issuing private placements under SEC Rule 144A, p. 16, *supra*.

security holders generally. The rules and regulations of the Municipal Securities Rulemaking Board (MSRB), national securities exchanges, the National Association of Security Dealers, and other groups have the same purpose.

Secondary Market Disclosure

Much attention has centered on the lack of sufficient secondary market information for investors in municipal securities. This situation has become worse since 1986 when industrial revenue bonds, housing bonds, and nursing and hospital bond issues accounted for almost three-quarters of the total dollar amount of payment defaults of all municipal securities. Because municipal issues are excluded from the registration requirements of the 33 Act and the disclosure regulations promulgated by the SEC for corporate issues, the patterns of information dissemination and disclosure that have developed over the years by issuers, underwriters, and trustees have been neither uniform nor consistent. In fact, investors in municipal bonds were often unable to obtain any information.

Since the corporate trustee is an essential party to the ongoing administration of the bond issue and may have information that is material to the financing transaction, it has been at the center of ongoing discussions by participants in the securities industry. Efforts to broaden the trustee's burden of disclosure of information beyond that required by the indenture have put the trustee in a difficult position. Although it is universally accepted that the trustee owes a fiduciary duty to its bondholders subsequent to an Event of Default, including the disclosure of any relevant information in its possession, how extensive that duty is has not been settled, including the issue of what is relevant (other than the occurrence of a default or an Event of Default) or the timeliness of the disclosure. Traditionally, indentures have provided little guidance to trustees on what can or should be disclosed, other than what is required by the TIA. Trustees have been reluctant to provide information that could be of financial benefit to those receiving the information without providing the information to all holders alike, and they have been concerned about their potential liability for any disclosure.[2]

It is clearly the issuer (and in the case of a conduit financing, the ultimate obligor) that must have the primary responsibility for continuing

---

[2] With evolutionary changes taking place in the trustee's traditional role, legal "safe harbors" will need to be created to protect trustees from the risk and liability it was never intended they assume and for which the compensation they receive is grossly inadequate.

market disclosure. The issuer has the most direct access to such information and is in the best position to evaluate its accuracy and materiality. When, however, the trustee has material information whose disclosure to the bondholders would effectively put it into the public domain, the trustee can—without violating its duty to the bondholders—release that information also to the marketplace.

To assist participants in the securities industry and those needing to develop consistent and uniform guidelines for the ongoing disclosure of information, corporate trustees, acting through the corporate trust committee of the ABA, have worked with other legal and securities organizations to establish workable practices and procedures, including draft provisions that can be incorporated into bond indentures providing for the public disclosure of material information on a periodic or ongoing basis by the issuer or the trustee. In addition, these provisions can describe the trustee's obligation to give the issuer information uniquely in its possession, the means of distributing this information, the compensation to the trustee for the additional responsibilities, and the indemnification of the trustee by the issuer for making this disclosure at the issuer's direction.

On July 3, 1995, the Securities and Exchange Commission adopted amendments to Rule 15c2–12 under the 34 Act to deter fraud and manipulation in the municipal securities marketplace by prohibiting the underwriting and subsequent recommendation of securities for which adequate information is not available.

These amendments were adopted as a result of the municipal markets' inability to implement the voluntary disclosure process just described. Since the SEC has little oversight or jurisdiction over the issuers of municipal securities, it promulgated these amendments for broker dealer firms for which it does have regulatory oversight.

The amendments prohibit a broker, dealer, or municipal securities dealer from buying or selling municipal securities unless the participating underwriter has determined that an issuer of municipal securities or an obligated party (the obligor in a conduit financing or, in some cases, a credit enhancer or a party other than the named issuer responsible for paying the debt) has agreed in a written agreement or contract for the benefit of the holders of such securities to provide certain annual financial information and event notices to certain information repositories and to prohibit a broker dealer or municipal securities dealer from recommending the purchase or sale of a municipal security unless it has procedures in place that provide reasonable assurance that it will promptly receive any event notices with respect to that security.

The rule is effective for issues distributed after July 3, 1996, and is not retroactive to any issue brought to the market before the enactment of the rule, which means that issues distributed before July 3, 1996, are not subject to either the financial disclosures or the event disclosures. However, it is presumed that once an issuer begins disseminating information about event disclosures and annual financial disclosures, the issuers will establish standards for disclosure for all issues, regardless of the issue date, and not just those required by the regulation.

The regulations list eleven specific event disclosures and the manner in which the event notices are to be disseminated. Even though these eleven events require a disclosure, they do not encompass all material events, and certain types of financings may require more or less disclosure. Issuers and their financial advisers must stay abreast of the transactions and judge whether the materiality of the events occurring in their financing transactions warrants an event disclosure.

These amendments may change some aspects of trustees' roles, and trustees must pay careful attention to their responsibility with regard to the disclosure process. Trustees may have to judge the materiality of an event and may be called on from time to time by issuers and obligated parties to participate in the determination process. Trustees should attempt to limit their role to that of a dissemination agent to transmit or send information to the market on behalf of the issuers unless the governing financing documents specify the events that require disclosure and they are events that the trustee can determine without independent judgment.

There will always be debate on the delineation of responsibility for disclosure, and the trustee will always be part of that debate. There will be debate also on the merits of disclosing. From a trustee's perspective, for more than sixty years, the corporate finance industry has adhered to the concept of event disclosure. Even though this concept is in its infancy with regard to the municipal finance industry, the more information that is made available to the marketplace, the more informed the investors will be, and the less likely they will be to blame the trustee for their unwise investment.

When information cannot be reported in the context of the indenture itself, as in the case of existing municipal bond issues, it is possible for the issuer (and in the case of a conduit financing, the ultimate obligor) to enter into a separate agency contract, according to which the trustee acts as an "information-reporting agent" for the issuer. Such an agency arrangement must be subordinated to the trustee's obligation to the bondholders. For example, information disclosed to the secondary market should not be more complete than or different from that given to the bondholders, nor should it be given to the marketplace before being released to the bondholders.

Reports of the Obligor and the Trustee

Each obligor with a security listed on any national securities exchange is required to file periodic financial statements and other reports with the SEC, with each exchange on which any securities are listed, and with the trustees under any indentures of the obligor. All these reports are public information and are available for inspection by any security holder.[3]

Each qualified indenture is also deemed to contain a provision requiring the obligor to transmit to the indenture's security holders summaries of such reports and other information as the SEC may prescribe by rules and regulations. No such rules or regulations have been issued; therefore, this provision is currently inoperative. Many companies, however, send copies of the annual reports for their stockholders to known holders of their debt securities. It is likely that almost every obligor would send a copy of the annual report at a bondholder's request.

Section 313 of the TIA requires the trustee to send an "annual" report to security holders under indentures qualified under the TIA if there has occurred within the previous twelve months (1) any change in the trustee's continued eligibility and qualification; (2) the creation of or any material change to one of the postdefault "conflict of interest" relationships defined in section 310(b)(1) through (10); (3) the character and amount of any advances made by it, as indenture trustee, that remain unpaid on the date of the report and for reimbursement of which it claims, or may claim, a lien or charge before that of the indenture securities, on the trust estate, or on property or funds held or collected by it if those advances not yet paid total more than one-half of 1 percent of the principal amount of the indenture securities outstanding; (4) any change to any indebtedness owed to the trustee in its individual capacity and the security, if any;[4] (5) any change to the property and funds physically in the indenture trustee's possession; (6) any release, or release and substitution, of property under the indenture, and the consideration received not previously reported; (7) any

---

[3] Arguing that bondholders do not receive sufficient information, a learned commentator suggested that such holders should have the same right to receive information and reports as do shareholders of a publicly traded company. Morey W. McDaniel, "Disclosure for Corporate Debt Securities, S & P Corporation," 16 *Rev. of Sec. Reg.* 907 (May 4, 1983).

[4] A drafting error in the TIRA added the words "any change to" to subparagraph (6) rather than (4). The SEC has advised trustees to prepare their reports consistent with congressional intent, as indicated here. SEC Release 33–6892 (May 8, 1991).

additional issue of indenture securities not previously reported; and (8) any other action taken by the trustee in performing its duties under the indenture that, in its opinion, materially affects the indenture securities or the trust estate.[5]

We have already discussed the notices the trustee must give of the occurrence of defaults or events of default under the indenture. Clause (8) of the "annual" report may omit, however, notice of a default being withheld according to appropriate indenture provisions for the reasons previously discussed.

In addition to the "annual" report, the trustee must also submit special interim reports of important transactions.[6] Besides reports of default, these include the following:

1. A brief report of the release, or release and substitution, of any property subject to the lien of the indenture, and the consideration, if any, if the fair value of such property is 10 percent or more of the principal amount of indenture securities outstanding on the date of the release. This report must be transmitted to security holders within ninety days after executing and delivering the release.
2. A report on the character and amount of any advances made by the trustee, for which it claims or may claim a lien on the trust estate before that of the indenture security holders if the amount of all advances remaining unpaid is more than 10 percent of the principal amount of indenture securities outstanding. This report must also be transmitted within ninety days.

Bondholder Lists

Under the TIA, the corporate obligor is required to furnish to the trustee, at intervals of not more than six months, all information coming into its possession, or that of its paying agents, about the names and addresses of security holders.[7] The trustee is also required to retain any information furnished to it or that it receives in its capacity as paying agent. The indenture usually provides that the trustee will preserve this information until it receives and prepares a new list (which typically is done in connection with the payment of the next maturing interest installment) and

---

[5] See TIA sec. 313(a). In our opinion, a similar report, as appropriate, should also be sent annually to holders of securities under non-TIA-qualified indentures, including municipal revenue bond issues (and particularly industrial development bonds).

[6] TIA sec. 313(b).

[7] Id. sec. 312.

that the trustee may then destroy the previous list. The purpose is to keep the information as current as possible.

In the case of debt obligations outstanding in bearer form, the only way that current information can be obtained about the names of the holders is from the collection of semiannual interest coupons. Under current law (i.e., effective January 1, 1984), presentors of corporate bearer coupons must indicate in their transmittal their name, address, and taxpayer identification number.[8]

When the issuer or the trustee wants to communicate with holders of bearer tax-exempt securities about a specific matter, such as an amendment to the indenture or other special matter, a procedure was developed by which substantial information could be obtained in connection with the collection of interest coupons, through a memorandum certificate of ownership. If notified at least thirty days before an interest payment date, the paying agent can prepare and deliver to the collecting agents a supply of these certificates with the request that they be completed and submitted along with the interest coupons. This provides a fairly complete list of holders as of the particular date.

A major drawback to this method of obtaining information is that it can be done only when interest is being paid. Once a default in interest occurs, no further coupons are presented, and the trustee should consider publishing a notice requesting the owners of the defaulted issue to send the trustee their names and addresses.

The most accurate list of holders is that obtained from the registration records. Whether the security is fully registered or registered as to principal only, the holder is assured of receiving all reports the trustee submits to the security holders. Of more practical importance, the holder is promptly notified of any redemption call that affects his or her holdings.

When the holder of an old corporate bearer instrument does not wish to have the security registered, an alternative is possible. The holder may advise the trustee of such holdings and request that his or her name be placed on file as the holder of particular securities. The trustee is required under the TIA to maintain the name on file for a period of two years.[9] In acknowledging such a request, the trustee should call attention to the two-year limitation and suggest filing a renewal request on or before a particular date.

Although the trustee is required only to mail copies of reports to the holders on this special list, most trustees treat it in the same manner as

[8] Interest and Dividend Tax Compliance Act of 1983, Pub. L.98–67, 97 Stat. 369, secs. 104, 105, and 108.

[9] TIA sec. 313(c)(2).

lists of registered holders. This is good practice, and copies of all redemption notices or other material of special interest to security holders should be sent to all holders on the two-year list maintained by the trustee.

The trustee's annual reports and notices of defaults or events of default must be submitted to all known holders of indenture securities, including the list obtained from the obligor, the list maintained by the obligor as the paying agent, the list of registered holders, and the special two-year list. Interim reports on releases or advances by the trustee are required to be submitted only to registered holders and holders on the special two-year list. As a practical matter, however, the interim reports are usually submitted to all holders, regardless of the source from which information was derived.

Under current practice, the largest (and sometimes the only) registered holder is DTC, through its nominee, Cede & Co. Information dissemination is complicated, as DTC keeps only the names of its participants, that is, the banks and brokers that hold the particular securities issue. It is therefore incumbent on the brokers and custodians to give to the beneficial holders any information they receive from the trustee.

Access to Confidential Information

Information about names and addresses of security holders is important to the obligor and to the trustee, and occasionally it may also be important to the security holders. Whereas this is particularly true in the event of a default or a threatened default, it may also be important to other proposed transactions. For example, certain holders may oppose a proposed amendment to the indenture and want to organize other holders who oppose it. When they feel that their rights may be prejudiced by any proposed action, they should be permitted to communicate their opposition and the reasons for it to other holders. This right is recognized by the requirement that under qualified indentures, three or more holders of the indenture securities may apply to the trustee and state their desire to communicate with other holders of indenture securities with respect to their rights under the indenture or under the securities.[10]

If such holders can establish by reasonable proof that they have been holders of indenture securities for six months or longer and can give the trustee a copy of the proxy or other communication that they propose to transmit, the trustee must give these applicants all the information in its possession about the names and addresses of security holders or must

[10]Id. sec. 312(b).

inform them about the approximate number of holders on the list maintained by it and the approximate cost of mailing the proxy or other communication that the applicants want to send. Upon the request of the security holders and the payment of the costs, the trustee is required to (1) offer the applicant access to the address data or (2) mail copies of the proxy or other information to all security holders known to it. If the trustee determines that mailing this information would not be in the best interests of the security holders, it must, within five days after receiving the proxy or other material, file with the SEC a copy of the material submitted and a written statement specifying the basis for its opinion that mailing the material would be contrary to the best interests of the security holders. The trustee then sends the applicant a copy of the statement sent to the SEC. The TIA provides for a hearing by the SEC and for a finding either sustaining or rejecting the trustee's contention. If rejected, the trustee must mail, reasonably promptly, copies of the material to all security holders known to it.

The trustee is protected with respect to the disclosure of information or the mailing of any material in accordance with the provisions of the statute or the order of the SEC.

Amendments to Indenture[11]

Often it is necessary to amend an indenture with a supplement. Most amendments can be made by agreement between the obligor and the trustee without reference to or approval of the security holders. The most common amendments of this kind are the following:

1. To create and provide the terms of additional series of securities authorized by the indenture to be issued.
2. To mortgage or pledge under the indenture specific property or additional property as security and to provide the terms and conditions on which the property may be handled by the trustee, consistent with other provisions of the indenture.
3. To modify, amend, or add to the provisions of the indenture in a manner permitting its qualification under the TIA.
4. To add to the obligor's covenants and agreements.

[11] When executing any supplemental indenture to an indenture entered into before November 15, 1990, the trustee must be exceedingly careful not to reaffirm the provisions of the original indenture now deemed included as the result of the TIRA. The unintended result could be to have a different (and higher) set of standards imposed on the trustee through a contractual agreement with the obligor. See also p. 87, *supra*.

5. To document the succession of another corporation to the obligor, and the assumption of the securities and the obligor's covenants and obligations by the successor corporation.
6. To cure any ambiguity or defective or inconsistent provision of the indenture as long as the rights of the security holders are not adversely affected.

Although these types of amendments do not hurt any substantive rights of security holders and so could be made without express authority in the indenture, it is desirable and good practice to include this authority in every new indenture, to prevent any objections to it being raised.

Sometimes it is necessary or desirable to make other changes in or amendments to the indenture or to eliminate specific provisions that may affect a substantive right of the security holders. In the absence of indenture authority, such changes cannot be made without the consent of all the security holders or of all holders whose rights may be affected.

It is therefore important to include in the indenture a section describing how such changes should be made and the authority required to do so. It is customary to permit these modifications with the consent of the holders of a majority or two-thirds of the principal amount of the securities outstanding, excluding any securities held by or for the account of any obligor. The indenture should explain in sufficient detail just how such consent is to be evidenced and the manner in which proof of security holdings is to be made.[12] Here again, it is best not to spell out such requirements in detail but, rather, to permit the trustee to make rules and regulations for these administrative matters.

Executed consents should be delivered to the trustee within a specified period or, alternatively, the indenture could be modified by a vote of the security holders at a formal meeting called for this purpose. In the latter event, provision should be made for voting by proxy. When the securities are outstanding in bearer form, notice of the proposed meeting should be published sufficiently in advance. In addition, whether or not required by the indenture—and except for registered holders, it is proper for technical reasons for the indenture not to so require—the trustee should mail copies of the notice to all security holders on the list it maintains.

Even though the obligor may be able to obtain the required consents without a formal meeting or approach to all security holders, it is good practice to publish or otherwise communicate to all holders a notice of the proposed amendment. This will apprise everyone interested of the

[12] See TIA sec. 316(c).

indicated change and give them an opportunity to express their opinion. The greatest communication problem is encountered when most of the issue is held in DTCs or street name, thereby making it more difficult to obtain the necessary consents.

When the trustee has received the required consents, it is then authorized to join in the proposed amendment.

Certain provisions should not be subject to change or amendment without the consent of all holders, or at least all of those who may be affected. Such matters include extending the time for paying the principal or interest on any securities; lowering the interest rate; modifying any sinking-fund or purchase requirements; changing any subordination provisions; altering the rights of holders of some securities without similar alteration of the rights of other holders; or reducing the percentage of the holders required to consent to any future amendment, to waive any default, or to waive compliance with any provision of the indenture.

Note that the trustee cannot be compelled to execute without its consent an amendment that changes its own rights, duties, and liabilities under the indenture.

Rights After Default

Limitations on the Rights of Individual Holders

Every indenture should contain limitations on the right of individual holders to take action to enforce the covenants provided in the indenture. One reason for appointing a trustee is to make it the "agent" for enforcing the security holders' rights as a class. To permit individual security holders to bring suit to enforce their individual securities as soon as a default occurs might prejudice the rights of the other security holders and subject the obligor to an unnecessary multiplicity of suits.

The usual provision is that no individual holder can institute a suit to enforce the covenants provided in the indenture, or unless after demand on the trustee by the holders of a specified percentage of the indenture securities and an offer of indemnity, the trustee refuses or neglects to take action. The percentage of security holders usually required to make such a demand is 25 percent, although this may vary.[13] Holders purchase their

---

[13] TIA sec. 316(b); Quirke v. San Francisco Railroad Company 277 F. 2d 705 (8th Cir. 1960); Friedman v. Chesapeake & O. Ry., 261 F. Supp. 728 (S.D.N.Y. 1966) *aff'd* 395 F.2d 663 (2nd Cir. 1968).

securities subject to the indenture's provisions, and such a provision restricting suits by individual holders has been enforced by the courts, even when it was established that it was impossible to secure the necessary percentage to make demands on the trustee. It has also been held that without showing compliance with the indenture's provisions, a bondholder cannot bring suit for the foreclosure of a mortgage or for an accounting of a breach of trust on the trustee's failure to foreclose; apply for the appointment of a receiver for the mortgaged property; accelerate the principal of the securities; or bring suit for the breach of a sinking-fund provision.

These restrictions on a holder's rights of action are strictly construed, however, and must be clearly stated in the bond or debenture itself. Accordingly, in one case in which the only reference to the indenture in the bond was the description and nature of the collateral security, it was held that the bondholder's right of individual action could not be defeated by a restrictive provision in the indenture. In an early case, a corporation had an issue of securities outstanding when all its property was taken over by another corporation for cash, debenture shares, and stock. The cash and debenture shares were used to reduce the corporation's liabilities, including the purchase and retirement of securities. When all liabilities except $1.3 million of securities had been paid and the corporation had $31 million of cash and debenture shares remaining, it proposed to distribute $26 million to its stockholders. A suit by the bondholders for an injunction was sustained, even though the corporation had $5 million left to apply to its securities and no demand had been made on the trustee. The court held that the bondholders had an inherent right to protect their securities.[14]

When the necessary percentage of holders has made a demand on the trustee and the latter has taken no action within the time required, the holders may bring suit themselves. If the indenture has been appropriately drafted and the trustee has instituted action for foreclosure or for enforcement of any of the other remedies, an individual holder cannot intervene in the proceedings as a matter of right.

Although the TIA neither requires nor prohibits restrictions on an individual holder's suits for enforcement, it includes a provision designed to prevent "strike suits" by individuals.[15] This provision authorizes any court, in its discretion, in any suit for the enforcement of any right or remedy under the indenture, or in any suit against the trustee for any action

[14] Hoyt, et al. v. E. I. du Pont de Nemours Powder Company et al., 88 N.J. Eq. 196, 102 Alt. 666 (1917. See also *In Re* Envirodyne 174 B.R. 986 (1994).

[15] But see TIA sec. 316(b), re bondholder suits for payment of principal and interest on the bonds.

taken or omitted by it as trustee, to require the filing by any party litigant of an undertaking to pay the cost of the suit. It also provides that the court may, in its discretion, assess reasonable costs, including reasonable attorneys' fees, against any party litigant in such a suit, having due regard for the merits and good faith of the claims or defenses made by the party litigant. The provision is not applicable to any suit instituted by a holder or holders of more than 10 percent of the indenture securities outstanding or to any suit by any holder for the principal of, or interest on, the security on or after the respective due dates stated on the security.[16]

Suit for Principal or Interest

Although provisions restraining suits by individual holders to enforce the indenture have been generally upheld, a different question is presented when the suit is for payment of the principal of, or interest on, the security.

It is clear that the indenture provision requiring demand on the trustee relates only to enforcing the remedies and does not restrain an individual's right to sue for the principal at the bond's maturity. Even when a substantial majority of the holders have consented to extending the maturity, a nonassenter may still bring suit at the regular maturity.

The TIA expressly recognizes the right of an individual holder to sue for principal or interest "on or after the respective due dates expressed in such indenture security."[17] Though rarely incorporated in indentures today, a provision is permitted authorizing the holders of not less than 75 percent in principal amount of the indenture securities outstanding (or if specified in the indenture, of any series of securities) to consent to postponing an interest payment for a period not exceeding three years from its due date.[18] This consent binds all holders. With this one exception, however, the right of any holder to receive payment of the principal of, or interest on, his or her security on and after the respective due dates stated in the security, or to bring suit to enforce the payment cannot be impaired without the holder's consent.[19]

The only qualification on this absolute right is that the indenture may state that the suit cannot be maintained if its institution or prosecution, or the entry of judgment, would result in the surrender, impairment, waiver, or loss of the indenture's lien on any property subject to the lien.

[16] Id. sec. 315(e).
[17] Id. sec. 316(b).
[18] Id. sec. 316(a)(2).
[19] Id. sec. 316(b).

Collective Action by Security Holders

1. Right to direct proceedings. The restrictions customarily placed on actions by individual holders do not apply to action by the security holders as a group, and a demand by a particular percentage can compel the trustee to take action or gives the holders themselves the right to do so.

Under every qualified indenture, the holders of a majority in principal amount of the indenture securities outstanding have the right to direct the time, method, and place of conducting any proceeding for any remedy available to the trustee or of exercising any trust or power conferred on the trustee under the indenture.[20]

Although this provision may be expressly excluded, it is a desirable one and, in most cases, should better protect the security holders' interests. It is customary and desirable from the trustee's perspective that a proviso be included permitting the trustee to refuse to follow directions that are unduly prejudicial to those bondholders not joining in any direction to it, that may be against the law, or that may involve the trustee in potential liability. The right given to a majority to control the trustee's action should help the trustee determine the proper remedy to pursue. Because after a default, the trustee is subject to the "prudent man" standard, to protect itself from potential liability the trustee might decide prematurely to accelerate the principal and/or institute a suit for foreclosure or file a petition under the Bankruptcy Code.[21] But these actions may, in fact, harm the holders' interests by, for instance, forcing the issuer or obligor to file for bankruptcy. In some cases, the trustee may be able to prevent liquidation or reorganization by refraining from exercising any rights or remedies under the indenture. Because the trustee is protected in acting or refraining from acting in accordance with the direction of a majority in principal amount of the security holders, cooperation by the holders may prevent hasty suits or help determine the proper remedy to pursue and the time and method for instituting suit, if that is appropriate.

2. Waiver of default. In addition to the right to direct the time, method, and place of conducting proceedings for enforcement, a majority in principal amount of the security holders have the right to waive any past default and its consequences under the indenture, other than a default in principal or interest. This waiver is binding on all holders.[22]

---

[20] Id. sec. 316(a)(1).

[21] See chapter 14, note 1, *infra*.

[22] TIA sec. 316(a)(1)(B). See also sec. 316(c) for provisions relating to record dates for soliciting consents.

This provision can be helpful in working out a readjustment plan to which a waiver of existing defaults is essential and for which the consent of all holders could not be obtained. Depending on the indenture, a waiver might also apply to past sinking-fund or purchase-fund installments, even though an extension of maturity, change in interest rate, or other prospective substantive changes in the indenture could not be made without the consent of the holders affected.

Any modification or amendment of the indenture can be made only with the consent of the percentage of the holders required by the indenture. As previously indicated, this would not include an extension of the principal's maturity, a reduction in interest, or a change in future sinking-fund requirements, which typically need the consent of all affected holders.

3. Removal of the trustee. Another remedy available to security holders, acting collectively, is removing the trustee. The indenture customarily provides that the trustee may be removed, and a new one substituted, by the action of a specified percentage—usually a majority in the principal amount of the security holders. When a new trustee is appointed by means of this action, the court will not disturb the discretion of the security holders and must recognize the new trustee.

Instances in which this remedy would be beneficial are the trustee's neglect or refusal to take remedial action or the existence of a conflicting interest that makes advisable the appointment of a successor.

This right may not always be an unmixed blessing, however. It may be possible for a group of holders to acquire a majority in principal amount of the securities in order to obtain control of the obligor in default and then use this control for purposes not related to protecting and enforcing their rights as security holders. The trustee, with the rights of the minority in mind, might refuse to accede to this group's demands for action. It could then be removed in accordance with the indenture and a new trustee appointed that would join in the majority's action. The right of removal by the requisite percentage of holders is absolute.

Problems arise if there is not an appropriate indenture provision, or if demand by the requisite percentage cannot be obtained. When a trustee refused to comply with a court order in a foreclosure proceeding, it was held that it could be removed at the suit of an individual bondholder. A trustee normally is not removed, however, if minority holders merely disagree with its policy. After a default, if the trustee is a general creditor, under the TIA it is deemed to have a conflict of interest and must resign unless it is a nonmonetary default and the SEC grants it a waiver.

4. Protective committees. As a practical matter, organizing the security holders to gain the consent or approval of a majority to direct or assist the trustee is not easy unless the securities are owned by a small number of holders with large investments in the securities. The main advantage in organizing a committee is their ability to obtain consents and permit some form of voluntary readjustment in those cases in which the default is not too serious and liquidation and reorganization can be avoided.

The delay means, however, that the trustee must determine for itself the initial steps that must be taken and then must take them.

The trustee represents all the security holders and must always be alert to the interests of the minority. Although it can help create a protective committee and cooperate with it, the trustee should maintain its independence at all times.

The trustee should not be a voting member of this committee, although it clearly should be aware of its proceedings and support its efforts and, if possible, work closely with the committee, but only to the extent that it does not conflict with the trustee's fiduciary responsibility to represent the entire class of security holders.

FOURTEEN

Bankruptcy and Reorganization

A corporation may become a debtor under the Bankruptcy Code[1] either voluntarily, by reason of its insolvency or an inability to pay its debts as they mature, or as the result of an involuntary bankruptcy petition filed by its creditors. Insolvency is not, however, a precondition for either a voluntary or an involuntary bankruptcy filing. Whenever an issuer files for bankruptcy protection, it triggers an Event of Default under most indentures. Before the Bankruptcy Code was enacted, filing a voluntary petition usually activated the indenture's remedial provisions and could result in the actual liquidation of the obligor's business and the sale of any properties mortgaged or pledged for the benefit of the security holders.

From the perspective of a secured creditor (e.g., a mortgage bond-holder) and a senior debenture holder, actual liquidation may represent the best opportunity to recover. But as a result of the diverse creditor and equity constituencies and the Bankruptcy Code's protective umbrella of the "automatic stay," an immediate liquidation upon a bankruptcy filing is not typical. In fact, it is evident that many courts interpret the underlying policy of Chapter 11 of the Bankruptcy Code to favor the debtor's rehabilitation even if this does not ensure maximum recovery by the creditors holding the senior debt.

Although the Chapter 11 process may not primarily benefit the security holders but, instead, the equity holders and despite the initial loss in security values that may accompany the commencement of a case in

---

[1] Pub. Law 95–598, 92 Stat. 2549 (1978), which codified and enacted Title 11 of the United States Code—Bankruptcy. Subsequent section numbers referred to are to Title 11.

bankruptcy, it is often in the interests of the security holders, as well as the debtor, that the issuer's capital structure be restructured and its business continued on a solvent and viable basis. The object of most Chapter 11 proceedings is a significant readjustment or reorganization of the obligor's affairs, brought about by extension, conversion, compromise, or, in some cases, expungement of the rights and claims of the indenture security holders and other creditors (or a combination of some or all of the foregoing actions). Often the equity interests are extinguished, and the security holders receive the equity of a solvent, restructured entity.

The obligor's debt may be restructured through either an out-of-court compromise between the obligor and its creditors or a judicial reorganization. In light of the expense of the Chapter 11 process, as well as its drain on the management's resources, every effort should be made to achieve a consensual workout without resorting to court proceedings. However, in some cases, even temporary relief may not be achievable without judicial intervention. Although a nonjudicial workout may be preferable, the indenture trustee usually does not have the authority to allow the debtor the necessary accommodations for any out-of-court voluntary adjustment without the holders' express consent. As indicated in the preceding chapter, most indentures do contain provisions permitting certain percentages of security holders to waive a past default or to amend certain indenture covenants. Permanent adjustments are usually difficult to accomplish unless the security holders are few and easily accessible. Therefore, when a permanent adjustment in the securities' terms is required, it is usually necessary to resort to some form of judicial proceeding. It may be possible, however, for the security holders to agree to accept new securities in exchange for the old without the intervention of a court proceeding. Much has been written on the various bankruptcy and reorganization statutes, and space will not permit a detailed discussion of this subject matter here. Most indenture administrative officers are at some time faced with the very serious problems in these proceedings and should therefore understand the applicable statutory provisions and the position of the indenture trustee in the proceedings.

THE BANKRUPTCY CODE

The U.S. Constitution specifically grants to Congress the right to enact bankruptcy legislation.[2] This power was exercised with the passage of the

[2] Art. I, sec. 8, cl. 4.

first National Bankruptcy Act in 1800, the Bankruptcy Act of 1898, the Bankruptcy Act of 1934, and the Bankruptcy Reform Act of 1978 (the Code) which became effective on October 1, 1979.[3]

The Code has seven chapters: (1) General Provisions; (3) Case Administration; (5) Creditors, the Debtor, and the Estate; (7) Liquidation; (9) Adjustment of Debts of a Municipality; (11) Reorganization; and (13) Adjustment of Debts of an Individual with Regular Income.

The filing of a petition under Chapters 7, 9, or 11 operates as an automatic stay, applicable to all parties in interest, of any action against the debtor.[4] The purpose of the stay is to promote the equality of distribution among competing creditors and, in Chapter 11 in particular, to give the debtor an opportunity to focus on its rehabilitation. The automatic stay bars the continuation or commencement of any action, judicial or administrative, against the debtor; the creation, perfection, or enforcement of a lien against the debtor; or any action to collect, assess, or recover a claim or set off a claim by a debt owed to the debtor. The stay continues until the case is closed or dismissed or a discharge is granted or denied, unless a creditor or any other party affected by the stay successfully petitions the court for termination or modification. After due notice and a hearing, the court may continue the stay or may modify or lift it to allow a lien or claim enforcement. In certain cases, the court may condition the stay's retention on the petitioning creditors' being given adequate protection of its interest during the pendency of the stay.[5]

Thus, the bankruptcy court becomes the pivotal point for resolving all issues and differences in determining whether any particular creditor may move to protect or improve its position.

Chapter 7 contains the basic provisions governing the collection, liquidation, and distribution of an estate in a liquidation case. It takes the place of the straight or "ordinary" bankruptcy under the former act. In such a case, a trustee is elected by the creditors to collect and reduce to

---

[3] Note 1, *supra*.

[4] 11 USC 362(a) and 922(a). Section 362(b) excepts certain actions from the stay, including acts to perfect an interest in the debtor's property to the extent that the bankruptcy trustee's rights and powers are subject to such perfection; the commencement or continuation of an action by a governmental unit to enforce its police or regulatory powers; and the setoff by certain financial market participants of mutual debt or claims arising in connection with certain financial market contracts. Section 1168 expressly provides an exception for "rolling stock," which affects railroad reorganizations.

[5] Id. sec. 362(d). See, however, section 362(f), which permits the court, without a hearing, to grant relief from the stay if "necessary to prevent irreparable damage to the interest of an entity in property."

money the debtor's property and to close up the estate as quickly as possible as is compatible with the creditors' best interests. If necessary, the trustee will examine proofs of claim and object to the allowance of any claim that is improper and will file a final accounting of the estate with the court.[6]

Chapter 9 gives municipalities[7] the sole right to institute a case. It has no provisions for the creditors of a municipality to institute an involuntary proceeding.[8] The municipality must, however, demonstrate that it is either insolvent or unable to meet its debts as they mature, that it is specifically authorized by state law to be a debtor, and that it desires to enter into a plan to adjust its debts. Under the Code, the municipality must show that it (1) has obtained agreement or, having negotiated in good faith, has not been able to gain agreement from those creditors who hold a majority of the amount of claims of each class that would be adversely affected; (2) is unable to negotiate with its creditors because negotiations are impractical; or (3) reasonably believes that a creditor may attempt to obtain a preference.[9] Notice must be given of (1) the commencement of a case, (2) the granting of an order for relief, and (3) any dismissal of a case. This notice must be "published once a week for three successive weeks in at least one newspaper of general circulation published in the (judicial) district in which the case is commenced and in such newspapers having general circulation among bond dealers and bondholders as the court designates."[10]

Chapter 9 was amended in 1988 to overcome certain structural problems in the public ownership of municipal facilities. A category of "special revenues" was defined that includes receipts derived from the ownership or operation of the municipality's projects or systems primarily used for transportation, utility, or other services; special excise taxes; incremental excise taxes; or other revenues derived from special functions of the debtor or specially levied taxes but excludes receipts from general property, sales, or income taxes levied for the debtor's general purposes. These special revenues are subject to a postpetition lien notwithstanding Section 552, which ordinarily defeats such liens. To ensure the continued operation of essential services, Section 928 provides that the lien on

---

[6] Id. secs. 702, 704.

[7] Id. sec. 101(29): defined as a "political subdivision or public agency or instrumentality of the state."

[8] Id. secs. 109(c), 901(a).

[9] Id. sec. 109(c)(5).

[10] Id. sec. 923; see also rule 2002, Rules of Bankruptcy Procedure.

special revenues is subordinate to the operating expenses required, for example, for electric-generating facilities. The amendments also insulate a bondholder's receipt of payments on its revenue bonds from the recapture provisions of Section 547 if such funds are received within ninety days of the filing of the municipality's Chapter 9 petition.

Chapter 11 is the sole reorganization chapter in the new Code available to nonmunicipal corporations. It forms a single system for the rehabilitation of a debtor and the adjustment of all claims against the debtor and its assets, secured and unsecured, as well as equity interests. In attempting to balance more equitably the competing rights of debt holders, secured and unsecured creditors, and holders of equity securities, it strives to make the reorganization process itself more expeditious, less expensive, and consistent with the realities of the competing interests. Subject to judicial extensions and reductions, Chapter 11 gives the debtor an exclusive opportunity to file a reorganization plan during the first 120 days after the court has ordered Chapter 11 relief. But if a Chapter 11 trustee is appointed, the debtor loses its exclusive right to file a plan. Any other party in interest, including an indenture trustee, may file a plan if (1) a Chapter 11 trustee has been appointed; (2) the debtor has not filed a plan within its period of exclusivity to file a plan; or (3) the debtor has not filed a plan that has been confirmed within the debtor's exclusive period to solicit votes on a plan, which is 180 days after the order for relief, unless modified by the court. After a notice and a hearing for good cause, courts often extend both the 120-day filing period and the 180-day solicitation period.

Once a reorganization plan has been completed, Section 1125 requires that a written disclosure statement, together with the plan or a summary of the plan, both as approved by the court after a notice and a hearing, be sent to all holders of the impaired claims or interests, in cases under Chapters 9 and 11. No acceptances (or rejections) of the plan may be solicited until the disclosure statement is distributed to each member of each impaired class. However, in rare instances, different disclosure statements may be sent to different classes, the test being whether the particular class has received adequate information of a kind and in sufficient detail that a hypothetical reasonable investor typical of that class can make an informed judgment about the plan.[11]

Although the statutory prerequisites to the confirmation of a plan are

---

[11] See rule 3017, Rules of Bankruptcy Procedure, for court considerations of disclosure statements.

detailed and complex, when satisfied, a plan can be confirmed if each class of creditors either has accepted the plan by the required percentages[12] or, if dissenting, the class of creditors will be treated at least as well under the plan as if the estate were liquidated under Chapter 7 or if secured creditors will receive value equal to interests in property securing their claims. In any event, no class of creditors or equity holders that is junior in right will receive any distribution by virtue of their prior claims or equity interests.[13] Although acceptance by a class of creditors requires a specified affirmative vote,[14] if a class is not impaired under the plan, it is deemed to have accepted the plan. Generally, if the proponent requests and if all other confirmation requirements are met except that all impaired classes have not accepted the plan, the court must confirm the plan.

Impairment is a new statutory concept, although it does have antecedents in Chapter XII of the old act. The Code deems a class of claims or interests to be impaired unless the plan treats the claim or interest in a manner that provides full and complete recovery, in cash, of the creditors' claims or interest; leaves unaltered the legal, equitable, and contractual rights of the holders of the claim or interest; or restores the full rights of interest in the debtor's property.[15] In effect, plan proponents may continue existing credit relationships unaffected and, by doing so, disenfranchise such creditors from voting on the plan. When a class does not accept a plan, it may be confirmed over the objection of a class of creditors if it provides a certain prescribed treatment for the nonaccepting classes. In particular, with respect to each nonaccepting impaired class, the plan may not discriminate unfairly and must be fair and equitable to each such class. In any event, at least one noninsider impaired class must accept the plan. This concept of confirmation over nonaccepting classes has been aptly dubbed *cramdown* and essentially satisfies the dissenters' claims in accordance with the absolute priority rule, which states that any nonaccepting class must be satisfied in full before any junior class can share under the plan. The prospect of cramdown and the desire of existing management to retain equity in the reorganized entity has an unmistakable bearing on the development of a consensus in producing a final plan of reorganization.

---

[12]The requisite majorities for acceptance by a class are at least two-thirds in amount and more than one-half in number of the allowed claims of such class that vote on the plan: sec. 1126(c).

[13]11 USC secs. 1126(c), 1129(a).

[14]Note 12, *supra*.

[15]Id. sec. 1129(a). See sec. 1124 for specific criteria to determine nonimpairment.

Some of the other significant provisions that directly relate to indenture trustees are (1) Section 364, which allows the debtor to incur unsecured debt in the ordinary course of business[16] as an administrative expense without a hearing; (2) Section 364, which also permits the debtor
under certain circumstances to obtain credit or debt secured by a senior
or an equal lien on property of the estate that is subject to an existing
lien;[17] (3) Section 503(b), which provides reasonable compensation to an
indenture trustee for services rendered in making a substantial contribution in a Chapter 9 and 11 case, including necessary expenses and reimbursement of its counsel's fees and expenses; (4) Section 547, which permits a debtor to avoid many transfers of property made to or for a
creditor of an antecedent debt within ninety days before the filing of a petition (the preference period is extended to one year if the creditor was an
"insider";[18] (5) Section 548, which permits the trustee in bankruptcy to
avoid fraudulent transfers by the debtor of an interest in its property if at
the time of the transfer, there was an intent to hinder, delay, or defraud
the entity to which the debtor was or became indebted or if the debtor received less than a reasonably equivalent value in exchange for the transfer and the debtor was or became insolvent at the time of, or as a result of,
the transfer; (6) Section 552, which appears to render after-acquired
property clauses in indentures automatically inoperative as of the date
that the bankruptcy case commences;[19] and (7) Section 1102(a)(i), which
directs the U.S. trustee to appoint a committee of unsecured creditors as
soon as practicable, to oversee the debtor and the reorganization process,
as distinguished from the court's involvement in the debtor's everyday
affairs.[20]

In Chapter 9 and 11 proceedings, the appointment of committee members, rather than their election, differs from the former Bankruptcy Act
and ensures that the committees are fairly representative and not solely
controlled by attorneys seeking committee counsel representations. If a

---

[16] A court allows this action only in extraordinary circumstances and only if the interests of
the original secured creditors are protected.

[17] Postpetition debtor-in-possession (or DIP) financing enables the debtor to stabilize its operations in the very early days after filing a petition for relief. A debtor may also obtain unsecured credit upon order of the court, even if not in the ordinary course of business. Id. sec.
364(b).

[18] Id. secs. 547, 548.

[19] The applicability of section 552, in the event of a municipality bankruptcy, has been curtailed by the addition of section 928(a).

[20] U.S. trustees generally are responsible for administering the cases and have a significant
amount of influence.

prepetition committee does not exist, the U.S. trustee is authorized to select a representative committee from among the largest creditors willing to serve. Even if it does exist, the U.S. trustee must appoint a committee, only rarely naming the preexisting committee as the official committee, with or without additions or changes.

Occasionally, multiple committees representing different classes of debt or equity may be necessary. The appointment of additional committees may not be automatic, however, but may require a conclusion by the court, upon application, that the particular committee requested is necessary to ensure adequate representation.[21] The importance of providing for "official" or "statutory" committees is that the expenses of the members, and the professional fees of those employed by such a committee—for example, attorneys, accountants, and financial advisers—are entitled to compensation from the estate based on the time, nature, and value of their services in relation to the cost of comparable services in a nonbankruptcy case. In practice, it is unusual and difficult to get such a special committee appointed. Usually a representative of debenture holders is appointed to the prepetition committee along with other representative creditors.

Chapter 11 does not require the appointment of a reorganization trustee but assumes the continuation of the debtor-in-possession. Any party in interest may, however, apply to the court for the appointment of a Chapter 11 trustee to operate the business. The request will be granted if the court finds that there are reasonable grounds for the appointment, which might include substantial evidence of fraud or mismanagement by the debtor or that the appointment is otherwise in the best interests of the creditors or stockholders.[22] As we noted, the appointment of a Chapter 11 trustee automatically deprives the debtor of the exclusive right to file a plan. If a trustee is not appointed (i.e., the debtor remains in possession and continues to operate the business), any party in interest may request the court to appoint an examiner, a request that will be granted if it is in the interests of the creditors or if the debtor's nontrade, nontax unsecured indebtedness exceeds $5 million.[23] The examiner's role is to investigate the debtor with respect to any adverse allegations, such as fraud or dishonesty, the debtor's financial condition, and any other matter relevant to the proceeding or formulation of a plan.

---

[21] 11 USC, sec. 1102(a)(2).
[22] Id. sec. 1104(a).
[23] Id. sec. 1104(b).

The Indenture Trustee and Security Holders in Reorganization Proceedings

The rights and functions of the indenture trustees in connection with the reorganization proceedings still have not been completely defined. Whereas indenture trustees are recognized as representing the indenture security holders, their rights of representation are strictly limited. In general, any matter relating to the security lien or priority of the indenture securities requires the indenture trustee's vigilance. But the indenture trustee has no power or authority to compromise the claims of the security holders, and so the extent to which it may properly participate in the formulation or advocacy of a plan that makes such a compromise is debatable. Nevertheless, without an actual bondholder on a creditors' committee, the public debt holder—apart from the trustee—often has no voice in the plan's development.

Notwithstanding the broad limitations imposed by the automatic stay on actions to enforce contractual rights and the prohibitions against rejecting a contract based solely on filing a bankruptcy petition, the filing of such a petition, voluntary or involuntary, is invariably an Event of Default under most, if not all, corporate bond indentures. Upon default, the trustee's standard of conduct with respect to its rights, duties, and obligations is raised to that of a "prudent man." Although not legally or contractually required to participate in statutory creditor committees, many corporate trustees of public debt do seek to serve on such committees.

The right of the indenture trustee to be heard on all matters arising during the proceedings is specifically recognized in Chapters 9 and 11. The indenture trustee may file a petition against a debtor, may intervene in any such proceeding as a matter of right, and is entitled to receive notice of all important matters arising during the proceedings.[24] These rights are recognized by the Code and are independent of the trustee's decision to participate as a member of a creditors' committee.

The specific provisions of the Code and the TIA with respect to the rights of the indenture trustee have not enlarged its authority to represent individual security holders. These provisions have recognized the importance of the indenture trustee as an agency representing the interests of security holders as a class during the proceedings, but the importance of representation by the security holders themselves has also been recognized and emphasized.

This emphasis on the individual holder has not, however, minimized

[24] Section 1109 and rule 2202(f), Rules of Bankruptcy Procedure.

the importance of collective action by security holders through committees. The right of any creditor to be represented in a Chapter 11 case by a committee is specifically recognized in Section 1102. Because of the complexity of a large corporate reorganization and the lack of information available to an individual holder, as well as the substantial expense involved, it is impractical for most individual holders to appear personally in the case. In addition to facilitating the conduct of the proceedings by having the various classes of creditors represented by committees rather than by a number of individuals, an objection will be more persuasive if it is entered collectively by a large number of a particular class. A committee will also be able, as a rule, to intervene in the proceedings, a privilege that offers a much greater opportunity for participation than does the general right of individual holders to be heard. If anything, the impact of collective action has been enhanced by requiring the acceptance of a plan by at least 50 percent in number and 66⅔ percent in amount of the creditors of any class as binding on the dissenters of that class. Therefore, a dissenting minority now has more at stake and should organize to protect itself. Since the activity of these committees is subject to court supervision, security holders should be better protected in being represented by a committee. However, although the committee "represents" holders, it does not have any rights that belong to the individual creditors.

GUIDANCE AND GUIDELINES

The following are a general guide to indenture trustee administration officers in reorganization proceedings. The circumstances of each case will vary, but these suggestions should apply in most situations:

1. Despite imposition of the prudent man standard of conduct and the understandable inclination of the indenture trustee to protect itself by court proceedings, the indenture trustee's petition for reorganization should be the last step to be taken. Experience has demonstrated that with few exceptions, such proceedings result in substantial delays and losses to indenture security holders. Every effort should be made to reach an out-of-court workout with the obligor and, to the extent possible, with a majority of the security holders. Interim arrangements should be made for the business operations to continue and the rights of the security holders to be protected. Filing a petition under the Code should be regarded as a last resort when no other means are available for protecting the inherent rights of the indenture security holders.

2. When a bankruptcy petition is filed by the debtor or other creditors, the indenture trustee should file an appearance promptly so that it will receive notice of all matters presented to the court, including the disclosure statement according to which the plan solicitation occurs. The trustee should also consider, with the advice of counsel, whether and to what extent it should send periodic information updates to the bondholders. In any event, the report should contain only information that is both factual and "public." The trustee may wish to have the bankruptcy court approve any information that it determines should be made available to bondholders.

3. The administration officer should make certain that every department of the bank is aware of the pending proceedings and is familiar with the general prohibitions against any dealing in securities represented in the bankruptcy case by the indenture trustee.

4. A critical duty of the indenture trustee is filing a proof of claim on behalf of all indenture security holders. The express authority to do so is included in most indentures, but the indenture trustee undoubtedly has implied authority even without such a provision.

5. According to Bankruptcy Rule 2019, in every Chapter 9 or 11 case, "every person . . . representing more than one creditor or equity security holder and, unless otherwise directed by the court, every indenture trustee shall file a verified statement with the clerk."[25]

   This statement must include the security holders' names and addresses, a description of the claims—including the time of acquisition and facts surrounding the employment of the indenture trustee—and a description of any claims or interests owned by the indenture trustee. The statement must be amended to reflect any changes in the relevant facts after the initial statement is filed. One of the sanctions for failing to comply is that the court may refuse to permit the indenture trustee to be heard or to intervene in the case. The Code has replaced the old Bankruptcy Act's

---

[25] Id. rule 2019. Filing the verified statement makes available to the Court and, consequently, to interested parties, the names of the debt holders. The requirement does not override the indenture requirements for obtaining bondholder lists prescribed by the TIA. Nevertheless, attempts to impound a list of creditors have been disallowed by the courts; see *In re* Itel Corp., 17 B.R. 942 (Bkrtcy. App., 9 Cir. 1982).

concept of "provability of claim" with that of an "allowed claim." This basically means that unless the debtor or a party-in-interest objects to it, the amount of the claim is allowed as filed. The trustee should keep in mind the problems created by an original issue discount, which is characterized as unmatured interest and is therefore disallowed under Section 502(b) of the Code.

6. When the indenture is a lien on the obligor's principal fixed properties and grants the trustee the right to income after a default, a motion should be filed promptly seeking the segregation of all income for the benefit of the indenture trustee and the security holders. This is important, for it may seriously affect either the rights of the security holders under the plan when it is presented or the right of the indenture trustee to object to the disposition of accumulated income during the proceeding. A motion for adequate protection and relief upon the stay should be filed promptly when appropriate.

7. Upon satisfying certain requirements, the Chapter 11 trustee or debtor-in-possession may apply for an order authorizing it to sell or dispose of specific items of property free and clear of the mortgage indenture and without seeking a release from the indenture trustee. The indenture trustee should insist that the order approving this petition contain a provision that the proceeds of any sale be held in escrow subject to the same liens and priorities as for the property disposed of and that these funds should be used only for distributions to the appropriate security holders or for acquisition of additional collateral. On the petition for approving individual sales under the general order, the indenture trustee should require evidence of a sufficient consideration of such sale.

8. Every petition filed in the proceedings should be examined carefully. A majority of these petitions deal with routine administrative matters and require no action or statement of position by the indenture trustee. If representing secured claims, the main objective should be to maintain the indenture's priority lien position on the debtor's property until a reorganization is completed. Any proposed action that seems to affect this position should be examined carefully, and if it appears likely to prejudice the position, it should be opposed vigorously.

9. The indenture trustee's primary responsibility is the maintenance and preservation of the bondholders' legal rights and

distribution priority. The trustee should initiate any action that seems appropriate or necessary to protect these rights. In particular, it should try to prevent the diversion of the proceeds of sale or liquidation of any of its securities to purposes not directly benefiting the security holders. When the indenture is unsecured, it is important that the indenture trustee be certain that the estate is not dissipated or, if it is, that as much of it that can be recovered is recovered.

10. Any application by the reorganization trustee for authority to incur debt or to issue certificates of indebtedness should be examined carefully. These obligations constitute a claim with priority over any prebankruptcy obligations. If a substantial amount of postpetition indebtedness is created, the security holders' position in the reorganized company may be compromised.

11. In the case of multiple lien positions, it may be necessary for the Chapter 11 trustee to prepare segregation formulas to allocate earnings and expenses to the various segments of the business subject to different lien priorities. Any new securities issued on reorganization must bear a direct relationship to prospective earnings, and indeed, the development of proper formulas for allocating these earnings is frequently one of the most important activities during the entire proceeding. Accordingly, the indenture trustee should participate actively in all relevant discussions and hearings. This is a matter for experts, and the indenture trustee should obtain expert assistance to support its case.

12. Whereas the committees directly representing the security holders' interests are usually very important, for the aforementioned reasons, the indenture trustee should not organize a committee or take an active role in their organization unless, on the advice of counsel, this is necessary or desirable under the particular circumstances.[26]

13. If the indenture trustee has lists of security holders, these should be delivered to the reorganization trustee or filed in court, and individuals attempting to form committees should have access to lists on file with the court. The trustee should

[26]For case law on the problem of the indenture trustee's being on a creditors' committee, see *Wood v. City National Bank & Trust Co.*, 312 US 262 (1941). Courts have also recognized that an indenture trustee may serve on a committee in a voting capacity; see *In re* The Charter Company, 42 B.R. 251 (Bkrtcy, MD Fla. 1984).

not make this information available directly except with the court's approval.

14. Once a committee has been organized and has intervened in the case, the indenture trustee should try to work closely with the committee on all matters relating to the protection of the security holders as a class. If the class does not include different levels of debt, the interests of the indenture trustee and the committee usually are identical. The interests of the unrepresented security holders are usually the same as those represented by the committee, for all will now participate to the same extent and in the same manner under the plan as finally approved. Normally, therefore, no position adverse to the committee is necessary for protection of the minority. The indenture trustee should always bear in mind, however, that it represents *all* the security holders. Each member of the creditors' committee has a duty to all members of the class, and therefore an indenture trustee serving as a voting member of a committee has a conflict of interest that it must address. While cooperating with a committee in every way possible (including serving as a member of the committee), the indenture trustee should never surrender its position of independence or prejudice its right to take a contrary stand. This is particularly true when the principal creditors serving on a committee are interested in issues other than the indenture securities. The indenture trustee must be mindful also of the potential conflicting interests between the professional bargain hunters who acquire the securities at severely reduced prices and those investors who were prebankruptcy debt holders.

15. The indenture trustee should take an active interest in all matters relating to the preparation and adoption of a plan, including a careful review of the disclosure statement. Appropriate objections should be made if the indenture trustee believes the statement is inaccurate, incomplete, or inadequate for the class of creditors it represents. Many trustees, conscious of their lack of authority to compromise the claims of security holders, believe that negotiations on a plan are a matter for the security holders and their committees and that the indenture trustee should play a passive role. This attitude is shortsighted and unrealistic. It is true that indenture trustees cannot make a commitment binding on their security holders, nor can anyone else.

This is a matter for individual holders, who must be given the right to express by vote their approval or disapproval once a plan is disseminated for acceptance. The indenture trustee has no right to vote on a plan but should participate freely to the same extent as other parties do, including committees, in all discussions leading to agreement on a plan. The trustee's participation in plan negotiations does not foreclose its right to object to confirming a plan that it believes is unfair or inequitable or that the security holders have rejected. Under normal circumstances, the indenture trustee should not itself try to prepare and file a plan. The only authority for it to do so is contained in Section 1121 of Chapter 11 when a Chapter 11 trustee is appointed or when the debtor does not file a plan and obtain acceptances within the specified time limits.

16. The indenture trustee should insist that the court's final order directing and providing for the plan's implementation contain a specific discharge of the indenture and the trustee's duties. If the plan contains these provisions, the canceled indenture securities may be properly disposed of by the distribution or exchange agent appointed by the court without being returned to the indenture trustee for cancellation and discharge. Unless this is done, the indenture trustee may find itself called on to do a great deal of detailed work for which it may be unable to obtain fees and expenses unless the court has approved them as an administrative cost.

17. The Code specifically authorizes the court, in directing the implementation of a plan under Chapters 9 and 11, to set a period of time during which all claimants must present their securities or claims for exchange. At the expiration of this period, the estate is closed, and all claims for unexchanged securities become void. Any property left in the hands of the exchange agent reverts to the debtor or to the entity acquiring the debtor's assets under the plan.[27] This is an important provision and is usually contained in all final orders of the reorganization proceedings. Failing to so provide may mean that an estate may never be technically closed.

18. When a debtor has been through a previous reorganization without providing for the final termination of an estate, a current

[27] 11 USC sec. 347(b).

bankruptcy case is an opportunity to secure an appropriate order and dispose of remaining property that may be held for exchange for old securities still outstanding from the previous reorganization. At the time the final order is entered in the current case, the court's authority should be secured for terminating any matters remaining in all previous proceedings.

19. In a Chapter 7 bankruptcy (liquidation), rather than a Chapter 11 reorganization, a court order establishing a limited period within which claimants must present their securities to receive their distributive share of the proceeds should also be obtained. Because there is no reorganized company in this situation to receive the balance of the proceeds, a procedure that has been used successfully is to provide for a second pro-rata distribution among those claimants that received the initial distribution. This enables the indenture trustee to close the estate within a reasonable period of time and is the most equitable disposition of the remaining funds. It is necessary, however, that such a method of distribution be incorporated in the initial order for distribution. In one case when this was attempted by a subsequent order, a state successfully intervened and claimed a vested interest in the remaining funds under an abandoned property law. When the initial order contains a provision for the complete distribution of all proceeds, no such rights can vest in the state.

COMPENSATION AND RECOVERY OF EXPENSES

Almost every indenture contains provisions giving the indenture trustee a contractual right to seek payment of its fees and recovery of its expenses from the obligor. Even when the obligor is in bankruptcy, there has been express recognition of this contractual entitlement.[28] Thus, the trustee should always file a proof of claim for its prepetition fees and expenses and also for any contractually based fees and expenses incurred after the petition. When settled, such a claim would receive consideration at the same level as that of any other unsecured creditor. However, given the uncertainties of a recovery, the trustee should also pursue a claim under

---

[28] *In re* Flight Transportation Corporation Securities Litigation, 874 F.2d 576, 583 (8th Cir. 1989); *In re* Revere Copper & Brass Incorporated et al., 60 B.R. 892 (S.D.N.Y. 1986).

Section 503 of the Bankruptcy Code, which allows a court to reimburse the indenture trustee for the actual and necessary expenses incurred in making a substantial contribution to a Chapter 9 or Chapter 11 case[29] and to pay the trustee "reasonable compensation for services rendered by [it] in making a substantial contribution in a case under chapter 9 or chapter 11 of this title, based on the time, the nature, the extent and the value of such services, and the cost of comparable services other than in case under this title."[30]

Unfortunately, indenture trustees often do not recover either their fees or their expenses (which are primarily counsel fees). The award of postpetition fees and the reimbursement of postpetition expenses under Section 503(b) is deemed to be an administrative expense of the bankruptcy estate and as such is given an administrative priority status. Because paying these expenses reduces the amount available to creditors and claimants, the courts have construed this section very strictly and narrowly.

Most troublesome of all the cases denying recovery to indenture trustees is an Eighth Circuit Court of Appeals decision that held that by merely performing its duties to its bondholders, even satisfactorily according to its obligation to act as a "prudent man," the indenture trustee was not, as a matter of law, entitled to compensation or recovery of expenses.[31] The court also concluded that the "bankruptcy estate should not have to pay for services which primarily benefit the debenture holders and only incidentally benefit the bankruptcy estate."[32]

This decision places the trustee in a difficult (some argue "impossible") position. The trustee must, as a matter of law under the TIA and contractually under most indentures, actively discharge its obligation under the indenture as an advocate for its bondholders, even if it means that other creditors might receive less in any reorganization, but if the trustee does do so, the bankruptcy court may deny its claim for fees and expenses. It is also evident that the indenture trustee must do a great deal more than simply file a proof of claim on behalf of its bondholders and otherwise perform in a perfunctory manner. Presumably, if the indenture trustee can show (i.e., prove) that its services provided a direct, significant, and demonstrable benefit to the entire estate; were not of a routine nature; and did not duplicate services rendered by other parties in the proceeding, it would stand a much better chance of being paid its fees and reimbursed

[29] 11 USC sec. 503(b)(3)(D).
[30] Id. sec. 503(b)(5), emphasis added.
[31] *In re* Fight Transportation Corporation, *supra*, note 29, at 581.
[32] Id. at 591.

for its expenses. It is essential that the administrative officer keep a detailed diary of the dates, time, and activities performed, including writing letters, responding to telephone calls from security holders, and attending all conferences and meetings involving the obligor.

Existing cases do not definitively answer this problem, nor do they even describe precisely what the nature and extent of the trustee's performance must be to recover from the bankrupt estate. The SEC, however, has formulated what it believes should be the appropriate legal standard:

> The Commission urges that an indenture trustee be entitled to compensation as an administrative expense pursuant to the substantial contribution test of Section 503(b) if its satisfies the following test:
> (1) the indenture trustee has, through its representation of the interests of bondholders, made demonstrable efforts towards furthering the reorganization process; and
> (2) the indenture trustee's services or those of its counsel do not duplicate the services of official participants or other indenture trustees.[33]

As a last resort, the trustee can attempt to recover under its lien against any distributions under an approved plan before distribution to the bondholders. However, the parties in interest may be authorized to review the proposed deduction for reasonableness. Since the amount of the proposed deduction may be material to the bondholders' decision to accept or reject the proposed reorganization plan, the trustee should include a description in the disclosure statement of its plans for obtaining compensation from the bondholders' distribution. This will avoid the possibility that after the plan is confirmed, the bondholders will be unpleasantly surprised by the indenture trustee's action. As long as any cash distributions exceed the trustee's claim for compensation, a dollar-for-dollar deduction will be easy to implement if the court approves. But if there is not sufficient available cash and the distribution consists of new debt and/or equity securities, the trustee may be in the rather unpleasant position of having to initiate a procedure before the court to value the noncash consideration received and to determine the appropriate deduction to be made. Given the additional potential for a dispute with the bondholders over valuation, it is unlikely that most trustees would pursue this route.

---

[33] Brief of the SEC, *In re* Baldwin–United Corporation, Case No. C-1-88-0056 (S.D. Ohio 1988), *appeal settled and dismissed*, BR Case No. 1-83-02495 (S.D. Ohio 1989).

Specialized Trusts and Agency Appointments

In the preceding chapters, we considered the most important duties and responsibilities of trustees under the customary indenture and private placement contract. Even these vary, however, because of differences in types of financing, the nature of the security, particular indenture provisions, and other factors. In general, these differences constitute matters of detail rather than a change in basic function or responsibility.

From time to time, a bank involved with corporate trusts is asked to serve in a somewhat different or more limited capacity, and we discuss in this chapter some of the more significant specialized trusts and/or agency appointments.

ASSET-BACKED SECURITIES TRUSTS

Asset-backed securities, a term generally used to describe debt issues secured by assets other than those securing the traditional mortgage bond issue, have become a major factor in the capital markets during the past several years.

The trustee usually can serve as a backup servicer. Before accepting the trusteeship of any type of asset-backed security issue, the trustee should understand the complexities of asset-backed securities and the additional duties and responsibilities required.

Although the issues that are sold publicly must be registered under the 33 Act and are subject to the disclosure and reporting requirements of the

33 and 34 Acts, the structure of the particular issue determines whether the TIA is applicable. If the underlying assets that are being securitized (typically, pools of mortgages or receivables) are sold to a trust, the debt securities issued by the trust constitute an undivided interest in the trust and are exempt from the TIA's provisions.[1] With this type of structure, when the trust is the issuer, a bank is appointed as trustee under a pooling and servicing agreement.[2] This agreement is not considered to be an "indenture," even though it contains many of the standard provisions of corporate indentures.

The pooling of mortgage loans by the Government National Mortgage Association (GNMA or Ginnie Mae) in 1970 was the earliest use of the securitization of a pool of assets and the issuance of securities backed by that pool. *Securitization* is simply the process under which pools of individual loans or receivables are packaged, underwritten, and sold to investors in the form of negotiable securities. The theory behind this financing technique is simply that the cash flows (which generally are predictable) from the underlying assets are used to pay the interest and principal on the securities. Until 1985, almost all asset-backed issues were basically mortgage-backed securities issued by GNMA, FNMA, and FHLMC. Thereafter, the market expanded rapidly as diverse asset pools were securitized. Although principally securitizing automobile loans and credit card receivables, other issues were backed by computer leases, loans against insurance policies (i.e., "death-backed bonds"), loans supporting employee stock option plans, home equity loans, hospital receivables, and even high-yield debt securities! In 1987 the total amount of issued asset-backed securities was $9 billion, and in 1997 the volume should exceed $140 billion.

When the first asset-backed issues were brought to market, investors scrutinized the issuing entities. Since most asset-backed securities are highly rated with limited potential for downgrading, investors later shifted their focus from the issuer to the quality of the collateral, the loss protection coverage, and the structure of the deal. In recent months, issuers have undergone increased scrutiny based on the issuer's capabilities to service the debt for such receivables as automobile loans and home equity loans.[3]

---

[1] The SEC has taken the position that these trust certificates are deemed to be equity securities and thus are exempt under TIA sec. 304(a)(1).

[2] A pooling and servicing agreement is executed by the seller (i.e., the entity selling the mortgage or receivables pool to the trust), the servicer or master servicer, and the bank as trustee.

[3] "Asset Backed Securities Face New Scrutiny," *Wall Street Journal*, Feb. 18, 1997, p. C1.

The rationale for this type of financing vehicle is that the issuer, sometimes referred to as the *seller* (primarily banks, finance companies, and insurance companies) can positively affect its balance sheet by reducing its assets, which are securitized, with a consequent reduction in the need for and cost of capital to support those assets. Second, asset-backed securities can usually be funded at a lower cost, as they are typically structured to receive at least an "AA" bond rating; thus the issuer is able to borrow at a lower cost than if it borrowed on its own credit.

Generally, investment bankers identify the specific assets to be pooled, according to two criteria. First, the assets must be homogeneous in order to facilitate the structuring so that the cash flows are steady and generally follow projections. Second, collateral will be selected that spreads the risk by limiting geographic—or, in the case of high-yield debt, industry—concentrations. Spreading the risk of default, linked with an economic downturn in a particular industry or geographic region, enables the asset pool to better absorb payment defaults.

If the selection of assets alone is not enough to obtain a high rating, other forms of credit enhancement may also be used. These credit enhancements may come in the form of the issue structure itself, a senior/subordinate structure, overcollateralization and reserve accounts; or a third-party enhancement in the form of a letter of credit or some form of bond insurance.

Investors find asset-backed securities attractive because of their high ratings and "bankruptcy remote" nature. The lower potential for default results from the absolute separation of the security holders' claims against the assets from the credit of the originator of the assets backing the bonds. This separation is created by an "issuer" of the asset-backed security. This issuer is usually a special-purpose vehicle created specifically for the purpose of issuing the securities. An essential part of initiating this transaction is the sale of the assets to the special-purpose entity, which may be a corporation, a partnership, or a trust created to hold the assets on behalf of the beneficial owners of the asset-backed securities. If a grantor trust is used, the owners of the asset-backed securities are also the owners of undivided interests in the asset pool. Such trusts are usually issued in pass-through form. If an owner trust form is used, the trust itself owns the assets and issues the more traditional type of debt securities that are collateralized by the assets. By using a special-purpose vehicle, the cash flows can continue to service the securities even if the originator of the transaction files for bankruptcy.

Asset-backed securities have been marketed in a variety of forms. The main forms are *pass-throughs*, in which the payments on the underlying assets go directly through to the bondholders, and *pay-throughs*, in which the payments on the underlying assets are the basis for the cash flows supporting the debt service on the outstanding securities. The cash flows are structured to meet the investors' needs. Collateralized debt obligations represent the debt of the issuer collateralized directly by the assets. The payments received on these assets are not dedicated to the payments on the securities.

Most asset-backed transactions require a servicer, which may either be related to the issuer or be independent. The servicer is responsible for tracking and collecting the payments due on the assets, for making the tax and mortgage payments on the mortgaged property, and for taking the necessary collection measures against the borrowers who fail to make timely payments. The servicer is also responsible for forwarding reports to the trustee documenting the assets' performance. The servicer's responsibilities may or may not include calculating the payment to be made to the security holders.

Some transactions have more than one servicer, in which case a master servicer is appointed. The role of the master servicer is to aggregate the information received from the various subservicers and forward it to the trustee.

The Trustee's Role

Because there is limited recourse to an issuer for asset-backed securities, the trustee's role becomes more involved than in a traditional form of debt financing. For the same reason that the issue is "bankruptcy remote," it could also be considered to be "issuer remote." Once the bonds are sold, few entities remain connected to the transaction. This financing structure requires the trustee to assume the responsibilities normally reserved for the issuer. Even though the trustee typically has little discretionary power and limited authority in a predefault situation, trustees for asset-backed securities are frequently called on to make decisions about the collateral,[4] to assume expanded responsibilities, and to advise, hire, and fire other parties to the transaction. For these reasons, the account officer and administrator must understand all the details of the particular transaction, including the cash flows and the collateral. It is essential that

---

[4] Although the underlying documents usually indicate that the trustee is to work with the servicer and may rely on its recommendations, the trustee must nevertheless independently exercise its discretion, especially when asked to release its lien on property not paid in full.

the documents associated with the financing, including the trust indenture and the pooling and servicing agreement be carefully reviewed to identify any nontraditional functions the trustee may be asked to perform.

When reviewing the documents, the account officer should prepare a "flow diagram" of the transaction to determine whether the required reports and cash flows will work operationally. For example, if the trustee must receive the master servicer's reports on the eighteenth of the month, but the subservicers do not need to report to the master servicer until the seventeenth, the parties will have difficulty meeting debt service payment deadlines. All duties must be clearly identified, and there must be complete understanding of which entity is responsible for each task. In certain situations, trustees may be required to advance any shortfall in the cash flows. Although the trustee is allowed to make recovery out of subsequent cash flows, a credit facility is usually required for the trustee to perform its duties. The decision to serve as trustee for asset-backed securities is thus often determined by the trustee bank's willingness to become a creditor.

The account officer must also review the reporting requirements and sample formats in the agreements. Underwriters usually require extensive reporting to the trustee. It is essential that the trustee receive sufficient and accurate information to enable it to calculate payments to the bondholders or to prepare other required reports.

One critical responsibility of the asset-backed trustee is tracking and monitoring the servicer's activities. An asset-backed financing can work only to the extent that the servicer performs its duties in a timely and accurate manner. The servicer's expertise is thus important to the financing. To ensure that there is no interruption in servicing the underlying collateral, if the designated servicer fails to perform or defaults, the trustee is normally appointed as the backup servicer. Although investment banks and rating agencies perform due diligence reviews of the servicer, the trustee should also review the servicer's qualifications before accepting the appointment.

Although most corporate trust organizations will perform some sort of "credit review" before accepting a new trustee appointment, for asset-backed transactions the servicer should be reviewed to see whether it can carry out its responsibilities over the term of the financing. This review should include the servicer's management qualifications and its data-processing and information systems. Other statistical information, including payment delinquency ratios, should be compared with that of other servicers in the same industry. The rating agencies and investment bankers tend to focus on the servicer's ability to service the assets. More critical to the trustee, and often overlooked by other parties to the financing structure, is the servicer's ability to translate the servicing activity into meaningful data to report to the investors. An otherwise excellent servicer may prove to be a significant threat to the viability of an issue if it does not understand the issue structure or if its systems cannot generate the required reports.

Once the issue is closed, the trustee must continue to monitor the servicer's performance by reviewing its reports and ensuring that the indenture covenants are met. If the servicer's parent organization is placed in receivership if its debt is downgraded or if the servicer is put up for sale, the trustee must know exactly what action it can take. The trustee must also decide what information it can and should disclose to the security holders and the investors.

More complex transactions backed by short-term assets, like credit card receivables or trade receivables, often have Amortization Events, in addition to Events of Default. *Amortization Events* typically involve credit quality issues such as delinquency ratios or inadequate overcollateralization. When the underlying collateral deteriorates in quality, the document may require the trustee to take immediate action to unwind the security issue. In comparison, Event-of-Default language often allows for periods of time to resolve problems, notify the holders, and involve the trustee.

Agency Functions

The usual appointments associated with asset-backed transactions are those of the registrar and paying agent as well as the collateral agent/custodian. They may also include the responsibilities of calculating payments to security holders and preparing and filing certain tax returns.

Asset-backed securities, such as federal agency–backed collateralized mortgage obligations (CMOs), mortgage pass-through obligations, and automobile and boat loan receivables, are backed by the same pool of assets over the life of the securities. Transactions backed by short-term assets, including credit card receivables, continuously pledge new assets to the pool as the other assets are paid down. In both cases, the trustee must periodically review the UCC financing statements or other appropriate documentation to ensure that the trust maintains its perfected security interest in the collateral.

In the case of home mortgages, government obligations (e.g., Sallie Maes), high-yield debt securities, and boat loans, the trustee may be asked to physically hold the securities or loan documents and to perform a due diligence review of the securities and the loan documents.

On or before the closing of a loan-backed transaction, the trustee or custodian may receive the loan documents that are pledged to the trust. The trustee must compare each loan file with the governing documents and the underwriter's listing and verify that all files have been received. Each file must be reviewed to verify that all required documentation is in the file; such documents usually include a mortgage note, mortgage, assignment of the mortgage to the trust, and title or other insurance policies. In credit card or trade receivables transactions, the collateral may consist of computer-generated files, supplied on magnetic tape or computer diskettes.

After the due diligence is completed, the custodian must identify all discrepancies and work with all interested parties to "cure" the problems. Typically these problems must be resolved by a specific time. At the end of the allowed time, the seller must replace or repurchase any loans with incomplete or incorrect documentation. The loan document files are then deposited in the trustee/custodian's vault for safekeeping.

During the life of the security issue, the trustee and the servicer process requests for mortgage assumptions, reamortizations, proofs of claim, satisfactions, easements, and other legal matters. The trustee must examine each request in the context of the relevant agreement, consult with counsel as required, and take appropriate action. When the trustee is physically holding securities as collateral, the trustee is responsible for collecting payments and processing substitutions of collateral.

The assets in these transactions generate substantial amounts of cash that must be deposited in a collection account, held by the servicer or collection agent and invested according to the terms of the governing documents. Payments received on mortgage-backed bonds are typically processed using the servicer's and master servicer's existing collection accounts, with a single remittance to the trustee before the payment date. Payments received from assets, such as automobile and boat loans, credit card receivables, and trade receivables, often are paid directly to an established account under the trustee's control. The collection agent or servicer is responsible for reconciling the cash received in the control account with the amount expected to be received. It is also the collection agent or servicer's responsibility to ensure that funds received between the designated cutoff dates are properly earmarked for the correct payment date. The governing documents should clearly define which party to the transaction will "advance" to the security holders those funds not received on time.

Often the collection agent's credit rating is considered when determining whether it is eligible to hold a collection account. The trustee must be diligent in monitoring the agent's credit rating and take any required action (including replacing the collection agent) should its credit rating fall to an unacceptable level.

The trustee may also be asked to make extensive calculations to determine the amount to be paid to the security holders, based on the data furnished by the servicer. The trustee must ensure that the documents clearly define its responsibilities. Data in a usable format, with clearly defined calculation requirements, must be delivered to the trustee on a timely basis. Finally, the trustee must be comfortable with the level of expertise in its own organization to make the necessary financial calculations.

One problem in performing these calculations is correctly determining the portion of the periodic payment that represents repayment of a portion of the principal and payment of interest on the security. Typically, these securities pay the principal during the life of the issue. The principal is paid based on a factor, which is a percentage applied to the original principal amount. The remaining principal amount is reported in terms of a factor that, when multiplied by the original face amount of the security, reflects the current outstanding amount. There is usually little risk of a redemption on asset-backed securities, but when there is a redemption, it is commonly known as a *clean-up call*. This results when 90 percent or more of the principal amount has been paid down, that is, the factor on the issue has fallen to 0.10 or less.

In addition to the usual Form 1099 tax reports, the trustee may be required to perform REMIC[5] tax reporting, that is, preparing and filing the trust's initial information return as well as its quarterly and yearly tax returns.

Serving as trustee for an asset-backed security issue is a complex appointment with greater risk and more liability than other debt trusteeships. Having to make decisions in shorter time periods and monitoring the daily cash flow require special expertise. For the past few years, the asset-backed trustee's role has broadened considerably, and the volume of new asset-backed securities is expected to grow significantly over the next several years, compared with the level of unsecured debt financings. The competition (including pricing) among trustees for these appointments will undoubtedly increase as well.

[5] Real Estate Mortgage Investment Conduit, as provided for in the Tax Reform Act of 1986.

EQUIPMENT TRUSTS

A special form of contract has been developed to finance the purchase of equipment by railroads and, since 1970, to finance the purchase of aircraft by the major airlines.

The basic concept of an equipment trust is ownership of the equipment by the trustee during the life of the loan. The obligations are in the form of equipment trust certificates, executed by the trustee, which represent a pro-rata interest in the rentals and other proceeds received by the trustee through the lease of the equipment to the user corporation. The proceeds received from the sale of the certificates are used to buy the equipment, and the lease for it is executed by the trustee to the user corporation. This is a net lease calling for rental payments over an eight- to fifteen-year period sufficient to pay all interest and principal on the certificates. In the case of railroads, the certificates mature serially, and the obligations are retired more rapidly than normal depreciation on the equipment. Because the corporation (or as more recently seen, an institutional investor) provides equity in an amount equal to 20 to 30 percent of the purchase price of the equipment and because most of such equipment is considered salable, these obligations command a ready market and usually a better price than the credit of many railroads or airlines alone would warrant.

In addition to its obligation to make the rental payments under the lease, the user corporation executes a guaranty on each certificate that runs directly to the certificate holder.

Normally the administration of these trusts is somewhat easier than that of the average trust indenture, although the initial documentation tends to be much more complex and very special problems are created if a default or equipment loss occurs under the lease.

CONSTRUCTION AND BOND FUND TRUSTS

Although occasionally an indenture requires administering a construction fund in connection with a new bond issue as part of the trustee's duties, the type of trust considered here is somewhat unusual. It may occur in connection with a revenue bond issue of a state or municipality or a public or quasi-public body created for a special purpose. Power districts, sewer districts, turnpike commissions, and similar entities are examples. Inasmuch as the security for the bonds issued consists of the revenue to be derived from the project to be constructed, the bond proceeds are required to be segregated and held in trust solely to pay the project's construction costs.

The function of the construction fund trustee is to hold the proceeds, invest them in such manner as to provide the greatest return consistent with the requirement for paying them out over a predetermined period, and disburse the funds and the income from them for the project's construction cost. The disbursement is made against certifications by the project engineers of actual expenditures made or obligations incurred for construction purposes. Although the trustee is entitled to rely on these certifications, it should check them to ascertain that the expenditures listed are of the type properly chargeable against the construction monies. In addition, the trustee should ensure that the types of investments are those specifically authorized by the indenture or bond resolution. As a practical matter, it is desirable to limit these to obligations of the United States or its agencies or to certificates of deposit in prime money-center banks.

One important consideration in establishing a construction fund is to provide for a revolving fund large enough to take care of ordinary day-to-day disbursements for a reasonable period of time. This permits all miscellaneous disbursements to be included in one certificate at monthly or other periodic intervals, at which time the revolving fund is replenished.

Once the project has been completed and an appropriate certificate to this effect received, the duties of the construction fund trustee are finished. Any disbursed funds are usually turned over to the bond fund trustee and used to retire a portion of the debt.

In addition to having a construction fund trustee for a revenue project, it is also necessary to designate a bond fund trustee. These may be separate institutions, or one trustee may be designated to perform both functions.

The duties of the bond fund trustee relate solely to the receipt and disbursement of the project's revenues once the project begins operation. Various types of special funds are usually created to provide for operating expenses, maintenance, bond service, reserves, and major replacements, additions, or extensions to the project. The revenues are received directly by the trustee and allocated to each fund according to the formula stated in the indenture. The funds are then disbursed for the proper purposes either according to a predetermined schedule or against certificates of the proper officials of the district, commission, or authority.

A bond fund trustee has no power of enforcement or other rights in an event of default or insufficiency of the revenues. If the revenues or other payments due are withheld wrongfully, the trustee could undoubtedly bring suit to recover them. Its duties relate solely, however, to the revenues or other funds to be paid to the trustee. It is not a representative of the bondholders for the purpose of enforcement.

ESCROW AGENT

The significant growth in the number and type of innovative financings has also increased the need for an escrow agent in many transactions. Essentially, an *escrow agent* is a disinterested party that holds something of value for two or more other parties in interest until a specified time has passed or until a specified event has occurred. The simplistic nature of an escrow appointment should not overshadow the fact that quite often the parties to the arrangement are either in disagreement or lack faith and trust in each other.

This type of "custody" arrangement has been used to hold the down payment toward the purchase of a plant facility, to secure a portion of the purchase price in a merger or acquisition transaction pending the execution of specified representations and warranties, to hold investors' payments for subscribing to securities, to hold life insurance policies covering the principals of closely held companies, and even to hold the source code documentation for computer software to ensure its users of continued support by the software developer.

An escrow agent does not want to hold title/ownership of the escrowed property and therefore, historically, has avoided like-kind exchanges of real property. But recent changes in IRS regulations allow the escrow agent to hold interest in the contract between two parties and does not require that the property be titled to the escrow agent. The title to the property goes directly from the seller to the buyer at the time of the exchange. These changes have made like-kind exchanges of real property more attractive to escrow agents.

An escrow agreement can be as simple or as complex as needs dictate. But if it is not carefully drafted, the escrow agent can be open to tremendous—and sometimes costly—liability. It is essential that the escrow agreement clearly identify the parties in interest, detail each one's duties and responsibilities, accurately describe the property to be held, and specify the circumstances of releasing the property from the escrow. The terms *verbal* and *discretion* can be a cause for concern and so should be avoided. If the property consists of cash and/or marketable securities, the escrow agent's duties and responsibilities regarding the investment, reinvestment, collection, and disposition of income; the registration of the securities; voting rights (in the case of stock); valuations; and reports should be carefully spelled out. All directives should be specific and in writing. The escrow agent should perform only those duties outlined in the agreement, no more and no less. Otherwise the escrow agent's performance could be questioned should there be litigation.

Appropriate provisions should also be included covering notifications and required methods of delivery, the resolution of disputes, the governing law, and the resignation, removal, and succession of the escrow agent. The escrow agent should also have the authority to deliver assets to a court of competent jurisdiction in case of unresolved disputes or failure of the parties to appoint a successor escrow agent should the need arise. It is equally important to provide for full indemnification of the agent against all loss, cost, damage, or expense that may arise or result from the performance of the agent's duties—its liability being only for gross negligence or willful misconduct.

Should a bank or trust obligor want to expand the functions of its escrow department, it can offer other services. Although the designation of "trustee" may replace "escrow agent," the responsibilities of the bank or trust obligor can essentially mirror the duties of an escrow agent. These functions are those that do not fit the typical trustee services provided by other trust areas of the financial institution.

For example, federal regulations require a nuclear power plant to set aside funds for any needed cleanup. These funds must be held by a disinterested party, generally appointed as a trustee. Although the bank or trust obligor is designated as the trustee, if duties relating to the securities are assigned to an outside investment manager and the trustee's duties are to hold funds, settle trades, and prevent the improper distribution of funds, the actual function performed is more in line with that of an escrow agent than a trustee. Thus the financial institution may choose to place these decommissioning trusts in an escrow department.

Voting trusts are used to comply with SEC regulations regarding majority ownership of securities. In its simplest form, a voting trust is set up for a closely held security with limited stockholders (fewer than ten is preferable) and no cash dividends. The agreement should be specific regarding proxy voting and limit the trustee's discretion, but the function of the voting trustee need be no more than holding the securities and voting the proxies.

Of course, the more complex voting trust arrangements involve numerous stockholders, cash and stock dividends, and transfers of ownership. Before committing the bank to these more complex relationships, the administrator should make certain that software and systems are available to make dividend calculations, distributions, transfers, and tax reporting. The functions performed imitate those of a stock-transfer and dividend-paying agent.

These last two examples of trustee relationships violate the escrow agent "rule" of not taking title/ownership of property. Thus, agreements must be closely reviewed and protection for the trustee provided.

The functions that can be performed and the services that can be provided by an escrow department are only as limited as the imagination. The focus should be on the ability to serve the clients while protecting the bank.

UNIT INVESTMENT TRUSTS (UITS)

During recent years, with the increased interest of private investors in the bond market and the desire to diversify portfolios, offerings of a "pooled" portfolio of bonds, much like mutual funds for stock issues, increased dramatically.[6]

An investment firm acting as a sponsor buys a selection of bonds for a particular UIT portfolio and then offers shares or "units" of the fund for sale to investors. Each unit represents a fractional, undivided share of all the bonds in the portfolio. This selection is determined by the type of fund the sponsor seeks to sell to investors. It may consist entirely of tax-exempt bonds of a particular state or the debt obligations of a particular industry, or it may be funded with securities of "growth" companies or, conversely, with debt obligations that provide high-income yield. The nature and type of the underlying portfolio are limited only by the sponsor's ingenuity and its perception of the potential investors' needs.

Because a UIT both issues securities and uses the proceeds to buy the underlying portfolio, it falls within the definition of an "investment company" in the Investment Company Act of 1940 (40 Act).[7]

The structure of the trust is governed by a trust indenture that designates

6 This investor interest has also resulted from the liberalization of tax legislation and regulation related to the establishment and funding of investment retirement accounts (IRAs) and Keoghs.

7 15 U.S.C.A. sec. 80a-3(a)(1) and 3(a)(3). UITs are also subject to the 33 Act but are specifically exempted from the TIA by its sec. 304(a)(2).

the trustee, the sponsor, and the evaluator and delineates their responsibilities. The indenture also states the duration of the trust and the conditions under which it may be terminated early.

Section 26 of the 1940 Act prescribes the minimum requirements for the indenture, stating that (1) the trustee must be a bank having aggregate capital, surplus, and undivided profits of not less than $500,000; (2) the trustee cannot resign until the trust has been liquidated or a successor trustee appointed; (3) the fees available to the trustee, sponsor, and evaluator must be stated, and; (4) the sponsor must maintain appropriate unit holder records and notify the holders in the case of substitution of any portfolio security.

The bonds are deposited with a bank as trustee that has a variety of duties, including safekeeping the securities until redeemed or called; collecting interest on the securities and their principal if called or redeemed; issuing to each investor a registered certificate of ownership or providing a book-entry record of these holdings; distributing checks representing the income on the shares on a monthly, quarterly, or semiannual basis or upon their reinvestment; and redeeming the trust's shares upon the investor's request.[8]

PROJECT FINANCING

The trustee's role in a project financing presents new challenges because of the added complexity. As the project finance vehicles have become more acceptable, investment bankers, project sponsors, and attorneys are being asked to structure increasingly complex transactions that employ the latest finance and risk management techniques. Derivatives, swaps, and options are routinely used to hedge interest rates, fuel costs, currency conversion, and foreign exchange risks. The corporate trustee must understand the importance of exchanging funds among multiple parties and must require the funds to be moved through various domestic and offshore project "waterfall" accounts in a timely and accurate manner. As always, the trustee must fully understand its responsibilities, rights, and powers, which are spelled out in the indenture or a like instrument, and exercise them with the same care as required by applicable law and custom and practice.

On international project finance transactions, the trustee is presented with a variety of challenges, including

[8] For a detailed discussion, see Jay B. Gould and Gerald T. Lins, "Unit Investment Trusts: Structure and Regulation Under the Federal Securities Laws," 43 *Bus. Law.* 1177 (Aug. 1988).

1. *Increased complexity.* International deals generally involve multiple parties and are much larger in scope and size than domestic transactions The parties are project sponsors, export credit agencies, bilateral/multilateral agencies, commercial bank syndicates, and capital market investors. Owing to the increased size of the working groups, the trustee plays a greater role in coordinating the various administrative and operational aspects of the transaction.

2. *Diverse legal/regulatory systems.* A critical feature is that certain project security documents may be governed by local laws, which require an understanding of different legal systems and regulation. The trustee is assigned security interests in the project's property for the benefit of the investors. With the help of local counsel, the trustee must understand the nuances of these laws and their effect on its rights and responsibilities.

3. *Global network.* For an international deal, the project's cash flows and payments are received and paid out in multiple currencies. Generally, local costs, such as for operations, maintenance, salaries, and fuel, are paid in the local currency, and the remaining cash is converted into a principal currency, such as U.S. dollars. Having a local presence or an established banking network is critical to handling, processing, and executing all the trustee's functions. Furthermore, the trustee should be able to make foreign exchange currency transactions so that funds can be repatriated into the investors' currency.

4. *Investment execution.* The success of a project financing requires that all investments and trades be settled in a timely manner to achieve the expected returns on the project's cash flows. Uninvested cash negatively affects the investors' and project sponsors' returns. In addition, some financing may require specialized or customized portfolio management capabilities with which the trustee should be able to work or offer to the participants.

5. *Trustee issues.* In project financings, amendments and changes are made frequently, to adapt to unanticipated circumstances before and after the construction phase. A small, private investor group can more easily deal with these than can a many-tiered or public market structure. In both instances, the trustee must play a key role in managing the amendments.

6. *Technology capabilities.* To administer complex deal structures effectively, the trustee must use technology to carry out its responsibilities and duties, including payments, investments,

account administration, foreign exchange and currency trades, swap payments, letters of credit, project documentation, and ticklers. Instructions and periodic reporting to and from project sponsors and investors benefit from on-line technology in international transactions.

Administration

The revenue stream generated by a project is the principal source of funds securing payment of all expenses incurred in the operation and financing of a project. Additional sources of revenue are insurance proceeds, liquidated damages, judgment proceeds, and payments from fuel suppliers.

All project revenues in the local currency are received by or on behalf of the trustee as the collateral agent. The collateral agent is responsible for moving funds and for properly funding the various project "waterfall" accounts. All revenues are initially passed through an operating account in the local host country. Operating costs, fuel changes, and local taxes are usually paid in the local currency out of the operating account.

After local expenses, the balance (after a foreign exchange transaction) is transmitted to the trustee's general account in the United States. All converted funds, now in the lender's currency, are used to pay interest and principal incurred in financing the project. After the lenders are paid, a series of project waterfall accounts are funded with the remaining cash. Accounts are generally reserves required to provide additional assurance in case of cash shortfalls or interruptions in cash flow due to unanticipated events. Waterfall accounts include operations and maintenance reserves and contingent reserves for the project. The collateral agent is responsible for properly funding the accounts and executing all related investment functions.

After all project expenses have been paid and the reserve accounts have been funded, the remaining cash is the profit that remains to be distributed to the project sponsors or equity investors.

The Trustee as Information Agent

As project finance structures increase in complexity, greater coordination is required among the various parties in the transaction. The trustee is the one party that remains throughout the life of the transaction and therefore is a central source for the exchange and communication of information among the various parties.

Increasingly, the trustee is called on to play this role as a coordinator of information through an "information agent agreement." Information flows in from various parties such as independent engineers, financial advisers, project sponsors, fuel suppliers, and contractors. This information is received, coordinated, and distributed to lenders, institutional and individual investors, and other related parties.

The trustee should make sure that it is not responsible for the accuracy of the information but that it is acting only as a conduit in distributing information to particular parties. This function is vital to international transactions in which, because of geographic and time distances, it is impossible for the various parties to communicate individually.

Servicing Debt Securities— Agency Functions

Corporate trust officers must be concerned not only with protecting the security of the indenture and administering its provisions but also with providing facilities for performing their many responsible and detailed duties in handling the securities themselves, from the time they are issued until they are finally retired and disposed of. In the larger institutions that handle a large volume of corporate trust business, these "operating" functions are usually performed by a separate staff under the management of a senior officer experienced in operating procedures and systems. In the smaller banks, however, which constitute a majority, a single officer may be responsible for both indenture administration and securities-servicing activities. Even in the large institutions, an administrative officer cannot function properly unless he or she understands the basic problems of servicing debt securities.

These functions are separate and distinct from the specific duties of the trustee, although their responsibilities necessarily overlap at many points. The functions are performed by the bank in an agency capacity, and it should receive separate appointing documents and instructions. Because the relationship is essentially that of an agency, it may be terminated by the issuer at any time without a change in the basic trustee relationship.

The securities agent's obligation is to exercise good faith and due diligence—an obligation that under the UCC cannot be varied by agreement, although the standards of performance may be subject to negotiation among the parties. The agent is also entitled to full protection and indemnity for any action taken or omitted to be taken on the instructions of the issuer, as long as the agent acts in good faith with due diligence and without negligence or misconduct.

In regard to its particular function, each agent has the same obligation to the holder or owner of the security and has the same rights and privileges as does the issuer in regard to these functions. The net effect is that the agent has the same liability as does the issuer and is subject to suit by a holder, regardless of whether or not the issuer is also sued.[1]

The bank designated as the corporate trustee is usually appointed as the corporation's principal agent to service the indenture securities, and in most instances, this designation facilitates handling the many problems involved. The issuer may, however, and sometimes does, designate other banks to act in one or more agency capacities.

New York City is the United States' principal financial center, and in the past, many purchasers of securities preferred to have facilities in New York City service their securities. But now the creation of the securities depository and particularly the Depository Trust Company (DTC) in New York has limited the need for a New York facility to provide immediate transfer and payment services. The advent of the book-entry-only security and the FAST security service offered by many transfer agents has limited the need for a New York City location to those issues listed on the New York Stock Exchange that require a place of presentment for transfers and payments.

Because many millions of securities are held in custodial or depository arrangements in New York, much money can be saved if they do not have to be shipped to other areas of the country. Accordingly, many older indentures require the obligor to designate an office or agency in New York City where demands or notices may be served and where the securities may be presented for payment, registration of transfer, tender, and exchange. When a bank outside New York City is named trustee, it is common to designate the bank as the principal agent to service the securities, with a New York bank named as either a coagent to perform all requisite agency functions or as a drop agent to receive items on behalf of the principal agent. The drop agent forwards items to the principal agent generally on the same day that the items are received. Although transfer agent regulations do not deem the "drop" to be equivalent to the principal agent's premises where the transfer is made, this agent must have appropriate procedures to ensure that items are promptly forwarded to it.[2] To

---

[1] For an excellent review of the cases and decisions related to these services, see Egon Gutman, *Modern Securities Tranfers* (rev. ed., 1989).

[2] See SEC rule 17Ad-1(g), 17 CFR 240.17Ad-1, and question (28) in SEC Interpretative Release 34–17111 (Sept. 2, 1980).

avoid the cost of shipping securities, the drop agent is usually authorized to cancel the securities on behalf of the main agent.

The agent's functions include that of authenticating agent for the trustee to authenticate securities to be issued on registration of transfer, exchange, or partial redemption. Occasionally, a coagent is named in one or more cities in addition to New York. The activities of all the agents must be closely coordinated, and appropriate controls should be maintained by the trustee and principal agent, with the other agents reporting and accounting to them.

The use of a New York City agent, even for outstanding older securities, is thus of limited use, with the services now offered through the depositories. Most of the older security issues have been qualified as depository eligible, which has resulted in most New York banks' depositing their security positions with DTC. The depository in turn has submitted the older security issues, which often include the bearer securities, to the transfer agent for registered securities, registered in DTC's nominee registration, CEDE & CO. The result is that the burden of safekeeping bearer securities has been shifted from the New York City agent and the depository to the transfer agent and trustee.

In recent years, some trustees and transfer agents have made a business decision to cancel and destroy significant supplies of negotiable bearer securities held in their vaults against registered securities outstanding. If a bearer security is requested, the trustee has the certificate(s) printed at its expense. The decision is based on the fact that printing costs are much lower than those for vault space and insurance coverage on the bearer securities.

Procedures tend to vary widely, depending on volume handled, local practices, and, in some cases, requirements of specific laws and regulations. This chapter focuses therefore on the most important aspects of the particular agency appointment and the relevant duties and responsibilities of the appointee. These securities-processing services are security registrar, interest-paying agent, principal-paying agent, exchange agent, conversion agent, tender agent, and accounting and destruction agent.

APPOINTING DOCUMENTS

The only documents normally required to support an agency appointment are (1) a resolution of the company's board of directors; (2) a copy of the indenture or supplemental indenture creating the issue (or in the case of a municipal security issue, a copy of the security resolution or ordinance);

(3) incumbency certificates; (4) a specimen of each authorized denomination of the bond or debenture; and (5) supplemental instructions from the issuer regarding the agent's specific duties and responsibilities. When the agent is also the trustee, the trustee will already have most of these documents, and so duplication is unnecessary.

When the agent is designated by name in the indenture itself, a general resolution approving the indenture is all that is required, although it is desirable that the resolution be broad enough to cover each agency appointment specifically. No special form is required, but it is suggested that the text of the resolution follow the indenture language as closely as possible, to indicate that this is the specific appointment the company covenanted to make. It is also recommended that the resolution contain general language designating the issuer's officials (by title) who are authorized to issue instructions to the agent. Although it is not necessary to name the agents in the securities themselves, the later processing is easier if the security contains the name of the bank to which it should be presented for payment, registration of transfer, and so on.

The incumbency certificates should include specimen signatures of the issuer's officers, particularly those who signed any of the bonds or debentures. If facsimile signatures are used, the specimen security suffices for this purpose, but the agent should still have the signatures of the officers authorized to instruct it. If the agent is a bank other than the trustee, it should also have specimens of the signatures of all officers of the trustee that authenticated the securities.

Finally, the agent should obtain such detailed instructions from an authorized official of the obligor as are necessary to enable it to carry out its duties expeditiously. These instructions include the source of funds to pay principal and interest, the disposition to be made of canceled securities, statements and reports to be rendered, and so on. As a practical matter, because the agent wishes this agency to follow a specific routine and usually knows more than does the issuer about what should be done, it is customary for the agent to explain to the issuer the procedure it intends to follow and to request the issuer's confirmation and approval.

Security Registrar

Before the UCC was adopted, there was no statutory requirement that corporate or municipal issuers maintain "books of record." However, for almost all publicly sold debt issues, the issuers assumed a contractual obligation to do so in the indenture, according to which the securities were issued and provided for an office or agency where registrations of transfer and payment could be carried out.

The registrar appointment is important to the modern, fully registered issue, and there are many reasons that the trustee should be designated as principal registrar to maintain the record of registered holders and of registrations of transfer. The list of holders is also necessary for other purposes, such as the selection of securities for partial redemption and the mailing of notices. Both time and expense are saved if the trustee is made responsible for maintaining this record. Interest and principal payments are usually made to individual holders by check (and by wire to depositories). It is important that this be done by the bank that maintains the record of holders. In any place where registration facilities are required that is not also the location of the trustee, the registrar or coregistrar should also be given the necessary authority to "authenticate" the obligations. This is an agency function, and the granting of this authority constitutes an appointment in addition to the registrar function.

Authentication on original issuance should be performed only by the trustee, as should the securities replacing mutilated, lost, stolen, or destroyed securities. These transactions entail creating additional indebtedness with respect to which the trustee has special fiduciary responsibilities. However, authentication of securities on transfer, exchange, or partial redemption does not involve the same degree of responsibility and, when desirable to avoid unnecessary expense to holders, may properly be authenticated under appropriate safeguards, by a responsible institution other than the trustee.

Many existing mortgage indentures are intended as permanent financing media, and because of certain language in the original indentures, there may be questions about whether an authenticating agent can be appointed for additional series of securities to be issued under these indentures. This is an example of the type of inflexibility that should be avoided when drafting indentures. In such indentures, every effort should be made to find a legal resolution, for it is obvious that the rights of holders of existing obligations will not be affected. If these legal questions cannot be resolved, the procedures for obtaining the consent of the requisite percentage of holders should be simplified.

A fully registered security means that both the principal and the interest are registered in the holder's name. From the holder's standpoint, there are a number of advantages to registration. Negotiability is restricted, and in the case of theft or loss, the expense of replacement is reduced, and the risk of losing the entire investment is almost eliminated. Interest is paid by check, and the chore of detaching and collecting interest coupons every six months is eliminated. In the event the security is called, or the trustee or issuer wishes to communicate with the holder, a notice or letter can be mailed directly to the registered holder. The main disadvantage is that the security cannot be disposed of by delivery to a purchaser but must be surrendered to the registrar to effect the registration of transfer.[3]

To register a transfer, the security must be accompanied by a form of assignment that has been executed by the transferor, assigning the holder's interest in the security in blank or to a specified transferee. The registrar will require that the holder's signature to the assignment be guaranteed. Most major security registrar banks normally require that the guarantee be by a member firm of the New York or American Stock Exchange or other acceptable regional stock exchange or by another commercial bank or one of its correspondent banks. Other registrars have similar requirements, modified to meet their particular needs and operating policies.

It has always been difficult to maintain current signature cards for the hundreds of banks and member firms of the stock exchanges. In the past, the trustee and transfer agent received each day many cards that needed to be filed immediately and discontinued signature cards pulled from the files. Each signature guarantee was to be checked against the signature cards. It was no longer economical to maintain this archaic system, so in 1994, the "medallion program" replaced the signature cards. The medallion is a registered stamp maintained by banks and brokerage firms and represents an official guarantee of the signature of the registered security owner. Institutions using the medallion initially pay a fee for it. The medallion stamp must be maintained in a dual-controlled environment to safeguard its use only for guaranteeing signatures of known registered security owners.

The registration of both principal and interest requires that a new security or securities be prepared and issued for every transaction, and they usually can be issued in any denomination that is a multiple of $1,000 (or in the case of municipal securities, in multiples of $5,000). If the registrar has been appointed as the authenticating agent, it will authenticate the new certificates, under advice to the trustee that it has canceled (obligor's signature only) an equal principal amount of securities, will include in

---

[3] See chapter 2, note 2, *supra.*

the certification the serial numbers of the certificates issued and canceled, and will ship the canceled securities to the trustee.[4]

If the registrar is not an authenticating agent, both the old and new certificates must be delivered to the trustee, which will cancel its authentication certificate on the old securities and authenticate the new ones to be delivered. Information on the particular transaction—including name, address, and taxpayer identification number of both the transferor and the transferee; the security numbers canceled and issued; and the principal amount—must be input to the registrar's security holder record file. A transfer or journal sheet is normally prepared reflecting each day's activity for the particular issue. Although most major security registrar banks maintain the permanent record as part of their automated record-keeping procedures, it may be desirable to produce daily "hard copy" of such transactions, either for research purposes if the information is not otherwise readily available or to forward it to the obligor. When more than one registrar is involved, only the principal registrar maintains individual registration records of the holders. All coregistrars must therefore furnish the information (usually a copy of their transfer sheets) to the principal registrar.

Almost all municipal debt securities issued before July 1, 1983, were in bearer form, and many provided for their registration at the holder's option. Most corporate obligations sold before 1968 were similarly issued. This registration privilege could be as to principal only or as to both principal and interest. In the case of corporate issues, the privilege had to be specified in the indenture.

Registration as to principal only means that the principal of the security is registered in the holder's name. The bearer interest coupons remain attached and are used for collecting the semiannual interest in exactly the same manner as if the security had not been registered. These securities also can be registered by presenting the security to the registrar accompanied by an executed assignment, with the signature guaranteed in the same manner as for a fully registered security. The registrar enters the date and name of the registered holder on the special registration panel on the back of the security, and the registration is authenticated by the signature of an authorized officer of the registrar opposite the name of the holder. A special transfer sheet is usually prepared by the registrar, showing the security number and a transfer from "bearer" to the name of

[4] It may be more desirable for the registrar to enter into an agreement with the trustee in which the registrar destroys the canceled certificates and gives the trustee a destruction certificate.

the holder. This transfer is posted to a subsidiary record file (or ledger sheet) under the name and address of the holder, which shows the date, number, and principal amount of the security registered as to principal in the holder's name. Any subsequent registration as to the principal of securities of the same issue in that holder's name is also posted to the particular record file by showing a debit to the transferor and a credit to the transferee.

A security registered as to principal is released in the same manner as a transfer, except that the word *bearer* instead of the name of the transferee is entered in the registration box. Full negotiability by delivery is then restored. An assignment in blank by the former registered holder is required to complete this "deregistration."

No posting to the trustee's principal record of securities issued file is required in the case of registration as to principal only or on transfers of such securities, for there is no change in the serial number or the principal amount of securities outstanding.

Several years ago, DTC created the Fast Automated Securities Transfer (FAST) program. Under this program, DTC leaves securities with the transfer agents in the form of a balance certificate registered in DTC's nominee name, CEDE & CO. The balances are adjusted daily based on DTC's deposit and withdrawal activities. Securities may be added at the time they are made DTC eligible or convert already eligible issues that had previously not been included in the FAST program. The transfer agent and DTC agree in writing on the FAST criteria. In summary, this agreement requires the agent to certify that (1) all transfer requirements have been met; (2) the balance for each FAST issue has been confirmed via the FAST balance confirmation system; (3) DTC will receive interest or dividend payments based on DTC's confirmed FAST balance; (4) the agent will accept from and return automated information to DTC relating to transfers; and (5) the agent must agree to participate in DTC's direct mail program to mail certificates to investors.

PAYMENT OF INTEREST

The agent's first obligation is to make certain that the requisite funds are obtained before each interest payment date. Many banks follow the practice of billing their principals for all interest payments due. This is an expensive but sometimes necessary step when required interest payments are based on variable rates. (The issuer's obligation to provide the necessary funds is an absolute one, and their officials should be capable—without a reminder—of making funds available on time and in the proper amount.) When the deposit with the paying agent is by check, it should be in enough time to enable the agent to complete the collection of the check and have funds available on the payment date. When the paying agent is willing to accept a deposit of immediately available funds on the payment date, extreme care should be exercised in following the usual and customary practice of mailing the interest checks on the business day preceding the payment date. This decision, including the advance mailing of the checks on a staggered basis, should be made only after weighing the possible consequences of the obligor's failing to deposit the requisite funds on the payment date.

Although almost all indentures provide for the payment of interest by check (occasionally one does see the use of "drafts" permitted). The use of wire transfers and direct deposit credits through automated clearinghouse (ACH) mechanisms is increasing. The Group of Thirty's Recommendations to pay all debt service payments to the depositories in same-day funds required significant controls of receipt and disbursement of debt service funds. All debt service funds received by the depositories by 2:30 P.M. eastern time are paid to the depository participants as a same-day payment. This practice significantly reduces the cost of funds to banks and brokers, which often paid their clients on the payable date, even though the depository typically did not pay interest and dividends until the day following the receipt of funds. The same-day funds payment convention does require coordinated communication with obligors and a closely monitored system of debt service receipts and disbursements.

Under qualified indentures, all funds deposited for the payment of interest and principal must be held in trust, whether or not they are held by the trustee. If the agent is a bank other than the trustee, it must—at the time of accepting its appointment—execute a letter of undertaking to the trustee to hold in trust, for the benefit of the security holders, all sums deposited with it for the payment of principal or interest on the securities and to give prompt notice to the trustee of default by the obligor in making any such payment.

The paying agent's responsibility is complicated by the necessity of complying with the relevant provisions of the Internal Revenue Code and with the regulations of particular taxing jurisdictions. All payments of interest on taxable security issues in excess of $10 must be reported to the federal government, and under specific provisions of the Interest and Dividend Tax Compliance Act of 1983, the paying agent may be required to withhold a portion of the payment.[5] For security issues sold before July 18, 1984, it is also necessary to withhold the requisite taxes on all payments to nonresident aliens and to process and file with the federal government the appropriate tax forms.

The requirements of particular state tax laws must also be considered. For example, any corporation incorporated in Pennsylvania or with a treasurer's office in that state is subject to the Pennsylvania corporate loans tax. Unless the corporation assumes this tax, it must be withheld from all payments to Pennsylvania residents. The corporation is entitled to a credit for payments to all non-Pennsylvania residents, but proof of such payments must be supplied. The agent must, therefore, obtain evidence on the residence of each holder to whom payment is made. In the case of bearer securities, the agent uses a memorandum certificate of ownership.

Payment of Registered Interest

Interest is usually payable semiannually, although in recent years, a number of variable-rate issues have provided for quarterly and monthly payments. Such interest is due and payable on fixed dates, with all accruals of interest being for the prescribed periods. A transfer of the obligation normally transfers the right to any interest accrued, with the purchaser paying this amount as part of the purchase price.

To give the paying agent enough time to pay interest on registered security issues, without disrupting the trading of the securities, a procedure was developed in the late 1960s in which the contract between the obligor and the holder provides for a record date before the end of the accrual period to determine which holders are entitled to the payment.[6] As a result, the transfer books need not be closed at all during this period.

Inasmuch as the basic obligation calls for paying interest on the interest payment date and the full six months' interest does not become payable as a debt until this date, the obligation to the holders of record as of a preceding date to pay on this date must be stated clearly in the indenture and on the face of the security.

[5] See chapter 13, note 10, *supra*. This withholding, referred to as *backup withholding*, is imposed if a nonexempt payee fails to give the payer an obviously correct taxpayer identification number and, for accounts opened after January 1, 1984, a statement that the holder is not subject to backup withholding. Both statements must be certified under penalty of perjury.

[6] The Municipal Securities Rulemaking Board (MSRB), with the concurrence of the SEC and the Government Finance Officers Association, strongly recommended using the standard record dates for registered tax-exempt issues, in *Notice Concerning Recommended Standards on Registered Municipal Securities* (May 6, 1983).

The standard uniform record date for interest payable on the first day of a calendar month is the close of business on the fifteenth day of the calendar month preceding the date of payment. If interest is payable on the fifteenth, the record date is the close of business on the last day of the preceding calendar month. In the event of a failure to pay on the due date, the established record date will have no effect, and the transfer of the security gives to the transferee all the holder's rights to the defaulted interest. This outcome should be stated clearly in the indenture, and provision should also be made to determine those persons entitled to payment of the defaulted interest. It is recommended that on being notified of the intention to pay the defaulted interest on a certain date (including arrangements satisfactory to the trustee for the deposit of the funds), the trustee establish a special record date, which should be not more than fifteen or fewer than ten days before the proposed payment date and not fewer than ten days after receiving the notice of the proposed payment. Notification of the proposed payment and of the special record date should be mailed to the security holders by the trustee not fewer than ten days before the special record date.

Interest owed to the "record date" holders of fully registered securities is paid by check, which is issued and mailed to them at the address shown on the registration records. Payments to DTC or to holders of private placement securities are usually transmitted by wire transfer. If the interest-disbursing agent is other than the registrar, the latter will prepare a certified list of registered holders, as of the record date, with the total holdings of each, and deliver it to the disbursing agent. These checks are usually mailed on the business day preceding the interest due date, to ensure that in most cases the holder will receive the check on the date the interest is due.

The total amount to be disbursed should be proved to the trustee's registered security control record to ensure that the registrar's security holder records are in proof with the trustee's control. Each transaction that changes the outstanding principal amount of securities should be posted to the trustee's record of securities issued file and the requisite control. When, however, an issue is outstanding in both bearer and registered form, it is necessary to maintain a subsidiary control of the outstanding fully registered securities. This practice facilitates a quick proof of the registered interest disbursements, certifications of registered securities outstanding, and other transactions relating to these securities. This record may be maintained as part of a automated securities transfer system or off-line in a manual ledger record. In the latter case, it is maintained by posting from a daily journal covering all the registration activities for each day. This journal records the total principal amount of fully registered obligations canceled or discharged or issued during the day for each separate issue on which there was activity. The totals are then posted to the registered securities outstanding control record for each such issue.

Payment of Bearer Interest

Because most corporate debt obligations issued before 1968 and almost all state and municipal obligations issued before July 1, 1983, are outstanding in bearer form, it is necessary to examine in some detail the means by which interest is collected by the holders thereof. This is accomplished by attaching to each such obligation a sheet of bearer coupons, one for each interest payment date to and including the date of maturity of the principal obligation. Until they become payable, these coupons are an integral part of the security itself, and together they constitute a single obligation.[7] Once they have matured and become payable, however, they become separate and distinct obligations and may be transferred by delivery separate from the security itself. Payment to the bearer, even when different from the holder of the security, discharges the debt.

As noted earlier, interest is usually payable semiannually, although infrequently provision is made for payment at different intervals. On a $20 million, twenty-five-year security issue consisting of all bearer securities of $5,000 denominations that remain outstanding to maturity without interim sinking-fund or redemption payments, 200,000 separate interest obligations must be processed. It follows that the function of the coupon-paying agent is one of the more important to be performed in servicing the pre–July 1, 1983, obligations of state and municipalities, old corporate security issues, and the so-called Eurodollar issues.

Because when due, the coupon becomes a separate obligation, it must incorporate a separate and distinct promise to pay. When the security is subject to prior redemption, all coupons maturing after the first possible redemption date should have this promise qualified by language such as "Unless the security hereinafter mentioned shall have been called for previous redemption and payment of the redemption price thereof duly

[7] It is, however, possible and proper to have the security "stripped" of its coupons, with the principal sold at a discount (much like a zero coupon security) and the coupons sold as a separate instrument. In the latter case, the investor receives semiannual payments, representing the amortization of investment plus interest on such investment.

provided." Each coupon should contain the name of the issuer, the date on which it will become due, the specific amount due, the place of payment, and a statement that it represents interest for a specified period on the security designated by serial number. The coupon is validated by the signature (usually facsimile) of the treasurer or other authorized official of the issuer. To facilitate identification and processing, the coupons attached to each security should be numbered in consecutive order, the first maturing coupon being 1, the second 2, and so on. All coupons maturing on the same date from securities of the same issue have the same coupon number.

The holder of a security may detach the coupons and forward them directly to the paying agent and receive a check in payment. Because this check must also be processed, this method of collection delays the receipt of usable funds by the holder, and so it is not the method most frequently used. From the agent's viewpoint, it is the most expensive method of payment. The normal collection procedure follows the same pattern as that used in processing checks, except that credit is usually not passed to the depositor's account until it is actually collected. Each bank provides special envelopes (generally referred to as *shells*) for its depositors in which coupons may be enclosed and deposited for collection. The holder writes his or her name, address, and taxpayer identification number on the shell, together with a description of the security, the denomination of the coupon, and the total face amount of coupons deposited. The bank of deposit then forwards the shell, together with all shells received from other depositors, to its correspondent bank in the city of collection. The latter accepts it as a deposit from the forwarding bank and assigns a collection number to the total deposit, which may represent many coupon shells for many different issues. After proving each collection, this bank then sorts the shells by issue and paying agent and presents the coupons to the respective paying agents. Most of this processing takes place before the maturity date, and the paying agent accepts coupons for processing about a week before the actual due date. On the due date, the paying agent pays the presenting bank for all coupons presented, up to and including that date. On the same date, each bank through which the coupon has been processed passes the preestablished credit to its depositor.

When default has been made in payment or when a particular coupon is mutilated or is otherwise irregular or has been detached from a previously called security, it must be returned through the same channels used in its collection, and each depositor's account must be charged back for the amount of the item.

In New York City, the major banks, and banks in certain other cities, provide for the collection of all coupons through a central clearinghouse. Each morning all collecting banks transport all their collection items to the clearinghouse, where they are delivered to the paying banks. For the total deposits and receipts, a net credit or debit is made to the bank's account at the Federal Reserve Bank. The aggregate of return items that have to be charged back is handled in the same manner. This arrangement facilitates the collection process and reduces to a minimum the number of checks that have to be prepared and issued by the agents. Together with the preliminary work performed by the banks in their capacity as collecting agents, this procedure has also minimized the costs to issuers for servicing their coupons.

The paying agent must examine each coupon presented to see that it is a valid obligation, that it is a matured obligation and one the agent is authorized to pay, that the security from which it was detached has not been previously called for redemption, that the coupon has not been canceled, that it is not otherwise mutilated, and that no stop order is on file with respect to the particular coupon.

The amount of each shell and collection item must also be verified. If everything is found to be in order, the coupons are canceled by perforation. The total number of coupons for each issue received each day is compared with the total number of collection items received, and the appropriate account is charged for the total payments. If payment is refused for any reason, the coupon is returned uncanceled to the presenting bank (or to the presenter if not a collecting bank) and, if an aggregate credit has been made, against an appropriate chargeback. When a clearinghouse arrangement is used, all coupons are usually processed and paid on the same day they are presented to the agent. Any coupons or shells returned for the reasons just cited should be returned immediately or, if presented through a clearinghouse, in the next day's clearing.

Most coupons are payable on the first or fifteenth day of the month, and the few days immediately preceding and following these dates are periods of heavy volume. During the remaining days of the month, the work processed during these periods is audited and verified by personnel other than those who handled the payment. In this operation, the coupons are broken down by the maturity date, and the total coupons paid for a designated period (usually monthly) are proved to the total charge made during the period to the coupon account.

Some banks still follow the expensive practice of maintaining a separate cash account for each interest maturity. Because in any event, it is necessary for the coupons to be segregated by coupon number (or maturity date), it is much easier to maintain the appropriate breakdown by subsidiary data record. When a single obligor has a number of separate issues of securities outstanding, it is acceptable to maintain a single cash account for all issues and to provide the necessary breakdown by issue and maturity by subsidiary records.

When a great volume of coupon payments is handled, the administrative officer's responsibility is to give the operations personnel the essential instructions and information in as concise and understandable a manner as possible. Any information that facilitates the verification of the obligation's validity is helpful.

A corporate issuer is required under qualified indentures to maintain a list, updated annually, of all its security holders' names and addresses. If this information is derived from the collection of interest coupons, the agents must maintain it in current form for filing with the trustee. The information is derived from the shells in which the coupons are received.

When two or more banks act as paying agents for a particular issue, the work of all the agents must be coordinated. The normal procedure is for one bank (usually the trustee) to be designated as the principal agent and for all funds to be deposited with that bank. If the other agents are correspondents of the principal agent, they are authorized to charge the account of the principal agent for payments by the coagents, and the principal agent is responsible to the issuer for all payments made. Once the coupons have been paid, verified, and canceled, and the coupon-paying account has been charged, the work of the paying agent is concluded. The problem of disposing of the canceled coupons is discussed later in this chapter in connection with accounting and destruction procedures.

PAYMENT OF PRINCIPAL

Theoretically, the same principles that govern the payment of the coupons should apply to the payment of the securities themselves. But the procedures followed are usually quite different. In the case of securities, the amount of money involved in handling each item is many times greater, and consequently the risk is much greater. Thus coupons are handled on a volume basis; securities, on an individual basis.[8] Whereas the

[8] Since the mid-1970s, a matured municipal and corporate security clearing system has been used by members of the New York Clearinghouse, following procedures similar to the daily clearing of coupons.

trustee is responsible for properly accounting for both securities and coupons, the latter are usually accounted for by total amount by maturity date, whereas principal obligations are accounted for individually, by serial number.

The security payment personnel work from instructions prepared by the account administrator. Although in the case of coupons, one set of instructions is normally sufficient for all maturities, it is desirable to prepare separate instructions for each principal payment. These instructions should contain all essential information so that the operations personnel do not have to refer to the indenture or other source material. In the case of a redemption payment, the amount of the premium payable must be shown, as well as the specific serial numbers of the particular securities called.

Because payment for principal obligations is made by check or sometimes by wire transfer, the identity of the individual presentor can be preserved.[9] During a heavy maturity period, each day's work represents a large dollar volume, and so it is necessary in any procedure to maintain proper controls. In a large-volume operation, it is desirable to have control maintained separate and apart from the personnel making the actual payment. For each item presented, there is indicated on the automated security log or, in the case of a manual processing system, a control ticket containing the name of the presentor, a description of the issue and its CUSIP number,[10] the aggregate face amount of the securities, and the serial numbers. One copy is given to the presentor (in the case of a window item), another is sent to a security control (audit) unit, and the other two copies accompany the securities to the payment desk. Here the securities are examined to determine that they are valid, that they are in good order with no mutilations, and that no stop payment order is on file for the particular securities. Other checks are made as indicated for a particular issue. The amount of the payment is computed and entered on the control ticket. The item is then recorded on the automated system, and a check is

[9] See chapter 13, note 10, and chapter 16, note 5, *supra*. In addition, payers are required under income tax regulations to report the "gross proceeds" paid to any nonexempt holder from the redemption of both corporate and municipal obligations.

[10] The term *CUSIP* is an acronym for the Committee on Uniform Security Identification Procedures, of the American Bankers Association. Since 1967, a standard alphanumeric numbering system has been used by all segments of the securities industry. The standard consists of nine characters: the first six are the issuer number, the next two are the issue number, and the last is a check digit. The numbers that appear on the face of each stock and security certificate are assigned by the CUSIP Service Bureau of Standard & Poor's Corporation under contract to the American Bankers Association.

printed, on which the number of the control ticket is entered. The securities are subsequently canceled, and the check is returned through the control clerk for delivery against the surrender of the receipt or for mailing to the presentor. The control clerk is responsible for seeing that a check is delivered for each control ticket processed. As a separate audit, the system or, in the case of a manual system, another person verifies the total securities canceled for the day against the total funds disbursed. A copy of the control ticket accompanies each block of canceled securities, and the original, with the number of the check issued entered on it, is filed for record purposes.

When part of the security issue is called before its stated maturity, the serial numbers of the securities presented must also be examined to ensure that they appear on the list of called securities.

Care should be taken that payment is made only to the registered holder or that an appropriate assignment is received. When payment is made to the registered holder, no assignment is necessary. Registered securities must also be delivered to the security registrar for proper discharge from the registration records.

In the case of a partial call, most registered securities of large denomination are called in part only. The holder of such an obligation is given a new security for the unredeemed portion. For a separate registrar, a special transfer sheet is prepared showing the reduction in the amount of such registered securities. It is important that the principal transfer agent communicate with all cotransfer agents before processing a partial call for redemption. All cotransfer agents should be required to submit journals to the principal agent no later than one business day after the transfer. The principal agent should post all activity before processing the call and notify the cotransfer agents that the books will be closed for a specified period.

Because all securities are controlled on the trustee's principal record of securities issued, one copy of the control ticket may be used to reflect the cancellation, reducing the trustee's control of outstanding securities. Since for purposes of the indenture, securities cease to be outstanding on the redemption date when the required funds are deposited in trust, the recommended procedure is for the entire principal amount called to be debited from the trustee's principal control record on the redemption date. A separate subsidiary control record should be established to reflect the actual surrender and payment of the securities, and the cash balance reflected in this record should always prove to the funds in the redemption account.

Exchange Agent

The function of an exchange agent is similar to that of a registrar in that it involves the exchange of securities of an issue for other securities of the same issue, provided that this is permitted by the terms of the indenture. In practice, a separate exchange agent is usually not appointed; instead, the registrar assumes this function.

One form of exchange is that of fully registered securities for the coupon bearer type, or the reverse, for pre-1983 issues when such bearer securities were authorized. Upon receipt of bearer securities with a request to issue an equivalent amount in fully registered form, the bearer securities are canceled, and a registered security, or securities, is prepared, with the transaction information input to the security holder records file. The canceled bearer securities and the registered piece are delivered to the trustee with a request to authenticate the latter. (If the registrar–exchange agent has been appointed as an authenticating agent, it authenticates the registered security, under advice to the trustee that it has canceled an equal principal amount of bearer securities, including in the certification the serial numbers of the securities issued and canceled.)

On a reverse transaction, issuing bearer for fully registered securities, the canceled registered piece is delivered to the trustee after discharge, and the appropriate number of bearer securities is requisitioned. After detaching all coupons for which interest has been paid, the trustee (or the authenticating agent) authenticates and delivers the requisite amount of previously unissued bearer obligations. A number of issues follow the practice of having the trustee "hold alive" any bearer securities that have been surrendered for exchange, on the theory that on an exchange back to bearer form, a supply of certificates will be available. Although this does reduce the cost to the issuer in the event that additional securities must be printed, it adds substantial liability to the trustee, which must safely control the authenticated bearer securities pending their possible reuse. This is a common practice with municipal securities, and systems have been designed with the appropriate controls in place to maintain current inventories of bearer securities deposited to vaults in exchange for registered securities.

Most banks, however, follow the practice of canceling all securities received for exchange, if permitted by the governing document, so that no securities bearing the same serial number can be reissued for any purpose. When frequent requests for exchange are likely, a supply of unissued bearer securities can also be lodged with the trustee for this purpose.

This is a more popular mode with the few remaining outstanding bearer corporate securities as well as with the Eurobonds.

When both coupon and registered securities are authorized, special provisions must be made to interchange the two forms between the record and payment dates. The coupon for the interest payable on the payment date should be detached from the bearer securities before being presented for exchange, or delivery in exchange, for an equal amount of registered obligations.

The function of the interdenominational exchange agent is important in fully registered issues to permit security holders to "split" or "consolidate" the number of pieces they hold. In the case of corporate securities issued in connection with a subscription offer to stockholders, denominations of $500, $100, and even $50 may be authorized. Often these denominations are freely interchangeable, although the more common provision is to permit their consolidation into securities of $1,000 denomination or multiples thereof, but no split of $1,000 securities into smaller denominations. The reason for this limitation is the substantial cost of servicing small-denomination securities.

During the 1980s, many of the larger banks acted as exchange agents for securities of highly leveraged companies being financially restructured. These transactions typically exchanged high-yield (i.e., "junk") securities for cash, extended-maturity and/or reduced interest-rate debt securities, and even common stock.

CONVERSION AGENT

The use of the convertible corporate type of debt security has varied in popularity during the past twenty years, as changes in economic conditions and the market's receptivity to such "equity kickers" have waxed and waned. In the case of a corporation that is rapidly expanding or whose credit is not considered top tier by investors, such a vehicle provides a means of raising equity capital, usually at considerably less cost than direct equity financing. During a period of rising stock prices, the conversion privilege is a valuable one, and many convertible debentures sell at substantial premiums above the price they would command as straight debt securities. The usual security into which such an obligation is made convertible is the common stock of the issuing company.

The indenture controls the terms and conditions on which the privilege may be exercised, and these terms and conditions should also be stated in the debenture itself in reasonable detail. The debenture may be made convertible into a fixed number of shares of stock, but the more usual provision is to fix a dollar price at which shares of stock may be purchased by using the principal of the debenture. This price is subject to adjustment to reflect any change in the ratio of number of shares outstanding (other than through conversion of other debentures of the same issue).[11] Provision may also be made for an arbitrary increase in the conversion price at stated intervals during the life of the debenture, to encourage conversions during the earliest period. A common practice is to set the initial conversion price at a figure somewhat higher than the current market price of the common stock. This offers the advantage of the company's having a less expensive debt security for a period of time, but one it will likely never be called on to pay, except by issuing common stock at a price higher than could be obtained by an immediate issue of the stock. To achieve the same purpose, sometimes the conversion privilege cannot be exercised until a stated time has elapsed after the debentures have been issued.

When the convertible debentures have been issued, the company must authorize and reserve for issuance the maximum number of common shares that could be issued when the entire debenture issue is converted. This authorization involves all the steps that would have to be taken if a number of shares were being concurrently issued publicly, including the necessary registration under the 33 Act and the listing of such additional shares on any securities exchange on which the stock is listed. The trustee should make certain that all proper steps have been taken.

The function of the conversion agent is to receive any debentures surrendered for conversion, compute the number of shares issuable, requisition the shares from the company's transfer agent, and, upon their receipt, cancel the debentures and deliver the shares to the presentor.

Often a fractional interest is involved, which may be handled in a number of ways. The almost universal practice, however, is to pay the value of the fractional interest in cash using the current market price of the stock to give the holder the equivalent value of the fractional interest. The indenture should state clearly the particular method to be followed.

Exercising the conversion right is a privilege to the holder of the debenture, who has the option of deciding when to exercise the privilege.

---

[11] For an excellent review of the problems in drafting antidilution provisions, see Tomczak, *Corporate Trust and Commercial Finance Agreements* (1984), sec. 1.45 *et seq.*

Conversion can frequently be forced by the company, however, by its calling the outstanding debenture issue for redemption. This places a termination date on the conversion privilege and, if the conversion is favorable, results in converting the entire issue. If the conversion privilege is not favorable, there is seldom reason for a redemption call.

It is desirable to have the conversion privilege continue until the maturity or redemption date of the debentures. Some issues provide for an earlier termination date of convertibility, and invariably substantial losses are sustained by security holders who receive no actual notice or misunderstand the provisions of their security. There is usually no good reason for an earlier termination, for it does not offer an advantage to either the company or its security holders and so should be avoided. The trustee should be diligent in endeavoring the change an arbitrary provision, and if unsuccessful, the trustee should insist that security holders be informed of their right to minimize their losses.

Another problem is the matter of accrued interest to the conversion date. The problem may be handled in a number of ways. Occasionally an adjustment is made, as between the accrual of interest and the accrual of dividends. This is an exceptional provision and is feasible only when the company has a fixed dividend policy with fixed dividend payment dates. The more common provision is to state that no adjustment for accrued interest or dividends will be made. It is up to the holder to time the conversion for the greatest advantage.

A convertible issue presents special problems when a record date is involved if a debenture is presented for conversion after the record date and before the interest payment date. Rather than suspend the conversion privilege during this period, the person converting should be required, as a condition of conversion, to deposit funds equal to the amount of interest that would otherwise be payable on the interest payment date on the debenture, or a portion of it, to be converted. These funds are then used to offset the payment made to the person in whose name the debenture was registered on the record date. This practice is desirable when the record holder has sold a debenture after the record date to an individual who converts before the interest payment date. As part of the sale, the seller normally delivers to the purchaser a check for the full interest due, conditional on the payment of interest by the obligor, with the exception that the seller will receive this amount back on the interest payment date. After receiving this check, the purchaser deposits equivalent funds at the time of conversion.

The necessity for requiring a deposit can be illustrated by a hypothetical situation in which, after a record date, dealer A buys twenty-five $1,000 debentures from twenty-five individuals and exchanges them for five $5,000 debentures. Dealer A then sells the $25,000 principal amount to various other dealers, of whom dealer B, having received a $5,000 principal amount, decides to convert before the interest payment date. As the result, the obligor is not required to deposit funds to pay interest on that $5,000 principal amount. Because the twenty-five individual holders of record are entitled to receive their interest on the payment date, the amount equivalent to interest payable of $5,000 debentures must be obtained from dealer B at the time the debenture is presented for conversion.

In the event that the obligor defaults in the payment of interest on the payment date, the funds deposited would be repaid to the person making the conversion. The provisions in the indenture establishing this condition for conversion must, however, be qualified to the extent that funds need not be deposited if the obligation converted has been called for redemption on a date before the payment date. Since there is no obligation to pay interest on an interest payment date on securities called for prior redemption, there would be no record date for such a payment. One question is the possibility of receiving from a debenture holder a check that cannot be collected before the interest checks have been mailed. If this check should prove uncollectible, a loss may result. This can be resolved by withholding delivery of the new securities long enough to allow for collection. Probably no special indenture language is required, but this problem should be kept in mind.

Note that most convertible debenture issues provide for a sinking fund. It is both customary and proper to provide that the obligor will receive credit against its sinking-fund requirement for all debentures converted into the company's stock.

SUBSCRIPTION AGENT

One of the collateral and important functions frequently performed is that of the subscription agent in issuing convertible debentures. In states where stockholders have preemptive rights, any issuance of stock or securities convertible into stock must first be offered to existing stockholders. Even when no preemptive right exists, the offer is frequently the most feasible way of completing a successful offering.

The offering is made by issuing subscription warrants to the existing stockholders. After the amount of the total offering has been calculated, an appropriate ratio to existing shares is determined, and each shareholder is given the right to subscribe to a pro-rata portion of the new offering. These rights are often valuable, with the measure of the value being the difference between the offering price and the market value of the debentures. Warrants are usually issued by the company's stock transfer agent and evidence the right to subscribe to a specified principal amount of debentures. The offer is normally underwritten, with the underwriters agreeing to buy all debentures not subscribed for through the exercise of warrants. Under the underwriting agreement, the life of the warrants is customarily limited to a period of two or three weeks from their date of issue.

The function of the subscription agent is twofold. First, the agent accepts and processes subscriptions to the debentures. This entails receiving warrants with checks in payment of the subscribed debentures. When issuable, the debentures are requisitioned from the trustee and delivered to the subscribers.

The second function concerns the purchase and sale of rights. A stockholder who is unwilling to subscribe to the debentures is still entitled to the value of the rights represented by the warrant. Others may wish to exercise only a portion of their warrant and sell the balance of the rights, and still others may wish to acquire a larger interest than their warrant entitles them to and therefore need to acquire additional rights. Because of the large number of small holders, trading these rights through normal brokerage channels might be very expensive. For the convenience of such holders, the subscription agent is permitted to buy and sell rights. It offsets the purchase and sale orders for each day's activity and either buys or sells the net position in the open market. The average price received on all transactions for the day is used to determine the price at which all purchases are computed. A small commission charge is imposed on the holders for this service.

Put/Demand Option Agent

For those issues with a "put" or "demand" option, the paying agent must be prepared to accept the securities against payment, usually at par, to the registered holder. In some issues, the securities are purchased by a remarketing agent rather than the issuer itself. Chapter 4 explained the role of the remarketing agent and the tender agent.

ACCOUNTING AND DESTRUCTION

The purpose of every security indenture is to secure payment of the obligations issued. The proper accounting for all such obligations is one of the trustee's main functions. Provision must also be made for the proper disposition of all obligations canceled because of transfer, payment, exchange, or conversion or for other reasons. Although these functions are usually performed by the trustee, they may be performed by the agent, but with full liability accruing to the trustee if the canceled securities are not properly controlled and disposed of by the trustee according to its policies and current regulations.

Accounting for Interest Obligations

A fully registered security represents the obligation for both principal and interest. When such a security is surrendered and canceled, the trustee is entitled to assume that all amounts due have been paid or otherwise discharged. It is desirable, however, for the trustee to maintain a more current account of interest payments. When it acts as registrar and interest-disbursing agent, its own records supply the requisite evidence of payment of all amounts of registered interest due. When the issuer or another agent disburses registered interest, the trustee should establish a procedure for ascertaining that all registered interest payments have been made. The most common and practical way to do this is for the trustee to receive and rely on a certification by the disbursing agent of the payments made. Whatever the form of the evidence received, it should be able to establish the fact of payment.

Accounting for coupon interest is a different matter. The coupons represent separate and distinct obligations, and the trustee should have satisfactory evidence of their payment or cancellation. A great deal of progress has been made over the years in simplifying the procedure of accounting for interest coupons. In the early days of corporate security issues, an elaborate procedure was followed. Large coupon ledgers were prepared that had a separate page for each security issued. As the coupons were paid, they were pasted on the appropriate page on this ledger sheet, with the date of payment entered. This provided a complete record, but the expense was substantial. For most corporate issues, this practice has been obsolete for many years, although some municipalities still follow it.

A major step forward was taken when issuers permitted trustees to dispose of canceled coupons by destroying them (usually by burning them). Concern for the environment and restrictions against burning now have given way to shredding the securities instead. Agents and trustees must take the business of destroying securities very seriously, to avoid the future presentation for payment those securities reported as destroyed. At first, an appropriate certification was prepared as evidence of such destruction. The burning was witnessed by both obligor officials and the trustee, but later, the trustee was permitted to perform this task alone. An elaborate exhibit was attached to the destruction certificate that included a description of the issue, the maturity date and amount of the coupons, and the security serial numbers. This costly procedure necessitated that all coupons paid be sorted in numerical order so that they could be listed on the appropriate schedules.

In the late 1940s, a number of trustees began to question the necessity of such an elaborate procedure. Investigation revealed that these detailed schedules were seldom if ever referred to. Such detail was, therefore, unnecessary for proper accounting. As a result of these studies, the accounting and destruction procedure was changed. Now this accounting needs only the total number of coupons and the total dollar amount for each coupon maturity date. The necessity of sorting and listing the coupons by security serial number has thus been eliminated, although some banks using computer-generated payment records still follow this practice.

To ensure proper accounting control, the trustee maintains a subsidiary destruction ledger or computer file. The total interest due is entered for each interest maturity date. The total registered interest disbursed and the total value of the coupons of that maturity shown by each destruction certificate are credited. The resulting balance, if any, shows the amount of coupons outstanding and unpaid.

When paying agents other than the trustee are paying a large percentage of the coupons, their subsequent shipment to and audit by the trustee requires an expensive and time-consuming arrangement. The trustee and the issuer should therefore authorize the paying agents to complete the disposition of the canceled coupons by satisfactorily destroying them. The trustee may then use the agent's certificate as evidence of the coupons' destruction.

Accounting for Principal Obligations

Each security canceled for any reason must be included in an appropriate accounting. The destruction certificates covering principal obligations are similar to those covering coupons, except that the securities' serial numbers are shown on the certificate or the supporting schedule. There is no reason for identifying and reporting the reason for the cancellation (i.e., transfer, exchange, payment, etc.) except with regard to any remaining inventory of unissued securities.

Registered securities are processed in a different manner than coupon bearer securities. When registered securities are canceled because of transfer or for any reason requiring the assignment of the security, their destruction is usually deferred for a reasonable period of time, usually one year, and an image or microfilm record is made of the security and the assignment before being destroyed. When the assignment is received separate from the security, it is usually imaged or microfilmed with the security and destroyed with it, together with any documentation supporting a "legal" transfer (e.g., one involving a corporation or a decedent). It is important that the laws of each jurisdiction be consulted when establishing canceled security retention and destruction periods.

LOST, STOLEN, AND DESTROYED SECURITIES

Securities are sometimes stolen or, more frequently, lost or misplaced by the holders. The holder then notifies the trustee (or in the case of a tax-exempt security, the fiscal agent or registrar) and requests that a stop order be placed against the security or coupon. Care should be used in acknowledging any such request, for the trustee may be placed in a position in which it cannot comply. Registered securities that have been endorsed and bearer securities and coupons are fully negotiable and so are valid obligations in the hands of a bona fide purchaser.[12]

The trustee or registrar (or fiscal agent) receiving a stop order should promptly refer to its records and communicate the information to all agents. In addition, the trustee or agent must promptly give this information to the Securities Information Center (SIC), the entity designated by the SEC to receive reports of loss or theft.[13] The SIC maintains a database of such information in order to respond to inquiries by institutions receiving, holding, or processing securities. Holders sometimes fail to notify the trustee that a lost security has been found, particularly in the case of coupons. Neither the trustee nor any agent should take it upon itself to

---

[12] Defined in UCC article 8 as "a purchaser for value in good faith and without notice of any adverse claim."

[13] Rule 17f-1 (17 CRF 240.17f-1, July 1, 1979).

remove a stop, even if a long period of time has elapsed, unless (1) the missing security has been surrendered to the trustee and is canceled by it or (2) before a replacement (or payment, as later discussed) has been issued, the holder who requested the stop order notifies the trustee and requests that it be removed.

When a stop order has been filed with the issuer (or trustee or agent) and the security is later presented, the issuer or agent is permitted to discharge its responsibility for the adverse claim[14] in any reasonable manner. It is recommended that the procedure outlined in the UCC always be followed.[15] The adverse claimant must always be notified by registered or certified mail, and the person presenting the security must be named. This notice must also grant the option of a court order or the filing of a sufficient indemnity bond.

Most indentures provide for the replacement of securities that have been lost, stolen, or destroyed, upon the presentation of satisfactory indemnity. This indemnity is usually a surety bond executed by the holder and a surety company, satisfactory to both the obligor issuer and the trustee. Some outstanding security issues have no provision for issuing replacement certificates, including a number of municipal and other public and quasi-public issues.

Under the UCC, the issuer (and the trustee) must issue a new security in place of the original if the owner (1) so requests before the issuer has been notified that the security has been acquired by a bona fide purchaser, (2) files with the issuer a sufficient indemnity bond, and (3) satisfies any other reasonable requirements imposed by the issuer.[16] Two conditions preclude the owner from receiving a replacement security: the failure by the owner to notify the issuer within a reasonable time after the owner has been notified, and a transfer of the original security has been registered before the issuer receives notice. If when presented, the original security was properly endorsed, the issuer is protected under this rule and may refuse the demand for a replacement.

After a security has been replaced, if a bona fide purchaser presents the original for registration of transfer or payment, the issuer must register the transfer unless the registration would result in an overissuance, in which case the issuer must either purchase and deliver a like security if reasonably available or, if not, pay the amount that the buyer paid for the

---

[14] A claim by someone not in possession of the security. It includes a claim that a transfer was or would be wrongful or that a particular person is the owner or has an interest in the security.

[15] UCC sec. 8–403.

[16] Id. sec. 8–405.

security with interest from the date of demand. The issuer may recover the replacement security from the buyer to whom it was issued (or anyone taking from this person except another bona fide purchaser) in addition to exercising any rights it may have under the surety bond.

Many indentures permit the obligor company to avoid the complications of issuing a replacement security by paying the lost security or coupon if it has, or is about to, become due and if the other conditions related to replacement are complied with. In the case of a convertible debenture, the indenture should specify that the right to convert is not destroyed by paying instead of issuing a new debenture.

MISCELLANEOUS FUNCTIONS

Certain other functions may be required to be performed by the trustee or the company's agents, depending on the terms of the particular issue. The main subsidiary functions are outlined next.

Validating Securities and Coupons

When a security is mutilated for any reason, the easiest solution is to cancel it and replace it with a new security. When only a single coupon has been mutilated, it is much simpler to validate the coupon, by having an official of the company sign a statement on the back of the coupon to the effect that it is a valid obligation. If this procedure is not feasible, the trustee itself may validate the coupon. The language used should be substantially as follows: "This coupon belongs to Security No. ——— and is a valid obligation of the obligor." The security itself should always be examined to ascertain that it is in fact a valid obligation.

Exchanges Under Judicial Reorganization or Recapitalization Plans

An important function is involved in implementing a reorganization or recapitalization plan. The agent is in effect acting for the reorganization proceedings and delivery of the cash and securities authorized.

Because of the complexity and diversity of such plans and arrangements, we will not describe the procedure in detail. In considering the acceptance of an appointment, the agent should ensure that the plan has been validly confirmed by the appropriate court order, that the claims and distributions schedule are clear, that proper direction and instructions concerning its functions have been received and approved by the court, that a definite termination date for the exchange has been set, and, most important, that the compensation to be paid for its services is sufficient to cover the expense and detail of the work involved.

Agent for Securities Not Issued Under an Indenture

The most important securities not issued under an indenture are those issued by states, municipalities and authorities. Generally, the same services are required as in the case of corporate obligations, with, however, a much greater emphasis at present on the paying agent's and registrar's functions. The procedures followed are similar except that the canceled securities are either shipped to the finance officer of the state or municipality, or the agent itself performs the accounting and destruction service customarily performed by the trustee in the case of corporate obligations.

In regard to corporations' direct placement financing, long-term notes are sometimes issued under purchase agreements not requiring the service of a trustee under an indenture. A bank is frequently, however, appointed the agent of the obligor company to service the note issue. It maintains a record of the note holders, makes interest payments, determines the allocation of periodic sinking-fund installments, acts as an exchange agent, and, in general, performs all the ministerial details that the company itself would otherwise be required to perform.

MUNICIPAL SECURITIES AND THE DEPOSITORY

Certificate Immobilization

The potential benefits of certificate immobilization and centralization have been understood in the corporate security sector for many years. However, until the enactment of TEFRA[17] legislation, municipal securities issuers had little knowledge of fully registered instruments, as bearer securities were the norm—municipal trades were traditionally settled by physical delivery versus payment (known as *DVP*) at the purchaser's premises. Anticipating the potential impact of DVP for registered municipal securities trades, the Municipal Securities Rulemaking Board established regulations to automate the settlement practices.

[17] See chapter 2, note 7, *supra.*

One of the rules that affected security registrars required the use of book-entry delivery systems to expedite the settlement process.[18] This required, in part and allowing for specific exceptions, that interdealer transactions be settled by book-entry delivery in a registered clearing agency (i.e., depository). Since then, most publicly traded municipal security issues have settled through a depository, the most significant being the Depository Trust Company in New York City. When a security becomes eligible, the underwriter directs the trustee/security registrar to register the securities in the depository's nominee name. The securities are then delivered to the depository against a trust receipt, generally one business day before the closing date. The depository assumes custodial responsibility for the securities by placing the physical securities in its vault. Upon joint notification by the trustee and the underwriter that all conditions for issuing the securities have been met (i.e., that the security issue has closed), the depository credits the appropriate value of the securities to the lead managing underwriter's account and processes book-entry deliveries to the accounts of the syndicate members and other purchasers of the issue.

For older issues allowing the issuance of physical securities, subsequent transfers of ownership may be through either book-entry notation on the participant's records or the withdrawal of physical securities from the depository's vault to be reregistered in the name of the purchaser or purchaser's representative, a process referred to as *withdrawal by transfer*. To eliminate the issuance of physical securities, most new security issues no longer allow the issuance of certificates. One balance certificate per authorized interest rate is issued in the name of the depository nominee, and holders are advised initially that they will not receive certificates. This effort has reduced the numbers of interest checks issued by paying agents and has served to speed the payment process. Nevertheless, a significant number of registered interest checks are still issued by transfer agents for securities that were not immobilized.

At the end of each business day, the depository nets all trades for each participant and either collects funds from or pays funds to them, depending on their net position.

Book-Entry-Only Securities

Municipal certificate immobilization through depository settlement gained momentum and quickly expanded to a procedure that had been employed by the U.S. government securities market for many years:

---

[18]MSRB rule G-12(f)(11), effective Feb. 1, 1985.

book-entry-only issuance (BEO). This program requires that issuers create a single "global" certificate for each maturity within a specific security issue. The underwriter instructs the security registrar to register the global certificates in the nominee name of the depository, with the certificates to be held in the depository's vault until final maturity or redemption. Any reduction in the authorized principal amount of securities outstanding, usually the result of a partial call for redemption, is posted on the depository's records and on the records of the trustee and security registrar. No physical securities change hands until the issue is paid in full, at which time the trustee or security registrar cancels and disposes of the global certificates.

The purchaser of BEO securities receives confirmation of a trade from its broker-dealer or bank. Subsequent activity, such as payments of interest and principal, is reflected on the customer's account record and is shown on periodic statements furnished by the broker-dealer or bank. Until the securities are sold or otherwise disposed of, the security position remains on the broker-dealer's or bank's participant account record at the depository. Ownership is transferred only thorough book-entry debits and credits to the purchaser's and the seller's participant account records.

In this environment, the trustee must recognize and prepare for the challenges presented by the issuance of BEO securities. Obviously, any revenue lost will hurt the organization's profitability, but also important is losing the capability of direct contact with those whom the trustee represents—the security holders.

The depository generally does not release participant records information without the issuer's written consent. Consequently, the trustee must obtain from the issuer a blanket authorization consenting to the release of information by the depository upon the request of the trustee. In a default, the trustee must be able to reach the security holders to obtain direction or consents and to provide critical information in an timely manner.

The need to standardize the processing practices of the trustee and security registrar has increased significantly with the growth of depository-eligible municipal securities. For a new security issue to be accepted as eligible by the depository, the trustee or agent may be required to execute an operational agreement that states, among other things, the required procedures governing the delivery of original issuance securities, the timeliness of certificate transfers, the reporting and notice formats and time frames, the methods of transmitting interest and principal payments, and the municipal call-processing procedures.

It is important that the appointed trustee and security registrar try to comply with the terms of the arrangement to ensure the continuing eligibility of the issue for which they are acting. The depository generally sends to the trustees and security registrars periodic performance reports so that any processing concerns can be identified and resolved promptly.

SEVENTEEN

Legislation, Regulation, and Risk Management

THE TRUST INDENTURE ACT OF 1939

The idea of regulation—particularly by the federal government—is a fixed and accepted principle in everyday business life and is assuming greater significance each year. Even so, there still are wide differences of opinion about the proper scope and purpose of such regulation and the limits to which it may properly be extended. In certain areas, regulation undoubtedly is important, but it should normally be limited to the establishment of minimum standards or modes of conduct deemed essential to the public interest to which all engaged in the particular activity are required to adhere. The value of regulation is directly proportional to the uniformity of standards that exist, or are capable of existing, in the particular activity.

The scope and value of government regulation are necessarily limited with respect to trust indentures. That is, trust indentures do not in themselves constitute a "business"; they are simply the instruments by which all types of businesses secure financing, and each type of financing produces its own type of indenture.

The trust indenture was developed with few restrictions imposed by governmental authorities. Legislation concerning the sale or distribution of securities was initially limited to the blue-sky laws enacted by various states that focused on fraudulent devices in the sale of securities.

Following the financial collapse of the 1930s, defaults under indentures became numerous, and many people's savings were depleted or, in some cases, wiped out. The concurrence of the drop in security values with the Great Depression brought the whole security structure to public attention. The result was the enactment by Congress of a series of security acts designed to protect investors.

The first legislation was the 33 Act, sometimes called the "truth in securities" act. With certain exceptions, this act requires filing a registration statement covering each public issue of securities and using a prospectus in connection with their sale and distribution. Stringent penalties are imposed for misrepresentations or misleading statements in either of these documents. The Securities Exchange Act of 1934 (34 Act)[1] was designed to regulate national securities exchanges, the listing of securities on them, and the purchase and sale of securities through these exchanges. This act also created the Securities and Exchange Commission (SEC) to administer both this and the 33 Act. Section 211 of the 34 Act directed the commission to "make a study and investigation of the work, activities, personnel, and functions of protective and reorganization committees in connection with the reorganization, readjustment, rehabilitation, liquidation, or consolidation of persons and properties and to report the result of its studies and investigations and its recommendations to the Congress." As a part of this study, the commission included a report on the activities of trustees under indentures.

Because of this report, the so-called Barkley bill was introduced in the Senate in 1937 and was referred to a subcommittee of the Committee on Banking and Currency. Although the measure was favorably reported by the committee, the Senate did not vote on it during that session. A similar bill was introduced in the House of Representatives in 1938 and in both the House and the Senate in 1939. The latter bill was enacted by Congress as the Trust Indenture Act of 1939 (TIA) and became effective on February 3, 1940.

The TIA was the first attempt by the federal government to regulate the indentures under which securities are issued. In its report, the SEC recommended extremely stringent provisions, including continuous supervisory administration by it, and the initial bill embodied these provisions. The legislation finally enacted was worked out by the SEC and a special committee of the American Bankers Association after extended hearings before committees of the House and Senate. The final version of the TIA differed substantially from the bill originally recommended but did not alter the basic concept of the trust indenture as a special financing contract among the parties.

[1] Codified in scattered sections of 15 U.S.C. secs. 77 and 78 (1976).

The TIA was enacted as Title III to the 33 Act, and its administrative provisions were drafted to dovetail with the SEC's administration of the securities act. In general, it required that all indentures, with specified exceptions, be submitted to the SEC for "qualification" along with the issuer's registration statement under the securities act.[2] The actual "regulation" provided by the TIA consisted solely of qualifying the indenture. Once the indenture was qualified, the SEC, with one minor exception, had no further jurisdiction over the indenture or the obligor, the trustee, or the security holders. The purpose of the act and the qualification of indentures was to ensure that every indenture contained the minimum standards imposed by the act and conformed to the requirements of the TIA.

In general, the legislation had three purposes: (1) to establish certain minimum standards with respect to specified acts and duties of the obligor and trustee to which all indentures must conform (by requiring the inclusion, or incorporation by reference, in each qualified indenture, of specified provisions that became an essential part of the contract); (2) to include minimum standards of responsibility and accountability for the trustees under indentures and to eliminate the broad exculpatory provisions formerly included; and (3) to eliminate any conflicting relationships between the trustee and the obligor and between the trustee and the underwriters for the obligor.

Although the original TIA did not eliminate defaults or losses to investors, it did not prove to be the burden that many trust companies had feared. The TIA went into effect in 1940 and became accepted as part of the normal routine of indenture administration. Whereas the prescribed provisions were required only in indentures qualified under the act, most of them came to be accepted as reasonable standards for all indenture administration for corporate as well as municipal debt securities and came to be included in almost all indentures, whether or not qualification was required.

Before the original TIA was enacted, all rights under the indenture contract were enforced by the common law of contracts and fiduciary obligations, with appropriate remedies for breaching the contract available in state courts. The legislative history of the act itself suggested that Congress intended that this approach be continued, instead of having the TIA be a matter of federal law, enforceable in federal courts.[3] In 1975, however, a federal district court in *Morris v. Cantor*[4] held that the TIA created

[2] TIA sec. 305(b). See section 304 for securities exempted from the act.

[3] See Dropkin, "Implied Civil Liability Under the Trust Indenture Act: Trends and Prospects," 52 *Tul. L. Rev.* 299, 322–24 (1978).

[4] 390 F. Supp. 817 (S.D.N.Y. 1975).

substantive liabilities for violating provisions of qualified indentures and that indenture security holders could enforce these liabilities as a matter of federal law in a federal court.[5] The judge concluded that the TIA "must be viewed as an indirect method of imposing nationally uniform and clearly defined obligations upon those associated with the issuance of corporate debt" and held that the act "created liability" as though it had directly mandated the same actions by trustees and issuers and, consequently, conferred jurisdiction on the district courts over lawsuits to enforce that liability.[6] Thus the existence of a private right of action was held to follow.

THE TRUST INDENTURE REFORM ACT OF 1990

The first comprehensive revision of the TIA became effective on November 15, 1990. Its principal purpose was to modernize the fifty-year-old TIA. As stated in the Senate committee report accompanying the reform bill in 1989,[7]

> During this period, however, the public market for debt securities has undergone significant changes. Innovations in the forms of debt instruments have produced securities, such as collateralized mortgage obligations, [which] were not contemplated in 1939. Technological developments and regulatory changes have resulted in new distribution methods including shelf offerings, direct placements and "dutch auctions." In addition, public securities markets have been profoundly changed by the increasing internationalization of the securities markets. Thus, current market practices conflict with many of the assumptions underlying the act, which were based on financial customs prevailing in 1939. . . . Enactment of Title IV would conform the Act to the present realities of the market and make it adaptable to future developments, while easing the administration of the Act.[8]

The following are the most significant features of the TIRA, which are discussed in detail in other chapters:

1. The trustee's resignation for a conflict of interest is postponed until there is a default under the indenture. Except in certain limited instances, a creditor relationship with the obligor has been added as a conflicting interest.[9] There is, however, one

---

[5] This result was recognized as a possibility in a footnote of Caplin v. Marine Midland Grace Trust Co., 406 U.S. 416, 426 n.17 (1971).

[6] 390 F.Supp. at 822.

[7] Report 101–155, Senate Comm. on Banking, Housing & Urban Affairs (Oct. 2, 1989).

[8] Id. at 29.

[9] TIA sec. 310(b).

conflict that is operative at all times: the absolute prohibition of the obligor and its affiliates from serving as trustees for its own securities.[10] To obviate the need to resign as the result of a "technical" default, the trustee's resignation is automatically stayed except in the case of a payment default, pending its application to the SEC that the default may be soon cured or that its continuing on as trustee will not be inconsistent with the bondholders' interests.

2. The need to state all the provisions of TIA Sections 310 through 317 in the indenture has been eliminated. The TIRA now mandates these provisions as a matter of federal law, with the optional provisions now deemed to be included unless they are expressly excluded.

3. The trustee's "annual" report need only be prepared and sent out to the security holders if there has been (a) any change in its eligibility and qualifications under Section 310(b); (b) the creation of or any material change in the relationships specified in Section 310(b) (1) through (10); (c) any change in any loans owed by the obligor to it or in any property or funds in its possession; or (d) the occurrence of any of the transactions spelled out in Section 313(a) (3), (6), (7), or (8).[11]

4. The obligor is required to give the trustee an annual no-default certificate, a requirement that already exists in most corporate indentures. The major difference is that the TIRA requires that it be signed by the obligor's principal executive officer, principal financial officer, or principal accounting officer.[12]

5. The obligor has the authority, but not the requirement, to establish a record date for determining those holders entitled to vote on or consent to any change in the indenture.[13]

6. The appointment of a successor trustee becomes effective only on the appointment of and acceptance by a successor. This provision, which is found in many indentures to prevent the orphaning of trusts, applies in all situations, including the trustee's voluntary resignation in anticipation of an obligor's default.[14]

7. The so-called clawback period has been shortened—from four to three months preceding the filing of a proceeding under the

[10] Id. sec. 310(a)(5).
[11] Id. sec. 313(a). See also chapter 13, note 4, *supra*.
[12] Id. sec. 314(a)(4).
[13] Id. sec. 316(c).
[14] Id. sec. 310(b), last sentence.

Bankruptcy Reform Act of 1978—during which any payments made to the trustee bank must be shared with the security holders. This change merely conforms the requirement to the preferential claim period in the Bankruptcy Act.[15]

8. The TIRA provisions apply to all outstanding indentures and supersede any inconsistent provision of any outstanding indenture. The only exception to the latter is the *optional* provisions not contained in pre–November 15, 1990, indentures.

9. Indentures can now be qualified with a trustee to be appointed after the registration statement is effective (under a Rule 415 shelf registration filing), provided that the issuer files an application simultaneously with the trustee's statement of eligibility. The application is effective automatically after ten days, unless the SEC issues an order finding the trustee ineligible.[16]

10. A foreign bank can, under certain circumstances, act as a trustee.[17]

11. The SEC has sweeping and open-ended exemptive authority to act by rule, regulation, or order to exempt any person, indenture, security, or transaction from any one or more of the act's provisions if it is necessary or appropriate in the public interest.[18]

12. Criminal sanctions for violating the TIA's provisions, which together with the SEC's new enforcement powers[19] and the retroactive effect of the TIRA, can be used against an issuer or trustee that fails to perform any of the specified duties. Although this may cause concern to corporate trustees, also note that TIA Section 309(e), which was not affected by the TIRA, provides that the SEC is not empowered to conduct an investigation to determine compliance with its provisions or to enforce the provisions. It is fairly obvious, however, that both issuers and trustees should make sure that they have timely and comprehensive procedures in place, to avoid any failure to comply with any of the provisions of this federal law.

To maintain some historical perspective with regard to this legislation, it is interesting to note that some of the concepts embodied in the TIRA originated in the proposed Federal Securities Code, a project begun in

[15] Id. sec. 311.
[16] Id. sec. 305(b)(2).
[17] Id. sec. 310(a)(1).
[18] Id. sec. 304(d).
[19] See Securities Enforcement Remedies and Penny Stock Act of 1990, P.L. 101–249.

1972 by the American Law Institute to review and codify the laws relating to securities distribution and markets, investment advisers, trust indentures, investment companies, and utility holding companies.[20] The code included provisions that the duties and responsibilities of trustees and others be interpreted, approved, and enforced exclusively as a matter of federal law, that certain enumerated provisions would be required to be included in every qualified indenture (e.g., notice of "payment" default), and that the SEC's enforcement authority would be expanded to a level comparable with that provided in other areas of securities law. The final official draft of the code, which was completed and approved by the American Law Institute in 1978, received the support of the SEC, but legislation to enact it was never introduced in Congress.

THE UNIFORM COMMERCIAL CODE (UCC)

The UCC has been adopted in forty-nine states, the District of Columbia, and the Virgin Islands. The only exception is Louisiana, which adopted only articles 1, 3, 4, 5, 7, and 8. Although the UCC deals with all facets of commercial practice, articles 8 and 9 are of particular importance in the corporate trust field.

Article 8 deals with investment securities and conforms or establishes certain basic principles:

1. It makes all investment securities negotiable. This enables greater flexibility in the form of these instruments without the fear of creating problems of negotiability.
2. It broadens the application of the rules relating to fiduciary transfers, placing responsibility on the fiduciary rather than the transfer agent, and in effect penalizing the transfer agent that requires excessive documentation.
3. It defines the responsibilities of an authenticating trustee, transfer agent, and registrar.
4. It imposes direct and independent responsibility and liability on the transfer agent or registrar for their acts. It is no defense to show that such action was strictly in accordance with a principal's direction.

[20] See generally, Richard Stark, "The Trust Indenture Act of 1979 in the Proposed Federal Securities Code," 32 *Vand. L. Rev.* 527 (Mar. 1979); SEC Release No. 33–6242 (20 SEC Docket No. 19 at 1483, Sept. 18, 1980).

5. It establishes guides for issuers and transfer agents in dealing with adverse claims.

Under the 1977 amendments to article 8, provision was made for the use of uncertificated securities, that is, a share, participation, or other interest in property or an enterprise of the issuer or an obligation of the issuer that was not represented by an instrument and whose transfer was registered on the issuer's books without a certificate being issued.

In 1994, the revised article 8 was approved by the American Law Institute and the National Conference of Commissioners on Uniform State Laws. As of mid-1997, it had been adopted by thirty-one states. The revision establishes rules concerning the system through which securities are held. It specifies the mechanisms by which ownership and other interests in securities are recorded and changed and also some of the rights and duties of the parties who participate in the securities holding system.

Revised article 8 deals with "direct" versus "indirect" holding systems. It minimizes the "certificated versus uncertificated" distinction reflected in the current article 8. The most significant distinction is whether one has a "direct" or an "indirect" relationship with the issuer, as when the investment is held through one or more intermediaries. In addition, the revision specifies that the interest of the ultimate beneficial owner does not constitute a direct property interest in the asset. A new term was established for this interest, namely, *securities entitlement*, which is the holder's package of rights and interests against a security's intermediary and its property.

Article 9 deals with secured transactions, and its impact on commercial transactions is probably more extensive than that of any other UCC article. Unlike article 8, which deals specifically with investment securities, article 9 was not drafted with corporate indentures primarily in mind. It is nevertheless important to this area, since it establishes uniform rules relating to all security transactions involving personal property, regardless of the form of the particular transaction or the security documents. The present trend toward more special-purpose secured financing—in which contract rights, equipment leases, receivables, other debt obligations, and the like constitute the principal security—makes desirable an understanding of the article's basic purposes and principles.

In addition to providing a single body of law for security transactions affecting personal property, the UCC made significant changes or clarifications in four important areas:

1. It provides statutory authority and rules for accounts receivable financing.
2. It specifically authorizes and makes effective arrangements for

both subjecting after-acquired property to a security agreement and arranging future advances under the agreement without the necessity of preparing, signing, and recording or filing supplemental agreements. This greatly facilitates security arrangements involving property that is constantly being disposed of and replaced, such as inventory.

3. It permits the debtor to mortgage its inventory, stock-in-trade, or similar property and to continue to operate the business in a normal manner and in accordance with the understanding and agreement of the parties, without the necessity of cumbersome provisions for the flow of proceeds.

4. It recognizes and provides for the special status of the purchase-money security interest.

Most corporate mortgages secure obligations that are outstanding for many years. Some railroad bonds have maturities extending for a hundred years or more, and many corporate mortgages, particularly those of public utilities and railroads, are open-end indentures, designed to serve as permanent financing media. As security, the obligor customarily mortgages all land, plants, equipment, machinery, fixtures, franchises, and all other items of property, real, personal, or mixed, then owned or thereafter acquired, which generally constitute its fixed plant and property account, permanent investments, and other classes of property exclusive of cash, receivables, merchandise, and the like.

Although in most normal commercial-financing arrangements, the intrinsic value of the collateral is readily measurable and adequate to secure the loan, the real security underlying a corporate mortgage is the "going concern" value of the business itself rather than the special value of the individual items of property. The importance of the security interest is the priority claim against the business's capital assets that are necessary to its continuing as a going concern. Because the specific items of property are constantly being replaced or otherwise changing, the effectiveness of the after-acquired property clause is of paramount importance.

Although no further action is required to continue the perfected status of the security interest in personal property covered by a corporate mortgage of real and personal property recorded before the UCC took effect, it is not clear what action, if any, should be taken with respect to personal property acquired after the effective date. If a supplemental mortgage is executed and filed or if there is additional financing under the mortgage, the requisite financing statement should be filed in the state's Department of State.

If the obligor has outstanding more than one mortgage covering its property and there is additional financing under a junior or refunding mortgage, financing statements under all mortgages have proper order of priority because of the "first to file" rule.

When partial releases of personal property are executed under a corporate mortgage, it would seem unnecessary to file for a partial release unless it involves the release of all such property in the jurisdiction. If necessary to protect the purchaser of the property released, executing the release on the bill of sale should be all that is required.

SECURITIES-PROCESSING REGULATIONS

Banks serve as major processors of securities and are regulated by three regulatory bodies. The board of governors of the Federal Reserve System is responsible for regulating state-chartered banks that are members of the Federal Reserve System. The Office of the Comptroller of the Currency, a unit of the U.S. Treasury Department, is responsible for regulating nationally chartered banks, and the Federal Deposit Insurance Corporation regulates banks that are not members of the Federal Reserve System. Each of these regulatory bodies supervises and enforces banking laws and regulations through regular examinations of their assigned banks.

Partially as a result of the intense criticism of the securities-processing industry, arising out of the heavy volume in securities trading during 1968–1970, a number of studies by congressional committees were made to determine the nature and extent of any additional legislation that would improve the clearance and settlement of securities transactions.[21] The most significant result was the enactment of the Securities Acts Amendments of 1975,[22] authorizing the establishment of "a national system for the clearance and settlement of securities transactions and the safeguarding of securities and funds related thereto."[23] To implement this objective, the 34 Act was amended by adding Section 17A[24] to provide for the federal regulation of clearing agencies and transfer agents. The SEC and the federal bank regulatory authorities were permitted to adopt

[21] In particular, U.S. Senate, Committee on Banking, Housing and Urban Affairs, *Report of the Subcommittee on Securities*, 92d Cong., 2d sess. (1972); U.S. House, Committee on Interstate and Foreign Commerce, *Report of the Subcommittee on Commerce and Finance*, 92d Cong., 2d sess. (1972).

[22] Pub. L. No. 94–29 (June 5, 1975).

[23] Id. sec. 2.

[24] Id. sec. 15.

rules and regulations governing the conduct of transfer agents and to enforce compliance.[25]

Under its authority, the SEC has promulgated rules implementing (1) the registration of transfer agents;[26] (2) the requirements for the almost universal fingerprinting of all persons selling securities, those handling or processing securities, monies, or books and records relating to them, and those having direct supervisory responsibility over persons engaged in such activities;[27] (3) the promulgation of minimum performance standards and record-keeping requirements for all registered transfer agents, including transfer turnaround requirements;[28] (4) the establishment of a reporting and inquiry system for all lost, stolen, missing, or counterfeit securities, whose prime objective is to prevent the misuse or fraudulent use of such securities, particularly as it relates to collateralizing loans;[29] (5) the regulations governing the maintenance of accurate security holder files and the safeguarding of funds and securities;[30] (6) the requirement that any registered transfer agent acting as a depositary in the case of a tender offer (or as an exchange agent in the case of an exchange offer) must establish special designated accounts with the national securities depositories to permit securities to move to and from the tender/exchange agent through a book-entry mechanism;[31] (7) the timely mailing of transfer agent journals by a cotransfer agent to the record-keeping transfer agent and a maximum time period in which to respond to dividend and interest inquiries;[32] (8) a requirement for filing an annual report on Form TA-2;[33] (9) the establishment of signature guaranty programs;[34] (10) the prior notification by transfer agents to a qualified registered securities depository (e.g., DTC) of the assumption or termination of services on behalf of an issuer or a change in a transfer agent's name or address;[35] (11) requiring transfer agents (effective 12/1/97) to conduct searches in an effort to locate lost security holders, and to maintain written procedures to effect compliance;[36] and (12) requiring transfer agents (effective 2/1/98)

---

[25] Securities Exchange Act of 1934, sec. 17A(d).

[26] Rule 17 2–1 (17 CFR 240.17 2–1, Oct. 22, 1975).

[27] Rule 17f-2 (17 CFR 240.17f-2, Mar. 16, 1976).

[28] Rules 17Ad-1/7 (17 CFR 240.17Ad-1 to 7, June 16, 1977).

[29] Rule 17f-1 (17 CFR 240.17f-1, July 1, 1979).

[30] Rules 17Ad-9/13 (17 CFR 240.17 Ad-9 to 13, June 21, 1983).

[31] Rule 17Ad-14 (17 CFR 240.17Ad-14, Jan. 19, 1984).

[32] Rule 17Ad-10 (17 CFR 240.17Ad-10, Apr. 1, 1986).

[33] Rule 17Ac2–2 (17 CFR 240.17Ac2–2, May 5, 1986).

[34] Rule 17Ad-15 (17 CFR 240. 17Ad-16, Jan. 6, 1992).

[35] Rule 17Ad-16 (17 CFR 240.17Ad-16, Feb. 1, 1995).

[36] Rule 17Ad-17 (17 CFR 240.17Ad-17, Oct. 1, 1997).

to file information on lost security holders with the Commission, on amended form TA-2.[37]

Each year, as of December 31, the trustee is required to report the type and the volume of its corporate trust and agency business on the Annual Report of Trust Assets—Form FFIEC 001, Schedule C—Corporate Trust. As new concerns and problems appear, additional regulations will be promulgated—unless the securities industry itself is able to resolve these to the satisfaction of the federal regulatory agencies.

RISK MANAGEMENT

During the past decade, increasing numbers of corporate trustees have placed greater emphasis on managing the potential risks inherent in the business. Risk management works best when it is an established unit in the bank. The unit typically reports to the senior officer in charge of the fiduciary lines of business. In some banks, the fiduciary risk manager may report directly to the bank's chief credit officer or chief executive officer.

The Office of the Comptroller of the Currency (OCC) revised Regulation 9, dated January 2, 1997, provides the basic regulations for managing trust business lines. Not only does Regulation 9 (Reg 9) establish the need for policies, account preacceptance, and postacceptance reviews; it also states the requirements for audits, record keeping, and control of assets and establishes the need for a fiduciary audit committee, to name just a few of its purposes. Corporate trustees often consult Section 9.6(c)—annual review and argue it is not applicable to corporate trusts. Although this section requires an annual account review at least once every calendar year, it specifically limits the review to those accounts for which the bank has investment discretion. It can be argued that corporate trustees typically do not have discretion over investments, since they are directed by the obligor. A good management tool is to mandate an annual account review of all trustee appointments. The review allows a structured opportunity for account officers to verify that all governing document requirements are being satisfied. See exhibit 10 for a sample checklist.

Reg 9, along with the other rules and regulations noted earlier, establishes the need for a structured risk management program. But risk management should not be confused with the function of the internal auditor, who satisfies Reg 9 by completing an annual internal audit.

[37] Rule 17a-24 (17 CFR 240.17a-24, Oct. 1, 1997).

Risk management officers should be an integral part of running a business. Although business line managers may see risk management officers as infringing on the business line management process, it is through the risk manager's specialized focus that business decisions can be improved. The business line manager's job is to focus on the revenues to be derived from new business to achieve financial goals. Consequently, he or she cannot possibly absorb the regulations and also be responsible for personnel, revenue growth, and new product delivery. Through the use of risk management, therefore, a continuing awareness of potential operational challenges, costs, policies, procedures, and regulations can improve the quality of internal audits and regulatory examinations. This in turn creates sound business practices.

Some banks also use a peer group review to improve daily operations. Typically, the department manager selects a sample of accounts to be reviewed for compliance with the governing document(s), policies, procedures, and regulations. The reviewing parties should be administrators who are not assigned to the accounts. The peer review helps identify systemic and isolated issues in the department. As automated compliance systems and imaging have become popular, it has become feasible for the department manager to conduct, by means of desktop technology, the peer review by random-sampling compliance items and the completion of automated ticklers.

Managing within the governing regulations and managing risk are considered by some managers as time-consuming and overpowering. The art of running the business, however, is to establish a leadership role by recognizing the need for regulatory compliance while not sacrificing client service and product development.

II

Management

Management is tasks. Management is a discipline. But management is also people. Every achievement of management is the achievement of a manager. Every failure is a failure of a manager. People manage rather than "forces" or "facts." The vision, dedication, and integrity of managers determines whether there is management or mismanagement.

—Peter F. Drucker, *Management*, 1974

What we need today, perhaps, is not new theory, concept or framework but people who can think strategically.

—Kenichi Ohmae,
The Mind of the Strategist, 1983

Introduction

During our years of involvement in the corporate trust industry, we have observed that when hiring people, bank trustees still use the same criteria as they did when we started in this business. The corporate trust industry provides technical training, often on a transactional basis, to help the corporate trust administrator or management trainee be productive as soon as possible. The only difference in today's management environment is that the required competitive efficiencies of the business demand fewer staff to do the work. Although transactional training will get the job done, it does not give new employees opportunities to understand the relationship of their job and its responsibilities to the overall corporate trust function and the business plan that drives it. A training program that links the organization's strategy and business plans to individual job requirements and accountabilities allows individuals to reach their personal goals while making achievement of the business plan more likely.

The human side of the enterprise includes managerial issues and concerns related to the components of the business, that is, strategy, planning, philosophy, process, organization of the work, training and development, performance evaluation, and advancement opportunities. Our experience during our years of teaching and working in the industry is that because these issues are viewed as the role of senior management, little attention has been paid to them in developing the corporate trust professional. Nonetheless, management is a skill and responsibility that must be learned and experienced at all levels, starting with taking responsibility for managing oneself.

The following chapters are not designed to teach the profession of management. Rather, the chapters represent only a framework in which corporate trust professionals can begin to appreciate and understand the complexities and dynamics of a professional environment.

Management is an interactive process, requiring trust, cooperation, and understanding between managers and subordinates. Effective management operates on three levels: manager to subordinate ("managing downward"), subordinate to manager ("managing upward"), and manager to manager and subordinate to subordinate ("managing laterally").

The implementation, ideas, and guidelines in the following chapters are dependent on the particular organization's structure and size. But the assumptions and premises should not be affected by the numbers of people or levels of management. The interest and inclination of the managers, who are in a position to influence the desired outcome, are the key factors in training and developing the corporate trust professional.

Numerous articles and books are available on the views and philosophies of management, and even managers (and those who would like to be managers) should find the following books to be helpful: *The Concept of Corporate Strategy* has a useful discussion of the formulation of corporate strategy and implementation.[1] *The Transformation of Management* covers the four great questions facing all managers at all levels in all types of organizations: mission (what are we trying to accomplish?), competition (how do we gain a competitive edge?), performance (how do we deliver the results?), and change (how do we cope with change?).[2] *Coaching for Improved Performance* is a practical approach to dealing with the obstacles to work performance and the means to counsel employees in overcoming these obstacles.[3] *Becoming a Manager* complements the other works by identifying those skills necessary to move from being a star performer to a competent manager.[4]

[1] Kenneth R. Andrews (Homewood, Ill.: Irwin, 1987).
[2] Mike Davidson (Boston: Butterworth-Heinemann, 1996)
[3] F. F. Fournes (New York: Van Nostrand Reinhold, 1978).
[4] Linda A. Hill (Boston: Harvard Business School Press, 1992).

Strategic and Tactical Planning

When examining the management aspects of the corporate trust function, it is necessary to look at it as a separate business or product line within a larger financial services institution. For any business to survive and succeed, it must be driven by a strategy that clearly defines its purposes or goals, so as to keep the business moving in a deliberately chosen direction. The structure of the organization, therefore, must support the chosen strategy. No student of management or of organization development would, however, suggest that a strategy is a static, immovable force. It and the structure must be adaptable to change; they must be flexible enough to permit the organization to modify its approach and even to dramatically change direction as the needs of its market, and of the environment in which it operates, change. The continuing consolidation of banks during the past six years has tested the flexibility of many corporate trust strategic plans as well as the resiliency of corporate trust professionals. For those banking companies and their staffs not involved with consolidations, strategic planning has emerged as a way to compete effectively in the consolidating businesses.

Corporate strategy has been defined as

> the pattern of decisions in a company that determines and reveals its objectives, purposes, goals, produces the principal policies and plans for achieving those goals, and defines the range of business the company is to pursue, the kind of economic and human organization it is or intends to be, and the nature of the economic and noneconomic contribution it intends to make to its shareholders, employees, customers, and communities.[1]

[1] Kenneth R. Andrews, *The Concept of Corporate Strategy* 13 (1987).

Another excellent definition was offered by Alfred D. Chandler in *Strategy and Structure*, that strategy is "the determination of the basic long-term goals and objectives of an enterprise and the adoption of courses of action and allocation of resources necessary for carrying out these goals."[2]

An organization's strategic business plan is based on its articulated strategy as expressed in terms of long-range direction, purpose, and corporate culture. One of the best-known and most widely read authors on management is Peter Drucker, who observed:

> 1. It is not a bag of tricks, a bundle of techniques. It is analytical thinking and commitment of resources to action. . . . 2. Strategy planning is not forecasting. It is not masterminding the future. . . . 3. Strategic planning does not deal with future decisions. It deals with the futurity of present decisions. . . . 4. Strategic planning is not an attempt to eliminate risk. It is not even an attempt to minimize risk. . . .
> . . . Strategy . . . answers the questions. What is our business, what should it be, what will it be. . . . It thereby determines what the key activities are in a given business or service institution. Effective structure is the design that makes these key activities capable of functioning and of performance.[3]

Strategy is thus the driving force from which all else in the organization flows and is the means to direct the organization in the pursuit of its mission, whose components we discuss next.

The strategic plan for the corporate trust business must flow from both the strategy and the strategic plan of its parent institution. Because the corporate trust function is not a fully independent entity, its strategy and planning process are guided by the institution's direction and demands, its guidelines, and its policies. Within any such parameters, however, corporate trust managers are responsible for developing its culture, plans, objectives, and supporting structure. The corporate trust manager, together with the members of the corporate trust organization, must drive the business within the context of its business plan. Axiomatic is the policy that "those who *implement* the plans must *make* the plans."[4]

THE NEEDS ANALYSIS

Before developing a strategic business plan, it is necessary to establish a process in which each of the essential elements leads into and influences the others. Figure 1 depicts this process flow and the interrelationships of the strategic and tactical business plans.

---

[2] Alfred D. Chandler, *Strategy and Structure* 13 (1962).

[3] Peter Drucker, *Management* 123, 523 (1974).

[4] Texas Instrument's Patrick Haggerty quoted in Tom Peters and Robert Waterman, *In Search of Excellence* 31 (1982).

This process contains an issues-and-needs analysis covering an "environmental scan" of the corporate trust- and securities-processing business, the present and projected economic capital-financing environment, the nature and extent of the competition for corporate trust appointments, the strategic posture of the institution, and the present state of the corporate trust function.

The *critical issues analysis* is simply an understanding and evaluation of those conditions under which the corporate trust function is operating and can expect to operate during the next three years.

The framework for such an analysis should focus on three levels:

1. The industry. (a) How has technology changed the trustee and securities services? (b) What legislation and regulation have affected the development, production, and delivery of these services? (c) How have judicial decisions affected the evolving role of the indenture trustee? (d) How are economic conditions and changes in the capital markets, including types of financing vehicles, being handled? (e) What is the competition for obtaining profitable appointments? (f) What has been the impact of clients' and security holders' changing demands and expectations?

2. The bank. (a) Does the bank's strategy enhance or detract from the corporate trust business? (b) Will the bank's response to changes in the limitations on or expansion of its activities help or hinder the corporate trust business? (c) Does the bank's management actively support or simply tolerate the corporate trust activities? (d) What demands does the bank's senior management make on the corporate trust function as a profitable business line? (e) Do other areas of the bank support product and market development? (f) Does the bank provide resources to support and expand the corporate trust business?

3. The corporate trust function. (a) What has been the financial impact of technological changes in the industry, of the volatile economic environment, of greater regulation and government intervention, of greater competition, and of greater demands by clients and security holders? (b) At what stage is the function in its organizational development, including managerial and technical/professional staffing; personnel training, development, and evaluation; and the needs and demands of a changing workforce? (c) What is the underlying basis for developing a new business, that is, the corporate trust's marketing responsibilities, and to what extent does it depend on the sales solicitation of

FIGURE I

Planning Process Flow

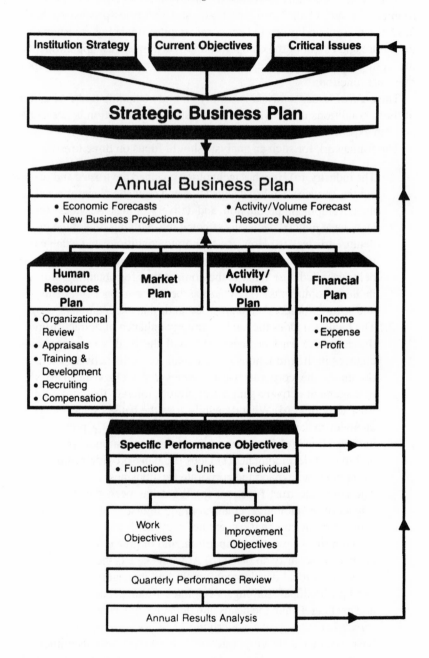

noncorporate trust people? How are internal sales managed? How are new services created or existing services modified? What has been the impact on marketing and sales of the bank's relationships with its corporate and municipal clients? (d) How does the existing technology support the corporate trust function? What are the major shortcomings or deficiencies of the processing and information systems? How much support can be expected from the institution's systems development staff? What major changes in or enhancements of the existing systems are needed for the business to remain competitive in pricing and marketing? What effect will the greater use of microcomputers and remote processing have on the delivery and cost of agency services?

When these questions have been answered, the next step is a *critical needs analysis*. In this instance, the issues identified earlier and the responses to them can be divided into two categories, those that have a longer-range impact, which should be addressed over three to five years, and those that must be addressed within one to two years. In each time category, the critical needs can be grouped as follows:

Financial management
Marketing development
Technological development
Organizational development
Organizational structure

In this part of the planning process, we identify those issues and needs essential to both the strategic and the annual business plans.

THE STRATEGIC PLAN

As discussed earlier, the components of the plan are an evaluation of the present state of the business (what are we doing?), an understanding of what the business will be like (what will we be doing?), and a posture reflecting the direction in which the business should go (what do we want to be doing?).

In addition to identifying critical issues and needs, we must examine the services offered and the markets for them by matrixing the various trustee and agency services against the several target markets, indicating for each (1) whether the service/market exists [E], is planned [P], or is possible [?]; (2) the attractiveness of the service/market on a scale of five to zero, in terms of profitable business and opportunity to increase volume and/or market share; and (3) the perceived competition for the service/market on a scale of five to zero.

The matrix for the paying agent service might look like this:

Service	Corporations	Governments	Banks
Paying Agent	E-5–4	E-4–5	P-3–5

A further refinement of this matrix would include an analysis of the financial components affecting each service/market in regard to (1) the relative significance of both fixed and variable costs (high—medium—low); and (2) the relative significance of the profit margins (high—medium—low) for both incremental and fully absorbed costs.[5] Our paying agent example might look like this:

	Cost	Profit
	Fixed/Variable	Incr./Fully Abs.
Corporations	M/M	H/M
Governments	M/H	H/M

Too often when fully absorbed costs are calculated and reviewed, fees or balances that are credited to other units of the bank are omitted. Letter-of-credit fees and government securities–trading fees are examples. Demand deposit balances, generated by corporate trust transactions, should also be considered when evaluating profit margins.

When reviewing the terminating or maturing accounts and potential new corporate trust business, we should analyze each of the major service/market categories: the trustee for the debt issues of corporations, governments, and other banks; the bond registrar for corporate and government debt issues; the transfer agent (and registrar) for corporate equity issues; and the paying agent for corporations and governments. For each of these components, we then should determine (1) the historical size and direction of the market and the environmental factors influencing the numbers and the direction (e.g., unsecured versus secured debt, straight versus convertible, fixed rate versus floating rate); (2) the nature and extent of the existing and projected competition for such appointments and of the perceived strengths and weaknesses of the strongest competitors; and (3) compared with the competition, the major existing

---

[5] Incremental profit is gross income minus fixed expense and corporate overhead, allocated to the function. Fully absorbed profit (sometimes referred to as NIBT, net income before tax) is gross income minus the total of all expenses (variable, fixed, direct, indirect, or allocated) attributable to being in the particular business.

and projected strengths and weaknesses of the corporate trust function in providing such services.

These analyses establish realistic parameters and opportunities for the business. The analyses may also persuade the senior management not to expand the business but either to let it run down or simply to sell it off. (This obviously is the risk inherent in fully understanding the dynamics, components, and profit potential in any business line!)

Assuming that the signs are favorable and the risk/reward analysis is positive, the next step is to decide on a *strategic overview and posture*, including a statement of the function's key objective or mission; a delineation of the services to be offered to the particular markets; the strategic theme reflecting the level of emphasis to be placed on particular services and markets; the business objectives in terms of market share, profit margins, year-over-year profit dollar growth, return on expense investment, or any other determinant or standard the institution establishes for its business lines.

Although it is not intended to be a definitive statement of the corporate trust function's overall mission or goal, this overview should contribute to the bank's growth and profitability by providing professional corporate trust services to its clients on a cost-effective and profitable basis.

When the strategic overview has been completed, it should be translated into the strategy to be applied to the continuation of the existing services and markets, the enhancement of such services, the broadening (or narrowing) of the target markets of each, and the planned development and delivery of new services to the same or different prospective markets. This strategic business plan should also consider and project the resources needed to carry out the plan. These resources can be divided into staff (number, type, mix), space (how much and where), and furniture and equipment, including technological support. The increasing use of personal computers, software programs, and the Internet can make technological support and research less onerous when creating new services. Also to be considered is the projected organization structure necessary to support the plan and the interdependencies of other units in developing, producing, implementing, and delivering the various services.

The final part of the strategic business plan is alternative and contingency planning. Because the previous parts of the plan were based on certain assumptions, which may prove not to be accurate or viable, we must consider alternative strategies. The areas of the strategic plan most susceptible to uncertainty are economic environment, legal and regulatory restrictions, competition, automation technology, and availability of trained staff.

THE ANNUAL BUSINESS PLAN

Each institution must establish a framework and process for its annual planning cycle, as well as the type and details of the plan itself. The plan's several separate but interrelated subplan components include a marketing plan, an activity/volume plan, an automation technology plan, a human resources plan, and, certainly, a financial plan.

The marketing plan covers not only the "how, when, and where" but also the projected results. The marketing plan constitutes the sales objectives that are believed to be viable and realistic based on market analysis and experience.

The activity/volume plan is simply a projection of the extent to which the existing and planned book of business will result in certain activities and the volume of each. These projections take into account the number of projected new trusteeships, the projected volume of certificates to be issued and canceled by the transfer agent, and the number of trustee and agent appointments scheduled to mature or terminate. Data are essential to evaluating and assessing the needs for resource support and to drawing up the income and expense plan. The corporate trust manager who insists on one system that can process the work, provide the required administrative ticklers and reports, and also create the necessary management reports from one database will produce a more accurate analysis when making the strategic and business plans.

The automation technology plan addresses the business's needs for delivering its services efficiently and effectively. The plan should specify the needs for systems maintenance and software enhancement, hardware, and, of course, the costs of completing the cost/benefit analysis.

The human resource plan focuses on the personnel needs of the function and its staff, including an assessment of the current staff—that is, its adequacy in terms of numbers and expertise, training and development—and an appropriate compensation program. This plan also translates these needs into organizational objectives and personal improvement objectives for the staff members. In the following chapters, we describe the main elements of organization and structure and the establishment of training and development programs and an evaluation process.

The final part of an annual business plan addresses the function's financial objectives. It covers the expected income from each of the major services, usually on a quarterly basis. The expense side is the allocation and use of all resources required to meet the income objectives. In almost every institution, this requires a detailed analysis of the fixed (e.g., space) and variable (e.g., overtime) costs of the business. Some of these expenses are charged directly to the function as a profit center, whereas others (e.g., corporate overhead) go through the institution's cost allocation systems.

The biggest expense, usually between 60 and 70 percent of the total, relates to people and therefore receives the most attention from managers as they seek to increase productivity. The technology plan has absorbed some of the expense formerly applied to personnel. Some companies have been able to achieve efficiencies while fixing the cost of production through automation. (Because of the impact of training, development, and performance planning on increasing productivity, chapters 20 and 21 address these topics separately.)

Finally, it is necessary to understand that the organization's structure must flow out of both the nature of the business itself and the strategy that drives the business. Peter Drucker put it this way: "Organization is not mechanical. It is not 'assembly.' It cannot be prefabricated! Organization is organic and unique to each individual business or institution. For we now know that structure, to be effective and sound, must follow strategy."[6]

[6] Drucker, *Management* 523.

Organization and Structure

Now that we have discussed what drives the business and the planning process, we shall look at the organizational entity and how the components fit together in the overall strategy.

In practice, the reporting relationships and interdependencies of the activities performed are determined (and even governed) by the senior managers who make the decisions. The very size of the organization and its geographic locations directly influence both the organizational make-up and the structure of the corporate trust function.

In its basic application, an "organization" should not be thought of as a chart containing a series of boxes connected by solid and dotted lines to reflect reporting relationships. (Such a chart is, of course, useful in larger organizations to help keep track of who reports to whom in what work unit.) Rather, an organization is simply the arrangement and relationship of the work done by people. It reflects the results of deciding what products or services to sell; which type of work units are needed to generate, produce, and deliver the product or service; how the work units will receive input and deliver output; and how they will work together to achieve a profitable result. Structure, then, is both the design of the organization and the design of the processes to make the organization effective in the areas of communication, reporting relationships, interdependencies among units, technology, and assignment of accountability. It is the management's conclusion about how best to create and maintain the necessary work units and their relationship to one another at a particular time.

When discussing organization and structure, we assumed that the function includes the following business activities: administering trust indentures, other debt-financing instruments and agreements, and agency-servicing agreements; servicing and processing debt and equity securities, maintaining related records and data files; and marketing both trustee and agency services to existing and prospective clients. This arrangement is often referred to as *product divisionalization*; that is, in most banks, the corporate trust function as an integrated business line or product center is a relatively self-contained business unit.

Some organizations do have separate divisions, with corporate trust–operating functions reporting separately from the administrative division. When the administration and operations divisions are separate, the organization should be maintained with a "boldface" dotted line on the organization chart. Service agreements between both divisions should be considered to establish the same quality and delivery standards that each division expects of the other. Typically, the only unit not reporting to the corporate trust manager, either directly or by a dotted line, is the unit that processes the cash and asset transactions and the client asset statements. Each of the key business activities interfaces with the others—the natural order of the work flows between and among them. The output of one becomes the input of another.

The final product, or the output of the function, is the result of the efforts, and value added, of each and all the work units in the process. As an integrated function, it is responsible and accountable for the expenses it incurs (including the overhead of simply being part of a larger organization) and the income it produces, resulting in a profit for the bank.

In many banks, in which not all the work units are under "corporate trust management," the practice of *transfer pricing* means charging the income-producing center for the costs of the work performed by the noncorporate trust work units. This approach works only if the rates to be charged are negotiated in advance; the activity volume is accurately captured; the resulting expenses are regularly monitored and evaluated; and it is, in fact, a cost-effective means of producing and delivering the services.

But too often in a transfer-pricing structure, the corporate trust account is assumed to carry the same volume and level of cost as do the other trust accounts in the trust organization. Likewise, the balance credits earned from corporate trust deposits are also not considered in the equation of revenue and cost. Corporate trust managers thus can immediately improve their cost structures with the appropriate analysis.

Transfer pricing does not address the real-people issues of full product ownership or the developmental options of the employees or the managers (these are examined in chapter 20).

In the corporate trust organization, it is generally agreed that a "functional" structure is the best for achieving the business goals described earlier. The integrated functional structure offers the most options for the most effective management of the people and their work. The classic problem of "we versus them" is greatly mitigated when all parts of the business line operate in a common environment under a management team responsible for the entire corporate trust function. On such a basis, the structure of the line units then is

	Function Head	
Marketing	Administration	Operations
Product Development	Trustee	Securities processing
Research	Agency	Funds and payments
Sales		Records

with such staff support units as are necessary.

(In a few, very large corporate trust banks, the product division is carried even further, establishing separate product centers—each having marketing, administration, and operations responsibilities—all in the overall corporate trust function.)

This arrangement, reflecting the major responsibilities of the business and the resulting interdependencies and accountabilities, is not, however, universal among the corporate trust banks. In fact, in some banks, each of the three main components is in a separate department, the only common manager being the bank's president! In those banks, corporate trust is usually defined as, and is limited to, the administration activity. However, even in this instance, attention to the organization and structure of the unit is critical.

Even under this optimal structure, the function is not a completely stand-alone business, that is, fully integrated both horizontally and vertically. It still requires the support of other line and staff organizations in the bank, including wire transfer, check reconcilement, government securities trading, personnel, auditing, and commercial banking units for marketing support.

Having looked at the corporate trust function as a whole, we will now examine each of the three main components.

MARKETING

New business is the lifeblood of the corporation trust function; there must be continuous infusions of new business appointments. Without a continuing inflow, the organization simply cannot survive, as fixed expenses will continue to mount, to the point at which the function cannot produce enough income to cover both the variable expenses and the overhead. In addition, no successful institution can offer a service indefinitely if the profits do not justify the investment in space, equipment, and people. Today, most successful banking organizations also demand that the business line demonstrate a year-over-year growth in its contribution to profits. Nonetheless, some banks still view the corporate trust function as an accommodation service—something it must offer to be perceived as a full-service financial provider—even though it does not contribute to the bank's net earnings. But the recent evidence of many corporate trust divestitures suggests that most banking services and products can no longer entertain an "accommodation service" view.

Corporate trust services, like most other non-asset-based banking functions, must be marketed on two different levels. First, corporate trust services must be marketed to the commercial banking officers who form the first line of salespeople in generating corporate trust appointments. Second, corporate trust personnel must directly market to corporate and municipal issuers. In the first instance, the banking officers become the eyes and ears of the corporate trust marketing, as they usually are in the best position to determine whether their clients need corporate trust services because of their frequent calls on clients. Unfortunately, the banking officers are also asked to do the same for all (or most) of the other services being offered by the bank—and corporate trust appointments may not be uppermost in their minds when seeking additional relationships with clients. Corporate trust managers have used a variety of incentives to keep their products at the top of the commercial bankers' list, often causing other product managers to offer similar incentives. Banking officers like to sell products and sweeten the products offered to their clients. Few of us will reject a monetary incentive, but timely, accurate, and responsive quality service is what banking officers regard as the real incentive.

It is for this reason that banking officers must be made aware of the corporate trust services offered, be comfortable in seeking such business, and know whom to call for technical sales help or to whom to refer a potential appointment. A great deal of corporate trust marketing therefore must be organized to ensure that these matters are addressed to as many commercial banking officers as possible. One easy way to do this is to "take a banker to lunch" and review the potentially profitable opportunities for the bank (thus increasing that particular banking officer's value to the bank as well). Although the news of quality service and experienced staff spreads quickly among the banking officers, the news of poor quality work spreads even faster. It is not always possible to achieve the desired marketing objectives by relying solely on others to do the sales work. In those instances in which the corporate trust function has the only relationship, or a technical sales call for a particular transaction would be more directly productive, it should be done by a knowledgeable corporate trust officer.

In either case, however, the responsibility for product development (i.e., what new or modified service to offer to which market segment) and basic research must be assumed by those people with the greatest knowledge of the nuances of the function's service and capabilities. Whether or not the marketing is specifically within the corporate trust structure, the required expertise and knowledge do not change. Fully understanding the nature and workings of corporate trust activities and the function's ability to deliver the services at a profit is essential to achieving any marketing objectives.

ADMINISTRATION

Once the appointment has been obtained, it must be administered in a professional manner, consistent with the particular duties and responsibilities of the appointment and with the knowledge of the potential liabilities. The organization and structure of the administration function is to supply one or more account officers and/or administrators (or teams of such) who discharge the bank's duties and responsibilities according to the appointment documents. This can run the gamut from a one-person unit to a structure that uses many people organized into separate work units or teams.

In the latter case, the people are organized in one of two ways, by allocating the work (1) on a functional or product basis, with a separate team handling each different type or appointment (e.g., being responsible only for municipal-housing issues) or just one aspect of the work involved in all accounts (e.g., giving comments on indentures or handling the various sinking funds) or (2) on a divisional basis, with each team responsible for all aspects of a variety of trustee and agency appointments. In practice, few corporate trust functions are organized on purely a functional or divisional basis but, instead, are somewhere between them. In the smaller banks, the tendency is toward a divisional structure, in which a few account officers and administrators do everything. In the larger banks, which probably have a very heavy volume of diverse appointments, more specialization is common, the result being a structure more reflective of a functional or product approach.

OPERATIONS

In almost every organization, the operations function was not created anew but grew along with a structure that responded to the type and volume of appointments over a period of years. The advent of the all fully registered corporate bond issues in the late 1960s, the proliferation of tax-exempt issues and creative financing vehicles, the increased numbers of smaller companies selling debt and equity securities, and the widespread use of computerized systems all have had a significant impact on the organization of the operations function and its structure. The proliferation of personal computers and the introduction of software that can extract required data from one central system and download it to operational and administrative workstations have also improved the productivity and quality of corporate trust product delivery systems.

It is not possible to define a precise model, given the diversity of activities that may be performed in the operations function. Even so, we can describe generally the basic areas of activity usually found in a corporate trust operations organization. These include (1) processing securities, (2) receiving and disbursing debt service funds, (3) maintaining records and data files and (4) billing for fees.

With respect to securities processing, the organization of work performed follows from the logical flow of the work required. This normally follows a pattern that includes

1. Receipt of the securities.
2. Examination of the securities.
3. Input of data to debit and credit security holder accounts.
4. Cancellation of incoming securities.
5. Issuance of new securities and/or payment vehicles.
6. Delivery of new securities and/or payments.

Each of these activities is part of both the receipt of work and the output of work—in effect, each of the parts must be organizationally structured to achieve the maximum efficiencies.

Securities may be received through either a collection or a clearing system, which generally is a bulk shipment of securities for the agent to process, or directly from an individual security holder (or broker) by mail or in person. The next step is examining each security to ensure, among other things, that it is in the appropriate form for the action requested, that is, registration of transfer, exchange, payment, and so forth. Assuming that the item is not defective and the action requested is possible, the security then goes to operations personnel who make the necessary changes in the security holder file.

When registering a transfer, the appropriate debit is posted to the transferor's account, with an offsetting credit to the transferee's account or, in the case of a new account, the posting of new account information. At the same time, systems are activated to produce new certificates in the name of the transferee. If the transaction is a redemption or maturity, the offsetting credit to the account debited is the production of a check or other payment vehicle. For a convertible issue, the offset to the cancellation of the surrendered certificates is the production (or requisition from the stock transfer agent) of the appropriate number of full shares of stock. The incoming securities are then canceled and ultimately disposed of, with the new certificates (or payment checks) being sent back to the person surrendering the securities. The securities may be mailed directly or returned over the window or back through the particular collection or clearing system, thereby completing the full cycle of the processing function.

The second major operational activity is receiving and disbursing funds. In almost every corporate trust organization, specific people are designated to follow, and book in, the required debt service funds or dividends. Because the role of the paying or disbursement agent is really that of a conduit, the other side of this activity is calculating the funds required to be disbursed and the actual disbursement. These typically are payments of interest on registered bonds and dividends on stock, payments of interest against the surrender of bearer coupons, and payments of principal because of a partial redemption or on the maturity of an issue. The activity is not performed in isolation but requires coordination between and among the account administrator and the operational units processing the securities.

The third major area of activity is maintaining records. Whereas much of the information required to be maintained is an integral part of the securities-processing and payment functions, other records must be kept, whether to establish appropriate audit trails, to meet SEC reporting requirements, to provide for accurate cash controls, to enable billing, or simply to supply management with information about activity and volume.

In addition, it is important that every operations officer pay attention to all proof and control activities in the function, including the daily reconcilement of all individual cash and securities transactions to the unit's control records. Maintaining records is the functional need that must be integrated into the organization, rather than the identification of which people or units do what work.

The fourth function is the fee-billing unit, which calculates all transaction and administrative fees and bills the corporate trust clients. Unfortunately, this unit is often isolated from the corporate trust operations function. The fee-billing unit can also be responsible for billing all clients for debt service. To provide billing integrity and efficiency, the corporate trust operations system should be the source of all billing data. A sound billing system produces automated bills, sends reminder notices for past due bills, maintains records for reimbursable expenses and ages outstanding bills in accordance with the bank's general policy on fee and expense recovery.

In most institutions, this operational work is structured along functional lines under the management of an experienced officer. Ideally, this person is a people manager, capable of dealing with complex automation needs, processing procedures, and techniques, all in a fast-paced and action-oriented environment.

We now turn to the training and development needs of the staff that implements the business plan.

Training and Development

Perhaps the most important part of a manager's job is establishing and maintaining an environment in which people are encouraged and helped to develop and improve their knowledge and skills. Unfortunately, training and development receive their greatest emphasis in the business plan phase of the annual budget process and later are de-emphasized as management demands adjustments in the expense portion of the business plan. It is generally agreed that to achieve the desired results, any developmental effort should be on a building-block basis. The cumulative effect of such an approach is that the individual becomes increasingly more knowledgeable and skillful (i.e., productive) in his or her existing position and demonstrates potential for increased levels and/or scope of responsibility. The end result is motivated persons with more value to themselves and more value to the organization. This in turn gives both the individual and the organization more options for the type and nature of their future responsibilities and the position in the organization at which they work.[1]

One concern of every manager is controlling risk, and a comprehensive training program can help with that. People who are well trained—whether through an in-house training program or external training resources—tend to be more motivated, with fewer performance risks.

[1] The Certified Corporate Trust Specialist designation offered by the Institute of Certified Bankers is intended to "hallmark" the industry's most experienced professionals. This program should also encourage other corporate trust practitioners to increase their level of competence and technical knowledge through a program of continuing education and development.

The starting point for any manager is to conduct a manpower audit. This audit measures the knowledge and skill of the existing staff against the needs of the organization as determined by its strategic and tactical business plans (as discussed in chapter 18). Included in the audit are the required numbers of people and their mix (specialists, generalists), the projected personnel turnover, and their personal vulnerabilities. It is in effect a personnel needs analysis that highlights the organization's particular recruiting, staffing, training, and development needs. A manpower audit also produces the names of those staff with the most and least potential. Management must decide whether those with the least potential can increase it through training and development. When working with people, managers too often devote 80 percent of their time to those staff members with the least potential and only 20 percent of their time to those who can implement the strategic plan and achieve the business plan.

As discussed earlier, the increasingly complex nature of the corporate trust business has led to more specialization of work by administrators and account officers, particularly in the larger organizations. It is evident that carried too far, this specialization may, over the long run, be counterproductive to the development of a well-rounded professional administrative staff. Much learning experience may be sacrificed under the guise of efficiency. In such situations, individual training and development needs must be factored into a comprehensive training program to ensure that diverse learning opportunities are made available.

The major drawback of training only specialists can be overcome by job rotation, provided that it follows a defined plan. To be effective, the timing of rotational moves and attention to structured training experiences require careful follow-up by the manager. However, the corporate trust organization is better served, and an individual is better equipped for greater responsibilities if he or she is not limited to a functionally driven set of accounts or work responsibilities but, rather, is thoroughly trained and experienced in all facets of administering debt and equity accounts, covering as wide a range of appointments as is possible.

Before beginning any type of comprehensive training program, it is essential to define the job, including its objectives, accountabilities, and the requisite knowledge and skills. These competencies are those related to technical, managerial (including self-management), and interpersonal factors. A good job description or position profile incorporates the essential elements of an account administrator's or officer's job, as follows:

KEY OBJECTIVE

To contribute to the bank's growth and profitability by providing expert innovative trust and agency services for issuers and holders of corporate, state, and municipal securities and by meeting the changing demands of the economy and of the banking and securities industry.

PRIMARY ACCOUNTABILITY

To represent the bank in all facets of corporate trust administration, including the review, negotiation, execution, and delivery of indentures and other financing agreements; the establishment and implementation of procedures relating to the administration of such agreements; the enforcement of these agreements in accordance with the Trust Indenture Act and other securities laws and regulations, with an emphasis on the rights of security holders and the risks and liabilities of the bank.

REPORTING RELATIONSHIPS

Reports to an administration manager (for officers). Has responsibility for supervising and training account administrators.

INTERFACE RELATIONSHIPS

Interfaces with operations units, commercial banking officers, existing customers, correspondent banks, investment bankers, law firms, and underwriters.

ACCOUNTABILITIES (LEVEL DETERMINED BY TRAINING AND EXPERIENCE)

Account Acceptance Performance

(1) Reviews, negotiates, and comments on new indenture and other financing instruments so that they meet the requirements for acceptance by the bank; (2) evaluates the bank's duties, responsibilities, and potential

liabilities; (3) handles all matters related to the closing, including the review of required documents, preparation of internal records, and instructions to operations units; and (4) develops and/or negotiates fees and pricing matters with client.

Account Administration Performance

Completes the following administrative transactions, as applicable, in a timely and effective manner: (1) establishing, maintaining, and using internal records, files, and instructions; (2) reviewing certificates and opinions; (3) analyzing financial statements; (4) receiving and moving funds and collateral; (5) preparing annual trustees' reports; (6) processing sinking funds and redemptions; (7) investing trust funds and valuations; (8) processing releases and withdrawals; (9) processing satisfactions, resignations, change-of-corporate name and consents, and waivers; (10) arranging security holder meetings; (11) processing successor trusteeships; (12) processing mergers and acquisitions; preparing annual account reviews and participating in peer account, policy, and procedure reviews.

Planning Performance

Develops specific objectives for annual performance, such as (1) recommending modifications of policies, procedures, and methods to improve administration services; (2) planning and establishing priorities in work flow and organization; and (3) participating in revenue-generating and expense-reducing planning.

Human Resource Performance (for account officers)

(1) Supervises the daily work flow of administrators and reviews all required documents; (2) provides training and development following the work standards and training guidelines for administrators; and (3) conducts appraisals of nonofficial staff and assists administration management.

Marketing Performance

(1) Promotes relationships with the current customer base and other contacts; (2) contributes to the planning process by helping identify new prospects; (3) evaluates prospective new business in conjunction with administration management; and (4) participates in new product development and sales material production.

KNOWLEDGE COMPETENCIES

(1) Principles of and developments in corporate and municipal finance; (2) federal and state securities statutes, particularly the TIA and applicable provisions of the UCC; (3) federal and state securities regulations, particularly those of the Federal Reserve Board and the SEC; (4) structure and content of basic documents, including bond mortgage, debenture indenture, private placement agreement, agency agreements for debt and equity, leverage lease documentation, commercial paper documentation, and depository and escrow agreements; (5) applicable bank and administration policies and procedures; (6) trends and developments in corporate trust industry, including applicable court decisions, securities-processing procedures and tax requirements; (7) administration's technical, managerial, and human resource–planning process; (8) investment-banking and underwriting functions; and (9) industry rules and practices, particularly those from the New York Stock Exchange (NYSE) and the Municipal Securities Rulemaking Board (MSRB).

SKILL COMPETENCIES

(1) Effectively negotiates trust and agency agreement provisions and related fees to meet the organization's standards; (2) administers trust and agency accounts in accordance with legal and bank policies and standards; (3) makes investments as directed by the obligor/principal by carrying out instructions and accurately calculating discounts, interest, and the like; (4) within specified guidelines manages default situations and bankruptcies; (5) provides operations units with timely and accurate instructions for processing all account transactions; (6) prepares, maintains, and uses internal administration records and files; (7) conducts research and responds to customers' inquiries about transactional projects; and (8) analyzes current and potential problems and makes recommendations/decisions based on this analysis.

MANAGERIAL COMPETENCIES

Planning

(1) Understands the objective-setting process and establishes meaningful and realistic performance objectives with supporting action; (2) ranks

current and projected work responsibilities and assignments by priorities; and (3) assesses the consequences of current and planned programs and work assignments.

Leading

(1) Trains and develops subordinates; (2) motivates subordinates to reach high standards of quality and to stretch own performance expectations; (3) develops and leads a transactional team or task force project; and (4) delegates work and responsibility, including scheduling work for maximum efficiency.

Organizing

(1) Manages own time, including scheduling and prioritizing work to be done; (2) regularly handles multiple assignments and completes them on time; and (3) recognizes and uses staff support resources as needed.

Controlling

(1) Monitors and controls work in progress; (2) implements the administration's performance standards and takes corrective action when necessary; and (3) monitors and conserves allocated expense dollars and other resources.

INTERPERSONAL COMPETENCIES

(1) Performance results—desires to excel and perform above standards; (2) customer contact—establishes and maintains working relationships to ensure responsiveness to customers' concerns and inquiries; (3) problem solving—works with others to develop relevant information, deciding on the best solution and implementing it; (4) influence management—achieves desired results through others over whom there is no direct control, including desirable changes in methods and procedures; (5) communicating—achieves understanding through oral and written communication, on a timely basis, with subordinates, peers, superiors, customers, and security holders; (6) sensitivity—recognizes the needs, feelings, and expectations of others and manages relationships to ensure productive results; (7) professional image—presents to customers and

colleagues a positive professional image in oral and written communication and personal appearance.

In conjunction with using a position profile, it makes sense also to have in place a fairly detailed description of the expected standards of performance for the position.

This guideline enables managers to determine, monitor, and evaluate the expected results or outcome of the training program. It also helps administrators and officers understand the expected standards of performance on which they will be reviewed and appraised (discussed in chapter 21).

The organization determines these standards according to the work to be done, the relationship among the people in the process, the organization's policies and procedures, and the quality of service that the organization wants for its clients.

When a position's accountabilities and requirements have been defined through the position profile and performance standards, the development of a training program simply flows from a logical analysis of how and when the particular components need to be addressed. The program itself should be comprehensive in its approach and detailed in its implementation. The program's individual components depend, of course, on the results of the needs analysis from the perspective of the corporate trust organization and the needs of the individual. It might be useful at first to retain a consultant, experienced in designing and developing performance-based training programs. The administrator should be judged on his or her educational background, previous jobs, and familiarity with the subject matter. He or she should then tailor the comprehensive program to each employee's needs (being in effect an "individual educational prescription").

Besides training in the technical aspects of the position, the administrator may need additional instruction and/or coaching on such seemingly basic requirements as the ability to write good business letters and memoranda, skillful verbal communication, and an understanding of elementary economics, finance, and accounting.

ELEMENTS OF A SUCCESSFUL TRAINING AND DEVELOPMENT PROGRAM

For a training program to be successful, management must demonstrate its commitment to it, starting with the senior business manager who must make training a priority objective, for both the business and each person in the organization. Management should include training as part of regular staff meetings and also attend training sessions when possible. Effective training is not a one-shot occurrence, but an ongoing process that builds on itself. Management's continuing involvement reinforces the importance of training.

The development of a carefully considered training program is essential to achieve senior management "buy-in," as well as its acceptance by the people involved. Elements of the plan should include efficiency gains anticipated, expense reductions, error reductions, improved management control, better audits, increased sales, and improved customer service.

When possible, numbers should be used to support the plan's results. The training program should also be designed to support the strategic objectives of the business unit and to produce the greatest overall benefit for the expense incurred.

KEY FEATURES OF A COMPREHENSIVE TRAINING AND DEVELOPMENT PROGRAM

There are a number of ways to train a corporate trust staff. Some organizations rely exclusively on outside conferences, workshops, and schools. Others use in-house training delivered by either their own staff or external consultants and teachers. A third approach combines internal and external resources and uses as wide a variety as possible of ways to achieve the desired results. The training should take place over a period of time during which the participants should be expected to acquire and implement the desired knowledge and skills.

The components of the program could include technical classes on specific core administrative and operational topics; broader classes covering sales training, investments, document review, and other advanced topics such as defaults and litigation; the bank's (or division's) policies and procedures; industry updates on current events and trends; use of an administrator's "handbook" containing relevant policies, procedures, and guidelines; availability of a library of relevant books, articles, judicial decisions, statutes, and regulations; orientation tours to other areas of the bank with which the corporate trust function interfaces; and attendance at industry-sponsored schools, seminars, and conferences.

The list of specific topics will grow quickly if input from the staff is solicited. To do that, a training coordinator should be designated to obtain feedback from all levels in the organization. Priorities can then be set to focus the developmental training on the organization's critical needs. The training program should be flexible and tailored to the needs of the participants.

Once the program's courses and content have been selected and prioritized, deciding how the material will be presented and by whom is the next step. Sometimes the organization has in place people who can make presentations in their specific area of expertise. Most organizations, however, must supplement their in-house expertise with that of external consultants and industry experts.

Any and all of these teaching vehicles or resources should be combined with on-the-job training (OJT). In fact, it is usually much better to use an actual transactional experience with appropriate reading and coaching, assuming that the manager of the OJT has specific goals. The training program should provide (and hold the manager accountable for) extensive coaching and counseling on the application and use of the knowledge and skills that the position requires. "Coaching goes far beyond the short-term need to help someone learn the mechanics of preparing a budget and setting a proposal up. It is the principal means through which people learn what makes the organization tick, what it stands for, and how they can contribute to it over time."[2]

As noted earlier, a comprehensive training and development program must focus on both the content and the timing of the subject matter to be covered. Exhibit 11 is a model for this approach, to be covered over a two-year period, which must be tailored to the individual as determined by his or her previous experiences, needs, and abilities. The program will grow as the years go by if the organization is committed to providing developmental training.

Training is the right of every employee. It provides the skills and knowledge needed to grow and develop professionally. Good people will not stay if they are not challenged and growing. Consistent, well-delivered training in a variety of areas is the key to motivating people to invest their future in the corporate trust business. It will be the most important competitive advantage of the successful corporate trust provider into the next century.

The results of the training initiative should be measured, with a database created to keep track of the training provided, who attended, the expense involved, and, most important, the benefits achieved. Measuring the results also supports any initiative to obtain additional resources for

---

[2] Tom Peters and Nancy Austin, *A Passion for Excellence* (1985).

expanded professional development.

It also is evident that training will be a much more visible part of future audit and regulatory examinations: it will be included in customers' "requests for proposals" and be considered by rating agencies and bond issuers seeking professional expertise in a trustee. The successful corporate trust provider must demonstrate an ongoing effort to improve the professionalism and technical competence of its staff.

Performance Planning, Evaluation, and Career Development

A business's effectiveness rests not only on the design of the structure and the skills of the people but also on how the system combines these elements and motivates and rewards its employees to reach the desired goals.

One decade ago, motivating and rewarding people usually meant giving them additional responsibility, recognized on the organization chart as "upward mobility." No longer does promotion always mean upward recognition. Because management positions today are filled with managers who have ten to twenty years until retirement and because technology and banking consolidations continue to find efficiencies in the business, managers must convince their staffs that professional growth may be a lateral expansion of knowledge and responsibility. Managers must teach their staffs that lateral professional growth can also earn the compensation expected with increased responsibility. Although these rewards may not be in the form of merit increases, incentive pools to allow lateral growth and special pools to reward special performance efforts must be available to foster lateral professional growth.

The discussion in the preceding chapters set the stage for our consideration of the interplay among structure, process, and people, particularly how an individual's performance, skills, and productivity can be effectively managed.[1]

Such a system, whether highly formalized or not, is derived from the business plan and the concomitant objective-setting process—a plan for what people are required to do. Using regular feedback, the organization

---

[1] Although chapter 20 covered account administrators and officers, most of the discussion in this chapter is equally applicable to operations supervisors and officers.

can determine how effectively the structure, process, and people are interacting to fulfill the organization's business strategy.

This system is universally referred to as the *employee evaluation* or *appraisal procedure*. *Performance appraisal* is simply the process of identifying, measuring, and developing people. A well-defined process not only evaluates current performance but also includes mechanisms to reinforce strengths and correct problems for the benefit of future performance. The process should also be designed to identify those employees with great potential who can be groomed for future advancement and responsibility.

The preceding chapter cited the need to identify the knowledge and skills that people must possess to perform their jobs as corporate trust administrators or account officers. But the position profile alone does not convey the dynamic perspective of the job. Rather, it requires a concerted effort by both the manager and the employee to understand the job required, the priorities necessary to meet the tactical objectives, and the concerns of the individual with defining his or her career aspirations.

Managers and their subordinates can interact only in an environment in which the managerial philosophy and the recognition of an individual's development are fully supportive. Without this, there can be no applied management of people, in either their personal development or the assistance required to enable them to contribute to the organization's desired objectives. Real people management produces a climate of trust and confidence and, consequently, greater receptivity to the feedback required for continued growth.

The process of identifying job skills, training employees, and developing programs provides not only the initial understanding of the job but also the definition and communication of job-relevant behavior, competencies, and skills as reflected in the business plan. Once the organization's strategic business plan has been developed and communicated, annual objectives can be set. Flowing from the specific objectives statement is an identification of the tasks needed to be done. Such planning permits congruency between organizational needs and individual expectations.

Planning enables us to make the most effective and economical use of manpower, equipment, facilities, and money. If we identify in advance our needs for people, we can develop individuals inside an organization so that they will be ready when the opportunity for promotion appears. Planning allows subordinates to know what is required of them and gives them an opportunity to participate in the decision making.

Planning in this respect is analyzing the needs of the organization and matching them to the strengths, talents, and expertise of its employees. Using a needs analysis approach, a manager identifies the specific areas in which each subordinate lacks the required knowledge and skills for the job and/or does not meet the expected standards of performance. In addition, the analysis should focus on the developmental opportunities that the particular administrator, supervisor, or officer needs for his or her growth in the organization, including individual coaching; participation in special projects outside the individual's routine work assignments; involvement in task forces, especially those with professionals outside the individual's own work unit; and job rotation. These are examples of lateral career growth opportunities within the individual's own organization.

A corollary to this analysis is the identification of those people who are evaluated as being in either the top 10 percent or the bottom 10 percent in terms of their performance and potential for advancement.

This analysis is best done when the employees' competencies, performance standards, and performance results expected in a particular position are in writing. The competencies should reflect the differing expectations dictated by level within a job family, for example, those of an administrator and an account officer. This also communicates the performance expectations for the next higher level position. Exhibits 12 and 13 give the minimum competency guidelines for those positions. The manager assesses and matches these expectations against the strengths and weaknesses of his or her subordinate to find areas for development. This cannot be a unilateral effort but, rather, must be the result of understanding and agreement between the manager and subordinate.

In this analysis, both the manager and the subordinate review (1) the position profile reflecting expected performance accountabilities, technical knowledge, and skill competencies, relevant managerial competencies, and interpersonal factors; (2) the specific objectives previously established; (3) the performance standards for the position's various activities and duties; (4) the reasons that expected work results or objectives were not achieved or not achieved on a timely basis; and (5) what obstacles are preventing the subordinate's expected growth and development. In essence, these are also the major points of review during an appraisal meeting, a subject discussed later in this chapter.

Because this process of performance review, identification of deficiencies and opportunities, establishment of personal improvement and work objectives, and implementation of training and development efforts constitutes a complete system circle, it is in effect a continuous cycle of planning, implementation, and review. In this regard, it is similar to the planning process described in chapter 18.

Now that the needs analysis has been completed and the specific areas in which the individual is deficient—or in which learning and experience opportunities would enhance the individual's development and advancement—have been identified, the next logical step is the negotiations, understanding, and agreement between manager and subordinate about the desired results of the training. This objective-setting process is also used to establish the expected results of designated performance responsibilities and activities. The subordinate and his or her manager must know where they are going before they can expect to get there. The more clearly the end result or outcome sought is visualized, the easier it will be to determine the best route, the best timing, and the best method of achieving it.

Often this process becomes so detailed and time-consuming that the participants rebel against it. Nonetheless, they continue to go through the motions (because it is expected) but produce nothing more than the same objectives year after year, or others that neither stretch the individual's talents and abilities nor lead to innovative or creative actions designed to resolve existing deficiencies or meet changing performance expectations.

In this connection, the following guidelines highlight some commonly encountered difficulties:

1. Objectives should focus only on the position's most significant aspects and the individual's major developmental needs within a year's period.
2. The number of objectives should be manageable, even as few as one or two, but certainly not more than five or six.
3. Each objective should be articulated so that the result or outcome can be verified at the end of a given period. The manager and the subordinate must be able to evaluate whether or to what degree the objective was achieved. This does not mean that all objectives, and especially those related to personal development and improvement, must or can necessarily be quantified.
4. If the result sought can be quantified, it should be in terms of quantity, quality, time, or cost.
5. The objectives should be challenging, yet reasonable, and should require stretch effort for their accomplishment. Writing a "maintenance" objective reflecting no change from existing performance is simply a waste of time and effort.
6. The manager and subordinate should agree on the priorities of each objective.
7. The objectives should be stated in writing and should include the results to be achieved, the standards or means of validating the results, the action plan or program steps necessary to meet

the objective, the expected timing or schedule for each step, and, if applicable, the cost of each step.

8. The manager should ensure that the objectives are consistent with the organization's business plan and that they, at the same time, will meet the deficiencies and opportunities identified in the needs analysis.

In essence, an objective is simply an important end result that adds value to the individual and the organization. Without the orderly and integrated development and implementation of the objective, the necessary congruence between the organization's business plan and its goals and the employees's developmental needs may not be realized.[2] The establishment of objectives, whether directly related to work results or a personal development need, must also include regular feedback. Employees must have an opportunity for two-way communication to review their progress in achieving the desired results. "Each individual needs to get accurate information about the difference between what he is trying to do and how well he is doing it. He needs to be able to use this information to correct or change his actions. Then, basically, he is steering himself."[3]

Although almost every manager would insist that he or she provides feedback to subordinates, it is usually on a transactional basis—the "one-minute praise" or, more likely, the "one-minute chewing out." Instant evaluation of and comment on a subordinate's performance is, of course, important, desirable, and necessary, but it should not take the place of an organized, scheduled, and reasonably detailed review of an individual's overall performance results during a given period.

Basic questions that need to be answered during a review are (1) Does the subordinate know what is supposed to be accomplished? (2) Are there obstacles beyond his or her control? (3) Does the subordinate know how to do his or her job? (4) Could the subordinate do the job if he or she had additional knowledge and skills? (5) What support should the manager provide? and (6) Is the expected performance result or objective still viable and necessary?[4]

This review should not take place only once a year, during an annual performance appraisal meeting. Rather, the subordinate's performance and developmental efforts requires more frequent appraisal. In many organiza-

[2] For additional discussion of this topic, see Drucker, *Management*, ch. 34 ("Management by Objectives and Self-Control").

[3] Gordon Lippitt, *Organization Renewal* 78 (1969).

[4] See Ferdinand F. Fournies, *Coaching for Improved Work Performance* 107–133 (1978).

tions, the manager establishes a quarterly performance review (QPR) that offers an opportunity for the necessary two-way communication regarding a subordinate's overall work performance, developmental results, identification of further needs, and review of the next quarter's steps and expected results. Because external factors—including volume of work, external situation, and even a change in business plans—may affect the individual's performance and objectives achievement, the QPR is a timely way to make adjustments and changes in direction, priority, and timing of the previously agreed-to performance results and objectives.

QPR can be an effective means of giving the manager an opportunity to discuss the subordinate's performance and to reinforce his or her commitment to support that subordinate's training and development process. If, in fact, performance is not up to standards or expectations, this also is a way for getting agreement that specific problems do exist, for discussing alternative solutions, for mutually agreeing on actions to resolve the problem, and for reaching an understanding that there will be more follow-up to ensure that the agreed-on action has been taken.

To be effective, the QPR should not be a spur-of-the-moment meeting. It should be held in a private, quiet area with enough time scheduled for a relaxed discussion. The manager should focus on specific performance results, with necessary supporting "data" or observations of behavior, and not on inferences or evaluations of behavior. When reviewing the achievement of objectives, the manager should review the progress that the employee is making in completing (or not completing) the appropriate steps. The results of training and development programs during the preceding quarter should be discussed. This meeting also permits both manager and subordinate to reevaluate the next quarter's expected performance results and to make any necessary modifications. In all of this, the QPR itself is an integral part of an overall developmental process.

At the completion of a business cycle, normally a year, the subordinate's performance is reviewed. This annual appraisal should look at all objectives and those factors that contributed to the subordinate's meeting or not meeting the agreed-on goals. The appraisal should include the evaluation of the subordinate's technical work performance, general performance factors, knowledge and skills, completion of objectives, and a developmental plan for the following year.

The annual appraisal process consists of three parts: (1) the completion of an appraisal document by the manager and the completion of the same form by the subordinate; (2) an appraisal meeting, similar to a QPR, in which the manager reviews both documents with the subordinate, focusing on the major differences between the evaluation and the self-assessment, as well as the demonstrated strengths and weaknesses of the subordinate; and (3) the establishment of a developmental plan for the following year, based on an understanding of and agreement regarding the needs of the subordinate and the organization.

Although the form of the appraisal document varies widely from institution to institution, and even within an institution, the essential elements (or competencies) of the position, the necessary knowledge and skills, the expected standards of performance, and the achievement of agreed-on objectives are included.

Acquisitions and Divestitures

AUTHORS' NOTE: *Although this topic is mainly of interest to senior corporate trust managers, it also is important that professionals in the business understand the factors that enter into such decisions. In addition, knowledge of the extensive implementation process that results from such a decision will enable the corporate trust professional to add value to such process.*

Understanding the factors and considerations in the decision to buy or sell a corporate trust business, and its implementation, is important. The past six years have witnessed a major consolidation in the corporate trust industry, at levels never seen before. Much of this results from either the purchase of one institution by another or the merger of two institutions to form a new banking institution. In addition, perhaps 40 percent of the remaining consolidations result from the sale of the corporate trust function to another bank.

It is expected that the consolidations of the securities- and information-processing industry, including corporate trust, will continue as banks, which now prefer to be known as *financial service organizations* (FSOs), realign themselves for the next century. The result will be a small group of FSOs that are global players in all aspects of providing securities- and information-processing services to both institutional and retail clients in many countries. Other FSOs will offer tailored services in a specific geographic market or will deliver specialized services. The latter will not devote many resources to developing products but will be basically distribution vehicles. They can be expected to form strategic alliances with major FSOs for product research and development, support, and perhaps even capitalization. Their strength will lie in delivering personalized and/or specialized services to a selected group of buyers, in a regional or local market.

In this changing environment for trust- and information-processing services, FSOs will evaluate their business to determine whether they should expand the business or divest it. Among the questions asked will be, What is the FSO's strategic direction, and how should it allocate its resources? If it includes these types of services, then the issue is whether it can dramatically expand the corporate trust function through new and repeat business from existing customers or only through acquisitions.

Management will question current and projected revenues, its expense profile (both direct and indirect) and its profitability in terms of return on equity, and its efficiency index (which is the reciprocal of its profit margin). In addition to determining the need for additional technology resources, this evaluation will include the FSO's current corporate trust market share position versus its current and projected competition in regard to the products offered, and the markets served. Executive management's decision will be based on an understanding of the business's dynamics, an accurate evaluation of potential revenues, and the relevant direct, indirect, and allocated expenses. For many FSOs, the quality and extent of ongoing relationships with customers also will be an important factor in the evaluation.

If a decision is made to expand the business through acquisition, then two scenarios must be considered: (1) the purchase of an "in-market" corporate trust organization, capable of being merged into the existing organization structure; and/or (2) the purchase of such an organization outside the FSO's current geographical area. This is commonly referred to as a *strategic-positioning move*, designed to establish an instant regional presence.

In the first scenario, the FSO buys an existing book of business and a known revenue stream. It is not likely to result in the hiring of many additional staff, unless there is a large increase in number or accounts and activity volume. Rather, this move is designed to enlarge the revenue stream while spreading the expense over a larger account base. It also may have the effect (real or perceived) of denying a competitor entry into the FSO's regional area.

In the latter case, even though the operations activities will be consolidated into the FSO's existing processing facilities, it is likely that the FSO will maintain the seller's administration facility, particularly if a local presence is necessary for it to maintain and expand the business. By expanding its franchise into a new geographical area, the acquiring institution will be able to leverage its existing product line and its sales and marketing efforts.

Management's decision to sell its corporate trust business may be driven by current economic considerations, such as an unacceptable profit margin, a lower-than-acceptable return on equity, or simply an insufficient revenue stream, even with an acceptable profit margin. Longer-range considerations include the necessity of investing in technology without perceived significant payback, no real growth potential without major acquisitions, or simply a decision that the use of the FSO's resources will yield greater benefits from other lines of business. In attempting to reach an "unbiased" decision of whether to expand or sell the business, management will need to evaluate the desirability of retaining a financial adviser or management consultant.

THE PLANNING AND PROCESS OF BUYING

Once the strategic decision has been made to grow through acquisition, management should draw up a list of potential targets that meet its standards for credit quality, fiduciary and operations controls, and payback and profitability levels. In practice, most acquisitions have been, and will probably continue to be, opportunistic, a reaction to a book of business being put up for sale.

If the seller has decided on a "private sale," it will approach the potential acquirer informally (after the latter has signed a confidentiality agreement) to determine whether the interest is real. If however, the seller has decided to open up the sale to competitive bidding, it will contact those institutions that it believes would be interested. Either way, it is also possible that the seller may retain an adviser or third-party intermediary to assist in this process.

After signing a confidentiality agreement, potential buyers receive an "offering memorandum" (described later in the chapter). Following an evaluation of this information, a potential buyer decides whether it is sufficiently interested to submit a nonbinding indication of interest. This is not a formal bid but, rather, enables the seller to determine whether the prospective buyer's level of interest, that is, price and conditions, warrants further consideration.

Whether the transaction is a private sale or a bidding situation, the prospective buyer submits its due diligence questionnaire to the seller.

This document is an extensive series of questions designed to supplement the information in the offering memorandum and to elicit full disclosure of the book of business, including its products, markets, controls, and systems. In addition, the questionnaire asks about detailed activity levels and volumes, as well as about the components of the business's revenue stream and direct expense data. Often, the potential buyer requests biographical information about the seller's senior officers and its organization and staffing levels. This information indicates the staffing levels that the buyer may need. A potential buyer also reviews personnel expenses.

The next step is for the potential buyer to conduct its due diligence review. This is a critical part of its evaluation, as it enables the buyer to visit the seller's facility, to examine samples of actual account files, audit reports, policy and procedure manuals, minutes of the corporate trust committee, and to review the status of all defaulted accounts and pending litigation. In addition, the potential buyer visits the operations area, including the seller's records rooms and certificate inventory vault, its security holder relations section, and its processing sections. In addition, the potential buyer reviews the seller's systems capabilities and hardware configuration. From the buyer's perspective, the more it can see and the more information it has, the more informed its bid will be and the less likely there will be unpleasant surprises later on.

The buyer must prepare carefully for this review, including plans to visit the seller's corporate trust facilities if they are not at the main office. The buyer must designate employees to look at specific areas, including a representative sample of different types of accounts, acceptance criteria, regulatory and audit reports, defaulted accounts, and litigation. In addition, documents showing acceptance criteria, covenant compliance (i.e., the tickers), fee processing, collateral processing, funds movement and investments, securities processing, and escheatment should be examined. Checklists are recommended for help in later evaluating what was seen during the due diligence review.

The last step for the buyer is to put together a carefully worded bid that includes the total price to be paid for the business and whether it will be paid all in cash or in cash and other value. The timing of the payment is also spelled out; normally most of the purchase price is paid at the sale closing, with an additional payment made some months later, depending on the retention of the accounts and associated revenue stream. The buyer may not wish to purchase, without special indemnification, accounts that it perceives as carrying extraordinary liability or not fitting its business profile. In any event, the names of such accounts should be disclosed before closing the sale. In addition, the bid may contain some commitment with regard to the retention of the staff and, if applicable, the maintenance of facilities in selected locations. The document may also comment on how the buyer plans to make the transition and conversion of accounts. This is a critical document for the buyer, as it is its formal offer to buy the business, with all the conditions spelled out.

The Planning and Process of Selling

If a decision is made to sell the business, a set of plans must be drawn up so that the highest price possible is paid for the business, with the least interruption to the clients in administering their accounts, and the most staff and clients can be retained.

At the outset, management must collect all the necessary data to be included in the offering memorandum. It is this initial document that is used to tell the prospective buyer the basic information about the book of business. A typical book has the following sections:

1. An *executive summary*, containing an overview of the business, key investment considerations, and the seller's reasons for selling the business.
2. A *business description*, an overview of the organization including the administrative/sales organization, administrative systems, operations organization, and operational systems.
3. A *book of business* with, as appropriate, account data by office location, capacity, and product type; maturity schedule projections; and new business and account termination history for reasons other than redemption or maturity.
4. The *operational performance*, covering the business's processing capability and volumes by selected categories and its processing quality.
5. The *financial performance*, encompassing three years of revenue, expense, and operating contributions; average daily cash and demand deposit account balances; and, as appropriate, fees and other revenue by location and product.

Collecting these data can be difficult if they are not readily available. All the available data should be presented in a clear, concise, and easily understood format. The seller should view this document as a marketing piece, perhaps the most important one it will produce, for it can result in either exciting a prospective buyer or dampening its enthusiasm for the business, which will be reflected in the subsequent bid.

Another critical component of the sale process is developing an extensive internal and external communications plan. This document must be carefully tailored to the FSO's organization and to the hierarchy of the corporate trust department's clients. Both components must address the initial announcement of the decision to sell, the announcement of the winning bidder, and the announcement of the closing date for the sale (i.e., the date of the business' legal transfer).

The internal component should arrange both the timing and the delivery of each of the three announcements. It is usual to brief the FSO's directors and executive management just before each of the announcements is made to the corporate trust staff. It is desirable to make these announcements to the corporate trust staff in a group meeting. If there are staff members in other locations, they can be tied in by using video- or telephone-conferencing facilities. Afterward, a general announcement is usually distributed to the rest of the FSO's business and support units.

The plan for making the external announcement should take into account the necessity of personally calling on key clients and either personally calling on or telephoning other clients and financial intermediaries. Coordinating with the commercial bankers for joint relationships is important. The value of administrators' personal visits to key clients should not be underestimated. Experience has shown that such contacts are important to retaining the client's business. In addition, a written press announcement should be prepared for the news media, will all inquiries directed to a designated spokesperson.

A plan should be drawn up with the personnel department to provide special support for the staff and to ask them to remain at the organization at least until the closing date. To encourage them, the FSO may implement a variety of special programs, including paying a cash retention award, distributing a bonus based on the value of the accounts transferred at the closing or the price paid for the business, and offering a severance program to those employees who are either not given jobs in the FSO or are not hired by the buyer.

Before scheduling the due diligence reviews, the accounts should be "scrubbed." That is, all open account compliance items should be reviewed and resolved, the account files and documents should be reviewed, any out-of-proof conditions should be resolved, and any open audit items should be resolved. This process should also help in the potential buyer's review of a sample group of accounts.

During the due diligence reviews, the seller should ensure that all the necessary documents and files are made available to the prospective buyers. To avoid any unnecessary interruptions to the staff, it is highly recommended that all such files and documents be assembled in a separate room away from the area where the seller's staff is located. One or two senior officers from the seller's management team should always be present and available to answer any questions and to help the buyers obtain necessary data. It is also recommended that the potential buyers not have access to either the seller's working area or the members of the staff, except through specific senior contacts.

Following the completion of the due diligence reviews, each prospective buyer submits a binding bid to the seller, as discussed earlier. The seller's managers review all the bids and evaluate both the financial component (i.e., the total price offered and the timing of the payments) and the nonfinancial considerations, such as the retention of existing staff, the transition/conversion process, and the seller's perception of retaining clients. Although the price is clearly the most important factor, the seller's managers must be "comfortable with the deal."

Once an offer is accepted, the arduous task of negotiating a definitive purchase contract begins. To facilitate the negotiations, the seller may require bidders to submit a proposed purchase contract with their bid. In addition, a servicing agreement is needed to cover the transition period between the closing date and the date when the accounts are legally transferred. Although the systems can be converted and the account files and documents can be handed over at or just before the closing, the legal transfer of the accounts may take more than a year to complete. Most states have no legal mechanism to transfer the accounts automatically. In addition, all agency agreements and most trust agreements require that a tripartite agreement be executed to make the transfer. This tripartite agreement is signed by the principal (in the case of an agency relationship) or the obligor (in the case of a trust agreement) and by both the re-signing agent or trustee and the successor agent or trustee.

Often overlooked by FSOs considering a divestiture of their corporate trust business is the need to maintain a small staff of professionals for at least a year (and often longer than that) following the closing. The post-sale professional staff provides oversight and maintains control over the FSO's potential liability while helping the buyer become familiar with its new book of business. In addition, the buyer's staff will have ongoing questions about preclosing data, records, and documents that may not have transferred. Obligors, financial intermediaries, and brokers may continue to call for several months. No matter how many notices have been sent to the security holders, there will be a constant and ongoing stream of calls coming in, likely to last for at least twelve months.

III

Reference Material

Exhibits

EXHIBIT I
Fiduciary Obligations Review

I. Acceptance of New Appointments

If the prospective obligor is not well known to the bank, background information should be obtained on the credit standing and reputation of the company and its management, as well as on the general reputation of the underwriters, attorneys, and other involved parties.

A "new name" trusteeship will be accepted if (1) the preliminary check reveals no adverse information and (2) either (a) no creditor relationship exists and there is no expectation of establishing such a relationship or (b) acceptance of the appointment is also approved by the banking department because of the credit standing of the obligor, even though a relationship exists. The pertinent credit files are to be noted as to the existence of the corporate trust relationship.

Any administrative officer may tentatively accept new accounts subject to final approval by a senior corporate trust officer and the corporate trust committee. A written report indicating the review and acceptance of the appointment is prepared and filed in the account contact file.

As part of the determination of the bank's eligibility and qualification to serve as a trustee, a determination is to be made that the bank is neither the obligor nor a person directly or indirectly controlling, controlled by, or under common control with the obligor. In addition, a "potential conflict" check is to be performed covering, inter alia, trust appointments under other indentures with the same obligor, ownership of stock of the obligor and underwriter by the bank and vice versa, common directors, and past underwritings by the bank's underwriting affiliate. Although not prohibited by the TIA, this is part of the trustee's "awareness review."

The rights, duties, obligations, and responsibilities of the trustee under the proposed indenture and applicable statutes are to be reviewed by an administrative officer and by outside counsel and referred to a senior corporate trust officer for review if a problem is encountered.

II. Annual Conflict Check

A conflict check is to be made to determine if an annual report to the security holders is required:

1. to ensure the bank's continued eligibility and qualification to serve as trustee under the indenture.

2. to determine the existence of any potential conflicts of interest as enumerated in section 310(b) of the Trust Indenture Act.

3. to ensure compliance with the reporting requirements of section 313 of the Trust Indenture Act.

III. Corporate Trust Committee

Established by the bank's board of directors for the purpose of group consideration of matters arising in the course of the administration of corporate trusteeships, and the reporting thereof to the board for its review of the administration of such accounts and the application of management policies to corporate trust matters. This committee, which is composed of senior corporate trust officers, the group head as chairman, [and the head of the Fiduciary Department as an ex officio member,] meets on the first [Wednesday] of each month. Some banks also include their trust risk manager as an ex-officio member.

The agenda for these meetings is to cover:

1. approval of minutes of preceding meeting.

2. review of appointments and terminations since preceding the meeting.

3. report and review of active defaulted accounts (i.e., those in which an event of default has occurred or those that are the subject of bankruptcy or reorganization proceedings).

4. review of other trustee accounts.

    a. any account, although not in default, that in the judgment of the committee warrants a monthly review because of existing financial or other special circumstances.

    b. each trust account on an annual basis (i.e., approximately 1/12 of such accounts are to be reviewed each month).

These reports are to be rendered by the accountable administrative officer and in addition to any specific information for the accounts in category a, to cover the following matters:

    (i) tickler items (i.e., whether the action or submission of documents by and to the trustee has been timely in accordance with the applicable indenture or other agreement).

    (ii) operational problems, if any.

(iii) administrative problems, if any.

(iv) potential TIA 310(b) conflicts.

(v) draws on credit enhancements.

(vi) overdrafts and uninvested cash.

(vii) prospects for new or additional business.

5. report on agency account matters (i.e., those not involving a trustee appointment).

IV. Performance Under Indenture Agreements

A. All items requiring periodic attention and/or documentation under an indenture or other agreement are to be monitored through a tickler system advice to the account officer for follow-up and completion sign-off each month. Items still open one month after action is required should be referred to a senior corporate trust officer.

B. All reports, opinions, and certificates received pursuant to an indenture requirement are to be reviewed for compliance, noted on acceptance, and filed in the account document file. Any variances or problems are to be referred to a senior corporate trust officer for further action.

C. All initial releases and/or substitutions of property or collateral for a given account are to be referred to counsel for review. If subsequent such transactions conform to the requirements of the indenture and follow substantially the same format as the original one, they need not be submitted to counsel. Any transaction that in the opinion of the account officer is nonroutine should be submitted to a senior corporate trust officer for review and, if a legal question is involved, referred to counsel.

D. Any variance in compliance with the provisions of the indenture or in the proper interpretation and application of pertinent indenture provisions to specific situations should be considered by a senior corporate trust officer; by counsel if a legal question is raised; and, if necessary, by the bank's senior management. All important transactions or activities after a default occurs are to be reviewed by senior corporate trust officers with counsel. Appropriate review is to be made monthly by the corporate trust committee or a designated default subcommittee.

E. The final satisfaction of an obligor's responsibilities under an indenture is not to be rendered until there has been strict compliance with the terms and conditions of the particular indenture or agreement. In the case of bankruptcy or reorganization proceedings, an appropriate discharge of the bank's responsibilities is to be secured from the court.

EXHIBIT 2
Preacceptance Review Worksheet

Debtor/Obligor Information

Name: _____

Contact: _____
          Name   Title

_____
          Street address

_____
          City   State   Telephone   Fax

Current corporate trust client: No ☐   Yes ☐

(If yes, attach current list of existing business)

Current corporate trust officer(s): _____

Current bank client: No ☐ Yes ☐   Relationship manager: _____

Location: _____   Telephone: _____

Issuer name (if other than obligor): _____

Other issuer information: _____

_____

_____

Acceptance data

Bank risk rating: _____ Debtor/obligor long-term debt rating: _____

Credit enhancement: No ☐ Yes ☐   Credit enhancement Type: _____

Credit enhancement issuer: _____

Rating: _____ Principal amount to be issued: _____

Capacity: Trustee: _____   Agent: _____   Other: _____

Issue description: _____

_____

_____

Prepared by: _____ Reviewed by: _____

Exhibit 3
TIA/Indenture Cross-References

Reference is made to the following provisions of the Trust Indenture Act of 1939, as amended, which established certain duties and responsibilities of the company and the trustee which are not set forth in this indenture:

Section	Subject	Section	Subject
310(b)	Disqualification of trustee for conflicting interest	315(b)	Notice of default from trustee to security holders
311	Preferential collection of claims of trustee as creditor of company	315(c)	Duties of trustee in case of default
312(a)	Periodic filing of information by company with trustee	315(d)	Provisions relating to responsibility of trustee
312(b)	Access of security holders to information	315(e)	Assessment of costs against litigating security holders in certain circumstances
313(a)	Annual report of trustee to security holders	316(a)	Directions and waivers by security holders in certain circumstances
313(b)	Additional reports of trustee to security holders	316(b)	Prohibition of impairment of right of security holders to payment
314(a)	Reports of company, including annual compliance certificate	316(c)	Right of company to set record date for certain purposes
314(c)	Evidence of compliance with conditions precedent	317(a)	Special powers of trustee
315(a)	Duties of trustee prior to default	318(a)	Provisions of Act to control in case of conflict

EXHIBIT 4

Checklist for New and Additional Issues Under Indentures

Obligor _____

Guarantors and/or joint issuers (if any) _____

Title of indenture _____

415 Shelf registration _____ Yes _____ No

Issue of $ _____ Under article _____ Section _____

Description of issue _____ CUSIP no. _____

Authorized issue under indenture $ _____ under this section $ _____

Total issued to date, under indenture
        (including this issue $ _____ under this section $ _____

Balance unissued under indenture $ _____ under this section $ _____

Indenture qualified under TIA? _____

OUR CAPACITIES

Indenture trustee _____ Registrar _____ P.A.-prin. _____ P.A.-int. _____

Conversion agt. _____ Fiscal agt. _____ Owner trustee _____

Destr. agt. _____ Tender agt. _____ Put agt. _____

Ledger maintained by _____ Coagents _____

TIME SCHEDULE

T-1 and T-2 to be prepared as of _____ furnished by _____ to _____

Registration statement to be filed on _____ Registration no. _____

Information meeting: Date _____ Time _____ Location _____

Bid meeting: Date _____ Time _____ Location _____

Delivery of bonds: Date _____ Time _____ Location _____

Delivery of underwriters list: Date _____ Time _____

Indenture executed: Date _____ Time _____ Location _____

Preliminary closing: Date _____ Time _____ Location _____

Closing: Date _____ Time _____ Location _____

CONTACTS

Banking officer _____ Tel. no. _____

Obligor: Name _____ Tel. no. _____

        Address _____

Obligor's counsel: _____

        Name _____ Tel. no._____

        Address _____

Underwriter: _____

        Name _____ Tel. no._____

        Address _____

Underwriter's (or purchaser's) counsel: _____

        Name _____ Tel. no._____

        Address _____

Our counsel: _____

        Name _____ Tel. no._____

        Address _____

Banknote co.: _____

        Name _____ Tel. no._____

Other: _____

        Name _____ Tel. no._____

Enter the following symbols in the column at the left to indicate action taken with respect to each requirement:

3 = Completed   P = Pending (pending card prepared)   Ø = Not applicable

I. Prior to filing:

_____ A. Obtain proofs of Indenture and other documents for review. Send copies to our counsel.

_____ B. Reserve rooms for meetings to be held at bank.

_____ C. Prepare new appointment/new issue form and distribute to appropriate parties.

_____ D. Complete conflict check.

_____ E. Furnish _____ executed and conformed copies of T-1 and T-2.

_____ F. Determine whether bank is qualified to act in all states in which mortgaged property is located and whether provision for individual or cotrustee is required or desirable.

_____ G. Send list of documents we require.

_____ H. If new indenture is involved, ensure that fee schedule is sent to obligor.

_____ I. Determine if we are to be appointed destruction agent.

_____ J. Prepare:

    _____ a. Informal credit review—memorandum.

    _____ b. Fees to be applied.

    _____ c. Memorandum accepting appointment, notifying banking department and credit files.

_____ K. Determine quantities of each denomination of securities and prefixes.

_____ L. Advise banking officer which officials from obligor will attend information meeting.

II. Between pricing and closing:

_____ A. Inform banking department promptly if closing to involve funds paid by investment and brokerage firms.

_____ B. Verify schedule for receipt of securities and lists.

_____ C. Review proofs of each securities denomination.

_____ D. Have trustee's counsel review proof of the security to be issued.

_____ E. Have operations division review proofs of each securities denomination.

_____ F. Obtain obligor's TIN, and advise operations division.

_____ G. Receive and review drafts of closing memo and closing papers.

_____ H. Obtain CUSIP number.

_____ I. Send instructions for original issuance to operations division (before receipt of securities and lists).

_____ J. Prepare and distribute operations instruction sheets.

_____ K. Determine when indenture is to be executed and by which officials.

_____ L. Consider necessity of obtaining county clerk's certificates on notarial acknowledgments.

_____ M. Determine disposition of funds (clearinghouse or federal) to be received at closing.

_____ N. Advise money desk if funds are to be deposited with us. Prepare deposit slip.

_____ O. Determine whether certified copies of bank bylaws, signing resolutions, or other documents are required.

_____ P. Prepare authentication certificate and any other papers or receipts required to be furnished by bank.

_____ Q. Open appropriate cash accounts.

_____ R. Open account for collateral.

_____ S. Advise banking officer which company official will attend closing.

_____ T. Check with operations division whether securities are ready to be released at closing.

_____ U. Instruct operations division to open appropriate accounts (interest, principal, cash in lieu of fractional shares, etc.).

_____ V. Determine if issue is subject to OID. Obtain discount factors.

III. At closing:

_____ A. Obtain supporting documents.

_____ B. Deposit proceeds of closing, and if instructed by the obligor, invest.

_____ C. Obtain receipt for securities from obligor.

_____ D. Receive, control, and deposit collateral.

_____ E. Release securities.

IV. After closing:

_____ A. Obtain opinion of our counsel.

_____ B. Prepare closing memo and distribute.

_____ C. Prepare letter for stock exchange listing if applicable.

_____ D. Write company for appointment as fiscal agent and withholding agent.

_____ E. Receive undertaking pursuant to provisions of section 317(b) of TIA if obligor appoints a paying agent other than the trustee.

_____ F. If issue is subject to original issue discount, instruct operations to file 1099-OID and provide factor schedule.

_____ G. Write company regarding lost security replacement procedure.

_____ H. If there is an individual trustee:

     _____ 1. Obtain undated resignation.

     _____ 2. Obtain power of attorney.

     _____ 3. Prepare cards for individual trustee file.

_____ I. Enter record date for trustee's annual report in conflict check file.

_____ J. Prepare approved tickler register control list. Consider sending copy to obligor.

_____ K. Prepare (or update) the following office records:

     _____ 1. Prepare authorities file.

     _____ 2. Prepare obligor address file.

     _____ 3. Update state of incorporation file and mortgage file.

     _____ 4. Update affiliates file from company questionnaire.

     _____ 5. Prepare owner trustee files if lease financing.

_____ L. Supplemental Indenture annotate reference copy of indenture.

_____ M. Write prior lien trustees.

_____ N. Prepare pending card for first interest payment.

       _____ 1. If first interest period is short or long, advise operations division to place legend on check. Consider enclosure.

       _____ 2. Two months prior to first interest payment date, check that issue is on registered interest list.

       _____ 3. Write to obligor regarding filing reports of interest paid to holders in particular states.

       _____ 4. If tax-exempt issue, advise operations division not to prepare 1099s.

_____ O. Prepare letter to obligor to accompany initial bill and fee schedule.

       _____ 1. Receive counsel bill.

       _____ 2. Advise billing unit to prepare our initial bill.

       _____ 3. Provide account synopsis, tickler dates, and sample statements as client's introductory package.

_____ P. If a convertible issue and bank is the conversion agent, send letter to obligor requesting that operations division be advised in writing of record dates for stock and the minimum deposit of funds sufficient for cash payments in lieu of fractional shares.

_____ Q. Document closing papers. Send appropriate documents to archives.

_____ R. Obtain conformed copies of Indenture for reference file and to fill requests.

_____ S. Prepare reminders to make arrangements for delayed deliveries.

_____ T. Receive recorded counterparts and legal opinion and file.

Date: _____ Prepared: _____ Approved: _____

EXHIBIT 5
Checklist for Agency Appointments

Obligor _____

Address _____

Agreement _____

Description of issue _____

CUSIP no. _____ Prin. amt. _____ Int. dates _____

OUR APPOINTMENTS (if coagent, so indicate):

Trustee, fiscal agent, or principal agent _____

     Ledger maintained by (registrar) _____

(Co)Registrar _____ Authenticating agent _____ Conversion agent _____

(Co)Paying agent: Interest _____ Principal _____ Tender agent _____

Accounting/destruction agent _____ Other _____

OTHER AGENTS:

(Co)Registrar _____

Authenticating agent _____

Conversion agent _____

(Co)Paying agent (interest) (principal) _____

Tender agent _____

Accounting/destruction agent _____

Escrow agent _____

Other _____

TIME SCHEDULE:	Date	Time	Place
Information meeting	_____	_____	_____
Bid/pricing	_____	_____	_____
Del. of underwriters list	_____	_____	_____
Preliminary closing	_____	_____	_____
Closing	_____	_____	_____

CONTACTS:

Obligor: Firm _____

             Address _____

             Name_____Tel. no._____

Obligor's counsel   Firm _____

                        Address

                        Name_____Tel. no._____

Bond counsel   Firm _____

                        Address _____

                        Name_____Tel. no._____

Underwriter   Firm _____

                        Address _____

                        Name_____Tel. no._____

Trustee   Firm _____

                        Address _____

                        Name_____Tel. no._____

Trustee's counsel   Firm _____

                        Address _____

                        Name_____Tel. no._____

Principal agent(s) Firm _____

                        Address _____

                        Name_____Tel. no._____

Banknote company Firm _____

                        Address _____

                        Name_____Tel. no._____

Enter the following symbols in the column in the left column to indicate action taken with respect to each requirement:

3 = Completed   P = Pending (pending card prepared)   Ø = Not applicable

BEFORE CLOSING:

_____ A. Prepare "Acceptance Form for New Issues" and distribute to appropriate parties.

_____ B. Consider fees and send schedule to issuer.

_____ C. Obtain and review proofs of security certificates.

_____ D. Obtain CUSIP number.

_____ E. Obtain issuer's taxpayer identification number.

_____ F. Determine quantities of each denomination of securities to be delivered to us by banknote company.

_____ G. If we are to do the original issuance, verify with underwriter:

_____ 1. list of registered holders.

_____ 2. time and place for delivery of securities.

_____ 3. time and place of packaging and preclosing.

_____ 4. time and place of closing.

_____ H. Prepare and distribute original issuance instructions to operations division if we are registrar or coregistrar.

_____ I. Prepare any documents we are to furnish at closing (e.g., signing resolutions, incumbency certificate).

_____ J. Advise appropriate officers of the bank as to closing and who will attend from the issuer.

_____ K. Open appropriate cash and/or investment accounts.

_____ L. Prepare and distribute standing account operating instructions.

_____ M. Check with operations division that securities are prepped and ready for release.

AT CLOSING:

_____ A. Obtain required documents, including:

_____ 1. documents appointing bank as agent.

_____ 2. executed (or conformed) counterpart of the indenture or agreement.

_____ 3. incumbency certificate of issuer's officers.

_____ 4. specimen certificates of each denomination.

_____ B. Deposit proceeds of closing into appropriate account(s), or wire funds at written direction of issuer.

_____ C. Obtain receipt for securities from issuer.

_____ D. Release securities to underwriter/syndicate manager.

AFTER CLOSING:

_____ A. Request appropriate documents from trustee to complete our records.

_____ B. If original issuance was done as a courtesy for another registrar, provide such with necessary information.

_____ C. Prepare closing memo and distribute. Ensure one copy is sent to appropriate banking officer and another put in the appropriate contact file(s).

_____ D. If securities are listed, prepare letter to New York Stock Exchange, covering supply of certificates held to facilitate transfers and exchanges by us as registrar or coregistrar.

_____ E. Ensure we have instructions from issuer or principal paying agent as to:

_____ 1. source of funds.

_____ 2. disposition of canceled securities.

_____ 3. where to send out bills.

_____ F. If we act as paying agent, write issuer for appointment as fiscal agent and withholding agent and send appointment letter to the IRS.

_____ G. Prepare all internal office records, including ticklers (consider sending copy to issuer).

_____ H. If issue includes a put or demand option, complete "Put/Demand Checklist."

_____ I. If we pay registered interest, prepare pending card for first interest payment.

    _____ 1. If first interest payment is short or long, advise operations division. Also note on instruction sheet.

    _____ 2. Set up tickler card to check that issue is on registered interest control list for first interest payment.

    _____ 3. If tax-exempt issue, send memo to operations division not to prepare 1099 forms; otherwise send memo to prepare the forms.

    _____ 4. If subject to OID, instruct operations division to file 1099-OID and obtain appropriate information from issuer.

    _____ 5. Write issuer regarding state reporting and pend to instruct operations division upon receipt of information.

_____ J. If we are coregistrar, obtain written instructions where to send transfer sheets and, if required, a supply of certificates from the trustee. Confirm in writing who will be responsible for maintaining records as registrar.

_____ K. Send letter to copaying agent(s) regarding procedure to follow if we are the principal paying agent.

_____ L. If convertible issue and we are conversion agent:

    _____ 1. Send letter to issuer requesting notification of record date for their common stock.

    _____ 2. Request notification from the issuer of changes in conversion price, if any.

    _____ 3. request from issuer minimum deposit of funds sufficient to pay cash in lieu of fractional shares.

_____ M. Follow to ensure that the initial bill is sent by operations division.

_____ N. Document closing papers.

_____ O. Consider sending letter of appreciation and introductory account package.

Date: _____Prepared: _____Approved: _____

EXHIBIT 6
Illustration of Allocation Formula for Pro-Rata Redemption

Objective: To select bonds for redemption in even multiples of $1,000 from all holders in such manner that all holders retain same proportion of outstanding bonds as nearly as possible.

Procedure: Prepare chart on which is listed for each outstanding registered holder (if more than one bond is registered in same name, determine if allocation is to be made separately for each bond or if holdings are to be considered in aggregate):

COLUMN A—The original principal amount.

COLUMN B—The present principal amount outstanding.

COLUMN C—The principal amount that should be outstanding after exact percentage allocation of all redemption payments, including the present. This is determined by multiplying amounts in Column A by a percentage determined as follows:

$$\frac{\text{Sum of Column B} - \text{Current redemption payment}}{\text{Sum of Column A}}$$

COLUMN D—Exact pro-rata allocation for each holding, determined by subtracting Column C from Column B.

COLUMN E—Adjusted to provide current pro-rata redemption in terms of $1,000 and integral multiples for each holding.

Application of this formula may be illustrated by considering a $10,000,000 issue originally sold to ten holders. The indenture provides for an annual sinking fund computed on the basis of 3 percent of the original amount for the first two years and 4 percent for the third year. Allocation of the sinking fund payments for the first three years would be as follows:

First Year

BOND NUMBER	COLUMN A ORIGINAL P/A OUTSTANDING	COLUMN B PRESENT P/A OUTSTANDING	COLUMN C 97% OF COL. A	COLUMN D COL. B MINUS MINUS COL. C	COLUMN E PRO RATA REDEMPTION
1	$3,500,000	$3,500,000	$3,395,000	$105,000	$105,000
2	1,800,000	1,800,000	1,746,000	54,000	54,000
3	1,250,000	1,250,000	1,212,500	37,500	38,000
4	950,000	950,000	921,500	28,500	29,000
5	878,000	878,000	851,660	26,340	26,000
6	720,000	720,000	698,400	21,600	22,000
7	540,000	540,000	523,800	16,200	16,000
8	175,000	175,000	169,750	5,250	5,000
9	140,000	140,000	135,800	4,200	4,000
10	47,000	47,000	45,590	1,410	1,000
	$10,000,000	$10,000,000	$9,700,000	$300,000	$300,000

Second Year

BOND NUMBER	COLUMN A	COLUMN B	COLUMN C 94% OF COL. A	COLUMN D	COLUMN E
1	$3,500,000	$395,000	$3290,000	$105,000	$105,000
2	1,800,000	1,746,000	1,692,000	54,000	54,000
3	1,250,000	1,212,000	1,175,000	37,000	37,000
4	950,000	921,000	893,000	28,000	28,000
5	878,000	852,000	825,320	26,680	27,000
6	720,000	698,000	676,000	21,200	21,000
7	540,000	524,000	507,600	16,400	16,000
8	175,000	170,000	164,500	5,500	6,000
9	140,000	136,000	131,600	4,400	4,000
10	47,000	46,000	44,180	1,820	2,000
	$10,000,000	$9,700,000	$9,400,000	$300,000	$300,000

Third Year

BOND NUMBER	COLUMN A	COLUMN B	COLUMN C 94% OF COL. A	COLUMN D	COLUMN E
1	$3,500,000	$3,290,000	$3,150,000	$140,000	$140,000
2	1,800,000	1,692,000	1,620,000	72,000	72,000
3	1,250,000	1,175,000	1,125,000	50,000	50,000
4	950,000	893,000	855,000	38,000	38,000
5	878,000	825,000	790,200	34,800	35,000
6	720,000	677,000	648,000	29,000	29,000
7	540,000	508,000	486,000	22,000	22,000
8	175,000	164,000	157,500	6,500	6,000
9	—[a]	—	—	—	—
10	47,000	44,000	42,300	1,700	2,000
11	105,000[b]	99,000[a]	94,500	4,500	5,000[c]
12	35,000[b]	33,000[a]	31,500	1,500	1,000
	$10,000,000	$9,400,000	$9,000,000	$400,000	$400,000

[a] Bond number 9 for $132,000 (original $140,000) canceled and new bonds 11 and 12 issued for $99,000 and $33,000, respectively.

[b] 75 percent and 25 percent of $140,000.

[c] Determined by lot.

EXHIBIT 7
Full-Redemption Procedure Guide

Obligor _____

Account no. _____

Indenture dated: _____ CUSIP no. _____

Issue description _____

Record date _____ Mail and/or publication date _____

Redemption date _____ Redemption amount $ _____

Premium (if any) _____ Accrued interest _____

Notice requirements (financial journal, first-class mail, registered mail, etc.) _____

Date funds are to be deposited _____

Enter the following symbols in the column in the left column to indicate action taken:
    3 = Completed   P = Pending (pending card prepared)   Ø = Not applicable

I. PRIOR TO REDEMPTION

_____ A. Immediately upon notification of redemption, review requirements of Indenture.

_____ B. If OID issue, receive from obligor revised OID calculations and forward to operations.

_____ C. If issue has a debt service reserve fund, review indenture provisions to determine if funds on deposit are to be used as credit against redemption proceeds.

_____ D. Verify with obligor the total amount of redemption proceeds, including accrued interest and the date the funds will be deposited.

_____ E. Notify any coagents of redemption.

_____ F. Forward to operations a request to call bonds.

_____ G. Prepare notice of redemption. Send to obligor, and counsel, if necessary, for approval)

_____ H. Send copy of notice to any copaying agents.

_____ I. Provide operations with a copy of notice.

_____ J. If redemption notice is required to be published, coordinate publication with appropriate advertising agent.

_____ K. Ensure that redemption notice is mailed to all registeredbondholders in accordance with indenture requirements.

_____ L. Forward copies of redemption notices to depositories, rating agencies, information services, stock exchange (if applicable), disclosure agent, and any other required agencies.

_____ M. Make arrangements for transfer of funds to any copaying agents.

II. ON OR AFTER REDEMPTION DATE

_____ A. Receive redemption proceeds from obligor.

_____ B. Obtain affidavit of mailing from operations.

_____ C. Obtain affidavit of publication from advertising agent.

_____ D. Notify any stock exchanges on which securities may be listed that sufficient funds were deposited by obligor.

_____ E. If bond issue secured by credit enhancement, make arrangements to return credit enhancement instrument to provider. (Review governing documents.)

_____ F. Review indenture provisions regarding return of any funds remaining on deposit.

_____ G. Instruct operations to prepare appropriate accounting.

_____ H. Initiate account termination procedures, including deletion/notation of appropriate records.

_____ I. Review pending file and dispose of any open items.

_____ J. Notify arbitrage rebate analyst of redemption and request final rebate calculation.

_____ K. Review unpaid bills, calculate final fee, and request operations to produce final bill.

_____ L. Review indenture regarding release of property (if any) and satisfaction. Prepare drafts and forward to trustee's counsel for review.

_____ M. Deliver letter regarding release and satisfaction, and final bill to obligor.

_____ N. After payment of final bill, execute and deliver release and satisfaction.

_____ O. Instruct operations to destroy remaining certificate inventory. Request certificate of destruction for account termination file.

_____ P. Establish ticklers to remind operations to mail second and third notices to any registered holders with unpresented bonds.

_____ Q. Determine when any undisbursed funds to be returned to obligor.

Dated: _____ Prepared: _____ Approved _____

EXHIBIT 8
Partial-Redemption Procedure Guide

Obligor _____

Account no. _____

Indenture dated: _____

CUSIP no. _____

Issue description _____

Record date _____ Mail and/or publication date _____

Redemption date _____ Redemption amount $ _____

Premium (if any) _____ Accrued interest _____

Notice requirements (financial journal, first-class mail, registered mail, etc.) _____

Redemption method (pro-rata, by lot, inverse maturity order, etc.)_____

Date funds are to be deposited _____

Reason for redemption (Sinking fund, optional prepayment, unexpended proceeds, etc.)

1. Under NYSE Rule 217, securities selected for redemption will not be good delivery after the date that called numbers become available (publication/mail date). Notice should be dated on the date that the books open and be mailed on that date.

2. Bonds with stops (and not previously replaced) can be called.

3. Previously reissued portions of called but unpresented bonds should not be called again if efforts to contact holders prove futile (i.e., registered letter is returned by postal authorities as undeliverable).

Enter the following symbols in the column at the left column to indicate action taken:
3 = Completed   P = Pending (pending card prepared)   Ø = Not applicable

I. PRIOR TO REDEMPTION

_____ A. Immediately upon notification of redemption, review requirements of indenture.

_____ B. If OID issue, obtain from obligor the OID calculations and forward to operations.

_____ C. If issue has debt service reserve fund, review governing documents to determine if reduction of reserve requirement is appropriate and if excess is to be applied as a credit to amount due from obligor.

_____ D. Verify with obligor the total amount of redemption proceeds, including accrued interest and the date that funds will be deposited.

_____ E. Notify any coagents of redemption.

_____ F. Forward to operations a request to call bonds and select bond numbers for redemption.

_____ G. Prepare redemption notice and mail copy to obligor and any copaying agents.

_____ H. Provide operations with a copy of redemption notice.

_____ I. If redemption notice is required to be published, coordinate publication with appropriate advertising agent.

_____ J. Ensure that redemption notice is mailed to all registered bondholders in accordance with indenture requirements.

_____ K. Make arrangements for transfer of funds to any copaying agents.

_____ L. Forward copies of redemption notice to depositories, rating agencies, information services, stock exchange (if applicable), disclosure agent, and any other required agencies.

ON OR AFTER REDEMPTION DATE

_____ A. Receive redemption proceeds from obligor.

_____ B. Obtain affidavit of mailing from operations.

_____ C. Obtain affidavit of publication from advertising agent.

_____ D. If bond issue secured by some type of credit enhancement, make arrangements to forward a notice of reduction to provider. Review governing documents for specific requirements.

_____ E. Deliver revised debt service schedule to obligor.

_____ F. Establish ticklers to remind operations to mail second and third notices to any registered holders of unpresented bonds.

Dated: _____Prepared: _____Approved: _____

Exhibit 9
Default Report Form

(For month ending: _____)

To: Default subcommittee_____

From: _____
        Administrator

Location/telephone:_____

Re:_____

1. Name of obligor (if other than issuer): _____

2. Principal amount outstanding:_____

3. Bond proceeds were used to: _____

4. Brief description of default: _____

_____

5. Date of default: _____

6. Is issue credit enhanced?   Yes _____   No_____

If yes, who is provider: _____

7. Does any other area of the bank have a relationship with the obligor?
Yes _____ No: _____

8. Is this account in a bankruptcy proceeding? Yes: _____ No _____

9. Trustee's counsel _____

of: _____
     Address

telephone: _____ fax: _____

10. Fees and expenses   incurred this month   paid this month

Legal: _____   _____

Extraordinary admin: _____   _____

Expenses: _____   _____

Fees and expenses will be paid by: Account: _____ Bank:_____

Indemnitor (specify): _____ Other (specify): _____

If bank is advancing fees and expenses, is reimbursement from another source likely
and if so, when is reimbursement anticipated? _____

Ordinary administration fee: $ _____ per annum current through _____

11. Number of registered holders as of: _____ is _____

If fewer than five, list them: _____

_____

_____

_____

_____

12. Date of last bondholder correspondence (explain if more than 90 days): _____

_____

13. Is this issue secured by real property?   Yes_____ No _____

If yes, is foreclosure contemplated?   Yes_____ No _____

14. When do financing statements expire? _____

15. Are insurance premiums current?   Yes_____ No _____

When does coverage expire? _____

16. Current status (include any litigation or bankruptcy developments): _____

_____

_____

EXHIBIT 10
Account Review Checklist

Account name _____ Account no. _____

Public issue/Pvt. placement_____ Corp/muni_____

Escrow agent_____

Our capacity _____

Descript. of outstanding sec. _____

REVIEW QUESTIONS	YES	NO
1. Is there any client service quality problem? If so, describe problem and action taken.	_____	_____
2. Have all account files been reviewed for completeness and accuracy?	_____	_____
With respect to the account/document files:		
a. In good order and in compliance with current policies?	_____	_____
b. All investment authorizations have been approved and filed?	_____	_____
c. All instruction sheets have been updated?	_____	_____
d. Authorities file has been updated?	_____	_____
e. Certificates, financials, etc., are being reviewed in accordance with current policies and performance standards?	_____	_____
f. Documents have been sent to archives in accordance with current procedure guidelines?	_____	_____
3. Have ticklers been prepared and approved?	_____	_____
Are ticklers up-to-date? If not, describe item, tickler date, and action taken.	_____	_____
4. Is the underlying collateral securing the issue being properly maintained?	_____	_____
Is refiling of financing statements required?	_____	_____
New refiling date is _____.		
5. Are all investments authorized by operative documents?	_____	_____
6. Has obligor/issuer met all debt service deposits/payments in a timely manner?	_____	_____
If not, describe problem and action taken.		

7. Are there any significant administrative
   problems?   _____   _____

   If yes, describe problem and action taken.

8. Are there any significant operational problems,
   including out-of-proof conditions?   _____   _____

   If yes, describe problem and action taken.

9. Are there chronic overdrafts or uninvested
   cash, either true or technical?   _____   _____

   If so, describe problem and action taken.

10. Indicate whether prospect for new or
    additional business (corp. trust or other).

Date of review _____Admr./account mgr._____

EXHIBIT 11
Training Guidelines for Administrators

SUBJECT MATTER	REFERENCE MATERIAL

A. DURING FIRST MONTH

1. *Orientation*
   Position profile, training program outline, competency expectations, performance standards, appraisal system, and corporate trust orientation — Handbook, training guidelines

2. Knowledge of debt and equity securities, differences between secured and unsecured and short-, medium-, and long-term maturities. — CTAM book

3. *Issuers of debt securities*
   Corporations, governments, states, state authorities, state agencies, and municipalities — CTAM book

4. Role of investment bankers and underwriters — CTAM book

5. Development of the trustee concept. Fiduciary responsibilities defined. — CTAM book

6. Functions and responsibilities of a corporate trustee — CTAM book

7. Securities Act of 1933
   Securities Exchange Act of 1934
   Trust Indenture Act of 1939, as amended — CTAM book, securities laws, handbook

8. *The trust indenture*
   As a mortgage, trust, contract — CTAM book
   An indenture

9. Public vs. private debt issues — CTAM book

10. *Functions of administration*
    a. Trustee functions — CTAM book
       Corporate trustee under trust indentures, construction fund trustee, bond fund trustee, owner trustee, and pledge agreement
    b. Agency — CTAM book
       Registrar, authenticating agent, fiscal agent, paying agent—corporate and municipal, exchange agent, conversion agent, destruction agent, escrow agent, tender agent, and depository

11. Coagency duties and responsibilities — CTAM book

12. Tickler system—Use and purpose — Handbook

13. Document files, correspondence files, and retention of records — Handbook

14. Organization and structure of bank, fiduciary department,   Handbook
    corporate trust function

15. Use of telephone, fax, office machines, and computer   Handbook
    terminals including e-mail

16. Introduction to corporate trust marketing function   Tours and
    related
    materials

17. Introduction to corporate trust operations function   Tours and
    related
    materials

B. DURING FIRST THREE MONTHS

1. Receipt of interest and principal   Handbook

2. *Preparation of debit and credit tickets and advices*
Preparation and knowledge of offsets, check collection,   Handbook
mailing advices, use of clearance accounts, transfer of
funds—money transfer, and clearinghouse vs. federal funds

3. *Private placements*
HOP agreements, Use and preparation of amortization   CTAM book,
schedules, pro-rata redemptions, computation of interest,   handbook
instructions to operations

4. *Corporate trust records*
Document files, use of correspondence file and contact   Handbook
file, use of pending cards, subsidiary administration files,
trustee records, cash and securities ledgers: Opening and
closing accounts and termination of accounts

5. Understanding and use of procedure book   Procedure book

6. *Internal instructions*
Preparation of operating instructions; address book,   Handbook
mailing instructions, and instructions for lists and labels

7. *Discussion of:*
Securities Act of 1933, Securities Exchange Act of 1934,   CTAM book,
Trust Indenture Act of 1939, and articles 8 and 9 of   handbook,
Uniform Commercial Code.   securities laws

8. *Usual provisions of a typical indenture*
(Composite picture of the scope of a typical indenture)   CTAM book

C. DURING FIRST SIX MONTHS

1. *Letter and memo writing*
Confirmations and certifications, presidential letters,   Handbook
bondholder inquiries, and cables, tested vs. untested

2. *Review and execution of releases*
   Indenture provisions, receipt of proceeds, substitution   CTAM book
   of property, prepayment of debt securities, and
   withdrawals—additions and betterments.

3. *Investments*
   Policy and functional areas involved, understanding of   Handbook
   various types of securities, order instructions, time limits,
   follow-up of transaction, maturities, reinvestments, and
   remittances—interest and principal

4. *Trustee reports*
   Annual TIA conflict check and trustee's annual report   CTAM book,
                                                                    handbook

5. *Preparation of instructions for agency appointments*
   Corporate and municipal agency appointments; corporate   Handbook
   and municipal issue calls, redemptions, and maturities

6. *Model indentures*
   Model provisions and simplified indenture   CTAM book,
                                                                    ABF model
                                                                    F/R debenture
                                                                    indenture,
                                                                    commentaries,
                                                                    simplified
                                                                    indenture

7. Operations orientation tour   Handbook

8. *Introduction to corporate trust's management philosophy
   and style*
   Planning process (and cycle), leading activities including   Handbook
   group participation, organizing work flow/structure, and
   controlling activities and programs

9. Discussion of appraisal program and salary administration   Handbook

D. BETWEEN SIX MONTHS AND ONE YEAR

1. Relationships with other banking/operations divisions

2. Detailed discussion of indenture provisions, issuance,   CTAM book,
   dating and interest accrual, insurance, maintenance,   commentaries
   financial, recording, sinking fund including: additions
   and betterments, cash (partial redemptions), and credit;
   default, conversion, concerning the trustee, and remedies
   of trustee and bondholders

3. Indenture Reading and Understanding   CTAM book,
                                                                    Commentaries

4. Credit enhancements, including letters of credit and bond
   insurance

5. *Closing functions as trustee for noncomplex public issues*
   Time schedule, ordering of certificates, review of
   documents, preparation of supporting documents,
   deposit of proceeds and collateral, documenting of
   closing papers, and preparation of trustee records

   CTAM book,
   handbook

6. Basic understanding of complex financings
   (e.g., structured transactions)

7. Preparation of ticklers   Handbook

8. Preparation of Form T-1   CTAM book,
                                                                    handbook

9. Filing of recorded counterparts   CTAM book,
                                                                    handbook

10. *Sinking funds and redemptions*
    Total, partial, and forced conversion   CTAM book,
                                                                    handbook

11. *Satisfactions*
    Accountings, disposition of documents, agency accounts,
    and payment of bond maturities   CTAM book,
                                                                    handbook

12. *Review of certificates, opinions, and financial statements*
    Checking indenture provisions, checking signatures, and   CTAM book,
    sign-off   handbook

13. Consents and waivers   CTAM book,
                                                                    handbook

14. Understanding replacement of lost, stolen, and   CTAM book,
    mutilated securities   handbook

15. Name change of obligor   CTAM book,
                                                                    handbook

16. Resignations   CTAM book,
                                                                    handbook

17. Organizing work and using available reference resources

18. Setting priorities

19. Following up on pending matters

E. BETWEEN ONE AND TWO YEARS

1. Introduction to financial planning and control programs

2. "Reading" and ability to give comments on new   CTAM book,
   indentures and supplements, private placement agreements,   model inden-
                                                                    tures, other
                                                                    financing

	documents commentaries, other indentures
3. *Closing functions as trustee or owner trustee for complex financings*	
Time schedules, ordering of certificates, review of documents, Preparation of supporting documents, deposit of proceeds and collateral, documenting closing papers, and preparation of records	Handbook
4. Merger of obligor	CTAM book, handbook
5. Successor trusteeships and indemnifications	CTAM book, handbook
6. Understanding of fee schedules and billing policies and procedures	
7. Introduction to default and bankruptcy administration	CTAM book

Reference Material Key

CTAM book	Landau and Krueger, *Corporate Trust Administration and Management*
ABF Model	American Bar Foundation, *Model Fully Registered Debenture Indenture*
Commentaries	American Bar Foundation, *Commentaries on Model Indentures*
Handbook	*Corporate Trust Administrator's Handbook*

EXHIBIT 12
Performance Competencies—Administrators

ADMINISTRATOR	SENIOR ADMINISTRATOR
1. Reviews new noncomplex indentures, agreements, and other basic documents for further review with account officer.	Reviews new complex indentures, agreements, and other basic documents for proper form and substance for review with account officer; understanding is sufficient to explain comments to our counsel.
2. Reviews all documents and certificates delivered in connection with the issuance of securities with the account officer and assists the account officer on all closing details.	Reviews all documents and certificates delivered in connection with the issuance of securities and handles all closing details with guidance from the account officer.
3. Completes review of all financial statements, certificates, and opinions for account officer.	Completes review and approval of all financial statements, certificates, and opinions.
4. Working knowledge of model indenture provisions and mechanics and of the least complicated negotiated provisions.	Understands model indenture provisions and mechanics and has good working knowledge of most negotiated provisions.
5. Handles details and follow-up with guidance for: a. receipt and disbursement of cash b. sinking funds c. releases d. investments e. withdrawals f. satisfactions g. preparation of trustee reports	Handles details and follow-up with guidance for: a–g: SAME h. consents and waivers i. name change of obligor j. resignations k. mergers
6. Prepares letters, memoranda, and internal instructions for account officer's approval and signature.	Prepares letters, memoranda, and internal instructions for own approval and signature or account officer's based on internal guidelines.
7. Exercises good judgment on what should be referred to account officer, offering optional solutions.	Exercises sound judgment when solving problems and when referring items to account officer. If referred to officer, exercises sound judgment in recommending the appropriate solution.

8. With account officer's guidance, sets priorities and organizes own work in an effective manner.

Sets priorities and organizes own work in efficient and effective manner.

9. Good understanding of trustee records maintained.

Complete understanding of trustee records maintained.

10. Handles work without constant supervision on fundamental tasks.

Handles all day-to-day work with only minimal guidance from account officer.

11. Dependent on account officer for guidance. Follow-up complete.

Dependence on account officer for guidance after presenting problem and possible solutions. Follow-up complete.

12. Recognizes an apparent problem. Presents complete information to account officer.

Recognizes an apparent problem and determines the real issue. Presents complete information and the best solution to account officer.

13. Originates and suggests to account officer new ideas to promote better safeguards and greater efficiency.

Originates new ideas to promote better safeguards and greater efficiency.

14. Applies appropriate level of job knowledge when solving problems and working under pressure.

SAME

15. Familiarity with the purposes and general applicability of the Trust Indenture Act of 1939, the Securities Act of 1933, and the Securities Exchange Act of 1934.

Familiarity with the purpose and specific application of the conflict and disclosure provisions of the Trust Indenture Act. Understands purpose and applicability of other relevant federal and state laws and regulations.

16. General understanding of debt and equity securities and the markets in which they trade; total understanding of the role played and the functions of the trustee, obligor, and the investment banker.

Good understanding of debt and equity securities and the markets in which they trade; total understanding of the role played and the function of the trustee, obligor, and the investment banker.

17. Basic knowledge of bank and administration policies as they relate to account administration.

Specific knowledge of bank and administration policies as they relate to account administration.

18. N.A.

Generally familiar with Administration planning and control programs.

19. N.A.

Basically familiar with all fee policies and procedures.

EXHIBIT 12 (*continued*)
Performance Competencies—Administrators

ADMINISTRATOR	SENIOR ADMINISTRATOR
20. Basically familiar with operations functions and key personnel of operations.	Complete knowledge of operations functions and key personnel of operations.
21. Basic knowledge of the organization structure of the bank, the trust department, and corporate trust function.	SAME, plus knowledge of other interfacing divisions.
22. General knowledge of other divisions and department functions in bank as they relate to the position.	SAME, but greater specific knowledge and understanding.
23. With account officer, cultivate relations with customers, counsel, and investment bankers.	With guidance from account officer, cultivate relations with customers, counsel, and investment bankers to put the bank in favorable position to market additional services.
24. Complies with position performance standards.	SAME

EXHIBIT 13
Performance Competencies—Account Officers

ACCOUNT OFFICER	SENIOR ACCOUNT OFFICER
1. Satisfactorily reviews new indentures, fiscal agency and authenticating agency agreements, etc. and identifies provisions missing or needing revision; gives comments with minimal assistance from administration manager.	Thoroughly reviews new indentures, fiscal agency and authenticating agency agreements, etc. and identifies provisions missing or needing revision and can draft substitute language; gives comments without assistance from administration manager.
2. Satisfactorily negotiates basic indenture provisions of the indenture or other agreements.	Effective negotiator in all areas of responsibility.
3. Understands basic debt financing methods.	Understands complex debt-financing methods.
4. Well qualified to administer trust or agency accounts and solve routine account problems.	Fully qualified to administer trust or agency accounts and solve complex account problems.
5. Handles routine accounts with minimal assistance from administration manager.	Handles complex, troublesome accounts and defaulted accounts with minimal assistance from administration manager.
6. Working knowledge of Trust Indenture Act and the purpose and significant provisions of the Securities Act and the Securities Exchange Act. Familiar with relevant UCC negotiable instrument and security interest provisions.	Fully understands Trust Indenture Act and is able to interpret provisions of the act in order to make decisions; understands the purpose and relevant provisions of the Securities Act and the Securities Exchange Act. Understands relevant provisions of the Federal Bankruptcy Code and UCC.
7. Writes satisfactory letters and memos; oral communication satisfactory on a one-to-one basis.	Effective use of oral and written communication skills; can conduct training seminars.
8. Recommends appropriate business decisions involving risk.	Within limits of authority, makes appropriate business decisions involving risk.
9. Identifies need for action concerning defaulted and financially troubled accounts.	Ability to make sound judgments with supportable recommendations on defaulted and financially troubled accounts.
10. Qualified to exercise limited independent action as the primary official account contact.	Within limits of authority exercises complete independent action as the primary official account contact.

EXHIBIT 13 (*continued*)
Performance Competencies—Account Officers

ACCOUNT OFFICER	SENIOR ACCOUNT OFFICER
11. Has basic knowledge of operations and marketing activities and functions of interfacing divisions.	Has extensive knowledge of operations and marketing activities; greater depth of knowledge of interfacing divisions including fiduciary. Maintains knowledge of bank structure and organization.
12. Familiar with administration planning and control functions.	Good understanding of administration planning and control activities.
13. Is thoroughly familiar with fee structure and schedules.	Recommends appropriate fees to administration manager.
14. Controls work in process; is supervised by administration manager.	Effectively controls own work in process.
15. Training skills being developed.	Well qualified to train, counsel, and evaluate administrators and develop account officers.
16. Not an experienced supervisor.	Has been trained in professional management skills; capable of supervising two or more subordinates.
17. Limited contribution to administration's marketing program.	Is responsible for participation in all sales and marketing activities.
18. Basic familiarity with ongoing developments in CT industry.	Good understanding of changes taking place in the CT and securities industries and trends within commercial banking functions.
19. Ability to perform needs analysis and establish specific objectives.	Establishes and consistently and in a timely manner accomplishes difficult specific objectives and special projects.
20. Sets priorities and organizes own work to ensure consistent, timely performance results.	SAME, plus that of assigned administrators.
21. Performance standards for own work are consistently met.	Performance standards for own work and that of assigned administrators are consistently followed.
22. Has been designated as a Certified Corporate Trust Specialist by the Institute of Certified Bankers.	SAME

THE TRUST INDENTURE ACT OF 1939
AS AMENDED BY
THE TRUST INDENTURE REFORM ACT OF 1990

CONTENTS

Sec. 301   Short Title

This subchapter may be cited as the "Trust Indenture Act of 1939."

Sec. 302   Necessity for Regulation

(a) Upon the basis of facts disclosed by the reports of the Securities and Exchange Commission made to the Congress pursuant to section 211 of the Securities Exchange Act of 1934 and otherwise disclosed and ascertained, it is hereby declared that the national public interest and the interest of investors in notes, bonds, debentures, evidences of indebtedness, and certificates of interest or participation therein, which are offered to the public, are adversely affected—

(1) when the obligor fails to provide a trustee to protect and enforce the rights and to represent the interests of such investors, notwithstanding the fact that (A) individual action by such investors for the purpose of protecting and enforcing their rights is rendered impracticable by reason of the disproportionate expense of taking such action, and (B) concerted action by such investors in their common interest through representatives of their own selection is impeded by reason of the wide dispersion of such investors through many States, and by reason of the fact that information as to the names and addresses of such investors generally is not available to such investors;

(2) when the trustee does not have adequate rights and powers, or adequate duties and responsibilities, in connection with matters relating to the protection and enforcement of the rights of such investors; when, notwithstanding the obstacles to concerted action by such investors, and the general and reasonable assumption by such investors that the trustee is under an affirmative duty to take action for the protection and enforcement of their rights, trust indentures (A) generally provide

that the trustee shall be under no duty to take any such action, even in the event of default, unless it receives notice of default, demand for action, and indemnity, from the holders of substantial percentages of the securities outstanding thereunder, and (B) generally relieve the trustee from liability even for its own negligent action or failure to act;

(3) when the trustee does not have resources commensurate with its responsibilities, or has any relationship to or connection with the obligor or any underwriter of any securities of the obligor, or holds, beneficially or otherwise, any interest in the obligor or any such underwriter, which relationship, connection, or interest involves a material conflict with the interest of such investors;

(4) when the obligor is not obligated to furnish to the trustee under the indenture and to such investors adequate current information as to its financial condition, and as to the performance of its obligations with respect to the securities outstanding under such indenture; or when the communication of such information to such investors is impeded by the fact that information as to the names and addresses of such investors generally is not available to the trustee and to such investors;

(5) when the indenture contains provisions which are misleading or deceptive, or when full and fair disclosure is not made to prospective investors of the effect of important indenture provisions; or

(6) when, by reason of the fact that trust indentures are commonly prepared by the obligor or underwriter in advance of the public offering of the securities to be issued thereunder, such investors are unable to participate in the preparation thereof, and, by reason of their lack of understanding of the situation, such investor would in any event be unable to procure the correction of the defects enumerated in this subsection.

(b) Practices of the character above enumerated have existed to such an extent that, unless regulated, the public offering of notes, bonds, debentures, evidences of indebtedness, and certificates of interest or participation therein, by the use of means and instruments of transportation and communication in interstate commerce and of the mails, is injurious to the capital markets, to investors, and to the general public; and it is hereby declared to be the policy of this subchapter, in accordance with which policy all the provisions of this subchapter shall be interpreted, to meet the problems and eliminate the practices, enumerated in this section, connected with such public offerings.

Sec. 303   Definitions

When used in this subchapter, unless the context otherwise requires—

(1) Any term defined in section 2 of the Securities Act of 1933 and not otherwise defined in this section shall have the meaning assigned to such term in such section 2.

(2) The terms "sale," "sell," "offer to sell," "offer for sale," and "offer" shall include

all transactions included in such terms as provided in paragraph (3) of section 2 of the Securities Act of 1933, except that an offer or sale of a certificate of interest or participation shall be deemed an offer or sale of the security or securities in which such certificate evidences an interest or participation if and only if such certificate gives the holder thereof the right to convert the same into such security or securities.

(3) The term "prospectus" shall have the meaning assigned to such term in paragraph (10) of section 2 of the Securities Act of 1933, except that in the case of securities which are not registered under the Securities Act of 1933, such term shall not include any communication (A) if it is proved that prior to or at the same time with such communication a written statement if any required by section 306 was sent or given to the persons to whom the communication was made, or (B) if such communication states from whom such statement may be obtained (if such statement is required by rules or regulations under paragraphs (1) or (2) of subsection (b) of section 306) and, in addition, does no more than identify the security, state the price thereof, state by whom orders will be executed and contain such other information as the Commission, by rules or regulations deemed necessary or appropriate in the public interest or for the protection of investors, and subject to such terms and conditions as may be prescribed therein, may permit.

(4) The term "underwriter" means any person who has purchased from an issuer with a view to, or offers or sells for an issuer in connection with, the distribution of any security, or participates or has a direct or indirect participation in any such undertaking, or participates or has a participation in the direct or indirect underwriting of any such undertaking; but such term shall not include a person whose interest is limited to a commission from an underwriter or dealer not in excess of the usual and customary distributors' or sellers' commission.

(5) The term "director" means any director of a corporation, or any individual performing similar functions with respect to any organization whether incorporated or unincorporated.

(6) The term "executive officer" means the president, every vice president, every trust officer, the cashier, the secretary, and the treasurer of a corporation, and any individual customarily performing similar functions with respect to any organization whether incorporated or unincorporated, but shall not include the chairman of the board of directors.

(7) The term "indenture" means any mortgage, deed of trust, trust or other indenture, or similar instrument or agreement (including any supplement or amendment to any of the foregoing), under which securities are outstanding or are to be issued, whether or not any property, real or personal, is, or is to be, pledged, mortgaged, assigned, or conveyed thereunder.

(8) The term "application" or "application for qualification" means the application provided for in section 305 or section 307 and includes any amendment thereto and any report, document, or memorandum accompanying such application or incorporated therein by reference.

(9) The term "indenture to be qualified" means (A) the indenture under which

there has been or is to be issued a security in respect of which a particular registration statement has been filed, or (B) the indenture in respect of which a particular application has been filed.

(10) The term "indenture trustee" means each trustee under the indenture to be qualified, and each successor trustee.

(11) The term "indenture security" means any security issued or issuable under the indenture to be qualified.

(12) The term "obligor," when used with respect to any such indenture security, means every person (including a guarantor) who is liable thereon, and, if such security is a certificate of interest or participation, such term means also every person (including a guarantor) who is liable upon the security or securities in which such certificate evidences an interest or participation; but such terms shall not include the trustee under an indenture under which certificates of interest or participation, equipment trust certificates, or like securities are outstanding.

(13) The term "paying agent," when used with respect to any such indenture security, means any person authorized by an obligor therein (A) to pay the principal of or interest on such security on behalf of such obligor, or (B) if such security is a certificate of interest or participation, equipment trust certificate, or like security, to make such payment on behalf of the trustee.

(14) The term "State" means any State of the United States.

(15) The term "Commission" means the Securities and Exchange Commission.

(16) The term "voting security" means any security presently entitling the owner or holder thereof to vote in the direction or management of the affairs of a person, or any security issued under or pursuant to any trust, agreement, or arrangement whereby a trustee or trustees or agent or agents for the owner or holder of such security are presently entitled to vote in the direction or management of the affairs of a person; and a specified percentage of the voting securities of a person means such amount of the outstanding voting securities of such person as entitles the holder or holders thereof to cast such specified percentage of the aggregate votes which the holders of all the outstanding voting securities of such person are entitled to cast in the direction or management of the affairs of such person.

(17) The terms "Securities Act of 1933," "Securities Exchange Act of 1934," and "Public Utility Holding Company Act of 1935" shall be deemed to refer, respectively, to such Acts, as amended, whether amended prior to or after August 3, 1939.

(18) The term "Bankruptcy Act" means the Bankruptcy Act or Title 11.

Sec. 304 Exempted Securities and Transactions

(a) The provisions of this subchapter shall not apply to any of the following securities:

(1) any security other than (A) a note, bond, debenture, or evidence of indebtedness, whether or not secured, or (B) a certificate of interest or participation in any

such note, bond, debenture, or evidence of indebtedness, or (C) a temporary certificate for, or guarantee of, any such note, bond, debenture, evidence of indebtedness, or certificate;

(2) any certificate of interest or participation in two or more securities having substantially different rights and privileges, or a temporary certificate for any such certificate.

(3) [left blank]

(4) (A) any security exempted from the provisions of the Securities Act of 1933, by paragraphs (2) to (8), or (11) of subsection 3(a) thereof;

(B) any security exempted from the provisions of the Securities Act of 1933, as amended, by paragraph (2) of subsection 3(a) thereof, as amended by section 401 of the Employment Security Amendments of 1970;

(5) any security issued under a mortgage indenture as to which a contract of insurance under the National Housing Act is in effect; and any such security shall be deemed to be exempt from the provisions of the Securities Act of 1933 to the same extent as though such security were specifically enumerated in section 3(a)(2) of such Act;

(6) any note, bond, debenture, or evidence of indebtedness issued or guaranteed by a foreign government or by a subdivision, department, municipality, agency, or instrumentality thereof;

(7) any guarantee of any security which is exempted by this subsection;

(8) any security which has been or is to be issued otherwise than under an indenture, but this exemption shall not be applied within a period of twelve consecutive months to an aggregate principal amount of securities of the same issuer greater than the figure stated in section 3(b) of the Securities Act of 1933 limiting exemptions thereunder, or such lesser amount as the Commission may establish by its rules and regulations;

(9) any security which has been or is to be issued under an indenture which limits the aggregate principal amount of securities at any time outstanding thereunder to $10,000,000, or such lesser amount as the Commission may establish by its rules and regulations, but this exemption shall not be applied within a period of thirty-six consecutive months to more than $10,000,000 aggregate principal amount of securities of the same issuer, or such lesser amount as the Commission may establish by its rules and regulations; or

(10) any security issued under a mortgage or trust deed indenture as to which a contract of insurance under title XI of the National Housing Act is in effect; and any such security shall be deemed to be exempt from the provisions of the Securities Act of 1933 to the same extent as though such security were specifically enumerated in section 3(a)(2), as amended, of the Securities Act of 1933.

In computing the aggregate principal amount of securities to which the exemptions provided by paragraphs (8) and (9) of this subsection may be applied, securities to which the provisions of sections 305 and 306 would not have applied, irrespective of the provisions of those paragraphs, shall be disregarded.

(b) The provisions of sections 305 and 306 shall not apply (1) to any of the transactions exempted from the provisions of section 5 of the Securities Act of 1933 by section 4 thereof or (2) to any transaction which would be so exempted but for the last sentence of paragraph (11) of section 2 of such Act.

(c) The Commission shall, on application by the issuer and after opportunity for hearing thereon, by order exempt from any one or more provisions of this subchapter any security issued or proposed to be issued under any indenture under which, at the time such application is filed, securities referred to in paragraph (3) of subsection (a) of this section are outstanding or on January 1, 1959, such securities were outstanding, if and to the extent that the Commission finds that compliance with such provision or provisions, through the execution of a supplemental indenture or otherwise—

(1) would require, by reason of the provisions of such indenture, or the provisions of any other indenture or agreement made prior to August 3, 1939, or the provisions of any applicable law, the consent of the holders of securities outstanding under any such indenture or agreement; or

(2) would impose an undue burden on this issuer, having due regard to the public interest and the interests of investors.

(d) The Commission may, by rules or regulations upon its own motion, or by order on application by an interested person, exempt conditionally or unconditionally any person, registration statement, indenture, security or transaction, or any class or classes of persons, registration statements, indentures, securities, or transactions, from any one or more of the provisions of this title, if and to the extent that such exemption is necessary or appropriate in the public interest and consistent with the protection of investors and the purposes fairly intended by this title. The Commission shall by rules and regulations determine the procedures under which an exemption under this subsection shall be granted, and may, in its sole discretion, decline to entertain any application for an order of exemption under this subsection.

(e) The Commission may from time to time by its rules and regulations, and subject to such terms and conditions as may be prescribed herein, add to the securities exempted as provided in this section any class of securities issued by a small business investment company under the Small Business Investment Act of 1958 if it finds, having regard to the purposes of that Act, that the enforcement of this subchapter with respect to such securities is not necessary in the public interest and for the protection of investors.

Sec. 305   Securities Required to Be Registered Under Securities Act

(a) Subject to the provisions of section 304, a registration statement relating to a security shall include the following information and documents, as though such inclusion were required by the provisions of section 7 of the Securities Act of 1933—

> (1) such information and documents as the Commission may by rules and regulations prescribe in order to enable the Commission to determine whether any person designated to act as trustee under the indenture under which such security has been or is to be issued is eligible to act as such under subsection (a) of section 310; and

> (2) an analysis of any provisions of such indenture with respect to (A) the definition of what shall constitute a default under such indenture, and the withholding of notice to the indenture security holders of any such default, (B) the authentication and delivery of the indenture securities and the application of the proceeds thereof, (C) the release or the release and substitution of any property subject to the lien of the indenture, (D) the satisfaction and discharge of the indenture, and (E) the evidence required to be furnished by the obligor upon the indenture securities to the trustee as to compliance with the conditions and covenants provided for in such indenture.

The information and documents required by paragraph (1) of this subsection with respect to the person designated to act as indenture trustee shall be contained in a separate part of such registration statement, which part shall be signed by such person. Such part of the registration statement shall be deemed to be a document filed pursuant to this subchapter, and the provisions of sections 11, 12, 17, and 24 of the Securities Act of 1933 shall not apply to statements therein or omissions therefrom.

(b)   (1) Except as may be permitted by paragraph (2) of this subsection, the Commission shall issue an order prior to the effective date of registration refusing to permit such a registration statement to be come effective, if it finds that—

> (A) the security to which such registration statement relates has not been or is not to be issued under an indenture; or

> (B) many person designated as trustee under such indenture is not eligible to act as such under subsection (a) of section 310;

but no such order shall be issued except after notice and opportunity for hearing within the periods and in the manner required with respect to refusal orders pursuant to section 8(b) of the Securities Act of 1933. If and when the Commission deems that the objections on which such order was based have been met, the Commission shall enter an order rescinding such refusal order, and the registration shall become effective at the time provided in section 8(a) of the Securities Act of 1933, or upon the date of such rescission, whichever shall be the later.

(2) In the case of securities registered under the Securities Act of 1933, which securities are eligible to be issued, offered, or sold on a delayed basis by or on behalf of the registrant, the Commission shall not be required to issue an order pursuant to paragraph (1) of subsection (b) of section 305 for failure to designate a trustee eligible to act under subsection (a) of section 310 if, in accordance with such rules and regulations as may be prescribed by the Commission, the issuer of such securities files an application for the purpose of determining such trustee's eligibility under subsection (a) of section 310. The Commission shall issue an order prior to the effective date of such application refusing to permit the application to become effective, if it finds that any person designated as trustee under such indenture is not eligible to act as such under subsection (a) of section 310, but no order shall be issued except after notice and opportunity for hearing within the periods and in the manner required with respect to refusal orders pursuant to section 8(b) of the Securities Act of 1933. If after notice and opportunity for hearing the Commission issues an order under this provision, the obligor shall within 5 calendar days appoint a trustee meeting the requirements of subsection (a) of section 310. No such appointment shall be effective and such refusal order shall not be rescinded by the Commission until a person eligible to act as trustee under subsection (a) of section 310 has been appointed. If no order is issued, an application filed pursuant to this paragraph shall be effective the tenth day after filing thereof or such earlier date as the Commission may determine, having due regard to the adequacy of information provided therein, the public interest, and the protection of investors.

(c) A prospectus relating to any such security shall include to the extent the Commission may prescribe by rules and regulations as necessary and appropriate in the public interest or for the protection of investors, as though such inclusion were required by section 10 of the Securities Act of 1933, a written statement containing the analysis set forth in the registration statement, of any indenture provisions with respect to the matters specified in paragraph (2) of subsection (a) of this section, together with a supplementary analysis, prepared by the Commission, of such provisions and of the effect thereof, if, in the opinion of the Commission, the inclusion of such supplementary analysis is necessary or appropriate in the public interest or for the protection of investors, and the Commission so declares by order after notice and, if demanded by the issuer, opportunity for hearing thereon. Such order shall be entered prior to the effective date of registration, except that if opportunity for hearing thereon is demanded by the issuer such order shall be entered within a reasonable time after such opportunity for hearing.

(d) The provisions of sections 11, 12, 17, and 24 of the Securities Act of 1933, and the provisions of sections 323 and 325, shall not apply to statements in or omissions from any analysis required under the provisions of this section or sections 306 or 307 of this title.

Sec. 306   Securities Not Registered Under Securities Act

(a) In the case of any security which is not registered under the Securities Act of 1933 and to which this subsection is applicable notwithstanding the provisions of section 304, unless such security has been or is to be issued under an indenture and an application for qualification is effective as to such indenture, it shall be unlawful for any person, directly or indirectly—

(1) to make use of any means or instruments of transportation or communication in interstate commerce or of the mails to sell such security through the use or medium of any prospectus or otherwise; or

(2) to carry or cause to be carried through the mails or in interstate commerce, by any means or instruments of transportation, any such security for the purpose of sale or for delivery after sale.

(b) In the case of any security which is not registered under the Securities Act of 1933, but which has been or is to be issued under an indenture as to which an application for qualification is effective, it shall be unlawful for any person, directly or indirectly—

(1) to make use of any means or instruments of transportation or communication in interstate commerce or of the mails to carry or transmit any prospectus relating to any such security, unless such prospectus, to the extent the Commission may prescribe by rules and regulations as necessary and appropriate in the public interest or for the protection of investors, includes or is accompanied by a written statement that contains the information specified in subsection (c) of section 305; or

(2) to carry or to cause to be carried through the mails or in interstate commerce

any such security for the purpose of sale or for delivery after sale, unless, to the extent the Commission may prescribe by rules and regulations as necessary or appropriate in the public interest or for the protection of investors, accompanied or preceded by a written statement that contains the information specified in subsection (c) of section 305.

(c) It shall be unlawful for any person, directly or indirectly, to make use of any means or instruments of transportation or communication in interstate commerce or of the mails to offer to sell through the use or medium of any prospectus or otherwise any security which is not registered under the Securities Act of 1933 and to which this subsection is applicable notwithstanding the provisions of section 304, unless such security has been or is to be issued under an indenture and an application for qualification has been filed as to such indenture, or while the application is the subject of a refusal order or stop order or (prior to qualification) any public proceeding or examination under section 307(c).

Sec. 307   Qualification of Indentures Covering Securities Not Required to Be Registered

(a) In the case of any security which is not required to be registered under the Securities Act of 1933 and to which subsection (a) of section 306 is applicable notwithstanding the provisions of section 304, an application for qualification of the indenture under which such security has been or is to be issued shall be filed with the Commission by the issuer of such security. Each such application shall be in such form, and shall be signed in such manner, as the Commission may by rules and regulations prescribe as necessary or appropriate in the public interest or for the protection of investors. Each such application shall include the information and documents required by subsection (a) of section 305. The information and documents required by paragraph (1) of such subsection with respect to the person designated to act as indenture trustee shall be contained in a separate part of such application, which part shall be signed by such person. Each such application shall also include such of the other information and documents which would be required to be filed in order to register such indenture security under the Securities Act of 1933 as the Commission may by rules and regulations prescribe as necessary or appropriate in the public interest or for the protection of investors. An application may be withdrawn by the applicant at any time prior to the effective date thereof. Subject to the provisions of section 321, the information and documents contained in or filed with any application shall be made available to the public under such regulations as the Commission may prescribe, and copies thereof, photostatic or otherwise, shall be furnished to every applicant therefor at such reasonable charge as the Commission may prescribe.

(b) The filing with the Commission of an application, or of an amendment to an application, shall be deemed to have taken place upon the receipt thereof by the Commission, but, in the case of an application, only if it is accompanied or preceded by payment to the Commission of a filing fee in the amount of $100, such payment to be made in cash or by United States postal money order or certified or bank check, or in such other medium of payment as the Commission may authorize by rule and regulation.

(c) The provisions of section 8 of the Securities Act of 1933 and the provisions of subsection (b) of section 305 shall apply with respect to every such application, as though such application were a registration statement filed pursuant to the provisions of the Securities Act of 1933.

Sec. 308   Integration of Procedure with Securities Act and Other Acts

(a) The Commission, by such rules and regulations or orders as it deems necessary or appropriate in the public interest or for the protection of investors, shall authorize the filing of any information or documents required to be filed with the Commission under this subchapter, or under the Securities Act of 1933, the Securities Exchange Act of 1934, or the Public Utility Holding Company Act of 1935, by incorporating by reference any information or documents on file with the Commission under this subchapter or under any such Act.

(b) The Commission, by such rules and regulations or orders as it deems necessary or appropriate in the public interest or for the protection of investors, shall provide for the consolidation of applications, reports, and proceedings under this subchapter with registration statements, applications, reports, and proceedings under the Securities Act of 1933, the Securities Exchange Act of 1934, or the Public Utility Holding Company Act of 1935.

Sec. 309   Effective Time of Qualification

(a) The indenture under which a security has been or is to be issued shall be deemed to have been qualified under this subchapter—

(1) when registration becomes effective as to such security; or

(2) when an application for the qualification of such indenture becomes effective, pursuant to section 307.

(b) After qualification has become effective as to the indenture under which a security has been or is to be issued, no stop order shall be issued pursuant to section 8(d) of the Securities Act 1933, suspending the effectiveness of the registration statement relating to such security or of the application for qualification of such indenture, except on one or more of the grounds specified in section 8 of the Securities Act of 1933, or the failure of the issuer to file an application as provided for by section 305(b)(2).

(c) The making, amendment, or rescission of a rule, regulation, or order under the provisions of this subchapter (except to the extent authorized by subsection (a) of section 314 with respect to rules and regulations prescribed pursuant to such subsection) shall not affect the qualification, form, or interpretation of any indenture as to which qualification became effective prior to the making, amendment, or rescission of such rule, regulation, or order.

(d) No trustee under an indenture which has been qualified under this subchapter shall be subject to any liability because of any failure of such indenture to comply with any of the provisions of this subchapter, or any rule, regulation, or order thereunder.

(e) Nothing in this subchapter shall be construed as empowering the Commission to conduct an investigation or other proceeding for the purpose of determining whether the provisions of an indenture which has been qualified under this subchapter are being complied with, or to enforce such provisions.

Sec. 310   Eligibility and Disqualification of Trustee

(a)   (1) There shall at all times be one or more trustees under every indenture qualified or to be qualified pursuant to this title, at least one of whom shall at all times be a corporation organized and doing business under the laws of the United States or of any State or Territory or of the District of Columbia or a corporation or other person permitted to act as trustee by the Commission (referred to in this subchapter as the institutional trustee), which (A) is authorized under such laws to exercise corporate trust powers, and (B) is subject to supervision or examination by

Federal, State, Territorial, or District of Columbia authority. The Commission may, pursuant to such rules and regulations as it may prescribe, or by order on application, permit a corporation or other person organized and doing business under the laws of a foreign government to act as sole trustee under an indenture qualified or to be qualified pursuant to this title, if such corporation or other person (i) is authorized under such laws to exercise corporate trust powers, and (ii) is subject to supervision or examination by authority of such foreign government or a political subdivision thereof substantially equivalent to supervision or examination applicable to United States institutional trustees. In prescribing such rules and regulation or making such order, the Commission shall consider whether under such laws, a United States institutional trustee is eligible to act as sole trustee under an indenture relating to securities sold within the jurisdiction of such foreign government.

(2) Such institution shall have at all times a combined capital and surplus of a specified minimum amount, which shall not be less than $150,000. If such institutional trustee publishes reports of condition at least annually, pursuant to law or to the requirements of said supervising or examining authority, the indenture may provide that, for the purposes of this paragraph, the combined capital and surplus of such trustee shall be deemed to be its combined capital and surplus as set forth in its most recent report of condition so published.

(3) If the indenture to be qualified requires or permits the appointment of one or more co-trustees in addition to such institutional trustee, the rights, powers, duties, and obligations conferred or imposed upon the trustees or any of them shall be conferred or imposed upon and exercised or performed by such institutional trustee, or such institutional trustee and such co-trustees jointly, except to the extent that under any law of any jurisdiction in which any particular act or acts are to be performed, such institutional trustee shall be incompetent or unqualified to perform such act or acts, in which event such rights, powers, duties, and obligations shall be exercised and performed by such co-trustees.

(4) In the case of certificates of interest or participation, the indenture trustee or trustees shall have the legal power to exercise all of the rights, powers, and privileges of a holder of the security or securities in which such certificates evidence an interest or participation.

(5) No obligor upon the indenture securities or person directly or indirectly controlling, controlled by, or under common control with such obligor shall serve as trustee upon such indenture securities.

(b) If any indenture trustee has or shall acquire any conflicting interest as hereinafter defined—

(i) then, within 90 days after ascertaining that it has such conflicting interest, and if the default (as defined in the next sentence) to which such conflicting interest relates has not been cured or duly waived or otherwise eliminated before the end of such 90-day period, such trustee shall either eliminate such conflicting interest or, except as otherwise provided below in this subsection,resign, and the obligor upon the indenture securities shall take prompt steps to have a successor appointed in the manner provided in the indenture;

(ii) in the event that such trustee shall fail to comply with the provisions of clause (i) of this subsection, such trustee shall, within 10 days after the expiration of such 90-day period, transmit notice of such failure to the indenture security holders in the manner and to the extent provided in subsection (c) of section 313; and

(iii) subject to the provisions of subsection (e) of section 315, unless such trustee's duty to resign is stayed as provided below in this subsection, any security holder who has been a bona fide holder of indenture securities for at least six months may, on behalf of himself and all others similarly situated, petition any court of competent jurisdiction for the removal of such trustee, and the appointment of a successor, if such trustee fails, after written request thereof by such holder to comply with the provisions of clause (i) of this subsection.

For the purposes of this subsection, an indenture trustee shall be deemed to have a conflicting interest if the indenture securities are in default (as such term is defined in such indenture, but exclusive of any period of grace or requirement of notice) and—

(1) such trustee is trustee under another indenture under which any other securities, or certificates of interest or participation in any other securities, of an obligor upon the indenture securities are outstanding or is trustee for more than one outstanding series of securities, as hereafter defined, under a single indenture of an obligor, unless—

(A) the indenture securities are collateral trust notes under which the only collateral consists of securities issued under such other indenture,

(B) such other indenture is a collateral trust indenture under which the only collateral consists of indenture securities, or

(C) such obligor has no substantial unmortgaged assets and is engaged primarily in the business of owning, or of owning and developing and/or operating, real estate, and the indenture to be qualified and such other indenture are secured by wholly separate and distinct parcels of real estate:

Provided, That the indenture to be qualified shall automatically be deemed (unless it is expressly provided therein that such provision is excluded) to contain a provision excluding from the operation of this paragraph other series under such indenture, and any other indenture or indentures under which other securities, or certificates of interest or participation in other securities, of such an obligor are outstanding, if—

(i) the indenture to be qualified and any such other indenture or indentures (and all series of securities issuable thereunder) are wholly unsecured and rank equally, and such other indenture or indentures (and such series) are specifically described in the indenture to be qualified or are thereafter qualified under this title, unless the Commission shall have found and declared by order pursuant to subsection (b) of section 305 or subsection (c) of section 307 that differences exist between the provisions of the indenture (or such series) to be qualified and the provisions of such other indenture or indentures (or such series) which are so likely to involve a material conflict of interest as to make it necessary in the public interest or for the protection of investors to disqualify such trustee from acting as such under one of such indentures, or

(ii) the issuer shall have sustained the burden of proving, on application to the Commission and after opportunity for hearing thereon, that trusteeship under the indenture to be qualified and such other indenture or under more than one outstanding series under a single indenture is not so likely to involve a material conflict of interest as to make it necessary in the public interest or for the protection of investors to disqualify such trustee from acting as such under one of such indentures or with respect to such series;

(2) such trustee or any of its directors or executive officers is an underwriter for an obligor upon the indenture securities;

(3) such trustee directly or indirectly controls or is directly or indirectly controlled by or is under direct or indirect common control with an underwriter for an obligor upon the indenture securities;

(4) such trustee or any of its directors or executive officers is a director, officer, partner, employee, appointee, or representative of an obligor upon the indenture securities, or of an underwriter (other than the trustee itself) for such an obligor who is currently engaged in the business of underwriting, except that—

(A) one individual may be a director and/or an executive officer of the trustee and a director and/or an executive officer of such obligor, but may not be at the same time an executive officer of both the trustee and of such obligor,

(B) if and so long as the number of directors of the trustee in office is more than nine, one additional individual may be a director and/or an executive officer of the trustee and a director of such obligor, and

(C) such trustee may be designated by any such obligor or by any underwriter for any such obligor, to act in the capacity of transfer agent, registrar, custodian, paying agent, fiscal agent, escrow agent, or depositary, or in any other similar capacity, or, subject to the provisions of paragraph (1) of this subsection, to act as trustee, whether under an indenture or otherwise;

(5) 10 per centum or more of the voting securities of such trustee is beneficially owned either by an obligor upon the indenture securities or by any director, partner or executive officer thereof, or 20 per centum or more of such voting securities is beneficially owned, collectively by any two or more of such persons; or 10 per centum or more of the voting securities of such trustee is beneficially owned either by an underwriter for any such obligor or by any director, partner, or executive officer thereof, or is beneficially owned, collectively, by any two or more such persons;

(6) such trustee is the beneficial owner of, or holds as collateral security for an obligation which is in default as hereinafter defined—

(A) 5 per centum or more of the voting securities, or 10 per centum or more of any other class of security, of an obligor upon the indenture securities, not including indenture securities and securities issued under any other indenture under which such trustee is also trustee, or

(B) 10 per centum or more of any class of security of an underwriter for any such obligor;

(7) such trustee is the beneficial owner of, or holds as collateral security for an obligation which is in default as hereinafter defined, 5 per centum or more of the voting securities of any person who, to the knowledge of the trustee, owns 10 per centum or more of the voting securities of, or controls directly or indirectly or is under direct or indirect common control with, an obligor upon the indenture securities;

(8) such trustee is the beneficial owner of, or holds as collateral security for an obligation which is in default as hereinafter defined, 10 per centum or more of any class of security of any person who, to the knowledge of the trustee, owns 50 per centum or more of the voting securities of an obligor upon the indenture securities;

(9) such trustee owns, on the date of default upon the indenture securities (as such term is defined in such indenture by exclusive of any period of grace or requirement of notice) or any anniversary of such default while such default upon the indenture securities remains outstanding, in the capacity of executor, administrator, testamentary or inter vivos trustee, guardian, committee or conservator, or in any other similar capacity, an aggregate of 25 per centum or more of the voting securities, or of any class of security, of any person, the beneficial ownership of a specified percentage of which would have constituted a conflicting interest under paragraph (6), (7), or (8) of this subsection. As to any such securities of which the indenture trustee acquired ownership through becoming executor, administrator or testamentary trustee of an estate which include them, the provisions of

the preceding sentence shall not apply for a period of not more than 2 years from the date of such acquisition, to the extent that such securities included in such estate do not exceed 25 per centum of such voting securities or 25 per centum of any such class of security. Promptly after the dates of any such default upon the indenture securities and annually in each succeeding year that the indenture securities remain in default the trustee shall make a check of its holding of such securities in any of the above-mentioned capacities as of such dates. If the obligor upon the indenture securities fails to make payment in full of principal or interest under such indenture when and as the same becomes due and payable, and such failure continues for 30 days thereafter, the trustee shall make a prompt check of its holdings of such securities in any of the above-mentioned capacities as of the date of the expiration of such 30-day period, and after such date, notwithstanding the foregoing provisions of this paragraph, all such securities so held by the trustee, with sole or joint control over such securities vested in it, shall be considered as though beneficially owned by such trustee, for the purposes of paragraphs (6), (7), and (8) of this subsection; or

(10) except under the circumstances described in paragraphs (1), (3), (4), (5) or (6) of section 311(b) of this title, the trustee shall be or shall become a creditor of the obligor.

For purposes of paragraph (1) of this subsection, and of section 316(a) of this title, the term "series of securities" or "series" means a series, class or group of securities issuable under an indenture pursuant to whose terms holders of one such series may vote to direct the indenture trustee, or otherwise take action pursuant to a vote of such holders, separately from holders of another such series: Provided, That "series of securities" or "series" shall not include any series of securities issuable under an indenture if all such series rank equally and are wholly unsecured.

The specification of percentages in paragraphs (5) to (9), inclusive, of this subsection shall not be construed as indicating that the ownership of such percentages of the securities of a person is or is not necessary or sufficient to constitute direct or indirect control for the purposes of paragraph (3) or (7) of this subsection.

For purposes of paragraphs (6), (7), (8), and (9) of this subsection—

(A) the terms "security" and "securities" shall include only such securities as are generally known as corporate securities, but shall not include any note or other evidence of indebtedness issued to evidence an obligation to repay moneys lent to a person by one or more banks, trust companies, or banking firms, or any certificate of interest or participation in any such note or evidence of indebtedness;

(B) an obligation shall be deemed to be in default when a default in payment of principal shall have continued for thirty days or more, and shall not have been cured; and

(C) the indenture trustee shall not be deemed the owner or holder of (i) any security which it holds as collateral security (as trustee or otherwise) for any obligation which is not in default as above defined, or (ii) any security which it holds as collateral security under the indenture to be qualified, irrespective of any default thereunder, or (iii) any security which it holds as agent for collection, or as custodian, escrow agent or depositary, or in any similar representative capacity.

For the purposes of this subsection, the term "underwriter" when used with reference to an obligor upon the indenture securities means every person who, within one year prior to the time as of which the determination is made, was an underwriter of any security of such obligor outstanding at the time of the determination.

Except is the case of a default in the payment of the principal of or interest on any indenture security, or in the payment of any sinking or purchase fund installment, the indenture trustee shall not be required to resign as provided by this subsection if such trustee shall have sustained the burden of proving, on application to the Commission and after opportunity for hearing thereon, that—

(i) the default under the indenture may be cured or waived during a reasonable period and under the procedures described in such application, and

(ii) a stay of the trustee's duty to resign will not be inconsistent with the interests of holders of the indenture securities. The filing of such an application shall automatically stay the performance of the duty to resign until the Commission orders otherwise.

Any resignation of an indenture trustee shall become effective only upon the appointment of a successor trustee and such successor's acceptance of such an appointment.

(c) The Public Utility Holding Company Act of 1935 shall not be held to establish or authorize the establishment of any standards regarding the eligibility and qualifications of any trustee or prospective trustee under an indenture to be qualified under this subchapter, or regarding the provisions to be included in any such indenture with respect to the eligibility and qualifications of the trustee thereunder, other than those established by the provisions of this section.

Sec. 311   Preferential Collection of Claims Against Obligor

(a) Subject to the provisions of subsection (b) of this section, if the indenture trustee shall be, or shall become, a creditor, directly or indirectly, secured or unsecured, of an obligor upon the indenture securities, within three months prior to a default as defined in the last paragraph of this subsection, or subsequent to such a default, then, unless and until such default shall be cured, such trustee shall set apart and hold in a special account for the benefit of the trustee individually and the indenture security holders—

(1) an amount equal to any and all reductions in the amount due and owing upon any claim as such creditor in respect of principal or interest, effected after the beginning of such three months' period and valid as against such obligor and its other creditors, except any such reduction resulting from the receipt or disposition of any property described in paragraph (2) of this subsection, or from the exercise of any right of setoff which the trustee could have exercised if a petition in bankruptcy had been filed by or against such obligor upon the date of such default; and

(2) all property received in respect of any claims such creditor, either as security therefor, or in satisfaction or composition thereof, or otherwise, after the beginning of such three months' period, or an amount equal to the proceeds of any such property, if disposed of, subject, however, to the rights, if any, of such obligor and its other creditors in such property or such proceeds.

Nothing herein contained shall affect the right of the indenture trustee—

(A) to retain for its own account (i) payments made on account of any such claim by any person (other than such obligor) who is liable thereon, and (ii) the proceeds of the bona fide sale of any such claim by the trustee to a third person, and (iii) distributions made in cash, securities, or other property in respect of claims filed against such obligor in bankruptcy or receivership or in proceedings for reorganization pursuant to the Bankruptcy Act or applicable State law;

(B) to realize, for its own account, upon any property held by it as security for any such claim, if such property was so held prior to the beginning of such three months' period;

(C) to realize, for its own account, but only to the extent of the claim hereinafter mentioned, upon any property held by it as security for any such claim, if such claim was created after the beginning of such three months' period and such property was received as security therefor simultaneously with the creation thereof, and if the trustee shall sustain the burden of proving that at the time such property was so received the trustee had no reasonable cause to believe that a default as defined in the last paragraph of this subsection would occur within three months; or

(D) to receive payment on any claim referred to in paragraph (B) or (C) of this subsection, against the release of any property held as security for such claim as provided in said paragraph (B) or (C), as the case may be, to the extent of the fair value of such property.

For the purposes of paragraphs (B), (C), and (D) of this subsection, property substituted after the beginning of such three months' period for property held as security at the time of such substitution shall, to the extent of the fair value of the property released, have the same status as the property released, and, to the extent that any claim referred to in any of such paragraphs is created in renewal of or in substitution for or for the purpose of repaying or refunding any preexisting claim of the indenture trustee as such creditor, such claim shall have the same status as such preexisting claim.

If the trustee shall be required to account, the funds and property held in such special account and the proceeds thereof shall be apportioned between the trustee and the indenture security holders in such manner that the trustee and the indenture security holders realize, as a result of payments from such special account and payments of dividends on claims filed against such obligor in bankruptcy or receivership or in proceedings for reorganization pursuant to the Bankruptcy Act or applicable State law, the same percentage of their respective claims, figured before crediting to the claim of the trustee anything on account of the receipt by it from such obligor of the funds and property in such special account and before crediting to the respective claims of the trustee and the indenture security holders dividends on claims filed against such obligor in bankruptcy or receivership or in proceedings for reorganization pursuant to the Bankruptcy Act or applicable State law, but after crediting thereon receipts on account of the indebtedness represented by their respective claims from all sources other than from such dividends and from the funds and property so held in such special account. As used in this paragraph, with respect to any claim, the term "dividends" shall include any distribution with respect to such claim, in bankruptcy or receivership or in proceedings for reorganization pursuant to the Bankruptcy Act or applicable State law, whether such distribution is made in cash, securities, or other property, but shall not include any such distribution with respect to the secured portion, if any, of such claim. The court in which such bankruptcy, receivership, or proceedings for reorganization is pending shall have jurisdiction (i) to apportion between the indenture trustee and the indenture security holders, in accordance with the provisions of this paragraph, the funds and property held in such special account and the proceeds thereof, or (ii) in lieu of such apportionment, in whole or in part, to give to the provisions of this paragraph due consideration in determining the fairness of the distributions to be made to the indenture trustee and the indenture security holders with respect to their respective claims, in which event it shall not be necessary to liquidate or to appraise the value of any securities or other property held in such special account or as security for any such claim, or to make a specific allocation of such distributions as between the secured and unsecured portions of such claims, or otherwise to apply the provisions of this paragraph as a mathematical formula.

Any indenture trustee who has resigned or been removed after the beginning of such three months' period shall be subject to the provisions of this subsection as though such resignation or removal had not occurred. Any indenture trustee who has resigned or been removed prior the beginning of such three months' period shall be subject to the provisions of this subsection if and only if the following conditions exist—

(i) the receipt of property or reduction of claim which would have given rise to the obligation to account, if such indenture trustee had continued as trustee, occurred after the beginning of such three months' period; and

(ii) such receipt of property or reduction of claim occurred within three months after such resignation or removal.

As used in this subsection, the term "default" means any failure to make payment in full of principal or interest, when and as the same becomes due and payable, under any indenture which has been qualified under this subchapter, and under which the indenture trustee is trustee and the person of whom the indenture trustee is directly or indirectly a creditor is an obligor; and the term "indenture security holder" means all holders of securities outstanding under any such indenture under which any such default exists.

In any case commenced under the Bankruptcy Act of July 1, 1898, or any amendment thereto enacted prior to November 6, 1978, all references to periods of three months shall be deemed to be references to periods of four months.

(b) The indenture to be qualified shall automatically be deemed (unless it is expressly provided therein that any such provision is excluded) to contain provisions excluding from the operation of subsection (a) of this section a creditor relationship arising from—

(1) the ownership or acquisition of securities issued under any indenture, or any security or securities having a maturity of one year or more at the time of acquisition by the indenture trustee;

(2) advances authorized by a receivership or bankruptcy court of competent jurisdiction, or by the indenture, for the purpose of preserving the property subject to the lien of the indenture or of discharging tax liens or other prior liens or encumbrances on the trust estate, if notice of such advance and of the circumstances surrounding the making thereof is given to the indenture security holders, at the time and in the manner provided in the indenture;

(3) disbursements made in the ordinary course of business in the capacity of trustee under an indenture, transfer agent, registrar, custodian, paying agent, fiscal agent or depositary, or other similar capacity;

(4) an indebtedness created as a result of services rendered or premises rented; or an indebtedness created as a result of goods or securities sold in a cash transaction as defined in the indenture;

(5) the ownership of stock or of other securities of a corporation organized under the provisions of section 25(a) of the Federal Reserve Act, as amended, which is directly or indirectly a creditor of an obligor upon the indenture securities; or

(6) the acquisition, ownership, acceptance, or negotiation of any drafts, bills of exchange, acceptances, or obligations which fall within the classification of self-liquidating paper as defined in the indenture.

(c) In the exercise by the Commission of any jurisdiction under the Public Utility Holding Company Act of 1935 regarding the issue or sale, by any registered holding company or a subsidiary company thereof, of any security of such issuer or seller or of any other company to a person which is trustee under an indenture or indentures of such issuer or seller or other company, or of a subsidiary or associate company or affiliate of such issuer or seller or other company (whether or not such indenture or indentures are qualified or to be qualified under this subchapter), the fact that such trustee will thereby become a creditor, directly or indirectly, of any of the foregoing shall not constitute a ground for the Commission taking adverse action with respect to any application or declaration, or limiting the scope of any rule or regulation which would otherwise permit such transaction to take effect; but in any case in which such trustee is trustee under an indenture of the company of which it will thereby become a creditor, or of any subsidiary company thereof, this subsection shall not prevent the Commission from requiring (if such requirement would be authorized under the provisions of the Public Utility Holding Company Act of 1935) that such trustee, as such, shall effectively and irrevocably agree in writing, for the benefit of the holders from time to time of the securities from time to time outstanding under such indenture, to be bound by the provisions of this section, subsection (c) of section 315, and, in case of default (as such term is defined in such indenture), subsection (d) of section 315, as fully as though such provisions were included in such indenture. For the purposes of this subsection the terms "registered holding company," "subsidiary company," "associate company," and "affiliate" shall have the respective meanings assigned to such terms in section 2(a) of the Public Utility Holding Company Act of 1935.

Sec. 312   Bondholders' Lists

(a) Each obligor upon the indenture securities shall furnish or cause to be furnished to the institutional trustee thereunder at stated intervals of not more than six months, and at such other times as such trustee may request in writing, all information in the possession or control of such obligor, or of any of its paying agents, as to the names and addresses of the indenture security holders, and requiring such trustee to preserve, in as current a form as is reasonably practicable, all such information so furnished to it or received by it in the capacity of paying agent.

(b) Within five business days after the receipt by the institutional trustee of a written application by any three or more indenture security holders stating that the applicants desire to communicate with other indenture security holders with respect to their rights under such indenture or under the indenture securities, and accompanied by a copy of the form of proxy or other communication which such applicants propose to transmit, and by reasonable proof that each such applicant has owned an indenture security for a period of at least six months preceding the date of such application, such institutional trustee shall, at its election, either—

(1) afford to such applicants access to all information so furnished to or received by such trustee; or

(2) inform such applicants as to the approximate number of indenture security holders according to the most recent information so furnished to or received by such trustee, and as to the approximate cost of mailing to such indenture security holders the form of proxy or other communication, if any, specified in such application.

If such trustee shall elect not to afford to such applicants access to such information, such trustee shall, upon the written request of such applicants, mail to all such indenture security holders copies of the form of proxy or other communication which is specified in such request, with reasonable promptness after a tender to such trustee of the material to be mailed and of payment, or provision for the payment, of the reasonable expenses of such mailing, unless within five days after such tender, such trustee shall mail to such applicants, and file with the Commission together with a copy of the material to be mailed, a written statement to the effect that, in the opinion of such trustee, such mailing would be contrary to the best interests of the indenture security holders or would be in violation of applicable law. Such written statement shall specify the basis of such opinion. After opportunity for hearing upon the objections specified in the written statement so filed, the Commission may, and if demanded by such trustee or by such applicants shall, enter an order either sustaining one or more of such objections or refusing to sustain any of them. If the Commission shall enter an order refusing to sustain any of such objections, or if, after the entry of an order sustaining one or more of such objections, the Commission shall find, after notice and opportunity for hearing, that all objections so sustained have been met, and shall enter an order so declaring, such trustee shall mail copies of such material to all such indenture security holders with reasonable promptness after the entry of such order and the renewal of such tender.

(c) The disclosure of any such information as to the names and addresses of the indenture security holders in accordance with the provisions of this section, regardless of the source from which such information was derived, shall not be deemed to be a violation of any existing law, or of any law hereafter enacted which does not specifically refer to this section, nor shall such trustee be held accountable by reason of mailing any material pursuant to a request made under subsection (b) of this section.

Sec. 313   Reports by Indenture Trustee

(a) The indenture trustee shall transmit to the indenture security holders as hereinafter provided, at stated intervals of not more than 12 months, a brief report with respect to any of the following events which may have occurred within the previous 12 months (but if no such event has occurred within such period no report need be transmitted):

(1) any change to its eligibility and its qualifications under section 310;

(2) the creation of or any material change to a relationship specified in paragraph (1) through (10) of section 310(b);

(3) the character and amount of any advances made by it, as indenture trustee, which remain unpaid on the date of such report, and for the reimbursement of which it claims or may claim a lien or charge, prior to that of the indenture securities, on the trust estate or on property or funds held or collected by it as such trustee, if such advances so remaining unpaid aggregate more than one-half of 1 per centum of the principal amount of the indenture securities outstanding on such date;

*(4) any change to the amount, interest rate, and maturity date of all other indebtedness owing to it in its individual capacity, on the date of such report, by the obligor upon the indenture securities, with a brief description of any property held as collateral security therefor, except an indebtedness based upon a creditor relationship arising in any manner described in paragraphs (2), (3), (4), or (6) of subsection (b) of section 311;

* See Footnote 4, Chapter 13, *supra.*

(5) any change to the property and funds physically in its possession as indenture trustee on the date of such report;

(6) any release, or release and substitution, of property subject to the lien of the indenture (and the consideration therefor, if any) which it has not previously reported;

(7) any additional issue of indenture securities which it has not previously reported; and

(8) any action taken by it in the performance of its duties under the indenture which it has not previously reported and which in its opinion materially affects the indenture securities or the trust estate, except action in respect of a default, notice of which has been or is to be withheld by it in accordance with an indenture provision authorized by subsection (b) of section 315.

(b) The indenture trustee shall transmit to the indenture security holders as hereinafter provided, within the times hereinafter specified, a brief report with respect to—

(1) the release, or release and substitution, of property subject to the lien of the indenture (and the consideration therefor, if any) unless the fair value of such property, as set forth in the certificate or opinion required by paragraph (1) of subsection (d) of section 314, is less than 10 per centum of the principal amount of indenture securities outstanding at the time of such release, or such release and substitution, such report to be so transmitted within 90 days after such time; and

(2) the character and amount of any advances made by it as such since the date of the last report transmitted pursuant to the provisions of subsection (a) of this section (or if no such report has yet been so transmitted, since the date of execution of the indenture), for the reimbursement of which it claims or may claim a lien or charge, prior to that of the indenture securities, on the trust estate or on property or funds held or collected by it as such trustee, and which it has not previously reported pursuant to this paragraph, if such advances remaining unpaid at any time aggregate more than 10 per centum of the principal amount of indenture securities outstanding at such time, such report to be so transmitted within 90 days after such time.

(c) Reports pursuant to this section shall be transmitted by mail—

(1) to all registered holders of indenture securities, as the names and addresses of such holders appear upon the registration books of the obligor upon the indenture securities;

 (2) to such holders of indenture securities as have, within the two years preceding such transmission, filed their names and addresses with the indenture trustee for that purpose; and

(3) except in the case of reports pursuant to subsection (b) of this section, to all holders of indenture securities whose names and addresses have been furnished to or received by the indenture trustee pursuant to section 312.

(d) A copy of each such report shall, at the time of such transmission to indenture security holders, be filed with each stock exchange upon which the indenture securities are listed, and also with the Commission.

Sec. 314   Reports by Obligor; Evidence of Compliance with Indenture Provisions

(a) Each person who, as set forth in the registration statement or application, is or is to be an obligor upon the indenture securities covered thereby shall—

(1) file with the indenture trustee copies of the annual reports and of the information, documents, and other reports (or copies of such portions of any of the foregoing as the Commission may by rules and regulations prescribe) which such obligor is required to file with the Commission pursuant to section 13 or 15(d) of the Securities Exchange Act of 1934; or, if the obligor is not required to file information, documents, or reports pursuant to either of such sections, then to file with the indenture trustee and the Commission, in accordance with rules and regulations prescribed by the Commission, such of the supplementary and periodic information, documents, and reports which may be required pursuant to section 13 of the Securities Exchange Act of 1934, in respect of a security listed and registered on a national securities exchange as may be prescribed in such rules and regulations;

(2) file with the indenture trustee and the Commission, in accordance with rules and regulations prescribed by the Commission, such additional information, documents, and reports with respect to compliance by such obligor with the conditions and covenants provided for in the indenture, as may be required by such rules and regulations, including, in the case of annual reports, if required by such rules and regulations, certificates of opinions of independent public accountants, conforming to the requirements of subsection (e) of this section, as to compliance with conditions or covenants, compliance with which is subject to verification by accountants, but no such certificate or opinion shall be required as to any matter specified in clauses (A), (B), or (C) of paragraph (3) of subsection (c) of this section;

(3) transmit to the holders of the indenture securities upon which such person is an obligor, in the manner and to the extent provided in subsection (c) of section 313, such summaries of any information, documents, and reports required to be filed by such obligor pursuant to the provisions of paragraph (1) or (2) of this subsection as may be required by rules and regulations prescribed by the Commission; and

(4) furnish to the indenture trustee, not less often than annually, a brief certificate from the principal executive officer, principal financial officer or principal accounting officer as to his or her knowledge of such obligor's compliance with all conditions and covenants under the indenture. For purposes of this paragraph, such compliance shall be determined without regard to any period of grace or requirement of notice provided under the indenture.

The rules and regulations prescribed under this subsection shall be such as are necessary or appropriate in the public interest or for the protection of investors, having due regard to the types of indentures, and the nature of the business of the class of obligors affected thereby, and the amount of indenture securities outstanding under such indentures, and, in the case of any such rules and regulations prescribed after the indentures to which they apply have been qualified under this subchapter, the additional expense, if any, of complying with such rules and regulations. Such rules and regulations may be prescribed either before or after qualification becomes effective as to any such indenture.

(b) If the indenture to be qualified is or is to be secured by the mortgage or pledge of property, the obligor upon the indenture securities shall furnish to the indenture trustee—

(1) promptly after the execution and delivery of the indenture, an opinion of counsel (who may be of counsel for such obligor) either stating that in the opinion of such counsel the indenture has been properly recorded and filed so as to make effective the lien intended to be created thereby, and reciting the details of such action, or stating that in the opinion of such counsel no such action is necessary to make such lien effective; and

(2) at least annually after the execution and delivery of the indenture, an opinion of counsel (who may be of counsel for such obligor) either stating that in the opinion of such counsel such action has been taken with respect to the recording, filing, re-recording, and refiling of the indenture as is necessary to maintain the lien of such indenture, and reciting the details of such action, or stating that in the opinion of such counsel no such action is necessary to maintain such lien.

(c) The obligor upon the indenture securities shall furnish to the indenture trustee evidence of compliance with the conditions precedent, if any, provided for in the indenture (including any covenants compliance with which constitutes a condition precedent) which relate to the authentication and delivery of the indenture securities, to the release or the release and substitution of property subject to the lien of the indenture, to the satisfaction and discharge of the indenture, or to any other action to be taken by the indenture trustee at the request or upon the application of such obligor. Such evidence shall consist of the following:

(1) certificates or opinions made by officers of such obligor who are specified in the indenture, stating that such conditions precedent have been complied with;

(2) an opinion of counsel (who may be of counsel for such obligor) stating that in his opinion such conditions precedent have been complied with; and

(3) in the case of conditions precedent compliance with which is subject to verification by accountants (such as conditions with respect to the preservation of specified ratios, the amount of net quick assets, negative-pledge clauses, and other

similar specific conditions), a certificate or opinion of an accountant, who, in the case of any such conditions precedent to the authentication and delivery of indenture securities, and not otherwise, shall be an independent public accountant selected or approved by the indenture trustee in the exercise of reasonable care, if the aggregate principal amount of such indenture securities and of other indenture securities authenticated and delivered since the commencement of the then current calendar year (other than those with respect to which a certificate or opinion of an accountant is not required, or with respect to which a certificate or opinion of an independent public accountant has previously been furnished) is 10 per centum or more of the aggregate amount of the indenture securities at the time outstanding; but no certificate or opinion need be made by any person other than an officer or employee of such obligor who is specified in the indenture, as to (A) dates or periods not covered by annual reports required to be filed by the obligor, in the case of conditions precedent which depend upon a state of facts as of a date or dates or for a period or periods different from that required to be covered by such annual reports, or (B) the amount and value of property additions, except as provided in paragraph (3) of subsection (d) of this section, or (C) the adequacy of depreciation, maintenance, or repairs.

(d) If the indenture to be qualified is or is to be secured by the mortgage or pledge of property or securities, the obligor upon the indenture securities shall furnish to the indenture trustee a certificate or opinion of an engineer, appraiser, or other expert as to the fair value—

(1) of any property or securities to be released from the lien of the indenture, which certificate or opinion shall state that in the opinion of the person making the same the proposed release will not impair the security under such indenture in contravention of the provisions thereof, and requiring further that such certificate or opinion shall be made by an independent engineer, appraiser, or other expert, if the fair value of such property or securities and of all other property or securities released since the commencement of the then current calendar year, as set forth in the certificates or opinions required by this paragraph, is 10 per centum or more of the aggregate principal amount of the indenture securities at the time outstanding; but such a certificate or opinion of an independent engineer, appraiser, or other expert shall not be required in the case of any release of property or securities, if the fair value thereof as set forth in the certificate or opinion required by this paragraph is less than $25,000 or less than 1 per centum of the aggregate principal amount of the indenture securities at the time outstanding;

(2) to such obligor of any securities (other than indenture securities and securities secured by a lien prior to the lien of the indenture upon property subject to the lien of the indenture), the deposit of which with the trustee is to be made the basis for the authentication and delivery of indenture securities, the withdrawal of cash constituting a part of the trust estate or the release of property or securities subject to the lien of the indenture, and requiring further that if the fair value to such obligor of such securities and of all other such securities made the basis of any such authentication and delivery, withdrawal, or release since the commencement of the then current calendar year, as set forth in the certificates or opinions required by

this paragraph, is 10 per centum or more of the aggregate principal amount of the indenture securities at the time outstanding, such certificate or opinion shall be made by an independent engineer, appraiser, or other expert and, in the case of the authentication and delivery of indenture securities, shall cover the fair value to such obligor of all other such securities so deposited since the commencement of the current calendar year as to which a certificate or opinion of an independent engineer, appraiser, or other expert has not previously been furnished; but such a certificate of an independent engineer, appraiser, or other expert shall not be required with respect to any securities so deposited, if the fair value thereof to such obligor as set forth in the certificate or opinion required by this paragraph is less than $25,000 or less than 1 per centum of the aggregate principal amount of the indenture securities at the time outstanding; and

(3) to such obligor of any property the subjection of which to the lien of the indenture is to be made the basis for the authentication and delivery of indenture securities, the withdrawal of cash constituting a part of the trust estate, or the release of property or securities subject to the lien of the indenture, and requiring further that if

(A) within six months prior to the date of acquisition thereof by such obligor, such property has been used or operated, by a person or persons other than such obligor, in a business similar to that in which it has been or is to be used or operate by such obligor, and

(B) the fair value to such obligor of such property as set forth in such certificate or opinion is not less than $25,000 and not less than 1 per centum of the aggregate principal amount of the indenture securities at the time outstanding,

such certificate or opinion shall be made by an independent engineer, appraiser, or other expert and, in the case of the authentication and delivery of indenture securities, shall cover the fair value to the obligor of any property so used or operated which has been so subjected to the lien of the indenture since the commencement of the then current calendar year, and as to which a certificate or opinion of an independent engineer, appraiser, or other expert has not previously been furnished.

The indenture to be qualified shall automatically be deemed (unless it is expressly provided therein that any such provision is excluded) to provide that any such certificate or opinion may be made by an officer or employee of the obligor upon the indenture securities who is duly authorized to make such certificate or opinion by the obligor from time to time, except in cases in which this subsection requires that such certificate or opinion be made by an independent person. In such cases, such certificate or opinion shall be made by an independent engineer, appraiser, or other expert selected or approved by the indenture trustee in the exercise of reasonable care.

(e) Each certificate or opinion with respect to compliance with a condition or covenant provided for in the indenture (other than certificates provided pursuant to subsection (a)(4) of this section) shall include (1) a statement that the person making such certificate or opinion has read such covenant or condition; (2) a brief statement as to the nature and scope of the examination or investigation upon which the statements or opinions contained in such certificate or opinion are based; (3) a statement that, in the opinion of such person, he has made such examination or investigation as is necessary to enable him to express an informed opinion as to whether or not such covenant or condition has been complied with; and (4) a statement as to whether or not, in the opinion of such person, such condition or covenant has been complied with.

(f) Nothing in this section shall be construed either as requiring the inclusion in the indenture to be qualified of provisions that the obligor upon the indenture securities shall furnish to the indenture trustee any other evidence of compliance with the conditions and covenants provided for in the indenture than the evidence specified in this section, or as preventing the inclusion of such provision in such indenture, if the parties so agree.

Sec. 315   Duties and Responsibility of Trustee

(a) The indenture to be qualified shall automatically be deemed (unless it is expressly provided therein that any such provision is excluded) to provide that, prior to default (as such term is defined in such indenture)—

(1) the indenture trustee shall not be liable except for the performance of such duties as are specifically set out in such indenture; and

(2) the indenture trustee may conclusively rely, as to the truth of the statements and the correctness of the opinions expressed therein, in the absence of bad faith on the part of such trustee, upon certificates or opinions conforming to the requirements of the indenture;

but the indenture trustee shall examine the evidence furnished to it pursuant to section 314 to determine whether or not such evidence conforms to the requirements of the indenture.

(b) The indenture trustee shall give to the indenture security holders, in the manner and to the extent provided in subsection (c) of section 313, notice of all defaults known to the trustee, within ninety days after the occurrence thereof: *Provided*, That such indenture shall automatically be deemed (unless it is expressly provided therein that any such provision is excluded) to provide that, except in the case of default in the payment of the principal of or interest on any indenture security, or in the payment of any sinking or purchase fund installment, the trustee shall be protected in withholding such notice if and so long as the board of directors, the executive committee, or a trust committee of directors and/or responsible officers, of the trustee in good faith determine that the withholding of such notice is in the interests of the indenture security holders.

(c) The indenture trustee shall exercise in case of default (as such term is defined in such indenture) such of the rights and powers vested in it by such indenture, and to use the same degree of care and skill in their exercise, as a prudent man would exercise or use under the circumstances in the conduct of his own affairs.

(d) The indenture to be qualified shall not contain any provisions relieving the indenture trustee from liability for its own negligent action, its own negligent failure to act, or its own willful misconduct, except that—

(1) such indenture shall automatically be deemed (unless it is expressly provided therein that any such provision is excluded) to contain the provisions authorized by paragraphs (1) and (2) of subsection (a) of this section;

(2) such indenture shall automatically be deemed (unless it is expressly provided therein that any such provision is excluded) to contain provisions protecting the indenture trustee from liability for any error of judgment made in good faith by a responsible officer or officers of such trustee, unless it shall be proved that such trustee was negligent in ascertaining the pertinent facts; and

(3) such indenture shall automatically be deemed (unless it is expressly provided therein that any such provision is excluded) to contain provisions protecting the indenture trustee with respect to any action taken or omitted to be taken by it in good faith in accordance with the direction of the holders of not less than a majority in principal amount of the indenture securities at the time outstanding (determined as provided in subsection (a) of section 316) relating to the time, method, and place of conducting any proceeding for any remedy available to such trustee, or exercising any trust or power conferred upon such trustee, under such indenture.

(e) The indenture to be qualified shall automatically be deemed (unless it is expressly provided therein that any such provision is excluded) to contain provisions to the effect that all parties thereto, including the indenture security holders, agree that the court may in its discretion require, in any suit for the enforcement of any right or remedy under such indenture, or in any suit against the trustee for any action taken or omitted by it as trustee, the filing by any party litigant in such suit of an undertaking to pay the costs of such suit, and that such court may in its discretion assess reasonable costs, including reasonable attorney's fees, against any party litigant in such suit, having due regard to the merits and good faith of the claims or defenses made by such party litigant: *Provided*, That the provisions of this subsection shall not apply to any suit instituted by such trustee, to any suit instituted by any indenture security holder, or group of indenture security holders, holding in the aggregate more than 10 per centum in principal amount of the indenture securities outstanding, or to any suit instituted by any indenture security holder for the enforcement of the payment of the principal of or interest on any indenture security, on or after the respective due dates expressed in such indenture security.

Sec. 316   Directions and Waivers by Bondholders; Prohibition of Impairment of Holder's Right to Payment

(a) The indenture to be qualified—

(1) shall automatically be deemed (unless it is expressly provided therein that any such provision is excluded) to contain provisions authorizing the holders of not less than a majority in principal amount of the indenture securities or if expressly specified in such indenture, of any series of securities at the time outstanding (A) to direct the time, method, and place of conducting any proceedings for any remedy available to such trustee, or exercising any trust or power conferred upon such trustee, under such indenture, or (B) on behalf of the holders of all such indenture securities, to consent to the waiver of any past default and its consequences; or

(2) may contain provisions authorizing the holders of not less than 75 per centum in principal amount of the indenture securities or if expressly specified in such indenture, of any series of securities at the time outstanding to consent on behalf of the holders of all such indenture securities to the postponement of any interest payment for a period not exceeding three years from its due date.

For the purposes of this subsection and paragraph (3) of subsection (d) of section 315, in determining whether the holders of the required principal amount of indenture securities have concurred in any such direction or consent, indenture securities owned by any obligor upon the indenture securities, or by any person directly or indirectly controlling or controlled by or under direct or indirect common control with any such obligor, shall be disregarded, except that for the purposes of determining whether the indenture trustee shall be protected in relying on any such direction or consent, only indenture securities which such trustee knows are so owned shall be so disregarded.

(b) Notwithstanding any other provision of the indenture to be qualified, the right of any holder of any indenture security to receive payment of the principal of and interest on such indenture security, on or after the respective due dates expressed in such indenture security, or to institute suit for the enforcement of any such payment on or after such respective dates, shall not be impaired or affected without the consent of such holder, except as to a postponement of an interest payment consented to as provided in paragraph (2) of subsection (a) of this section, and except that such indenture may contain provisions limiting or denying the right of any such holder to institute any such suit, if and to the extent that the institution or prosecution thereof or the entry of judgment therein would, under applicable law, result in the surrender, impairment, waiver, or loss of the lien of such indenture upon any property subject to such lien.

(c) The obligor upon any indenture qualified under this title may set a record date for purposes of determining the identity of indenture security holders entitled to vote or consent to any action by vote or consent authorized or permitted by subsection (a) of this section. Unless the indenture provides otherwise, such record date shall be the later of 30 days prior to the first solicitation of such consent or the date of the most recent list of holders furnished to the trustee pursuant to section 312 of this title prior to such solicitation.

Sec. 317   Special Powers of Trustee; Duties of Paying Agents

(a) The indenture trustee shall be authorized—

(1) in the case of a default in payment of the principal of any indenture security, when and as the same shall become due and payable, or in the case of a default in payment of the interest on any such security, when and as the same shall become due and payable and the continuance of such default for such period as may be prescribed in such indenture, to recover judgment, in its own name and as trustee of an express trust, against the obligor upon the indenture securities for the whole amount of such principal and interest remaining unpaid; and

(2) to file such proofs of claim and other papers or documents as may be necessary or advisable in order to have the claims of such trustee and of the indenture security holders allowed in any judicial proceedings relative to the obligor upon the indenture securities, its creditors, or its property.

(b) Each paying agent shall hold in trust for the benefit of the indenture security holders or the indenture trustee all sums held by such paying agent for the payment of the principal of or interest on the indenture securities, and shall give to such trustee notice of any default by any obligor upon the indenture securities in the making of any such payment.

Sec. 318   Effect of Prescribed Indenture Provisions

(a) If any provision of the indenture to be qualified limits, qualifies, or conflicts with the duties imposed by operation of subsection (c) of this section, the imposed duties shall control.

(b) The indenture to be qualified may contain, in addition to provisions specifically authorized under this subchapter to be included therein, any other provisions the inclusion of which is not in contravention of any provisions of this subchapter.

(c) The provisions of sections 310 to and including 317 that impose duties on any person (including provisions automatically deemed included in an indenture unless the indenture provides that such provisions are excluded) are a part of and govern every qualified indenture, whether or not physically contained therein, shall be deemed retroactively to govern each indenture heretofore qualified, and prospectively to govern each indenture hereafter qualified under this title and shall be deemed retroactively to amend and supersede inconsistent provisions in each such indenture heretofore qualified. The foregoing provisions of this subsection shall not be deemed to effect the inclusion (by retroactive amendment or otherwise) in the text of any indenture heretofore qualified of any of the optional provisions contemplated by section 310(b)(1), 311(b), 314(d), 315(a), 315(b), 315(d), 315(e), or 316(a)(1).

Sec. 319   Rules, Regulations, and Orders

(a) The Commission shall have authority from time to time to make, issue, amend and rescind such rules and regulations and such orders as it may deem necessary or appropriate in the public interest or for the protection of investors to carry out the provisions of this subchapter, including rules and regulations defining accounting, technical, and trade terms used in this subchapter. Among other things, the Commission shall have authority, (1) by rules and regulations, to prescribe for the purposes of section 310(b) the method (to be fixed in indentures to be qualified under this subchapter) of calculating percentages of voting securities and other securities; (2) by rules and regulations, to prescribe the definitions of the terms "cash transaction" and "self-liquidating paper" which shall be included in indentures to be qualified under this subchapter, which definitions shall include such of the creditor relationships referred to in paragraphs (4) and (6) of subsection (b) of section 311 as to which the Commission determines that the application of subsection (a) of section 311 is not necessary in the public interest or for the protection of investors, having due regard for the purposes of such subsection; and (3) for the purposes of this subchapter, to prescribe the form or forms in which information required in any statement, application, report, or other document filed with the Commission shall be set forth. For the purpose of its rules or regulations the

Commission may classify persons, securities, indentures, and other matters within its jurisdiction and prescribe different requirements for different classes of persons, securities, indentures, or matters.

(b) Subject to the provisions of chapter 15 of Title 44 and regulations prescribed under the authority thereof, the rules and regulations of the Commission under this subchapter shall be effective upon publication in the manner which the Commission shall prescribe, or upon such later date as may be provided in such rules and regulations.

(c) No provision of this subchapter imposing any liability shall apply to any act done or omitted in good faith in conformity with any rule, regulation, or order of the Commission, notwithstanding that such rule, regulation, or order may, after such act or omission, be amended or rescinded or be determined by judicial or other authority to be invalid for any reason.

Sec. 320   Hearings by Commission

Hearings may be public and may be held before the Commission, any member or members thereof, or any officer or officers of the Commission designated by it, and appropriate records thereof shall be kept.

Sec. 321   Special Powers of Commission

(a) For the purpose of any investigation or any other proceeding which, in the opinion of the Commission, is necessary and proper for the enforcement of this subchapter, any member of the Commission, or any officer thereof designated by it, is empowered to administer oaths and affirmations, subpena witnesses, compel their attendance, take evidence, and require the production of any books, papers, correspondence, memoranda, contracts, agreements, or other records which the Commission deems relevant or material to the inquiry. Such attendance of witnesses and the production of any such books, papers, correspondence, memoranda, contracts, agreements, or other records may be required from any place in the United States or in any Territory at any designated place of investigation or hearing. In addition, the Commission shall have the powers with respect to investigations and hearings, and with respect to the enforcement of, and offenses and violations under, this subchapter and rules and regulations and orders prescribed under the authority thereof, provided in sections 20 and 22(b),(c) of the Securities Act of 1933.

(b) The Treasury Department, the Comptroller of the Currency, the

Board of Governors of the Federal Reserve System, the Federal Reserve Banks, and the Federal Deposit Insurance Corporation are authorized, under such conditions as they may prescribe, to make available to the Commission such reports, records, or other information as they may have available with respect to trustees or prospective trustees under indentures qualified or to be qualified under this subchapter, and to make through their examiners or other employees for the use of the Commission, examinations of such trustees or prospective trustees. Every such trustee or prospective trustee shall, as a condition precedent to qualification of such indenture, consent that reports of examinations by Federal, State, Territorial, or District authorities may be furnished by such authorities to the Commission upon request therefor.

Notwithstanding any provision of this subchapter, no report, record, or other information made available to the Commission under this subsection, no report of an examination made under this subsection for the use of the Commission, no report of an examination made of any trustee or prospective trustee by any Federal, State, Territorial, or District authority having jurisdiction to examine or supervise such trustee, no report made by any such trustee or prospective trustee to any such authority, and no correspondence between any such authority and any such trustee or prospective trustee, shall be divulged or made known or available by the Commission or any member, officer, agent, or employee thereof, to any person other than a member, officer, agent, or employee of the Commission: *Provided*, That the Commission may make available to the Attorney General of the United States, in confidence, any information obtained from such records, reports of examination, other reports, or correspondence, and deemed necessary by the Commission, or requested by him, for the purpose of enabling him to perform his duties under this subchapter.

(c) Any investigation of a prospective trustee, or any proceeding or requirement for the purpose of obtaining information regarding a prospective trustee, under any provision of this subchapter, shall be limited—

(1) to determining whether such prospective trustee is qualified to act as trustee under the provisions of subsection (b) of section 310;

(2) to requiring the inclusion in the registration statement or application of information with respect to the eligibility of such prospective trustee under paragraph (1) of subsection (a) of section 310; and

(3) to requiring the inclusion in the registration statement or application of the most recent published report of condition of such prospective trustee, as de-

scribed in paragraph (2) of subsection (a) of section 310, or, if the indenture does not contain the provision with respect to combined capital and surplus authorized by the last sentence of paragraph (2) of subsection (a) of section 310, to determining whether such prospective trustee is eligible to act as such under paragraph (2) of subsection (a) of section 310.

(d) The provisions of section 4(b) of the Securities Exchange Act of 1934 shall be applicable with respect to the power of the Commission to appoint and fix the compensation of such officers, attorneys, examiners and other experts, and such other officers and employees, as may be necessary for carrying out its functions under this subchapter.

Sec. 322   Court Review of Orders; Jurisdiction of Offenses and Suits

(a) Orders of the Commission under this subchapter (including orders pursuant to the provisions of sections 305(b) and 307(c)) shall be subject to review in the same manner, upon the same conditions, and to the same extent, as provided in section 9 of the Securities Act of 1933, with respect to orders of the Commission under such Act.

(b) Jurisdiction of offenses and violations under, and jurisdiction and venue of suits and actions brought to enforce any liability or duty created by, this subchapter, or any rules or regulations or orders prescribed under the authority thereof, shall be as provided in section 22(a) of the Securities Act of 1933.

Sec. 323   Liability for Misleading Statements

(a) Any person who shall make or cause to be made any statement in any application, report, or document filed with the Commission pursuant to any provisions of this subchapter, or any rule, regulation, or order thereunder, which statement was at the time and in the light of the circumstances under which it was made false or misleading with respect to any material fact, or who shall omit to state any material fact required to be stated therein or necessary to make the statements therein not misleading, shall be liable to any person (not knowing that such statement was false or misleading or of such omission) who, in reliance upon such statement or omission shall have purchased or sold a security issued under the indenture to which such application, report, or documents relates, for damages caused by such reliance, unless the person sued shall prove that he acted in good faith and had no knowledge that such statement was false or misleading or of such omission. A person seeking to enforce such liability may sue at law or in equity in any court of competent jurisdiction. In any such suit the court may, in its discretion, require an undertaking for the payment of the costs of such suit and assess reasonable costs, including reasonable attorneys' fees, against either party litigant, having due regard to the merits and good faith of the suit or defense. No action shall be maintained to enforce any liability created under this section unless brought within one year after the discovery of the facts constituting the cause of action and within three years after such cause of action accrued.

(b) The rights and remedies provided by this subchapter shall be in addition to any and all other rights and remedies that may exist under the Securities Act of 1933, or the Securities Exchange Act of 1934, or the Public Utility Holding Company Act of 1935, or otherwise at law or in equity; but no person permitted to maintain a suit for damages under the provisions of this subchapter shall recover, through satisfaction of judgment in one or more actions, a total amount in excess of his actual damages on account of the act complained of.

Sec. 324   Unlawful Representations

It shall be unlawful for any person in offering, selling or issuing any security to represent or imply in any manner whatsoever that any action or failure to act by the Commission in the administration of this subchapter means that the Commission has in any way passed upon the merits of, or given approval to, any trustee, indenture or security, or any transaction or transactions therein, or that any such action or failure to act with regard to any statement or report filed with or examined by the Commission pursuant to this subchapter or any rule, regulation, or order thereunder, has the effect of a finding by the Commission that such statement or report is true and accurate on its face or that it is not false or misleading.

Sec. 325   Penalties

Any person who willfully violates any provision of this subchapter or any rule, regulation, or order thereunder, or any person who willfully, in any application, report, or document filed or required to be filed under the provisions of this subchapter or any rule, regulation, or order thereunder, makes any untrue statement of a material fact or omits to state any material fact required to be stated therein or necessary to make the statements therein not misleading, shall upon conviction be fined not more than

$10,000 or imprisoned not more than five years, or both.

Sec. 326   Effect on Existing Law

Except as otherwise expressly provided, nothing in this subchapter shall affect (1) the jurisdiction of the Commission under the Securities Act of 1933, or the Securities Exchange Act of 1934, or the Public Utility Holding Company Act of 1935, over any person, security, or contract, or (2) the rights, obligations, duties, or liabilities of any person under such Acts; nor shall anything in this subchapter affect the jurisdiction of any other commission, board, agency, or officer of the United States or of any State or political subdivision of any State, over any person or security, insofar as such jurisdiction does not conflict with any provision of this subchapter or any rule, regulation, or order thereunder.

Sec. 327   Contrary Stipulations Void

Any condition, stipulation, or provision binding any person to waive compliance with any provision of this subchapter or with any rule, regulation, or order thereunder shall be void.

Sec. 328   Separability of Provisions

If any provision of this subchapter or the application of such provision to any person or circumstance shall be held invalid, the remainder of the subchapter and the application of such provision to persons or circumstances other than those as to which it is held invalid shall not be affected thereby.

Glossary

Many of the following definitions are from the *Corporate Trust Reference Manual and Securities Processing*, 3d ed. (American Bankers Association); *A Guide to Registered Municipal Securities* (Government Finance Officers Association), and a glossary prepared by the Cannon Financial Institute.

AD VALOREM TAX A direct tax based on the value of a property. Counties, school districts, and municipalities usually are—and special tax districts may be—authorized by law to levy such taxes on property other than tangible personal property.

ADVANCE REFUNDING A financing structure under which new bonds are issued to repay an outstanding issue before its first call date. Generally, the proceeds of the new issue are invested in government securities that are held in escrow.

AGENCY ACCOUNT An account whose title to the property constituting the agency does not pass to the trust institution but remains with the owner of the property (who is called the principal and in which the agent is charged with certain duties with respect to the property).

AMERICAN DEPOSITORY RECEIPT (ADR) A security that represents shares of foreign stock or bonds; a negotiable receipt for foreign securities held by the foreign correspondent bank of an American depository bank.

ARBITRAGE The simultaneous buying and selling of separate but related currencies, securities, or goods in separate markets (often foreign) in order to profit from the difference in their prices.

ARBITRAGE BOND A bond whose proceeds are reasonably expected (at the time the bonds are issued) to be used directly or indirectly (1) to acquire higher-yielding investments or (2) to replace funds used directly or indirectly to acquire higher-yielding investments.

ASSESSMENT BOND   A type of special-tax municipal bond, repaid from related taxes such as real estate or property taxes.

ASSET-BACKED SECURITY   A security for which the income and principal payments are secured by specific assets such as a pool of mortgages or car loans.

ATTORNEY-IN-FACT   An agent acting for the security holder under a power of attorney to effect a transfer.

AUCTION-RATE SECURITY   A security that uses an auction, or bidding, mechanism to periodically reset the rate at which dividends or interest payments are to accrue. Although the auction mechanism was first applied to corporate preferred stock issues, it is now used to structure debt offerings as well.

AUTHENTICATION   A manual certification appearing on a bond or note executed by the trustee (or its agent) under an indenture, or by a fiscal agent under a fiscal agency agreement, under which the bond or note is issued, stating that it is one of the bonds or notes named in the relevant indenture or fiscal agency agreement.

BACKUP WITHHOLDING   A method established by the Interest and Dividend Tax Compliance Act of 1983 that requires paying agents to withhold 31 percent of interest, dividend, and principal payments to investors who have not filed an exemption certificate, certified taxpayer identification number, or social security number with the paying agent.

BALLOON PAYMENT   A scaled method of bond interest payment (or mortgage payment) whose final payment is proportionally higher than previous payments.

BANKER'S ACCEPTANCE (BA)   A corporate bank draft (usually for a future delivery of foreign goods) whose payment has been guaranteed and stamped "accepted" by the corporation's bank.

BASIS POINT   A term used in stating bond interest; 100 basis points equal 1 percent.

BDUG   The Bank Depository User Group of Depository Trust Company (DTC), a user panel assembled to work with DTC on refining and enhancing DTC services.

BEARER SECURITY   A negotiable security that is not registered in regard to interest or principal. It is presumed in law to be owned by its holder. The title to bearer securities is transferred by delivery.

BENEFICIAL OWNER   The true owner of securities that may be the bearer or registered in the name of another, such as a nominee.

BEST EFFORTS   An underwriting method in which the investment banker sells as much of an issue as possible.

BID PRICE   The price at which the market maker buys a security. Bid and asked prices are quoted by market makers on over-the-counter stocks.

BLUE-SKY LAWS   A popular name for various state laws enacted to protect the public against securities fraud.

BAN (BOND ANTICIPATION NOTE)   A municipal note maturing in less than one year issued in advance of a new bond issue. Proceeds from a bond issue repay the note with interest.

BOND CERTIFICATE   An interest-bearing debt obligation under whose terms a borrower contracts, among other things, to pay the holder a fixed principal amount on a stated future date and normally a series of interest payments during its life. A long-term debt instrument. In this sense, it may also be called a *debenture* or *note*.

BOND COUNSEL   An attorney (or firm) retained by an issuer to give a legal opinion that a municipal issuer is authorized to issue the proposed securities and has met all the legal requirements necessary for issuance and that the interest on the securities will be exempt from federal income tax and, when applicable, from state and local taxes.

BONDHOLDERS   Investors who lend money to an enterprise for a stated period of time and receive interest and repayment of principal. Their claims on a corporation's assets take precedence over the claims of preferred and common stockholders.

BOND OPINION   An opinion usually covering (1) whether the bonds are valid and binding obligations of the bond issuer; (2) the source of payment or security for the bonds; and (3) whether and to what extent the interest on the bonds is exempt from federal income tax and from taxes imposed by the state in which the issuer is located.

BOND POWER   An assignment separate from the certificate used for bonds.

BOND PURCHASE AGREEMENT   An agreement between an issuer and the underwriter of the bonds that states the terms of the sale, including price, premium or discount, interest rate, closing conditions, restrictions on the issuer's liability, and any indemnity provisions.

BOND REGISTRAR   A corporate agent responsible for registering transfers and maintaining records of registered debt security holders.

BOND RESOLUTION   The document(s) representing action by a municipal issuer authorizing the issuance and sale of securities. The resolution also describes the nature of the obligation and the issuer's duties to the bondholders.

BOOK-ENTRY SETTLEMENT   An accounting method for securities transactions and funds movements, in which no physical movement of the certificates or funds is necessary. Instead, debits and offsetting credits (and vice versa) are posted to the accounts of the transaction's principals. These parties are usually members of the same securities depository, clearinghouse, or the Federal Reserve System, or they maintain special accounts with a common bank or broker.

BROKER CONFIRMATION   A receipt sent to a customer by a broker after executing a trade. The "confirm" indicates the customer's name, broker account number, description of security, quantity, price, dollar amounts, delivery and receiving parties, and so forth. Also called *trade confirmation* or *trade confirm*.

BROKER/DEALER   A party who makes securities transactions on behalf of its customers, as well as for its own market position. A broker may not buy and sell from its own account, and it charges fees for the services performed. A dealer may purchase and resell the securities to its customer, charging a markup for its services. A broker/dealer may serve the customer as either a broker or a dealer.

BULLDOG BOND   A sterling-denominated bond marketed in the United Kingdom by a non-British entity.

BULLET ISSUE   An issue of securities with no amortization feature, in which the principal amount is repaid in full at the maturity date.

BUSINESS DAY   A day that always is specified in the indenture or fiscal agency agreement but usually means
    1. in the Euromarkets, when two related markets are open for banking business; in the Eurodollar market, a day when both London and New York banks are open for business.
    2. in the U.S. domestic market, any day on which business can be conducted, except Saturdays, Sundays, or legal or statutory holidays.

BUY-IN   If the selling party to a securities trade fails to deliver, the buyer may buy the securities through other sources at the prevailing market price. The defaulting seller is liable for the difference in price. (The buyer must notify the seller of its intentions to buy the securities elsewhere before resorting to the buy-in.)

CALLABLE SECURITY   A bond issue, all or part of which may be redeemed before maturity under specific conditions spelled out in the indenture's provisions.

CALL OPTION   A short-term security that gives the owner the right to buy a security at a fixed price until a stated future date.

CALL PROTECTION   The period of time during which the issuer cannot call the security for redemption.

CALL PROVISION   A feature of bonds or preferred stock that allows the issuer to repurchase part or all of an issue before it matures.

CAPITALIZATION   The total amount of the various securities issued by a corporation. Capitalization may include preferred and common stock, bonds debentures, and surplus.

CAPITALIZED INTEREST   The portion of an issue's proceeds that will be used to pay interest on the bonds for a specific period of time, usually the period of construction of a project financed by the issue.

"CASH" SETTLEMENT   A cash settlement usually takes place on the trade date, avoiding the usual five-day settlement delay.

CEDE & CO.   The Depository Trust Company's nominee name, used on all registered securities that the DTC holds in storage.

CEDEL AND EUROCLEAR   The Eurobond Clearing systems, which provide safekeeping, custody, and clearance services for holders of Eurobonds and Yankee bonds.

CERTIFICATES OF ACCRUAL ON TREASURY SECURITIES (CATS)   CATS represent ownership in serially maturing interest payments or principal payments on specific underlying U.S. Treasury notes and bonds. Each CATS entitles the holder to receive a single payment at its maturity.

CERTIFICATE OF DEPOSIT (CD)   An interest-bearing, negotiable certificate representing a deposit with a fixed maturity issued by a commercial bank and traded on a yield basis with interest computed for the actual number of days held on a 360-day year.

CHAPTER 11   A chapter of the federal bankruptcy code. Among other provisions, it directs the Securities and Exchange Commission (SEC) to aid the bankruptcy courts in corporation reorganizations. The SEC advises on plans submitted by the court and comments on fairness of the reorganization plan to the corporation's investors.

CHARTER, CORPORATE   A corporation's constitution granted by its state of incorporation, which specifies the rules and limitations of ownership, operation, funding, security issuance, and the like.

CHINESE WALL   The popular term for a provision of the Glass–Steagall Act that required all trust accounts to be maintained and managed separately and apart from the bank's commercial side.

CLASSES OF STOCK   Common: Represents the principal ownership of the corporation, the first class to be issued and the last to be retired.
Classified common: Division of the common stock usually into two classes, class A and class B, to differentiate controlling or voting power.
Preferred: A cross between common stock and a bond. Holders receive dividends before profits are distributed to common stock holders.
Cumulative preferred: If not paid by the stockholders, dividends are accumulated and paid at a future date.
Noncumulative preferred: The stockholder is paid dividends if they are earned, without any cumulative provision.
Participating preferred: The stockholder receives a specified dividend and may also be entitled to additional earnings generally available to common stockholders.
Classified preferred: 4.25 PFD, class A PFD, class B PFD, and so forth. These distinctions usually refer to different rates or voting privileges.

Convertible preferred: Stock that carries a provision enabling the stockholder to convert it into common stock.

CLEARINGHOUSE FUNDS   (1) Funds used to settle equity, corporate, and municipal bond settlement transactions; or (2) a term meaning "next-day availability" of funds.

CLOSE-END (MORTGAGE) BONDS   A type of security (usually first mortgage bonds) that prohibits the future sale of a junior issue with the same priority of lien on the corporate assets covered by the original indenture.

CLOSELY HELD COMPANY   A corporation with a small number of owners, all living in one state at the time its stock is issued. The issue need not be registered with the SEC.

CLOSING DATE   The date on which a new issue's proceeds are paid to the borrower by the lead manager against delivery of the securities in a temporary or definitive form.

COLLATERAL AGENT   A private financial institution, typically a bank and often the trustee, that serves as an agent for the credit enhancement provider. It holds and maintains the collateral that is pledged to the trustee to secure the obligations of the credit enhancer under the credit facility.

COLLATERAL AGREEMENT   The agreement under which a credit enhancement provider pledges the collateral (e.g., cash or readily marketable securities) to a collateral agent to hold as security for the bonds.

COLLATERAL TRUST BOND   A bond secured by securities owned by the issuer that is deposited with an indenture trustee.

COLLATERALIZED MORTGAGE OBLIGATION   A bond with two or more classes of maturities secured by a pool of mortgages or mortgage instruments (e.g., Ginnie Maes).

COMMERCIAL PAPER   A negotiable, unsecured, short-term note issued in bearer form by a large and well-known corporation. Usually sold on a discount basis with a maximum maturity of nine months.

COMPETITIVE BIDDING   A sealed-envelope bidding process employed when various underwriter groups are interested in handling the distribution of a securities issue. The issuer awards the mandate or contract to one group based on the highest price paid and the lowest interest cost.

COMPOUND INTEREST   Interest paid on original capital and on the interest that has been added to the capital. Interest can be compounded daily, weekly, monthly, quarterly, semiannually, or annually.

COMPTROLLER OF THE CURRENCY   An official of the U.S. government, appointed by the president and confirmed by the Senate, who is responsible for chartering, examining, supervising, and liquidating all national banks.

CONDUIT FINANCING   Bonds issued by a governmental unit to finance a project to be used primarily by a third party, usually a corporation engaged in private enterprise. The security for such bonds is the credit of the private user rather than the governmental issuer. Generally, such bonds do not constitute obligations of the issuer because the corporate obligor is liable for generating the pledged revenues (e.g., industrial revenue bonds).

CONSTRUCTION FUND   A fund, usually held by the trustee under an indenture, into which the proceeds of an issue are deposited for payment of authorized project costs.

CONTINUOUS NET SETTLEMENT (CNS)   A securities trade settlement option that condenses multiple transactions into a single net security settlement and a single net money affirmation, in which the identity of the contra side is lost. The bank and broker settle all security and money transactions with the clearing corporation.

CONVERSION   An indenture provision giving the holder of a bond or note the right to exchange it for other securities of the issuer (usually shares of common stock).

CONVERSION AGENT   A bank designated by the issuer of convertible securities to convert, at the investor's request, the issuer's debt or equity securities into the number of shares of stock specified in the trust indenture or stock-offering agreement. The conversion agent requisitions the shares of stock from the stock transfer agent and draws a check for any cash fraction upon surrender of the convertible securities.

CONVERTIBLE DEBENTURES   Securities that may be exchanged for common stock of the same company at a set conversion price stated in the bond indenture.

CO-OP (A BANK FOR COOPERATIVES)   A bank that makes loans to farmers' associations by issuing bonds. These are not guaranteed by the U.S. government but are secured obligations of banks that are under governmental supervision.

CORPORATE REORGANIZATION   A major change in a corporation's capital structure and financial operation, often requiring new issues and/or exchanges of securities.

CORPORATE RESOLUTION   A formal document issued by a corporation to make a statement, ratify actions, or grant authority to individuals to act for the corporation on specific matters.

CORPUS   The property in a trust account, whose title vests in the person entitled to the future estate.

COUPON BOND   A bearer bond with coupons attached. The interest on the bond is collected by detaching and presenting the coupons as they become due.

COVENANT   A provision—either affirmative or negative—in an indenture, stating an undertaking or agreement by the issuer in regard to specific matters.

COVERAGE   The portion of pledged revenues available annually to pay debt service, compared with the annual debt service requirement. The ratio is one indication of the margin of safety for the payment of debt service.

CREDIT ENHANCEMENT   An external credit support of a debt obligation, including letters of credit, municipal bond insurance, and third-party guarantees.

CREDIT ENHANCEMENT PROVIDER   Insurance companies, banks, savings and loans, municipal bond sureties, or other private financial institutions that provide additional security for tax-exempt bonds by guaranteeing or insuring the bonds' repayment.

CURRENT YIELD   Annual interest (or dividends) divided by the current market price of a bond (or stock).

CUSIP   Acronym for Committee on Uniform Securities Identification Procedures. A uniform numbering system widely used to identify securities and their issuers. It includes corporate, municipal, state, federal, and some foreign issues. The CUSIP number appears on the certificates and in documents relating to securities processing.

CUSTODIAN   An agent, usually a bank, that safekeeps securities for its customers and collects dividends and interest. It also buys, sells, receives, and delivers securities if so instructed by the customer.

DATED DATE   The date of a bond issue, printed on each bond, when interest usually starts to accrue, even though the bond may actually be delivered at a later date.

DEALER   An individual or firm in the securities business acting as the principal rather than the agent. Typically, a dealer buys for its own account and sells to a customer from its own inventory.

DEBENTURE   An unsecured debt certificate backed by the issuer's general credit.

DEBT SERVICE   Payments of interest and principal on total borrowings that must be made by the borrower during the period in which its debt is outstanding.

DEBT SERVICE RESERVE FUND   A fund usually held by the trustee under an indenture established for the payment of debt service on bonds in the event that the pledged receipts are insufficient.

DEEP DISCOUNT BOND   A bond sold at a substantial discount below its par value, bearing either interest at a rate significantly below the current interest rates or no interest at all.

DEFAULT   The failure by the issuer of bonds or notes to comply with one or more of its obligations in the indenture under which the bonds are issued.

DEFEASANCE   A general term pertaining to the termination of the rights and interests of the bondholders and the extinguishment of their lien on any property or collateral according to the terms of an indenture or bond resolution. The term may also refer to the termination of an issuer's obligations under such contracts upon the refunding of the issue or by provisions for the future payment of interest and the repayment of principal.

DELAYED DELIVERY   A partial delivery of new issue securities to the lead manager after the closing date, in accordance with an agreement.

DELIVERY VERSUS PAYMENT (DVP)   A physical delivery of securities against the payment of the purchase price. Normally, payment is due on the scheduled settlement date even if securities are delayed.

DEMAND OPTION   The right, which may be evidenced by a certificate, given to the holder of a debt security to sell it back to the issuer at any time before the security's maturity.

DEPOSITORY AGENT   An agent retained by the maker of a tender offer to receive securities forwarded to the agent by the owners, to hold the securities, and to make payment in cash and/or securities to the owners when authorized by the maker of the tender offer.

DEPOSITORY TRUST COMPANY (DTC)   The New York depository serving institutional participants such as banks, brokers, insurance companies, and other high-volume securities traders.

DERIVATIVE   An investment instrument that derives its value from the value of other securities. Options and futures are examples.

DIRECT PAY LETTER OF CREDIT   A letter of credit that covers an amount equal to the principal of and interest on the bonds and that is withdrawn by the trustee on each bond payment date in an amount equal to the full amount of principal, interest, and premium, if any, due for the bonds. This letter may also reinstate the interest component after any interest is withdrawn, unless the issuing bank notifies the trustee to the contrary within a certain period of time after the withdrawal.

DISCOUNT   The amount by which a security is selling below its par value. In the case of an original issuance, this is referred to as the *original issuance discount* (OID).

DIVIDEND   A proportion of net earnings paid periodically by a corporation to its stockholders as a return on their investment.

DIVIDEND, STOCK   The payment of additional shares of common stock by the corporation to the stockholders.

D.K. (DON'T KNOW)   A D.K. results when the purchaser's clearinghouse or bank refuses to accept a security delivery simply because it "doesn't know" about it and is not expecting it.

DROP LOCK BOND   A hybrid debt security that is issued as a floating-rate instrument but becomes a fixed-rate bond when its rate falls below a predetermined trigger rate.

DUE BILL   An assignment or similar instrument given by the seller in a trade to transfer title to dividends, interest, or other rights legally due to the buyer.

DUE DILIGENCE   An investigation conducted by underwriters and their counsel and, in some cases, also by the bond counsel and the issuer's counsel to determine whether all material items in connection with the issuer, the issue, and the security for the issue have been accurately disclosed in the official statement and that no material disclosure has been omitted.

DUTCH AUCTION   An auction in which securities are awarded at the price that represents the lowest accepted bid. All bidders pay the lowest bid accepted.

ENDORSEMENT   The signature written on the back of a negotiable instrument (or in an accompanying power) that transfers the instrument to another party. The signer must have the legal right to transfer the instrument if the endorsement is to be valid.

ENDORSEMENT IN BLANK   The signature of an authorized person on the back of a negotiable instrument, or on a separate power, that does not indicate the specific name of the party to whom the instrument is being transferred. Endorsement in blank makes the instrument as transferable as if it were in bearer form.

ENTERPRISE ACTIVITY   A revenue-generating project or business that supplies the necessary funds to pay the debt service on bonds issued to finance the facility. The debt of such projects is self-liquidating when the projects earn sufficient monies to cover all debt service and other requirements imposed under the bond contract.

EQUIPMENT TRUST BOND   A bond secured by machinery and equipment issued according to an equipment trust.

EQUITY SECURITY   A security evidencing ownership of a corporation, including preferred and common stock of all types.

ERASURE GUARANTEE   Any irregularity in the assignment guaranteed by the broker or the commercial bank before the transfer is registered.

ESCHEAT   The revision of property to the state when there are no legal heirs or claimants.

ESCROW   An agency physically holding cash, securities, or documents until certain conditions called for in an agreement between two parties are met.

ESCROW AGENT   An institution, usually a bank, designated by two or more parties to hold securities, funds, or documents that are to be delivered upon compliance with the conditions contained in the escrow agreement, usually within a specified period of time.

EURO   A standard basket of European Union member currencies.

EUROSTERLING BOND   A sterling-denominated bond issued in bearer form only, marketed solely outside the United Kingdom and the United States.

EUROCLEAR   An international securities depository, founded in 1968, with headquarters in Brussels, Belgium, to hold cross-border securities for its members.

EUROCOMMERCIAL PAPER   Commercial paper sold by foreign corporations.

EURODOLLAR   A U.S. dollar deposited in any European bank outside the United States.

EURODOLLAR BOND   A U.S. dollar–denominated bond marketed wholly outside the United States (primarily in Europe). No registration statement is required to be filed with the SEC.

EURODOLLAR CERTIFICATE OF DEPOSIT   A negotiable, dollar-denominated, short-term bearer certificate that represents deposits in foreign banks or foreign branches of U.S. banks.

EUROMARKET   A general term for the European capital markets that comprise, among other things, the markets for Eurobonds, Euro FRNs, Euro CDs/FRCDs, and Euro-syndicated credits.

EVENT OF DEFAULT   A specific kind of default whose occurrence and continuance permit the trustee (or a holder of bonds or notes) to exercise the remedies in the indenture under which the bonds or notes were issued.

EXCHANGE AGENT   A bank, usually the bond registrar, designated by an issuer of securities to exchange the bonds of an issue for other bonds of the same issue (e.g., registered bonds for bearer and interdenominational exchanges) or to exchange the bonds or stock for other securities of the same issuer or of a different company as a result of a merger or acquisition.

EXERCISE PRICE   The price set in an option. Also called the *striking* or *strike price*. The owner of the option has the right to buy or sell the security named in the option at the exercise price within a set period of time.

EXTENSION LETTER OF CREDIT   A letter of credit that provides for a single withdrawal in the event of the acceleration of the bonds in an amount equal to all payments made on the bonds during the period of a specified number of days (usually ninety-one) before the occurrence of (1) an act of bankruptcy that triggers acceleration or (2) the drawing on the letter of credit if no act of bankruptcy has occurred.

FAIL   The failure of the seller to deliver securities to the buyer on the settlement date and/or the failure of the buyer to accept and pay for the securities. Also called a *settlement fail*.

FANNIE MAE (FEDERAL NATIONAL MORTGAGE ASSOCIATION)   A privately owned company that adds liquidity to the residential mortgage market by buying mortgages from the original lenders, such as savings and loans, banks, and insurance companies. Fannie Mae buys mortgages guaranteed or insured by government agencies, as well as conventional mortgages. To raise funds, it sells debentures, notes, and mortgage-backed certificates to the investing public and occasionally to the U.S. Treasury.

FARM CREDIT ADMINISTRATION   An independent U.S. government agency that offers credit and financial services to farmers, ranchers, and allied businesses. See also Co-op (a bank for cooperatives), FICB (Federal Intermediate Credit Bank), and FLB (Federal Land Bank).

FDIC (FEDERAL DEPOSIT INSURANCE CORPORATION)   An agency of the U.S. government that insures depositors' accounts at most commercial banks and mutual savings banks.

FEASIBILITY STUDY   A report of the financial practicality of a proposed project and its financing that may include estimates of the revenue that will be generated and a review of the physical, operating, economic, or engineering aspects of the proposed project.

FEDERAL FUNDS
1. Excess reserve balances of a member bank on depositary at a Federal Reserve Bank. This money may be made available to eligible borrowers on a short-term basis.
2. Funds used for the settlement of money market instruments and U.S. government securities transactions.
3. A term used to mean "same-day availability" of funds. See also CLEARING-HOUSE FUNDS.

FLB (FEDERAL LAND BANKS)   Responsible to Farm Credit Administration. FLBs arrange long-term loans to farmers and ranchers, secured by mortgages on farm or ranch properties. FLB bonds are issued to finance these loans. See also FARM CREDIT ADMINISTRATION.

FEDERAL RESERVE REQUIREMENTS   The dollar amount that banks must deposit with a Federal Reserve Bank or hold in cash on their own premises. The purpose of the reserve requirement is to ensure that a bank remains liquid and does not lend more money than it can afford. An individual bank may have more or less funds on reserve than its requirements dictate. A bank with a deficit borrows federal funds—or so-called fed funds—from a bank that has an excess amount on reserve. The borrowing bank pays interest to the lending bank for the overnight use of the fed funds.

FEDERAL RESERVE SYSTEM (FRS)   Known as "the Fed," this is the central banking system as established by the Federal Reserve Act of 1913. It regulates the nation's supply of money, determines the legal reserve requirement of its member banks, oversees the mint, transfers funds, promotes and facilitates the clearance and collection of checks, and examines its member banks.

FHA (FEDERAL HOUSING ADMINISTRATION)   Responsible to HUD, the Department of Housing and Urban Development, this agency insures residential mortgages, settles claims in cash for defaulted mortgages, and issues registered, transferable debentures that have an unconditional U.S. government guarantee.

FHLB (FEDERAL HOME LOAN BANK SYSTEM)   The federal system that supervises all nationally chartered savings and loan associations and mutual savings banks. State-chartered thrift organizations may also be eligible for membership. One purpose of the FHLB is to make funds available for home loans and mortgages.

FHMA (FARMERS HOME ADMINISTRATION)   An agency of the Department of Agriculture that aids loan programs in rural areas. Its outstanding securities have a U.S. government guarantee.

FICB (FEDERAL INTERMEDIATE CREDIT BANK)   A bank that is responsible to the Farm Credit Administration and provides short- and medium-term financing to financial institutions that serve the farm credit market. See also FARM CREDIT ADMINISTRATION.

FINANCIAL ADVISER   With respect to a new issue of municipal bonds, a consultant who advises the issuer on matters pertinent to the issue, such as structure, timing, marketing, fairness of pricing, terms, and bond ratings.

FINS (FINANCIAL INDUSTRY NUMBERING SYSTEM)   A numerical code (similar in structure to the CUSIP numbering system) identifying financial institutions such as banks and brokerage firms. Used in security trade documents, depository accounting procedures, and the like.

FISCAL AGENT   Am entity, normally a bank or trust company, authorized to enter into a fiscal agency agreement with an issuer of bonds or notes (usually a government entity). The agreement provides for control of the issue and its servicing, but the fiscal agent does not have fiduciary responsibilities.

FLOAT   A colloquial term meaning the earnings on uninvested balances held by a bank.

FLOATER   A common term used to describe a security with a variable-interest rate.

FLOATING RATE   An interest rate that is not a fixed percentage of principal. The issuer typically "pegs" the future rate it will pay to the future rate of a basic short-term financial instrument (such as a specific U.S. Treasury issue) and pays a small stated percentage above the rate.

FLOWER BOND   A class of treasury bonds no longer being issued, but previous issues will mature through 1998. If the bondholder dies before the bond matures, the heirs may redeem the bond at full face value to pay federal estate taxes.

FORWARDING AGENT   An institution, usually a bank, that receives securities during a tender offer and forwards them daily to the appropriate depository agent with an accounting record.

FRACTIONAL RIGHTS   The residual portion of the total rights received by a stockholder in a rights offering that is too small to allow the purchase of a full share.

FREDDIE MAC (FEDERAL HOME LOAN MORTGAGE CORPORATION)   An organization that supplies mortgage credit for residential housing, mostly through federal home loan banks. (The FHLB system serves thrift institutions, much as the Federal Reserve System serves commercial banks.) Freddie Mac issues bonds, debentures, notes, and certificates.

FREEDOM SHARE   A nonmarketable U.S. Treasury savings note. Although freedom shares were not issued after 1970, many were outstanding until 1994. Payable on presentation to certain banks, as well as the Bureau of Public Debt. Also known as a *U.S. savings note*.

FULLY GUARANTEED OBLIGATION   An obligation of some federal agencies that is fully guaranteed by the U.S. government for both principal and interest.

FULLY REGISTERED BOND   A bond that is registered for both principal and interest in a holder's name.

GENERAL-OBLIGATION BOND (GO)   A municipal bond issued by any level of government below the U.S. government and is backed by the issuer's full faith, credit, and taxing power.

GINNIE MAE (GOVERNMENT NATIONAL MORTGAGE ASSOCIATION)   A corporation wholly owned by the U.S. government that buys mortgages from banks and other private lenders and resells them to investors. It issues and guarantees mortgage-backed bonds and pass-through certificates.

GLOBAL CERTIFICATE   A single certificate, in either bearer or registered form, representing an entire issue or maturity of an issue of securities. Global certificates are used in registered book-entry systems in which issuers are obligated under state law to issue at least one certificate per maturity. For book-entry-only bonds, the issuer delivers the global certificate(s) to the securities depository where they are retained until maturity. Global certificates may also be used, especially in the Euro market, when definitive bonds are not available at the closing.

GOOD DELIVERY   A term referring to all conditions of a securities delivery that must be met by the seller. These include the correct type of security and issuer, the right quantity and denomination, the presence of outstanding interest coupons if any, proper endorsement, and timeliness of delivery.

GRANTING CLAUSE   The section of a trust indenture that states the security for the obligations to be issued. It includes a recital of the consideration, a specific grant to the trustee, and a legal description of the real property if it is to be mortgaged.

GROUP OF THIRTY (G30)   An international group of senior financial managers that analyzes global financial issues. The Group issued a study in 1989 with nine recommendations for securities processing in global markets that are now unofficial guidelines for all markets to follow.

GUARANTEED INVESTMENT CONTRACT (GIC)   An investment offered by financial service institutions that pays investors a fixed rate of return, usually close to the current yield on high-grade bonds, for a stated term generally not exceeding ten years.

GUARANTEED MORTGAGE CERTIFICATE   A certificate backed by mortgages and also by a guarantee. The FHLMC issues certificates of this type in registered form, backed by conventional residential mortgages.

GUARANTY AGREEMENT   An agreement by a third party, for consideration, to pay debt service on an issue that is the primary obligation of another party or the promise of the primary obligor under a sale and leaseback by a separate agreement to pay debt service on the issue.

HOLDER OF RECORD   The person whose name appears in the corporation's records.

HOME OFFICE PAYMENT AGREEMENT   An agreement pertaining to the private placement of debt securities in which, regarding the payments of principal being made to the holder without presenting the security for notation of payment, the holder agrees that it will, before its disposition, present the securities to the issuer (or its agent) for notation of payment or issuance of new security reflecting the unpaid balance.

HUD (DEPARTMENT OF HOUSING AND URBAN DEVELOPMENT)   The U.S. department responsible for three groups that circulate funds for the construction and major improvement of housing and urban renewal. See also FHA, GINNIE MAE, and HUD PUBLIC HOUSING NOTES AND BONDS.

HUD PUBLIC HOUSING NOTES AND BONDS   Notes and bonds issued by local communities to fund public housing or urban renewal. HUD guarantees approved securities for payment of interest and repayment of principal.

INCOME BOND   A bond issued only to replace older bond issues on which a corporation has defaulted. Both the principal amount and interest rate on the income bond are greater than on the bond it replaces. Interest is paid only if earned, but unpaid interest accrues, to be paid when and if possible. Also called an *adjustment bond*.

INDUSTRIAL REVENUE BOND   A bond issued to support a community's economic development. The funds raised are used to construct facilities for lease to a corporation whose operations will bring jobs to the community. Repayment is based on the corporation's lease payments.

INTEREST COVERAGE   Strictly speaking, this is not actually a ratio but, instead, an important consideration in extending credit—particularly long-term credit—to a corporation. The purpose of this measure is to determine the relationship between a company's earnings and its annual interest charges, and it is computed by using net earnings before interest and income taxes are paid. If an extension of new credit is being contemplated, the interest charges on the new debt should also be included. It is customary to take the average earnings over a period of years and, if the industry is a cyclical one, to consider the earnings during the poorest year. Important to the extension of long-term credit is the company's history of ample coverage of all fixed charges.

INVESTMENT BANKER   A firm that deals with corporations' long-term capital needs. When a company needs to raise new capital, the investment banker advises it on whether to issue debt or equity securities. It also recommends the amount and terms of the financing and helps sell the securities. Investment bankers are also called *underwriters*.

ISIN   International security identification number, a twelve-digit number used to identify securities that are traded across borders.

ISITC   The Interface Standards for Institutional Trade Communication committee, formed by a group of U.S. banks and investment managers to develop and maintain standards used for securities message communication among participants in the U.S. securities industry.

ISO   The International Organization for Standards, with headquarters in Switzerland, which serves as the global overseer of standards. Individual countries have their own internal groups, which are affiliated with the ISO.

ISO 6666   The published international standard for security numbers that affirms the ISIN as the standard security identifier for cross-border securities.

ISO 7775   The published international standard for security message formats that generally conforms to the formats used on the Society for Worldwide Interbank Financial Telecommunications (SWIFT) network.

ISSUED AND OUTSTANDING   The portion of debt and equity securities authorized for sale by a corporation's board of directors that has been sold by the corporation and is currently owned by the public. It excludes securities that have been repurchased from the public and are either held in the corporation's treasury or have been retired.

ISSUER   A public or private entity that signs an evidence of obligation, such as a note, bond, or stock certificate, in return for which the issuer receives cash, goods, or services.

JUMBO   A general term for a large-denomination certificate.

JUNIOR LIEN   A security that represents a claim on the issuer's income or assets subordinate to the claim of another security.

JUNK BOND   A generic description of a high-yield debt security typically issued by commercial borrowers to finance leveraged buyouts, generally subordinated to the borrower's other indebtedness.

KRAY & CO.   The nominee name of Midwest Securities Trust Company, used on the registered securities that the MSTC holds in storage for its participants.

LEGAL TRANSFER   The transfer of securities registered in the name of decedents, fiduciaries, trusts, corporations, partnerships, clubs, institutions, and so forth. The transfer of items not generally recognized as good delivery items.

LETTER OF CREDIT   A financial instrument issued to a company (or individual) by a bank that substitutes the bank's credit for the company's (or individual's) credit. It is frequently used by companies ordering goods from foreign suppliers with which they have no credit relationship.

LETTER OF ERASURE   A letter signed by an authorized person indemnifying the transfer agent and the corporation against liability when transferring an erased or altered assignment.

LETTER OF INDEMNITY   A letter signed by an authorized person indemnifying the transfer agent or indenture trustee and the issuer against liability when replacing a lost, stolen, or mutilated certificate.

LETTER OF TRANSMITTAL   A form used in transmitting securities to the depository agent in the case of a tender offer.

"LETTER" STOCK   Also called *restricted stock*. A special issue of common stock that a corporation is legally permitted to sell, without SEC registration, to a small group of investors. The buyer must sign a letter of intent stating that the purchase is for investment purposes and will not be sold. Letter bonds can also be issued.

LEVERAGE LEASE   A financing vehicle involving the acquisition of property by an investor (usually through a trustee) and providing a minor portion of its cost (with the lenders providing the balance) and the leasing of the property to the lessee. The lender's investment is usually represented by bonds under an indenture.

LIBOR (LONDON INTERBANK OFFERED RATE)   Eurodollar deposits between banks. There is a different LIBOR rate for each deposit maturity.

LIMITED OPEN-END INDENTURE   A mortgage arrangement that sets a limit on the principal amount of bonds that may be issued in the future under the same indenture and with the same priority of lien on corporate assets.

LIMITED-PURPOSE TRUST COMPANY   A state-chartered and -regulated trust company that is permitted to perform specified trust functions.

LOST AND STOLEN SECURITIES PROGRAM   A program, under the Securities and Exchange Commission's Rule 17f-1, reporting and inquiring about the loss, counterfeiting, and theft of securities. The Securities Information Center (SIC) is the central agency that handles reports and inquiries through its automated database.

LOWER FLOATER   A general term for a security with a variable-interest rate and also a tender feature.

MARK-TO-MARKET   The process of valuing a portfolio, a securities position, or a trade, by multiplying the number of shares (or the principal amount in the case of bonds) by the current market price per share (or per bond).

MARKET MAKER   A dealer that buys and sells specific issues in the over-the-counter market or on stock exchanges.

MARKET ORDER   An order for securities in which the buyer/seller does not specify an exact dollar price but agrees to trade immediately at the best price.

MASTER SERVICER   The entity specified in the prospectus supplement for a bond issue secured by mortgage loans that will administer and supervise the performance by servicers of their duties and responsibilities under serving agreements regarding the collateral for the securities.

MORTGAGE-BACKED CERTIFICATE   A debt certificate secured by a pool of mortgages. Such certificates issued by Fannie Mae are secured by conventional mortgages and guaranteed for interest and principal.

MORTGAGE BOND   A debt security backed by a legal interest in specified real property of the issuer, according to a trust indenture.

MULTICURRENCY ACCOUNTING   A term describing the accounting for international securities in both the currency of the local market in which the security is traded and the base currency of the investor.

MUNICIPAL BOND   A bond issued by a state or local government, or its agencies or authorities, or by a possession or territory of the United States. These bonds are often called *tax-exempts*, for interest paid on most of these issues is exempt from federal income tax and also state and local income taxes in the state of origin.

MUNICIPAL NOTE   A debt security issued by a municipality for a period of less than one year. See also BAN, RAN, and TAN.

MUNICIPAL SECURITIES RULEMAKING BOARD (MSRB)   An independent, self-regulatory organization established by the Securities Act Amendments of 1975 that has rule-making authority over dealers, dealer banks, and brokers in municipal securities.

NATIONALLY RECOGNIZED MUNICIPAL SECURITIES INFORMATION REPOSITORY (NRMSIR)   An organization authorized by the MSRB to receive from municipal securities underwriters and others disclosure materials pertaining to such securities and to retain those materials for public access.

NEGATIVE PLEDGE AGREEMENT   An agreement by an issuer or by the entity providing security for an issue not to create any new debt or to pledge or encumber its revenues and/or assets except under specified limitations or conditions.

NEGOTIABLE   The condition of an instrument, the legal interest in which can be transferred by delivery, without the need for endorsement. Bearer securities are inherently negotiable, whereas registered securities can be rendered negotiable by the completion of a power of assignment.

NET INTEREST COST (NIC)   A common method of computing the interest expense to the issuer of bonds, which usually serves as the basis of award in a competitive sale. The NIC allows for premium and discount and represents the dollar amount of interest payable over the life of an issue, without taking into account the time value of funds.

"NO ACTION" LETTER   An SEC staff letter stating that the staff has decided not to recommend to the commission that it take any enforcement or injunctive action against a particular issuer, or other party to a transaction, based on the facts and circumstances stated in the letter to the staff that requested the letter.

NO-CALL PROVISION   An indenture provision prohibiting the optional redemption of a debt issue before a specified date or its maturity.

NOMINEE   A financial services entity that holds its customers' securities as custodian and/or investment agent for trust portfolios; a mechanism for simplifying securities deliveries among banks, brokers, institutions, and individuals, as well as simplifying dividend and interest payments by issuers.

NONREFUNDABLE PROVISION   An indenture provision prohibiting the optional redemption of debt securities for a specified period by using funds borrowed at an interest rate lower than that borne by such securities.

NOTICE OF REDEMPTION   A publication of the issuer's intention to call outstanding bonds before their stated maturity date, in accordance with the bond contract.

OFFERING CIRCULAR   A document usually prepared by the underwriters of an issue stating basic information about the issuer and the issue to be offered in the primary market.

OFFICIAL STATEMENT   A document published by a municipal issuer disclosing material information on a new issue, including the purpose of the issue, how it will be repaid, and the financial, economic, and social characteristics of the issuing entity.

ONE-AND-THE-SAME GUARANTEE   Certification used in the event that the signature of the security holder differs slightly from the name appearing on the face of the certificate.

OPEN-END MORTGAGE BOND   A bond issued under an indenture that allows additional series of bonds to be issued in the future under the same indenture.

OPTION   A right to buy (call) or sell (put) a fixed amount of a given security (usually stock) at a specified price within a limited period of time.

ORIGINAL ISSUE DISCOUNT(OID)   The excess over the issue price of the stated redemption price at a security's maturity. Individual security holders are required by law to report as income a portion of the discount each year until maturity.

PAR VALUE   The face value of a share of stock or debt certificate having no relation to its market value.

PASS-THROUGH CERTIFICATE   A security that represents undivided interests in pools of mortgages. Principal and interest payments from the mortgagors are passed through, as received, to certificate holders. Because mortgagors may prepay mortgages, the pass-through payments to certificate holders fluctuate.

PAYABLE DATE   (1) The date established by a corporation's board of directors for the payment of a dividend to the stockholders of record. The payable date is usually fifteen to twenty days after the record date. (2) The date fixed in an indenture or bond resolution for the payment of interest or principal.

PAYING AGENT   An institution, normally a bank, authorized by the issuer to pay the principal of (premium if any) or interest on any debt securities on behalf of the issuer.

PHILADEP & CO.   The nominee name of Philadelphia Depository Trust Company, used on registered securities that Philadep holds in storage.

POINT   One percent of par value. Because bond prices are quoted as a percentage of $1,000, a point is worth $10, regardless of a bond's actual denomination.

POISON PILL   Rights or warrants granted to stockholders that can be exercised if a raider obtains a specified percentage of the company's shares.

POLLUTION CONTROL BOND   A type of municipal bond, similar to an industrial revenue bond, whose proceeds are used to fund the construction of air and water pollution-control facilities.

PRELIMINARY OFFICIAL STATEMENT (POS OR RED HERRING)   A preliminary version of the official statement used by the issuer or underwriters to describe the proposed issue of municipal bonds before the determination of an interest rate and offering price. Normally, bonds cannot be accepted on the basis of the preliminary official statement, and a legend to that effect appears

on the face of the document in red print, which gives the document its nick-
name—red herring.

PREMIUM   The amount at which a security may sell above its par value. In the case
of a new issue of stock or bonds, the premium is the amount the market price
rises over the original selling price.

PRIVATE ACTIVITY BOND   A bond issued by a municipality that is not classified
as a governmental bond. It is tax exempt if it constitutes s qualified bond as determined by the Tax Reform Act of 1986.

PRIVATE PLACEMENT   The sale (to a limited number of institutional investors)
of securities not involving a public offering and exempt from registration under
the U.S. Securities Act of 1933.

PROJECT NOTE   A municipal note with a maturity ranging from three to twelve
months that provides short-term financing for federally assisted public housing
and urban renewal projects. HUD may guarantee the principal and interest of
these notes.

PROSPECTUS   An official document that must be given to buyers of new SEC-reg-
istered issues. It describes the issuer's products and business and the industries
in which it competes, its physical facilities, management background, and the
like and presents historical financial statements, as well as the issue and intended use of the funds to be received. The SEC neither approves nor disap-
proves the prospectus, which is an abstract of the lengthy registration statement filed with the SEC.

"PRUDENT MAN" RULE   Also known as the *prudent person rule*. A common
law standard of conduct, which requires a fiduciary or trustee to deal with the
trust estate as if it were the fiduciary's or trustee's own property. In effect, the
rule is a standard of due diligence and care.

PUBLIC HOUSING BOND   A debt security issued by a state or local government
to provide funds for loans made to developers, home buyers, and lending institutions that service home buyers. HUD may guarantee some of these bonds.

PUBLIC UTILITY REVENUE BOND   A municipal bond issued to raise funds to
create or improve electric, gas, water, and sewer services.

PUT OPTION   A right, which may be evidenced by a certificate, given to the
holder of a debt security to sell it back to the issuer on one or more fixed future
dates before the security's rematurity.

RAN (REVENUE ANTICIPATION NOTE)   A municipal note maturing in less
than one year, issued in expectation of revenue from particular projects.

RATING AGENCY   A private company that rates the creditworthiness of bonds;
the three best known are Moody's Investors Services, Standard & Poor's Corporation, and Fitch Investor's Service, Inc.

REBATE CALCULATION   A mathematical calculation to determine whether funds held in accounts for tax-free bond issues have earned more than permitted by law (an amount greater than the interest paid on the outstanding tax-free bonds). The calculation must be made annually and the excess segregated and remitted to the Internal Revenue Service every five years.

RECORD DATE
1. The date set by a corporation's directors that determines eligibility to receive the current declared dividend.
2. In the case of bonds, the dates fixed in the indenture that determine eligibility to receive the current interest payment. The standard record dates are the fifteenth day of the month preceding a payment on the first day of the following month and the last business day of the month preceding the payment on the fifteenth day of the following month.

RED HERRING   A short, preliminary form of a prospectus available to potential investors in a new issue before the prospectus is published. It contains company and industry information, financial statements, and so on but does not indicate the price per share, which is determined just before the issue is offered for sale. It is called a red herring because the front cover bears a legend printed in red announcing that it is not the final official prospectus.

REFUNDING   The issuance of new debt securities to replace an older issue.

REGISTRAR   A bank, normally the trustee or fiscal agent for a debt issue, that maintains the records of bearer certificates registered as to principal only and certificates in fully registered form. The registrar processes the registrations of the transfers and exchanges of securities.

REGISTRATION STATEMENT   The statement (or document) containing any amendment filed with the SEC in connection with the proposed sale of securities to the public.

REGULATION 9   The regulation of the Office of the Comptroller of the Currency that established standards and procedures for national banks acting in a fiduciary capacity and managing collective investment funds.

REINVESTMENT AGENT   A bank, usually the paying agent, designated by the issuer of securities to reinvest upon the written request of the security holders all or part of the dividends or interest to be paid to the security holders.

REMARKETING AGENT   A bank or investment banking firm that agrees to remarket bonds tendered or "put" by their owners after the initial issuance.

REMIC (REAL ESTATE MORTGAGE INVESTMENT CONDUIT)   A tax-advantaged vehicle created by the Tax Reform Act of 1986 to hold real estate mortgages and to issue securities representing interests in those mortgages.

REPURCHASE AGREEMENT (REPO)   A contract between a seller and a buyer of U.S. government and other securities under which the seller agrees to buy back the securities at a specified price after a stated period of time. In the interim, the seller has the use of the buyer's funds, a service for which the seller pays a fee.

RESOLUTION TRUST CORPORATION (RTC)   Established by the Financial Institutions Reform, Recovery, and Enforcement Act of 1989, the RTC is responsible for the sale and disposition of assets of thrift institutions that were in receivership on November 1, 1989, or that failed after that date, until August 9, 1992.

REVENUE BOND   A state or local government bond on which the interest and principal are paid from the revenues produced by the project financed by the bond issue. Water, sewer, gas and electrical facilities, roads, and bridges are typical projects.

REVERSE REPO   A repurchase agreement originated by a customer who needs securities temporarily but does not want to buy them outright. The customer holds the securities for the duration of the reverse repo agreement or places them in another repo agreement to yet another party. Also called a *resell agreement*.

ROUND LOT   The usual unit of trading in a security or a multiple of them. A round lot of stock is generally one hundred shares; for bonds, $1,000 par value is typical.

RULE 10B-5   A regulation of the SEC, under the 34 act, that makes it unlawful for any person to employ any devise, scheme, or artifice to defraud; to make any untrue statement of a material fact; or to omit any true statement of a material fact or to omit a material fact necessary in order to make the statements made, in light of the circumstances under which they were made, not misleading; or to engage in any act, practice, or course of business that operates or would operate as a fraud or deceit on any person, in connection with the purchase or sale of any security.

RULE 144 A   A regulation of the SEC, under the 33 Act, that exempts from registration the resale of privately placed securities to "qualified" institutional investors, thus creating a viable secondary market for such securities.

RULE 387   The New York Stock Exchange rule governing the extension of delivery-versus-payment (DVP) privileges by its member brokers. Basically, brokers can extend DVP privileges to customers who participate in the institutional delivery system and provide for book-entry settlement if the issue is eligible for depository services.

SALLIE MAE (STUDENT LOAN MARKETING ASSOCIATION)   A privately owned, U.S. government–sponsored corporation founded to help students repay educational loans. Under its warehousing program, Sallie Mae makes large loans to lending institutions that then grant loans to students. Under its loan purchase program, Sallie Mae makes direct loans to students.

SAMURAI BOND   A Japanese yen–denominated bond marketed in Japan by a non-Japanese entity.

SECONDARY MARKET
1. A term referring to trading securities not listed on an organized exchange.
2. A term referring to trading securities other than a new issue.

SECURITIES ACT OF 1933 (33 ACT)   A statute requiring, among other provisions, the filing of a registration statement before the public sale of certain securities, the disclosure of substantial information about the issuer and the issue, as well as provisions for furnishing prospectuses upon the distribution of the security.

SECURITIES AND EXCHANGE ACT OF 1934 (34 ACT)   A statute providing for the regulation of securities exchanges and over-the-counter markets, as well as the establishment of the SEC.

SERIAL ISSUE   A bond that matures on a scheduled basis over several years, thereby allowing the issuer to amortize the loan over a period of years. Almost all municipal bonds are serial issues.

SETTLEMENT DATE   The date on which a contract for the purchase or sale of securities is to be completed or settled.

SHELF REGISTRATION   A procedure allowed by the SEC permitting qualified issuers to file a single registration covering its long-term securities' financing plans for a two-year period.

SIGNATURE GUARANTEE   A guarantee (normally obtained from a commercial bank or securities dealer) of the seller's endorsement, which appears on the stock or bond power accompanying the security being sold. This guarantee affirms (1) that the person who signed the power is the person in whose name the securities are registered or is authorized to act on behalf of that person and (2) that the signature is genuine. The actual signature guarantee has been replaced by the medallion program.

SINKING FUND   The periodic retirement (by repayment or purchase) of portions of a debt issue before the issue's stated maturity, according to the indenture's terms.

SLGS (STATE AND LOCAL GOVERNMENT SERIES)   U.S. government securities issued to municipalities at various interest rates to ensure that issues of tax-free bonds do not violate arbitrage rules. These bonds do not trade in the open market and are carried in book-entry form only at a Federal Reserve Bank.

SPREAD   The difference between the bid and the asked price (or yield) in the quotation of a security or between two security issues of differing maturities; the difference between an underwriter's bid on a bond issue and its resale price to the public; or the difference between what the funds cost a bank and the rate at which it lends the funds.

STANDARD & POOR'S   A financial services firm that rates bonds and offers financial publications and computerized information that provide pertinent facts about thousands of issues.

STANDBY LETTER OF CREDIT   A letter of credit that covers an amount equal to the principal of and a portion of the interest on the bonds and that provides for a single withdrawal in the event of the bonds' acceleration.

STOP ORDER   A notification by a holder of a security requesting the obligor, the trustee, or its agent(s) not to register or transfer the security or to pay it on maturity or redemption.

STREET NAME   When a certificate is registered in the name of a bank, brokerage firm, or its nominee, it is said to be in street name. Securities are sometimes registered in this manner to facilitate delivery, collection of dividends and proxies, and so forth. All securities purchased on margin must be registered in street name.

STRIPPING   Removing the interest coupons from bonds, with the intent of selling the coupons separately from the certificates.

SUBSCRIPTION
1. The procedure of buying securities by exercising rights or warrants.
2. The purchase of part of a bond issue on the original issuance by members of the selling syndicate.

SURETY BOND   A bond from a surety company that enables the replacement of a lost or stolen security.

SYNDICATE   A group of underwriters formed to buy (i.e., underwrite) a new issue of securities from the issuer and offer them for resale to the general public. One member is designated as the lead manager to administer the syndicate's operations.

TAN (TAX ANTICIPATION NOTE)   The most common type of municipal note, sold in anticipation of tax receipts.

TAX ANTICIPATION BILL   A special class of security, occasionally sold by the U.S. Treasury to corporations. It usually matures one week after the tax date but can be turned in at full value when the taxes are paid, thus earning an extra week's interest.

TAX TAILS   A series of short-term taxable bonds added to a tax-exempt bond to pay the cost of issuance expenses not allowed under federal regulation because they are more than 2 percent of the bond's proceeds.

TENDER AGENT   A private financial institution, usually a bank, that serves as an agent for the trustee or the remarketing agent to accept bonds that are tendered or "put" under the provisions allowing the bondholders to require the bond issuer to repurchase the bonds at certain times or intervals.

TENDER OFFER
1. An offer to buy made to holders of a particular issue by a third party. A detailed offer is made by public announcement in newspapers and by personal letter to each stockholder.
2. An offer by a corporation to buy back a portion of its own shares. This is normally done when the corporation has excess cash and when it believes the market price of its stock is unreasonably low. The reduced share count may result in higher future dividends per share on the remaining shares.

TOMBSTONE   An advertisement placed by underwriters announcing the sale of a new issue, giving the name of the issuer, a description of the issue, its interest rate, its maturity, and the names of the underwriting syndicate.

TRANCHE   A term used to designate a particular class or series of securities in a specific issue that is different from the other classes or series of that issue in some fundamental entitlement such as interest rate, maturity date, or another inherent right.

TREASURY STOCK   Previously issued stock that a corporation has brought back from its stockholders. Not entitled to vote or receive dividends.

TURNAROUND RULES   A set of rules imposed by the SEC on registered transfer agents according to section 17A of the 34 act.

UNDERWRITER   An entity that purchases a large block of securities at the initial offering. The underwriter acts as a wholesaler between the issuing entity and a syndicate or between the issuing entity and the general investing public.

UNDERWRITING AGREEMENT   The contract between an investment banker and a corporation, containing the final terms, conditions, and prices of the issue.

UNIFORM ACTS   A series of model acts designed to standardize state laws governing a particular activity. State legislatures may modify their existing laws or conform new laws to the proposed Uniform Act.

UNIT INVESTMENT TRUST (MUNICIPAL)   A fixed portfolio of municipal bonds sold to investors in fractional, undivided interests, usually in denominations of $1,000. The same bonds are held in the portfolio until they mature or are redeemed.

UNSECURED DEBT   An obligation not backed by the pledge of an issuer's assets. Unsecured bonds are called *debentures* or *notes.*

VARIABLE-RATE SECURITY   A short- or a long-term security whose interest rates—either floating or variable—are adjusted as often as weekly, monthly, or quarterly. The rate is a function of a market indicator, such as the prime rate, the U.S. Treasury bill or bond rate, or a combination of both.

WARRANT   A certificate, either attached to a debt security or issued separately, that gives the holder the right to purchase a specified amount of another security (either a debt security or common stock) issued by the borrower, for a limited period of time, which may lapse before, on, or after the maturity of the debt security.

WITHDRAWAL BY TRANSFER   A method by which a depository participant can obtain physical securities from the depository to forward to a buyer. The depository takes securities from inventory, has them registered in the name of the new owner, and sends the new certificates to the participant or buyer.

YANKEE BOND   A U.S. dollar–denominated bond marketed publicly in the United States by a non–U.S. corporation or governmental entity. A registration statement for this issue is required to be filed with the SEC.

YIELD TO MATURITY   The discount rate that makes the current value of a bond's cash flow until maturity equal to the bond's market price. Yield to maturity takes into account all the interest payments to be received until maturity, plus the difference between the current market price and the par value that the investor will receive at maturity; it expresses this total return on capital on an annual basis.

ZERO COUPON   A term applied to debt securities that are offered initially by the issuer without provision for periodic payments of interest. The final payment at maturity covers the principal and all interest due for the life of the security.

Index